Miraculously Builded in Our Hearts

A DARTMOUTH READER

Miraculously Builded in Our Hearts

A DARTMOUTH READER

Edited by EDWARD CONNERY LATHEM

and DAVID M. SHRIBMAN

HANOVER · NEW HAMPSHIRE · 1999

DARTMOUTH COLLEGE

Distributed by University Press of New England

HANOVER AND LONDON

Publication of this book was made possible
through sponsorship provided in memory of

KENNETH F. MONTGOMERY

DARTMOUTH CLASS OF 1925

by his children, Kenneth H. Montgomery and Rita Montgomery Heydon.

EDITORS' ACKNOWLEDGMENTS

The editors extend special thanks to Kenneth C. Cramer, Archivist-Emeritus of Dartmouth College, who provided painstaking and tireless research assistance; to College Archivist Anne Ostendarp and Archival Specialist Barbara Krieger, as well as to the Reference Services staff in Baker Library, who were unfailingly helpful and gracious in various ways; and to Arline E. McCondach, who typed the manuscript with both infinite good cheer and careful attention to detail.

Grateful acknowledgment is also made for permissions that have been granted to reprint herein text from the following copyrighted works: Matthew Bernstein, *Walter Wanger, Hollywood Independent* (Berkeley: University of California Press, 1994); Earl H. Blaik with Tim Cohane, *You Have to Pay the Price* (New York: Holt, Rinehart and Winston, 1960); "A Candid Conversation with Dartmouth's John Sloan Dickey," in *Yankee*, June 1969; James Dodson, "A Civil Voice in the Wilderness," in *Yankee*, June 1991; Corey Ford, "My Dog Likes It Here," in *Ford Times*, October 1953; Paul Gambaccini, *Radio Boy* (London: Elm Tree Books, 1986); Eugene Griffin, "New Dealism Forced on Dartmouth," in *Chicago Daily Tribune*, October 18, 1948; Judson D. Hale Sr., *The Education of a Yankee* (New York: Harper & Row, 1987); Benjamin Hart, *Poisoned Ivy* (Briarcliff Manor, N.Y.: Stein and Day, 1984); Jean Alexander Kemeny, *It's Different at Dartmouth* (Brattleboro, Vt.: Stephen Greene Press, 1979); C. Everett Koop, *Koop: The Memoirs of America's Family Doctor* (New York: Random House, 1991); Aaron Latham, *Crazy Sundays: F. Scott Fitzgerald in Hollywood* (New York: Viking Press, 1971); William Loeb, "Dartmouth Buys A 'Lemon,'" in Manchester, N.H., *Union Leader*, May 8, 1970; Henry S. Robinson, *Autobiography Of A Third World Citizen* (1986); and Ricardo T. Worl, "A Tlingit Brother of Alpha Chi," in *First Person, First Peoples*, edited by Andrew Garrod and Colleen Larimore (Ithaca: Cornell University Press, 1997). An expression of indebtedness and appreciation is tendered, as well, to the Estate of Robert Lee Frost for permission to quote from five letters written by Robert Frost in 1915 to Harold Goddard Rugg. —E.C.L. & D.M.S.

Distributed by University Press of New England, Hanover, New Hampshire 03755

Contents

Preface

by DAVID M. SHRIBMAN

IT MIGHT OTHERWISE be a place faraway, forgotten and forlorn, surrounded as it is by mountain fastnesses, much of the year buffeted by the wolf-wind wailing in the doorways, buried by the snow drifts deep along the road, chilled by the great white cold that walks abroad. But to the thousands of men and women of Dartmouth, it is a special place—of lore and learning and legend, of challenge and commitment and change, of trial and triumph and tremulous moments too numerous to count. No college started so modestly and succeeded so majestically. No college marries so gracefully the whimsy of the young and the wisdom of the old. No college claims more loyalty from its charges.

"Dartmouth is not a college," my wife, half in derision, half in awe, is fond of saying. "It is a cult." And there is something to that. It is the only college where the students wear sweatshirts that carry the name of their own college, not someplace else (unless, of course, the sweatshirt says GREEN, which means the same thing, or COLLEGE, which can only mean one College). Here the students know the words not only to "the college song," but to many of the College's songs. Here the lessons learned are lifelong, and they are not only about the causes of the Civil War, or the reasons why stars die, or the rhythms of Whitman and Dickinson and the Harlem renaissance, or even the mysteries of algebraic combinatorics. Here the College is always—always —referred to in writing with an upper-case C.

And just as the College is an extraordinary college, the twentieth century has been an extraordinary century for our College. At the turn of the last century, Dartmouth was, as Prof. Francis Lane Childs 1906 characterized it in a fabled 1957 lecture, "still local, narrow and ill-equipped." Today's College is international, broad-minded and exceedingly well-equipped. It is modern in every way; no cow has been sighted grazing lazily on the College Green for decades. Dartmouth is, moreover, bigger and better in every way. At the turn of the century, the enrollment of the College was 315 men. At the close of the century the enrollment of the College is 4,200 men and women. At the turn of the century the endowment of the College was just over $2 million. At the close of the century the endowment of the College is nearly $2 billion. At the turn of the century President William Jewett Tucker spoke of Dartmouth's obligation to "fill to the full the college ideal." At the close of the century, President James Wright would speak of Dartmouth in his inaugural address as a "university in terms of our activities and our programs, but one that remains a college in name and in its basic values and purposes."

At the beginning of this century Dartmouth had no central dining facility, its classrooms no electricity, its dormitories no central heating. There was no Baker Library. There was no Massachusetts Hall, no New Hampshire Hall. There were nearly no baths, and no showers. (Students who wanted to bathe had to go to the gymnasium—or to Sanborn Hall, where the fee was twenty-five cents a bath—or else use such washtubs as they had in their own rooms.) In the next hundred years Hanover would turn from sleepy village to bustling town; the College would be transformed from a remote outpost of teaching to an internationally recognized center of learning; Dartmouth Hall would be consumed in a nightmarish fire and be rebuilt in a display of alumni resolve; tuition would grow from about $100 a year to about $8,000 a term; the name "Hopkins" would refer, in turn, to a visionary College administrative-staff member, then to the longest-serving modern College president, and finally to the center of the studio and performing arts.

At the turn of the century a writer in the *Dartmouth Magazine* could speak of "the College love that always thrilled the heart." A writer today could remark upon much the same thing. On the eve of World War I, Wilder Dwight Quint 1887 set out to discover what students did at Dartmouth, and he found, as he reported in *The Story of Dartmouth*, that "primarily they work at such varied forms of the higher education as they may select out of a liberal variety." That's true today, though the varied forms are unimaginably more varied. Ernest Martin Hopkins thought the central aim of a liberal arts college was to "develop a habit of mind rather than to impart a given content of knowledge." That is the central aim of James Wright's Dartmouth, too.

In the past century, that habit of mind has produced a remarkable record of achievement. It has also left behind a remarkable chronicle of reminiscences and tributes, exhortations and *pensées*, diatribes and manifestos. The story of the last century—Dartmouth's Century, you might say, except for the fact that the next century might well be Dartmouth's, too—is the story of the men and women who found, loved and left Dartmouth, only to discover that the sense of wonder they found here never disappeared—and that their love for the place never left them, either.

These reminiscences and tributes, exhortations and *pensées*, diatribes and manifestos, are the leaves of Dartmouth's tree, and here at the autumn of the century my friend Edward Lathem 1951 and I felt an unmistakable and irresistible need to rake them, to pile them up, to jump into them, and to reassemble the pile again. No one— not the College Trustees, not the worthies in the Development Office, not the buyers at the Bookstore or the Co-op—told us to do this. But, then again, no one tells a young child to make his autumnal leaf pile, or to jump into it. Some deeply imbedded impulse screams: You must do this.

So we did. We looked through the multicolored leaves of this College, through books and magazines and newspapers, notebooks and scrapbooks. We searched through archives; we read letters written by people we never met. We enjoyed every minute of it. And, to fill a need here and there, we commissioned a number of entries especially for this anthology. The selections that follow are mostly excerpts from previously published material, though even the very best pieces were vulnerable to the ruthless caprice of the editors' pencils (you will notice the bracketed ellipses, which indicate editorial excisions).

In many ways this volume is a companion to the much-loved *A Dartmouth Reader*, edited by Francis Brown 1925 and published in 1969, at the time of the College's bicentennial celebration. Mr. Brown's book reached all the way back to 1769, to the founding of the College, and left off in the very last year of the tumultuous 1960s. But so much has happened since 1969. Since then, the familiar phrase "men of Dartmouth" has come to represent only half the students on campus, and the word "blitz" is something students send to each other by computer, not something Hitler did to London or something the football defense did to Princeton or Cornell. Since then, interstate highways and communications technology have made Hanover far less remote, and the high-octane students have made the campus far more yeasty.

We intentionally focused our volume on our century, when the College changed and when it, in so many ways, rededicated itself to the highest ideals of its founding and its past. But even in restricting ourselves to the twentieth century, we faced the problem that haunted Mr. Brown three decades ago: "I felt like the old preacher who, in announcing the hymn, said let's sing all twelve verses, they're all too good to omit any one." The Dartmouth hymnal has only grown since then. There was so much we wanted to include, so little we were willing to discard. Over the months that extended to three years we rummaged and winnowed—and every once in a while we even bickered. But overall we are happy with our literary leaf pile. And we are still speaking to each other, Ed and I.

While preparing this volume we developed fresh appreciation for that peculiar slice of humankind known as the men and women of Dartmouth, who in Hanover learn to analyze the verse of Milton, explore fluid dynamics, wrestle with Lu Xun, confront Aquinas, discover radiogenic isotope geochemistry, climb Moosilauke, build their own kayaks, sharpen an ax with a dual-grip handstone and slip across a snowy campus on cross-country skis to an early-morning class on Flaubert. We know, of course, that the still North remembers them, the hillwinds know their name. We know, too, that the granite of New Hampshire keeps the record of their fame. We just wanted to put part of that record between cloth covers. Here it is.

In his first letter to Lord Dartmouth, Eleazar Wheelock said of the College he founded: "By the blessing and continual care of heaven, it has lived, and does still live and flourish." To which we add, twenty-three decades later: Amen.

David M Shribman

Class of 1976.

Miraculously Builded in Our Hearts

A DARTMOUTH READER

See! By the light of many thousand sunsets
Dartmouth Undying like a vision starts:
Dartmouth—the gleaming, dreaming walls of Dartmouth,
Miraculously builded in our hearts.

–from "Dartmouth Undying"
by Franklin McDuffee 1921

Coming of "the New Dartmouth"

by WILLIAM JEWETT TUCKER

⇒⇒⇒ The Rev. William Jewett Tucker (Class of 1861) became Dartmouth's President in 1893. His administration not only carried the College into the twentieth century, it also constituted a monumental turning point in the College's history, bringing about what was designated "the New Dartmouth"—an institution both enlarged and enriched in scope and in vigor, as well as possessed of a decidedly distinctive character. This text is taken from Dr. Tucker's autobiography, *My Generation* (1919).

PROFESSOR FOSTER, head of the department of history, has told me that about the time of the close of my administration he called, in an examination on the colonial period, for a comparison between the early history of the college and its latest development. One student remarked incidentally, comparing Dr. Wheelock and myself, that both "were gamblers by instinct." I was as much pleased as amused with the insight of the student. Dr. Wheelock certainly took, according to the view of the average man, a great chance when he ventured on his errand into this northern wilderness. My errand was undertaken under very different conditions, but measured by the definite object to be achieved which was to determine its success or failure, this latter venture of faith had in it to the ordinary, and to the interested onlooker, a large element of chance. This object was nothing less than to attempt to give to the College its possible institutional development—to develop it to its full institutional capacity. The colleges with which Dartmouth had been most intimately associated in its early history—Harvard, Yale, and Princeton —had gradually drawn away in the pursuit of their own educational ideals. Harvard and Yale had already defined themselves as universities, and Princeton was taking steps to reach the same end. What further development should Dartmouth attempt, consistent with its traditions, and possible of realization? No alumnus of Dartmouth cherished the desire to see the College become a university. Apart from the adverse sentiment which the attempt of the State (in the Dartmouth College controversy), to convert the College into a university had created, it was clearly seen that the limitations of its environment would make the attempt, so far as any satisfactory result might be concerned, quite impracticable. But the purpose was legitimate and practicable, and the opportunity was present, for Dartmouth to expand and to seek to fill to the full the college ideal. This was the purpose entertained, altogether distinct from the ambition to realize the university ideal, but in itself honorable, and satisfying.

The means for carrying out this purpose, so far as they fell within the province of administration, were both moral and material. To my mind the emphasis in the choice of means rested at three points. First, Dartmouth was in a peculiar sense an historic college. Its history was its great asset, both moral and material. It was necessary that its history should be capitalized at its full value. To this end the College of the present was to be brought into vital contact with the College in its origin and early development. The essential thing was to open wide the channel for the transmission of the spirit of the College. Dartmouth had no advantage in the transmission of culture. Her advantage, and it was very great, was in the well-nigh unrivaled possession of an originating spirit at once creative, adventurous, and charged with spiritual power. [. . .]

Second, the creation of a high college sentiment, not mere college spirit, was essential to the full institutional development of the College. I have placed much stress upon the educational value of the human element during the college stage. It is of special value in creating the institutional spirit in constructive periods. "The mind of the college" can be lifted at such times above the ordinary causes of enthusiasm and set upon the growths and advancements of the college itself. Such periods produce a fine community of feeling among members of the faculty, students, and alumni. The institutional effect of growth in numbers is not to be minimized, but the real significance of numbers lies in what they represent. Assuming quality as a fixed necessity, the most desirable result is the broadening of the constituency of a college. In the present case, the object sought in the increase of the student body was the nationalization of Dartmouth.

The third point upon which emphasis was placed was that any plan of reconstruction and expansion must be commensurate with the existing opportunity. This as compared with those already mentioned was the material point, but it involved the whole question of educational advance. The contrast is often drawn between teaching and equipment to the disparagement of the latter. There may be reason for this disparaging contrast, but it was entirely out of place in that period of educational reconstruction which followed the introduction of the sciences and of the scientific method. Teaching became in large degree a question of equipment. Colleges had to be rebuilt. The college plant had an educational value which no instructor could despise. No increase of salary could make amends for meager facilities. Such was the situation at Dartmouth at the beginning of the period of reconstruction and expansion. It was altogether an educational crisis. Next to a spirit of hospitality toward the new subject-matter of the higher education was the necessity of making adequate provision for it; and this demand, when met, necessitated in turn the rehabilitation of the material of the older discipline.

I will not anticipate what is to be said more in detail as I describe the modernizing process which went on at Dartmouth, but I may fitly say at this point that I quickly became aware of the dynamic force latent in the College, as I sought to bring it up to its full institutional capacity, and I may repeat what I have already strongly urged, that college administration has to do with spiritual quite as much as with material forces. The college administrator, whatever may be his other qualifications, must be able to recognize the meaning and to feel the force of the "corporate consciousness of the college." [. . .]

What is termed the romance of Dartmouth is in truth a spiritual romance. It began in the appeal of the idea embodied in Wheelock's Indian School to the spiritual imagination of the Mother Country. It took shape and color in the visit of Samson Occom to England, where he was received not only with curious interest, but with ardent sympathy and eager coöperation, as evidenced in the subscription of ten thousand pounds in behalf of the school, the list headed by His Majesty with a subscription of two hundred pounds, and containing the names of three thousand individuals and churches. The romantic character of the origin of the College appears more clearly in the fact that as the mirage of the higher education of the Indians disappears, there rise in place of Wheelock's Indian School the substantial walls of Dartmouth College, fitly bearing the name of the statesman as well known in his time for his friendship for the colonies as for his missionary zeal. And if anything further were needed to complete the "romance of Dartmouth," it may be found in the reflection that none of these conditions attending its origin could have happened except in the decade in which they occurred. Ten years from the date of Occom's visit to England and six years from the date of the Charter of the College, the colonies were at war with the Mother Country. Dartmouth was the ninth and last of the colonial colleges. [. . .]

It is an abrupt transition from the epoch when Dartmouth was making its traditions to the time when, in common with the historic colleges, it entered upon what I have termed the modernizing process —the era of reconstruction and expansion. [. . .]

The modernizing process at Dartmouth was somewhat belated. The delay, however, was not altogether to the disadvantage of the College. It gave the opportunity to determine the nature of the expansion of which the College was capable. The modernizing of the colleges was not an external process imposed upon all alike without regard to the individuality of each. It was in all cases an internal process, subject to certain inflexible conditions, but in no respect a purely standardizing process. In the case of Dartmouth, it was determined to make use of the process to test the *capacity* of the College for expansion, having in mind both the vigor of its constitution and the opportunity for stimulating and strenuous exertion. In other words, the policy adopted was not that of a programme. It was a policy of inward development, determined and measured by the reach of its resources, by the response of its constituency, and by the return of its increase and enlargement upon itself. Expansion was to mark the limit of the productivity of the College under the most stimulating treatment consistent with safety. The process of expansion presented itself in a series of problems—the financial, the physical, and the strictly educational. The physical involved the reconstruction of the college plant; the educational, the enlargement of the curriculum and the increase of the faculty. [. . .]

The educational expansion of the College necessarily adjusted itself to existing conditions. It meant in part the introduction of entirely new subjects like biology and sociology into the curriculum, in part the organization of unorganized or attached subjects like history and economics into departments, in part the disproportionate increase of the teaching force in some departments as especially in the modern languages, and generally an enlargement of the Faculty. More money naturally was expended for equipment in the direction of the sciences than in any other; but as a further and very definite part of the expansion effected came in through the relative place assigned to the new humanities, history, economics, sociology, and the newer forms of political science the increase of expenditure here, both in equipment and teaching force, was relatively great. [. . .]

The extension of the subject-matter of the curriculum enlarged the intellectual horizon of the College; so also did the introduction in considerable numbers of new men into the Faculty, many of whom were from other colleges. [. . .]

While taking note of the changes attending the enlargement and reconstruction of the Faculty, it is of interest to note the change which took place in the student body, especially in the distribution of students according to locality. It will be seen how definitely the process of nationalizing the College had begun to take effect within the period of reconstruction. In the Catalogue of 1893–94 the registration stood by localities—New England, 427; Middle States, 34; Near West, 21; Beyond the Mississippi, 11. In the Catalogue of 1908–09 the registration stood—New England, 839 (Massachusetts, 502, New Hampshire, 197, other New England States, 140); Middle States, 149; Near West, 98; Beyond the Mississippi, 48. [. . .]

Foreseeing the exactions of the presidency on the administrative side, I had renounced in advance all hope of teaching. In this respect [. . .] instead of assuming the teaching function I did not hesitate to avail myself of the most valuable aids in my administrative duties. Professor John K. Lord was made Acting President of the Faculty in the absence of the President. This appointment meant much more to me than the freedom of often prolonged absences among the alumni. It meant the privilege of constant and most helpful advice. Later, and especially during the period of my illness while still in office, the promotion of Mr. Ernest M. Hopkins, who had been my private secretary, to be Secretary of the College, enabled me to relieve myself of certain definite responsibilities. [. . .]

The external changes brought about by the modernizing process were soon apparent, but their effect upon the internal life of the College could not be quickly seen or easily estimated. The effect, for example, upon scholarship was for some time in doubt. On the whole the immediate effect was not favorable. The inherited scholarship of the classroom was the resultant of well-formulated subjects, of a logical routine, and of a compulsory discipline. All these conditions were changed to the degree in which the new régime took effect. [. . .] The new courses appeared fragmentary when compared with the routine long at work in the classics and mathematics. And the elective system called for a sudden shift of will power from the college authorities to the individual student. There was, of course, much stimulus to scholarship latent in the new subject-matter and in the principle of the elective system, but the interruption of the college discipline was felt earlier than the stimulation of the new freedom.

If any one had assumed that the modernizing process was to be altogether an intellectual process, he would soon have been convinced that it required for its success strong moral supports from without, and the utilization of the moral forces within the student body. The uncertain but really decisive factor in the whole matter was the student himself, involving his moral quite as much as his intellectual attitude. [. . .] From the first I believed in the incorporation of the students, individually and collectively, into the movement for reconstruction and expansion. I believed that it was entirely possible, as it was certainly in every way desirable, that they should be made to share in the "corporate consciousness of the College." To the degree in which they understood and felt this larger consciousness, they would be qualified to take a leading part in remoulding college sentiment as a means of reaching and applying higher standards. With this end in view, I sought to interpret the history and traditions of the College in their relation to present plans. [. . .] "Dartmouth Night" was instituted, to bring the undergraduate body into sympathetic and intelligent contact with the alumni, the living and the dead. [. . .]

College education in this country was from the very beginning set to some definite end outside and beyond itself. This end has been for the most part satisfied in the relation of the colleges to the professions. A liberal education has never been allowed to become the mere perquisite of a leisure class. We have accepted the English requirement that it must be "fit for a gentleman," but we have added the implication—a gentleman at work. With us the natural complement of a liberal education has been a professional life.

Dartmouth has always kept faith with the professions, and never more strictly than in support of the recent efforts for the advancement of professional standards. There have been times, it is true, of an unapprehended danger to the promotion of professional standards from the stirrings of the university idea. The position of Dartmouth, relatively remote from the centers, but central to a large and somewhat distinct territory, has frequently suggested the ambition to assume the functions of a university, which if realized would have added one more to the aggregation of minor professional schools. The presence of the medical school, existing almost from the first in various relations to the College, has been a local reminder of natural possibilities in this direction. Even so sane a mind as that of President

Lord was at one time seriously infected with the university idea. In 1841, stimulated by the largest enrollment in the history of the College, placing it on a full numerical equality with any of the New England colleges, he urged upon the Trustees the restoration of the Chair of Divinity to active use, saying that "another step," referring to the possible provision for a law professorship, "will then place the College in the position of a university, to which Divine Providence has been so evidently leading it, and for which public opinion is in a great degree prepared." [. . .]

The university idea made a still stronger appeal to the vivid imagination of President Smith, and during his administration came much nearer to realization. It was his aim to concentrate the higher educational interests of the State at Hanover, and through his efforts the New Hampshire College of Agriculture and the Mechanic Arts was first located there. The Thayer School was established in his administration practically on the basis of a graduate school. There was the definite promise, according to public announcement, of three large bequests which had they become available in his time, would have materially aided in the working-out of his large plans. Their failure to "arrive" till it was too late for his uses, was a pathetic illustration of the saying as applied to successions in a college presidency—"one soweth and another reapeth." The subsequent removal of the Agricultural College to Durham, which took place just before the close of President Bartlett's administration, closed the door to further efforts in behalf of a university based on State needs or resources. The sympathies and activities of President Bartlett were altogether in favor of the development of the College as such. [. . .]

In one way or other—in its earlier history by the force of circumstances and in later times by fixed purpose—Dartmouth had been preserved from becoming the danger to the professions which the small university, with its inferior facilities for reaching the higher professional standards, presents. [. . .] When I recall the historic position of Dartmouth and its relation to the apparently conflicting demands of liberal and professional education, I am ready to accept in its behalf the congratulatory words of President Hadley of Yale [. . . : "]For nearly three half-centuries Dartmouth has occupied an exceptional position: [. . .] during later generations as an institution whose work for the cause of higher learning is thrown into salient relief by the fact that where so many institutions claim to do more than they actually accomplish, Dartmouth accomplishes more than she claims."

From a Senior's Letters Home

by DOUGLAS VANDERHOOF

>>> Various aspects of College life during the academic year 1900–01 are touched upon in these passages from letters written to his parents in San Francisco by Douglas VanderHoof 1901, excerpts that also reflect facets of the early personal development of a man who was subsequently to have a long and distinguished career, as both physician and teacher of medicine, in Richmond, Virginia.

September 16, 1900—Wrote you from Montreal last Tuesday evening. Arrived in Hanover the next morning & started right in work Thursday. Have got my courses arranged to suit me in every particular, for which I am very glad as, according to the schedule two of my five subjects conflicted coming at the same hour of the day. But by special arrangement I can do my laboratory work by myself at my own convenience, being present at the scheduled hour only for the lectures. Have started in on human anatomy under Gil Frost & it is going to be a fine course. My book costs me $6.80—but it is the latest edition & of course will be used by me for the next three years in my medical work. Have seen "Billy" Patten & he seems to be pleased with what I brought. Had the first recitation in embryology under him yesterday & in a few days we will start in hatching chickens eggs in the incubator. Ernest Cross & I both elected scientific German & we find that there are only two others in the course. It is hard & dry to begin on but will be a very valuable course. Am also taking a course in higher Botany which is in the Pharmacy line, & treats of the adulteration of foods, etc. A somewhat similar course, altho' going about it in a different way, is my organic chemistry[.] Altho' I mention this last, it is by no means least, as it is one of the stiffest courses in college—& very essential for medical work. [. . . .] It seems strange to be a senior, & you can hardly realize how badly I miss some of the 1900 boys. [. . . .] There is a fine lot of freshmen in town, the largest entering class in the history of the college. I have started in on my drawing instruments & have already taken some orders, & will go around this afternoon. Expect to make a good thing out of it. Prof. Hazen very kindly recommended me to the class, as selling good instruments etc, so every spare moment I am chasing around to see what I can do.

October 1—I am beginning to wonder if I have not taken up almost too stiff a schedule. This anatomy is extremely technical & requires absolute knowledge. For tomorrow we have one of the bones of the arm which has 16 muscle attachments alone besides all the other joints—Every join-hole—every ridge-bump—or knob—every depression—groove & notch has a name & must be learned. ₍. . .₎ In all probability I shall go west to Chicago with the banjo & mandolin clubs, if they take the western trip. I had my trials on the mandola last Friday night—Got a good piece & practised hard & it went off first rate. Of course I did not have to try for the banjo, as my reputation in that line is already established here—ahem—

October 7—Last Friday was Dartmouth Night, an annual function in Hanover. It is a mass meeting of the whole college, with speeches etc. This was one of the best nights for years, all the trustees of the College being here, as well as some of the big alumni from Boston & elsewhere. The speeches were all very good, & of course great enthusiasm was aroused. You know, next Commencement when I graduate, is the 100th anniversary of Daniel Websters graduation in 1801, so great efforts are being made to have it a big affair. At that time Prexy announced that the corner stone would be laid for Alumni Hall ⌈Webster Hall⌉, which is to be a big hall for lecturing purposes & entertainments—a small theater in fact. It is something very much needed as the old Gym is no place for such entertainments₍.₎ Of course this is only one feature of the building. There is a building being started on one corner of the campus which is to be a combined Commons (eating hall, for 200) dormitory & club house. It made me feel sad to think I was to graduate & miss all these things. But when I expressed such sentiments to Dr Patten the morning after the mass meeting, he said that I could enjoy these buildings when I came back next year as an alumnus. ₍. . .₎ Enjoyed a good sermon & communion at St Thomas this A.M. & a very good crowd turned out. The choir is also an improvement on last year. This is a very busy time as chinning season will soon be here when the fraternities choose their delegations from the freshmen class. I am chairman of the chinning committee of my frat, but I told the boys I was too busy to do any of the work ₍. . .₎.

October 11—Are you receiving the Dartmouth regularly? You probably also noticed that I was elected secretary of my class a couple of weeks ago, altho' I had forgotten to tell you. Had a written quiz in chemistry the other day & Dr Richardson complimented me highly on the paper I passed in, which is pleasing because Organic Chemistry is such a stiff course & it shows I am doing well in other lines besides biology.

October 28—In anatomy we have had all of the bones of the body except the skull, & we start on that this week. We are getting soaked in that Scientific German, with a nine page reading lesson for tomorrow, but I am beginning to read quite readily, & as now we are reading in zoology, having finished physics & geology, it is more interesting. Yesterday afternoon took a long tramp with Sib over the golf links & next Spring, if I can only arrange my studies satisfactorily, I shall try to get time to play some golf.

November 5—The dorm. as well as the whole town is just about deserted, as every body has gone in a night shirt parade to Lebanon for a republican rally. The college band went & every fellow carried a torch & as there was a special train most every body took advantage of the trip out of town. They will all probably have a pretty lively time, but I preferred to remain at home, as in all probability they wont get back till way after midnight, & as I am very tired I think the sleep will do me more good than the politics. ₍. . .₎ I suppose all S. F. is excited over the election. Well things are pretty lively here, but it doesnt affect me much to think I miss my vote by one month! & to think that in a little over one month your little son—shall become a man. Quite exciting—isn't it? But I really think that agreement about smoking should allow me to begin when the Xmas vacation commences, instead of waiting until almost its close—Don't you think so? Especially as I have ordered a corking little Theta Delt pipe to have on hand when I commence.

November 9—I dont know as I have told you what a great chef I am getting to be. You know every Saturday night, at the Casque & Gauntlet House, we always have some kind of a feed—a rarebit, cream chicken, tomato newberg or something else, & Henry Taylor usually runs the chafing dish. Well last week he was down in Boston, & as we had a lot of the Juniors around it was necessary to have a bang up feed. So the boys said I must make some cream oysters. Well, I have never made them before but have eaten them enough to know how they look. So ahead I went & must confess quite distinguished myself for every body called for "seconds" so they must have been good. Have been doing a little tutoring past week, as one fellow has to make up all his comparative anatomy of last semester, & another has been out most of this term & wants help on his chemistry.

November 25—C. & G. banquet comes off the day after the recess begins, & you cant realize how badly one wants to smoke after such good spreads and then most of the vacation I shall be on the glee club trip. But I suppose I already know what you will say—but as long as I have waited so far, a few days wont make any difference etc. And that I ought to have courage enough to wait etc—Of course I shall be bound by what you say, & will do as you wish.

Thanksgiving A.M.—Greetings to you on this my fourth Thanksgiving from home. It has been snowing all day, & our winter has commenced in good earnest. Can you imagine six inches of snow, out in sunny California! Yesterday afternoon went skeeing & had a grand time as it was the first real exercise I had had for some time. Then we would put three skees together & four of us pile on, most any way & off we would go toboganning. [. . .] There are very few fellows in town & things are awfully quiet, which seems in full harmony with the silent snowfall out of doors. In spite of all my caution I have managed to catch a little cold. Took 14 grains of quinine day before yesterday, & at night tried to sweat it out, & hope to lose it soon.

December 9—Last Wednesday night a quintette from the mandolin club, & a quartette from the glee club went down to Meriden, N.H. 12 miles from here where there is a prep. school & made our first appearance of the season to a very enthusiastic audience. We drove down there in a big sleigh & as the concert began early—at 7:00[—] we were thro' by 9:00 & got home in good season about 11:00. It was bright moonlight & a most glorious ride. Haugan & I gave a banjo duet which called forth more applause than the quintette did. We have two concerts around here next week, & then have a trip which begins the Thursday after Christmas, going to some of the principal cities in Massachusetts, excepting Boston.

January 6—Our midyear exams begin the last of this month & last 10 days or two weeks, so of course this is a busy time with everybody, & particularly so with me. [. . .] I note what you say in regard to smoking moderately, & of course you are right. And while I have been smoking a good deal this vacation, principally because there was nothing else to do, now that I have so much plugging to do I am going to smoke very little as I think it is best for me.

January 20—Twenty four below zero today and 20 below yesterday. Can you imagine it out where you see flowers & green grass nearly all winter? Well, the schedule of exams is out & my schedule couldn't be better arranged if I had fixed it myself. It's hard to get exams arranged so as to suit everybody & very often several, or all, may come in the space of a few days which makes it very hard. I have German Wednesday—Embryology Saturday—Chemistry Tuesday week—Botany Wednesday week & Anatomy the following Saturday—which gives me a good long time to get ready for each of them & as of course we have no recitations to attend during that time. I have now taken every biology course offered here at Dartmouth except one in higher Botany under Dr. Moore. I have elected this but as I am the only one who has elected this subject Dr Moore is going to give me a special course in Cryptogamic Botany which includes the study of various fungi, bacteria etc.

February 4—It was a week ago since I last wrote & that was only a few lines. Well as I look back on the last week's work & its results I feel that it was a week of triumph for my chemistry botany & anatomy exams were all met & passed in good shape. [. . .] You know the medical school up here is only a poor one horse affair & I should never think of going here. [. . .] I got a catalogue & statement from John Hopkins Univ. & a letter from the dean & I am very much pleased with the way things are taken up & am convinced more than ever that it is the best medical school in the country. One thing is that they allow only college graduates to enter so that the classes are small—not over 60 men which every one says is a great advantage. [. . .] One objection I have to John Hopkins is that women are admitted there being seven in this years freshman class. They are mostly Wellesley girls altho I saw several Bryn Mahr & Smith girls. But in this respect it is no worse than the University of California. I received the catalogue of the Univ. of California Medic school & agree with father that it is not much good when compared with such schools as John Hopkins & Harvard. I am so anxious to get right into real medical work that I can hardly wait for next fall to come.

February 15—We gave our concert in Hanover last Tuesday night & left Wednesday morning, giving a concert in Reading Mass. Wednesday night & our concert here in Steinert Hall last night—a packed house. Tonight we play in Everett which is no more than a suburb of Boston & that is our last concert but our cuts are excused till Monday morning so we shall stay here till Sunday as the B.A.A.—Boston Athletic Assn—meet comes off Saturday night, & Dartmouth runs against Columbia in the relay races, & the glee club is going to attend in a body. [. . .] I am having just a grand time & I think it is so fortunate for me that I am in the mandolin club. This little trip is a pleasant change after the hard work since Christmas. But I have got a lot of work ahead of me yet & expect to buckle right down from now till Easter vacation, after that my work will be lighter.

February 24—I have been intending to write you some time about my affairs here. I owe $47.00 as a balance on last years term bill, for roomrent etc. & my bill for this year is $97.00 for room & electric light, & 6.00 for tuition, as tuition is 106.00 including library dues, & my scholarship gives me $100.00. making at total of 150.00 due the treasurer. This is supposed to be paid by March 10th as you will see on page 166 of this year's catalogue, which I believe I sent you, or on page 164 of last year's catalogue. Of course I cannot graduate until this is paid & I am very anxious to get it settled up, & if you are in a position to pay it, I will draw a draft on you & give it to the treasurer, or if not for the entire amount now at least a part of it, so that there will be only so much less to pay in June. Let me know as soon as you can about this, if you will, as March 10 is just two weeks from today. Of course I owe nothing for board which is very fortunate. My diploma costs 8.00 & then there are various expenses at Commencement which each member of the class has to bear such as class tax, buying cap & gown etc.

March 5—The slight perturbations (you see I am studying astronomy) caused by my glee club trips have all been counterbalanced by continuous application & now I am down to routine work once more, & feel that I have got to do just exactly so much each week & accordingly have everything laid out in systematic order. My laboratory work mounts up to 24 hours a week as a minimum, besides my recitation work which requires a good deal of preparation. This week I have some tutoring to do, which has also to be fitted in during some hours

of the night and day. I fear I am going to have some trouble in getting
you a suitable room for Commencement week. [. . .] I had a fine place
engaged for you in the same house where I roomed freshman year.
But the party to whom the Frosts rented it have left town, which
leaves me in the lurch. The rooms at the hotel were all taken up long
ago, but that is a miserable house anyway. But don't worry for I shall
find a place before long. I should like to know when you are coming
on. I am expecting a letter from father soon in answer to mine of a
week & a half ago & I hope I will be able to square up with the treasurer soon. The usual senior class tax of twenty dollars has been levied
to cover the cost of the graduation exercises which amount to over
2000 dollars. Such as $750.00 for the Salem Cadet Band—500.00 for
printing & 250.00 for decorations—dinner—ball etc. Then we have to
get our pictures taken for exchanging with friends etc. Pach of Boston
is to come up here & has made very low rates $8.00 for fifty—cabinet
size. I am seriously debating what to do for prom week. Of course we
have a frat dance & there is the prom etc. Sibley is going to have a
Wellesley girl up, & wants me to invite a friend of this girl, Avis
Morrison. I met her at Belfast Christmas vacation sophomore year. I
should like to have Avis Coburn again from Smith for she is a corking
dancer but don't like the idea of having the same girl up for two years
in succession. Looks like too much of a steady affair.

May 6—I have some very good news to tell you, & I am sure you
will be as pleased to hear it as I was today. Prof. Emery called me to
his office & informed me that I had made a commencement appointment, for one of the English orations, & that I stood *seventh* in my
class of one hundred and twenty. Only those men who have a rank
above 85% make the appointments, & in my class there are 22 that did
this. An unusually large number, so you see what it means to stand
well up in a class like this. This also means that I am sure to make Phi
Beta Kappa, & I also have the privilege of speaking at Commencement. Out of this 22 six are chosen by competition to speak at Commencement, & of course as a good many either are unable or are dis-
inclined to take the trouble they will drop out & will ask to be
excused. I should like to try, so will not ask to be excused. These six
are chosen purely on their oratorical ability, & rank doesn't have anything to do with it—except that they have to be above 85%. It will
mean a good deal of extra work to write a good spiel & speak it well,
but I should like to try it. I shall send you notices about it later.

The Tuck School Is Founded

≫ꝰ This news story reporting the establishment at Dartmouth of the nation's first graduate school of business was carried during the autumn of 1900 in newspapers in widely scattered parts of the country. The text here reprinted bears a Boston dateline of November seventeenth.

ERHAPS THE MOST notable experiment among those now being made in fitting college men for business was begun this year in the opening of the Amos Tuck School of Administration and Finance as a graduate department of Dartmouth College. Its name—administration and finance—indicates its scope. It is founded to train young men in the broad principles governing the great modern businesses, not to fit them definitely for definite positions, but to bring them intellectually in touch with the great problems which are involved in business control and extension, and to send them out into the world with that invaluable "right point of view" which ought to be worth half the battle.

The Tuck School was founded in memory of the late Amos Tuck, of New Hampshire, by the generosity of his son, Mr. Edward Tuck, of Paris, who turned over to the college, last spring, securities amounting to $300,000. Mr. Tuck is a graduate of Dartmouth in the class of 1862, and is a collegemate, therefore, of President Tucker. He began life in the diplomatic service in the American legation in Paris; later, for a considerable time, he was a member of the Franco-American banking house of Monroe & Co. Since his retirement from active participation in that business, he has been connected with various enterprises in this country. He is one of the directors of the Chase National Bank of New York, and a large holder of the stock of the Great Northern railway.

His father, Amos Tuck, was a typical son of the Granite State. He was one of the most prominent figures in the political history of New Hampshire and New England during the early part of the anti-slavery conflict. [. . .] For six years he was a member of congress, and during that time he was one of the really intimate friends of Mr. Lincoln, their friendship continuing to the end. Leaving congress, he

17

resumed the practice of law in Exeter. He was a man noted for his resolute courage in difficult political situations. He was a graduate of Dartmouth in the class of 1835, and a trustee of the college from 1857 to 1866.

Hanover, the seat of Dartmouth College, is a quiet New Hampshire town, and distant from any great city, but the Tuck School has been able to count on the interest of financiers and leaders of great businesses in the most important commercial centers in the country, from New York and Boston to Chicago and St. Paul [....]. For such a school would mean, if it is successful, and if the example of Dartmouth is followed in other American college centers, that the American business man of the future, while not lacking in the force and special knowledge of his predecessor, is to have a wider culture, a broader outlook, and a sounder knowledge of the principles which lie at the base of commercial affairs.

In making up the curriculum, the Dartmouth authorities tried to put themselves in the place of the college graduate who, like so many of his class nowadays, has determined not to enter a profession, but to engage actively in affairs. They realized that a graduate school should not and could not be a "commercial college"; that it must present not so much details as principles; and that these principles must be based not only on the general culture of a college education, but on a special study of finance, economics, history, law, and politics. They realized that the young man leaving such a school must be prepared, not for mere clerkship—which was a matter of practical training—but for a position of responsibility and control, and knowing that in such a position a man's outlook must be of the widest, they made up the two years' course which was begun in September with the formal opening of the new school.

It was their aim, to quote the carefully prepared announcement which was given out last summer, "to prepare men in those fundamental principles which determine the conduct of affairs, and to give specific instruction in the common law and the laws pertaining to property, in the management of trusts and investments, in the problems of taxation and currency, practical banking and transportation, in the methods of corporate and municipal administration, in the growth and present status of the foreign commerce of the United States, and in the rules governing the civil and consular service. The attempt will be made to insure to college graduates who have in view administrative or financial careers, the preparation equivalent in its purpose to that obtained in the professional or technical schools. The training of the school is not designed to take the place of an apprenticeship in any given business, but it is believed that the same amount of academic training is called for under the enlarged demands of business as for the professions or for the productive industries."

The greatest care was taken to make the first entering class, however small it might be, a body of serious, studious, determined young men, who should reflect credit, when they went out into life, on the institution from which they had come. Too much stress cannot be laid on the fact that the Tuck School is a graduate school, with two years of instruction following a thorough college preparation. To enter it a student must have received a degree from a college of recognized standard. The only exception is that seniors in Dartmouth of proved ability who have taken the proper preparatory courses in their first three years in the college, may elect the first year in the Tuck School in place of the fourth year in the college, receiving the A.B. degree at the end of that year and the Tuck certificate a year later. Students from other colleges entering the senior year at Dartmouth in order to avail themselves of this privilege, must present with their certificate of transfer a record of their standing, so that they may show themselves equally capable with the regular Dartmouth men who have been allowed to enter the school. Special students will be received with caution, and only on proving fitness for the particular courses they desire to take up.

It is interesting to note the novel standpoint of even the general courses which have been adopted for the Tuck School. The first year's history includes a review of the geography of Europe, followed by the political history of the continent from the French revolution down to 1878. This is followed by a similar course dealing in essentially the same way with the political history of the United States. In the second year the modern history course consists of lectures on the political history of the South American and Central American States, Mexico, and the English colonies; and under the direction of the instructor the students will construct for the political history of Europe since 1878 and of the United States since 1877. Next in order will come a study of diplomacy, dealing with the origin and the evolution of modern diplomacy, the qualifications and methods of typical modern diplomats, the course of certain noteworthy negotiations, from the congress of Vienna to the Venezuela case, including the evolution and history of the Monroe doctrine; the organization of

American and foreign diplomatic and consular services, and the duties laid down by the United States government for its agents in foreign countries.

There is nothing like this course in diplomacy in the curriculum of any other American college. President Tucker has expressed publicly, in a much quoted address, his hope for better trained men in our public service, and this new course at Dartmouth may be taken as his contribution to the solution of a problem that has long troubled the critics of American institutions.

Another most interesting course in the Tuck School gives the history of American industrial development, including the development of the great manufacturing industries, the growth of corporations, trusts, and monopolies; the history and problem of transportation; stock and produce exchanges; the relations of capital and labor; and the effect of modern methods of business on producer and consumer. The courses in sociology are especially noteworthy, including anthropological geography, social statistics and applied sociology, demography, and social institutions. Demography, for example, is the study of the population or the units of all forms of social life. It involves the economic value of the various nations and peoples as producers and consumers of commodities, and includes the study of the different groups or classes into which population tends to fall. The course dealing with social institutions, on the other hand, treats the psychology of the forms of associated life, viewing human institutions as an expression of the spiritual life of the people. In this connection, an attempt is made to interpret sympathetically trade unionism, mass and class feeling, and all important group aspirations and rivalries.

Other courses which must obviously be included in a curriculum like that of the Tuck School relate to banking and investment of finance; and in the department of transportation, transportation itself, the foreign commerce of the United States, and international trade relations. [. . .]

The founding of the Tuck school at once brings to Dartmouth broader connections with active life. The curriculum will be strengthened by the introduction of non-resident lecturers who will conduct courses in banking, investments, accounting, insurance, municipal organization, the legal conditions of international trade, and other related subjects. [. . .]

It may be seen from this summary of courses that Dartmouth intends that the graduates of its Tuck School shall not only become, if they develop the ability required, "captains of industry," but shall be trained also in the broader duties of citizenship and public responsibility.

≫⁓ Tuck School's creation was also focused upon within the November 24, 1900, number of *The Commercial and Financial Chronicle*, in an article that began:

The munificent gift of $300,000 by Mr. Edward Tuck [. . .] has enabled Dartmouth College, in opening [. . .] the Amos Tuck School of Administration and Finance, to place commercial education in this country upon its proper basis and to prepare the way for carrying it further than is yet done in Europe. Commercial education has of late been much exploited. Commercial courses have been widely introduced into the public schools and the catalogues of the universities have begun to offer special courses that will be of value to students contemplating a business career. One university president has come out deprecating the movement and suggesting that to take the law course is all that any would-be merchant need do. Several of the leading universities have, indeed, opened special schools parallelling those in Arts and Sciences in the regular university course; but it seems to be immensely difficult to secure acceptance for the idea that education has any place in business life or that a business man should be as highly educated as any. Some years ago when old Daniel Drew was a prominent figure in Wall street, a friend said to him: "Uncle Daniel, what a man you would be if you had been educated!" "Oh," was the reply, "it would have spoilt me." The tradition to that effect seems still to hang about many minds, but the community is fast outgrowing it, and few successful business men of today are willing to look with complacency upon having a son succeed to the management of a business of which he has no more knowledge than any clerk. [. . .]

Here is the distinction of the Tuck School. For the first time commercial education is put definitely upon the plane of the advanced sciences. Dartmouth College had the advantage of a highly successful model. The Thayer School of Civil Engineering connected with that college was founded some years ago by Gen. Sylvanus Thayer, of the United States Army, for the purpose of educating civil engineers of the highest grade. [. . .]

When, therefore, the Tuck gift came into the hands of the trustees of Dartmouth they were not long at a loss as to the best way to use it.

The method of the Thayer School will be applied to advanced commercial education. Leaving the business colleges to do their work for clerks, and the high schools to teach the rudiments of accounts, and such as will to offer courses that are parallel to the regular college courses and will inevitably tend to narrow and restrict the education offered to sons of merchants, the Tuck School boldly limits itself to picked men who have completed at least three years of college work and are candidates for the regular college degree. This seems the largest possible liberal education. The student is to be fitted to be an educated man before he starts on his career as a business man. [. . .]

Much will depend upon the character of the instruction; but the fact that it is a department of the work of a college so old and so distinguished as Dartmouth is, for the high grade of its scholarship and the exceptional number of strong men it has produced, is a guaranty of the result. [. . .]

Quotations from
William Jewett Tucker

From the standpoint of imparting both moral and spiritual values, Dr. Tucker greatly impacted the lives of those who attended Dartmouth during his presidency. This was particularly achieved through his talks, given each week to the entire student body, during Sunday Vesper Services.

While an undergraduate, Eugene R. Musgrove 1905 compiled a notebook of "Quotations from President Tucker," comprised of more than fifty manuscript pages. The following selections have been drawn from that source by Fred Berthold Jr. 1945, Professor of Religion, Emeritus, and first Dean (1957–63) of the William Jewett Tucker Foundation.

NO MAN OUGHT to be satisfied with anything less than integrity.

Progress always waits for those who do not want the best things for themselves.

It is a wholesome business for one to turn practised judgment upon himself. Consistency requires him to do this.

Nothing hurts a sane and honest man so much as to find himself engaged in special pleading for himself.

The sense of inconsistency is about the most painful sense which a man can hold in his conscience. Conscience may relent somewhat toward one who falls away from his ideals, or who even violates a law, but it has no mercy for a man who does not play fair with his fellow men.

Great is the advantage to society from the man who expects much, because he gives much. He sets the standard of giving and receiving.

"Whatsoever," Jesus says, "ye would that men should do to you, even so do ye also to them." That one word "whatsoever" measures the difference between men. With some men it is a little word meaning no more than the barter of petty trade. With other men it is a full word standing for the exchange of the richest products of mind and heart in the market places of the world.

It is perhaps the chief business of education to create the asking, and expectant, but discriminate mind. There is less danger from the overasking, the grasping mind, than there is from the mind without desires and without demands. Descrimination is the after part of education. First the creation of wants, the kindling of desires, then the refinement of the awakened and enlarged nature.

Life today is asking more questions, investigating more problems, daring to do braver things. There is no escape from the test in any department of life, or on the part of any man. To him that hath it shall be given, and he shall have abundantly. Men delight to give to the man who is intent on the true riches. His desires, his purposes, and struggles, as well as his achievements enrich the common life.

Such is the gracious and ennobling order of the providence of God—first the surrender of personality through obedience to commandment and through loyalty to common ideals, and then the recovery of personality, disciplined and refined, to win a place in the presence of men and of the world.

Keep your faith in men, I pray you, as you keep your faith in God. Faith in God has been defined as trusting Him against appearances. Believe in men against appearances. Use the true, not the false in human nature, and persist in doing this. So shall you gain access to the heart of humanity.

Do not mistake oddity for independence.

We can easily broaden and not deepen. We should do both.

When we are overcome by a great sorrow, there is no way to carry it out except to carry it out in the open, out in the breadth of a great faith. There are no little places in this world in which to put great things, and a sorrow is a great thing. There is no place big enough for it, save in the heart and in the plan of God.

The one great qualification of a Christian is not, as it once was, preparedness for death, but it is preparedness for life. When Dr. Lyman Beecher was asked, in the closing moments of his life, if he was ready to die, he replied emphatically: "No! I would volunteer over again."

Most men can deal with things, but few men can deal with men.

Every advance in power carries with it obligations which, if they are not met, relegate power to the rude and elementary.

What is a man's soul worth if he hasn't self respect?

Do not fear to give to men freely of that which has cost you the most. Who wants the second things of any man's giving? The greater the man, the more we want him at his best. The increment of your lives is yours. When you give that, you give yourselves.

Nature may outlast man, as far as he is a part of her life, but she does not rid herself of his ceaseless and resolute questioning. She may bury him out of sight, but the seed [s]he buries will spring up to vex and torment her. Gradually, the secret of nature is yielding to the invincible search of man.

It is according to the eternal plan that the capital of the world, its moral as well as its material capital, should be made up out of the earnings of humanity.

Moral courage rests altogether upon the sense of values. Men fight for what they know the worth of, and believe in, and therefore dare not betray.

The original capacity of any man is of God; the increment of his life is that which he earns for himself, and is the test not only of our own social judgments but also the test of the divine judgment.

Get into your minds the idea of the permanent. Covet permanent acts, permanent ideas, permanent hopes. Put your thoughts into the souls of men: men never die.

The office of faith is twofold—to enlarge a man's vision, and to make the man, like St. Paul, be obedient to the vision.

There is need today of personal religion as the one power that can ask of every one who is looking forward to some accomplishment, Is the purpose right? More voices are calling for success than for duty. Religion makes a man look beyond the voices of success and listen for the still small voice of duty.

Knowledge is the understanding of things as they are. Wisdom is the understanding of things as they ought to be. This age, because of its great discoveries, emphasizes knowledge rather than wisdom. And we, who are in and of this age, hear its voice and feel its power. We often lack that wisdom which the prophet calls the ultimate end of knowledge.

Someone has aptly said that "Nature doesn't last unless we mix man with it." This is what we do among these hills of Dartmouth. Men find themselves here. They learn their large relation to man, nature, and God.

Every man of any imagination likes to feel that he has, or may have, a place among the more permanent things of the world. There is nothing so great, certainly nothing so impressive, in this world of limitations and change as the power to live, and still to live. Here lies the glory of institutions above the glory of men. The college was before we were, and will be when we are no more, but as we are in it and of it, we share its permanency.

A man does not get very far on his way in the midst of the stern and often [. . .] disturbing facts of life without feeling the need of drawing upon such resources of the spirit as are in him. It is the presence or absence of this deeper sense of things which determines not only a man's personal happiness, but in a large degree his power over others.

The end of personal freedom is not freedom, but responsibility, action, the stronger and more efficient life.

Life means a great comradeship. Am I worthy such comradeship?

Cowardice is one form of selfishness.

Books are more than tools. Willingly as the great explorers and interpreters in the intellectual world lend themselves and their work to our uses, they give themselves more joyfully to our companionship. They allow themselves to become ours by inalienable rights of ownership.

You cannot do good by being local; you must perform a service as wide as the world. A man must be cosmopolitan in order to be human.

"Dedicating" Harvard's Stadium

➤➤ Toward the close of the 1903 football season, Boston's newspapers prominently carried commentary relating to the up-coming Dartmouth-Harvard contest, which was to be the first game played within Harvard's grand, newly completed stadium. *The Boston Herald* in one of its articles commented: "The Hanover boys have been down to Cambridge year after year, with the claim that they were going to 'take it out' of the Harvard team, and year after year Harvard has put in a team of subs and has come out ahead. Last year, however, it was by a very small margin that the Crimson won, or at least it was not until the last few minutes of play that Harvard pulled out ahead, and this year Dartmouth is credited with a remarkably strong team." Then, on the day after the November-fourteenth encounter had taken place, the *Herald*'s headlines read: "HARVARD SHUT OUT BY DARTMOUTH / Tough Defeat in the New Stadium. / The Crimson Eleven Was Completely Outplayed. / Thrown Back on Every Rush...." At Hanover, the undergraduate newspaper, *The Dartmouth*, carried in its November-twelfth edition a detailed account of the victory, as well as of its jubilant impact locally, in an extended story from which these passages have been taken.

SATURDAY WAS a notable day in Dartmouth's athletic history, for the sturdy men who represent Dartmouth on the gridiron realized their highest ambition by defeating Harvard. Eleven points to nothing, and two hundred and thirty-six yards to forty-eight, in the first game in the Crimson's new stadium, tell in brief the story of a victory as glorious to the Green as it was humiliating to the Crimson. As *The Boston Traveller* put it, "The brawn and beef of the Granite State boys pushed under, over, and through the Crimson line as though Harvard was represented by men of straw. It was a complete defeat, a defeat without an excuse."

Dartmouth completely outclassed Harvard. Neither offense nor defense left anything to be desired. The team-work was marvelous. It was a splendid sight to see the eleven men get into every play as a unit; to see them charge together, rally round the man with the ball, and push, pull, and shove for every inch. Dartmouth's line, although nine-

27

teen pounds heavier than Harvard's, from tackle to tackle, got the jump on the Crimson nearly every time, and opened up big holes for the backs. The defensive work proved that Coach Folsom and his assistants had brought out a team capable of presenting one of the most stubborn and determined fronts of any team now playing the game.

Captain Witham ran his team with admirable judgment, and it is the opinion of the *Globe* that he "should be reckoned with when the all-American elevens are made up this fall." Dartmouth's attack spread across Harvard's whole line, and Dartmouth found admittance at every point [. . .].

The scene after the game [. . . defies] description. The contrast was impressive. While the Harvard supporters remained in their seats and cheered the defeated team with commendable loyalty, the Dartmouth men instantly flooded the field to indulge in more than the usual congratulatory enthusiasm. A procession of several thousand men then started for Harvard Square, where the crowd scattered. Dartmouth alumni and undergraduates alike continued their jollification at the Quincy House, where the members of the team made merry at dinner by singing songs and giving cheers, at the Adams House, and at the Columbia Theatre.

One of the finest features of the day, however, was the celebration in Hanover. This classic village had not seen such a time in years. When the three hundred stay-at-homes learned that their team had scored on Harvard in a few minutes after the toss-up, their enthusiasm knew no bounds. They immediately secured continuous telegraphic service, and a good running story of the game was read to the expectant throng. When the last message arrived, the students withdrew to collect material for a huge bonfire—and the work was not confined to the Freshman class!

At seven o'clock one of the most enthusiastic meetings ever held in celebration of the athletic victory took place in Old Chapel. Every man who did not go to Boston was there to cheer the team and listen to the speeches given by members of the faculty. President Durgin of the Senior class presided.

President Tucker was the first speaker. In his introductory remarks he spoke of the severe illness of Freshman Hayes and requested that the parade be confined to the Campus. He then spoke of the great victory of the day and what it meant to Dartmouth. It was due to the men on the team, Coach Folsom, and the Athletic Council, who "had bragged little and done much." We should all have great respect for the men on the team who have submitted themselves to this double discipline and have worked so well.

Dean Emerson, speaking of Harvard's stadium, said that it was a copy of the Coliseum and that Dartmouth had certainly "called to see 'em." [. . .] The possibilities of the Dartmouth team were as great as of any team in the country. The victory meant that Dartmouth's name would go down as the first team that won in the new stadium.

Prof. J. K. Lord said that he thought the occasion was almost too great for speech, that like the little boy, he felt so good that he wanted to hug himself. The victory has left a coat of green on the stadium and it will take a good many coats of crimson and blue to wear it away. [. . .]

Professor Laycock said that it was a notable opening of "our" stadium. [. . .]

Prof. G. D. Lord thought that it was not necessary to belittle Harvard. We have reached out to Harvard for a great many things that she was willing to give us, but to-day we have taken something that she was very reluctant to part with. Great credit is due to the first team and all the other men who have assisted in perfecting it.

After the meeting the excited students formed in line and, headed by the band, marched round the campus, down College Street, up Lebanon and Main, down Allen Street, up School and West Wheelock to the campus. They called on Prof. Charles H. Richardson and Prof. Charles F. Richardson, who made enthusiastic remarks. The fire was lighted at 8:30 o'clock, and it was one of the biggest blazes in recent years. Around the fire the men sang songs and cheered wildly, and then indulged in a nightshirt parade, which ended one of the most memorable athletic celebrations in Dartmouth's history.

Dartmouth Hall Burns

꙳》 Articles about the great conflagration that occurred in Hanover on February 17, 1904, were carried on the front pages of newspapers throughout New England and in papers far beyond the immediate region, as well. This account appeared on February eighteenth in the *Boston Evening Transcript*.

DARTMOUTH HALL, about which centred much of the history of Dartmouth College, and which has sheltered Dartmouth men for four generations, burned to the ground this morning. Fire broke out at eight o'clock, as the chapel bell calling the students to morning prayers was ceasing, and at ten o'clock the century-old building was merely a heap of blazing ruins. The loss is $25,000, partially covered by insurance. About twenty-five students, who roomed on the top floor of the hall, lost most of their furniture, books and other belongings. No one was injured during the progress of the fire. Most of the students had left the hall for morning prayers, and the few belated ones were dressed and about to leave the building. For a time Wentworth and Thornton halls, which flank Dartmouth Hall, were in danger; but they were saved by the hard work of the students and townspeople.

At eight o'clock the entire college was assembled in Rollins Chapel for the customary morning exercises. Cries of "fire" were suddenly heard, and Dean Emerson, hurriedly entering, announced that Dartmouth Hall was on fire. The fire started on the third floor in the room immediately under the clock. By the time the volunteer fire department arrived with a hose reel flames and smoke were pouring from several of the windows. There was a lack of water pressure, and, though lines of hose were quickly laid inside the building, the fire gained rapid headway. Within fifteen minutes of the first alarm the tower and a portion of the roof were all ablaze.

From this point the flames gained rapidly. The third floor was used for dormitory purposes, but so rapid was the spread of the flames that the students were able to save practically nothing. Several in their efforts to save a few valuables were cut off from the stairs and had to descend by means of ladders. It soon became apparent that all efforts to save "Old Dartmouth" were useless. The flames were revelling in a huge wooden building, dry as tinder, timbered and boarded with resinous primæval pine, felled a century and a quarter ago, which has been drying and seasoning ever since. Conditions were perfect for a monster bonfire, and such the destruction of Dartmouth Hall became from the spectacular point of view.

When it became evident that Dartmouth Hall could not be saved, the firemen turned their attention to Wentworth and Thornton halls, which flanked the burning building. As these dormitories were only thirty or forty feet away, they were in danger of catching fire, not only from the sparks, but from the heat of the blazing pile. The students occupying these dormitories removed their furniture and other valuables as a precautionary measure. Lines of hose were carried into the buildings and also laid on the roofs.

At half-past nine the Lebanon fire department, to which Chief Ford had telephoned for help, arrived with a hose wagon and ladder truck, coming over five miles of hill country road deep with snow.

Several more lines were laid, and by keeping the walls and roofs of the dormitories wet, Thornton and Wentworth halls, being of brick, were saved, though their safety was not assured until the walls of Dartmouth Hall had fallen inward and the burning building was reduced to a huge bonfire.

The cause of the fire is not certainly known, but it is believed that the fire started from a match thrown in a wastebasket.

The greatest excitement prevailed during the progress of the fire, which was fought under the most adverse conditions. The morning was bitter cold, and the freezing spray from the fire streams coated the firemen with ice. [. . .]

Dartmouth Hall—"Old Dartmouth," as Dartmouth men have affectionately called it for generations—while intrinsically perhaps the least valuable of the college buildings, was the richest in history and legend. It was of three stories, the only wooden building owned by the college. It was virtually contemporaneous with the founding of the college, the foundation having been [laid] in 1769, and Dartmouth Hall having been commenced in 1784. The money for its erection was secured from grants from the Provincial Assembly of New Hampshire, from private subscriptions, and from public lotteries, as was the custom of the time. There is no doubt that a portion of the money raised in England by Wheelock and Occum, part of which came from the Earl of Dartmouth whence the name of the college, went into the construction of Dartmouth Hall. None the less, a debt remained on the building, which was a source of embarrassment to the college authorities for many years.

Dartmouth Hall was completed in 1791, and was one of the oldest college buildings in the country. It has been recognized as one of the best examples of college architecture in the Colonial period. Now that it has been destroyed, the only existing examples of like character are Nassau Hall at Princeton, from which Dartmouth Hall is said to have been modelled, and University Hall at Brown. The timbers in Dartmouth Hall were hewn from trees felled on its site and on the campus below. Some of them, whose rough-hewn proportions were visible in the cellar of the building, were no less than seventy-five feet long and maintained throughout that great length all the massiveness of their fifteen inches square. Many a mast for the king's ships went into Dartmouth Hall.

For forty years Dartmouth Hall met all the requirements of the college for recitation rooms, library, and dormitory. It was originally heated, during the proverbial Hanover winter, by fireplaces; but in 1822 stoves were introduced and the old fireplaces were bricked up. As late as ten years ago, the recitation rooms were heated by huge wood-burning furnaces in the cellar, while the rooms occupied by students were warmed by stoves. This great fire risk the old hall survived; and when, in 1899, steam heat was introduced from a central heating plant some hundreds of yards away, it was thought that the fire risk had been reduced to a minimum.

The portion of the building about which centred the tenderest memories was the "Old Chapel." This was evolved by a remodelling of the central portion of the building in 1828, and until the construction of Rollins Chapel in 1885 this chapel, rising through two stories in the centre of the hall, was the focus of the religious life of the college. Here worshipped all the classes from that of '28 to '89; and after Rollins Chapel was built, it was in the "Old Chapel" that the classes gathered for their oratorical work, and, on Wednesday afternoons, the whole college to exult in the oratorical struggles of perspiring seniors. Here, too, have been held the college mass-meetings, before great games and on other important occasions; and here have occurred the exercises of "Dartmouth Night," an annual event which has done much to solidify the graduates and undergraduates of the college, and especially to introduce successive classes of freshmen to the peculiar Dartmouth atmosphere. About the "Old Chapel" centred much of the tradition of the college—from the departure of Dartmouth's sons to war, to the introduction of a donkey, of happy memory, upon the platform whence the stern and reverend president of the college was to speak.

With Dartmouth Hall the names of all the great men of the college are inseparably connected. Here they all recited; here they worshipped; here many of them roomed. Webster lived in Dartmouth Hall his senior year, occupying the northeast corner room on the third floor, overlooking what is now the college park. Here too roomed Choate, and a hundred more. Every room in the old building was redolent of memories of the past. Of late only the top, or third floor of Dartmouth Hall has been used for dormitory purposes. The "Old Chapel" took up the central part of the building through the first two stories; and in either wing were recitation-rooms—Latin and French in the right wing, first and second floors; and Greek and German in the first and second floors of the left wing. [. . .]

With fire streams still playing into the blazing cellar of "Old Dartmouth," and waiting only for the word that the fire was under control and no more buildings burned, the Boston alumni set their faces to the future and began to plan for rebuilding. Melvin O. Adams, their representative on the board of trustees, left for Hanover by the eleven o'clock train, to consult with President Tucker in person, though they had a hurried telephonic conversation this morning while Dartmouth was still burning. Meantime, a mass meeting of Dartmouth men of this vicinity has been arranged, to be held in Lorimer Hall, Tremont Temple, Saturday, Feb. 20, at three o'clock in the afternoon, when ways and means will be discussed.

From the expressions heard this morning from many Dartmouth men, including officers of the college, it appears to be already decided, informally, but by spontaneous agreement, that Dartmouth Hall not only must rise from its ashes—that goes without saying—but in the same architectural form. That is, the new building must be a replica of the old one, but of more enduring and fire-resisting material. The classic dignity of the destroyed building, surmounted by its graceful cupola, has appealed to the artistic instincts of generations of Dartmouth men; and the great body of graduates will find consolation for the loss of the historic structure only in the knowledge that the new building shall perpetuate the form of "Old Dartmouth," and, so far as may be, its memories.

≫≫ On the same day as the fire, Sophomore Francis Lane Childs 1906 (later to be for nearly half a century one of the College's most esteemed teachers of English) wrote to his mother at Henniker, New Hampshire: "I suppose perhaps the most eventful day of all my college life is nearly over—the day on which old Dartmouth burned. It seems to have created much the same effect as a death would have, except that it was attended with so much excitement." Then, four days later, on February twenty-second, he sent this follow-up report—a communication providing, also, comments on some of his personal concerns and activities of the moment.

DEAR MOTHER:—Now that everything is calmed down and we are once more back in the regular routine I will write again. I don't know when you will get this, for it seems to me the mails down that way must be most awfully erratic. [. . .] I sent you some papers Saturday morning and will send some more to-day. The [Boston] Transcript account is the best one in any of the dailies, and the [Hanover] Gazette account is also pretty correct. The Manchester Union is all off its base—you could see that when it states the fire broke out at "3 o'clock last night." Of course the account in the Dartmouth is all right. I want you to keep all these papers, also the [Boston] Journals. But everyone up here is thoroughly disgusted with the Journal—it is so swell-headed. The very idea of claiming that it is at "*the Journal's*" suggestion that Dartmouth Hall will be rebuilt on the old site preserving the same proportion and outlines as the old hall. No one here had any thought of doing otherwise, and it was talked of before the fire was wholly out. [. . .]

The fire still smokes in a few places, tho it is raining a little this morning, which will probably help to finish it. You have no idea how strange it looks not to see "old Dartmouth" any more. I seems as tho the college was not all here. The classes held in it—all the Latin, Greek, French, Spanish, & most of the German—nearly sixty in all, most of them reciting three times a week, are distributed throughout the other buildings. [. . . .]

I think it speaks well for the loyalty of Dartmouth alumni when you consider that the fire only broke out at 8 o'clock Thursday morning, and at 10.10, before the end walls and part of the back had fallen, a hall in Boston had been obtained and a meeting of the alumni of Boston and vicinity had been called for Saturday afternoon. Of course, the old Hall—the link between Dartmouth of the 18th century, and Dartmouth of the 20th can never be replaced—it can live only in the memory of the alumni and undergraduates who have passed so many precious hours within her walls, but when we consider that we shall have a new building, modern and costly, which in outline and proportion will suggest the old Dartmouth—and that besides this the plans for Webster Hall and the new dormitory will also be carried out—that a quarter of a million of dollars has been voted to do these things—we cannot but think that, barring the sentiment lost—and that will be preserved in so far as it can be—the College may have gained.

The washing came all right Friday. I was awfully glad of the apples. I picked up my washing in a hurry the night I sent it, and forgot my dirty handkerchiefs which were in one of my chiffonier drawers instead of in my laundry-bag as they should have been. I guess you will think there are enough this week to make up. [. . .]

Saturday afternoon we went skeeing. The last hill we came down, I fell, and Arthur & Neely were tickled, for it is the first time I have fallen since the first day we went out, while they have fallen several times every day, and both of them have scraped the skin well off their noses. I have not hurt myself at all yet, and hope I shall not.

But Saturday night we had the most fun there has been doing for a long time. We went over to Norwich to see "Ten Nights in a Bar Room" by a travelling show. About a hundred fellows went over and they put the show completely on the bum. It was pretty punk, anyway; the poorest apology for acting I ever saw—it couldn't hold a candle to the free medicine shows that come to Henniker. The fellows all cheered & sang and stamped between the acts, and when the actors came out to sing between acts the fellows all sang with them, which proved somewhat disconcerting, especially to the lady performers (there were two). The hall was a little one with the stage in the long side of it, and the curtain and stage fittings were not as good as we kids used to rig up for our "shows" in the barn; the curtain failed to work once or twice. You know the play is very pathetic and when any very sad parts were reached, the sympathetic audience would groan and sob; this sometimes resulted in making an actor laugh right in the midst of a heart-broken speech, and it spoiled the effect somewhat. The manager got pretty sore and put the curtain down on us several times, but the fellows would yell "money back" until he would go on.

Before the show began they (the company) sent out and got a constable and several assistants who tried to allay the disturbance, but without much effect. At last, during the scene where little Mary is dying, the manager got red-hot mad (the fellows were so touched by the pathos, that they were nearly in hysterics) and coming front he ordered the officer to arrest a certain man in the front row. The fellows all yelled "Bunch up," the dying girl and the leading lady fled from the stage, and it looked as tho there would be something doing. The fellows stuck together and of course the officers did not dare do anything more than argue. One drew a revolver, but of course he did not dare to use it. I doubt if it was loaded anyway. Well, after lots of talk, the fellows promised to keep quiet if the show would go on. So, omitting an act and a half, the company presented the last act amid perfect quiet. Then after it was over, the fellows got together and gave a "wah-hoo-wah" for the whole show, and for the principal actor and went home. It was an awful lot of sport. Harold Rugg took his opera glasses and tho we were not more than a dozen feet from the stage we levelled them at the leading lady when she came on to sing, to her great consternation. There was a small bunch of Norwich people there, including some women, but, having lived all their lives in Norwich, they were used to students and seemed to enjoy it almost as much as the fellows. I even heard one old lady gaily recounting the days when the Norwich University and the Dartmouth students used to have pitched battles out on the hill. I said they enjoyed it—all but one, who declared she "was never was so disgraced in all her life! She was going right straight home! The idea of Hanover students coming over and disturbing a nice, peaceable entertainment!" But her husband wouldn't go till the fun was over, so she had to stay. Well, the fellows had their fun, and the show got some $25 or $30 more than they would if they had not gone over, and considering that they got stranded and had to leave their trunks at the last town before Norwich, so needed our assistance financially, I think it was fair all around.

I can think of nothing more to write so will close. Love to all. [. . .]

A Visit from Lord Dartmouth

≫ The preparations for rebuilding Dartmouth Hall took an especially felicitous turn when it developed that the Earl of Dartmouth, accompanied by his wife and elder daughter, would be able to visit Hanover in the autumn of 1904, and that His Lordship would at that time lay the cornerstone for the new structure. On October twenty-first, just in advance of the Earl's arrival, *The Dartmouth* undertook to provide its readers with some biographical information about Lord Dartmouth and his ancestors—information that included these paragraphs.

T HE PRESENT AND SIXTH EARL OF DARTMOUTH, William Heneage Legge, was born May 6, 1851, and is the son of the fifth earl and Augusta, daughter of the Earl of Aylesford. He was educated at Eton, where he was a contemporary of Lord Randolph Churchill, Lord Rosebery, and Arthur Balfour, the present premier of England. His college was Christ Church at Oxford. Lord Dartmouth is a member of the Carlton, St. Stephen's, and the Travelers' clubs in London. A very prominent Free Mason, he has been provincial grand master for Staffordshire since 1893. Upon succeeding to the earldom in 1891 he was made lord lieutenant of Staffordshire. He is a privy councillor, was member of Parliament for West Kent from 1878 to 1885, and was for several years the whip of that party in the House of Commons. For a time he was a conspicuous figure at court, and was vice chamberlain of the household to the late Queen Victoria, from 1885 to 1892. In recent years, however, he has devoted himself to the management of his large estates and also to literary research, to which his attention was turned by the wonderful collection of literary treasures among his family papers, including all the correspondence of Pepys, of "Diary" fame, with the first Lord Dartmouth, a large number of letters from Dean Swift, Lord North, King William III., George III., and John Wesley. [. . .] King Edward has recognized Lord Dartmouth's interest in literary research by appointing him one of the members of the Royal Commission on Historical Manuscripts.

Lord Dartmouth is a very rich man, his earldom ranking with that of Lord Derby as one of the greatest in England. The family estates comprise 19,000 acres in Staffordshire and neighboring counties, and the ancestral homes of Lord Dartmouth are Patshull House, near Wolverhampton, which was built about two hundred years ago, and Woodsome Hall, near Huddersfield, which has been in the possession of the family from the sixteenth century. [. . .]

The Countess of Dartmouth was Lady Mary Coke, [. . .] daughter of that patriarch of the British peerage, Lord Leicester. By this marriage, which took place in 1879, Lord Dartmouth is a brother-in-law to the Bishop of Southwark.

⇛⇛⁓ The *Concord Evening Monitor* on Wednesday, October twenty-sixth, carried a story, bearing a Hanover dateline, that in part reported:

The town is in gala attire and in fitting shape to receive its noted guest, who is the great-great-grandson of the patron of the college in its early days. College Hall, the social headquarters of the college, is decked with the Stars and Stripes and the Union Jack, they being side by side around the pillars on the balcony. The banners of national pride and patriotism are everywhere in evidence around the town, and particularly on college buildings.

The earl and his party arrived at West Lebanon, about four miles from here on the 1:24 train Tuesday afternoon. [. . .]

At 4 o'clock, the earl, countess and Lady Dorothy, with C. T. Gallagher and President Tucker, went to the alumni oval, where a game of football was played between the first and second teams. The Earl of Dartmouth dined with the students at College Hall at 6 o'clock, when every possible honor was bestowed upon him. The dining-room was filled in every nook and corner and the menu was one specially prepared for the guest of honor. The balcony of the dining-room was decked with harvest trimmings which lent brightness to the room. [. . .] The earl and party were seated on the right side of the hall on a slightly raised platform. At the earl's left sat President Tucker, and the others seated at the guests' table were Prof. D. C. Wells, Prof. William Patten, Prof. C. F. Richardson, J. R. Merriam, president of the College club, and Fletcher Hale, president of the Dramatic club. After the guests were seated, the students gave the college yell for Lord Dartmouth, and he recognized the ovation with bows and smiles.

During the latter part of the dinner a pleasing incident occurred which interested the earl very much—the electric lights suddenly went out and for a few moments the dining hall was in darkness. During this time the boys sang college songs and songs used at football games.

>>> *The Dartmouth* of October twenty-eighth gave an extended account of the various formal events associated with Lord Dartmouth's presence on Hanover Plain.

The exercises attending the laying of the corner-stone of the new Dartmouth Hall were held Tuesday and Wednesday with dispatch and success. [. . .]

The celebration attracted a very large number of alumni, all of whom were abundantly pleased and satisfied. The decorations were artistic. American and British flags were prominent at College Hall and at the Inn, but the principal feature was an electric arch over the entire length of the Dartmouth Hall site, making brilliant the words, "1791—Dartmouth—1904." Excellent music was furnished by the College band of twenty pieces, H. W. Rainie '06, leader, assisted by six musicians of Nevers' band of Concord. [. . .]

Dartmouth Night, the first important event of the week, was celebrated on the Alumni Athletic Field Tuesday evening under very favorable weather conditions. The grand stand, although reserved chiefly for the guests of the College, trustees, alumni, and the faculty, was extended by covered seats to accommodate the entire student body. Heavy strips of canvas were fastened about the open tops and side spaces for protection. A separate covered stage, artistically decorated with red, white, and blue bunting, the College green, and electric lights, stood directly opposite the grand stand. Fifteen hundred people were present.

The program consisted of singing by the glee club, a series of stereopticon views relating to the first half century of the College and historical tableaux illustrating Dartmouth's origin and early days. These tableaux, given by the dramatic club, Fletcher Hale '05 president, were shown on the covered stage and were most excellently presented with appropriate scenery, costume, and action. [. . .]

The exercises in the College Church Wednesday morning attracted an audience that filled the historic building. At ten o'clock the trustees and faculty formed in procession at the Inn and escorted the guests to the Church, under the marshalship of Col. Charles Kimball Darling

'85. The guests, prominent alumni, trustees, and members of the faculty had seats on the platform, which had been extended for the occasion. Undergraduates and alumni filled the body of the house and friends filled the galleries. The room was decorated with American and British flags. Pres. William Jewett Tucker presided, and the exercises were as follows:

Venite in D, College chorus, Prof. C. H. Morse, conductor; prayer, the Rev. Samuel Penniman Leeds, D.D. 1870; Luther's hymn, "A Mighty Fortress is our God"; historical address, "The Origins of Dartmouth College," Prof. Francis Brown '70, D. D. Dart., D. Litt. Oxon; presentation by Lord Dartmouth of the correspondence between Eleazar Wheelock and the second Earl; conferring of the honorary degree of Doctor of Laws upon Lord Dartmouth; psalm CXXXVI, sung by alumni and students; benediction, the Rev. Frederick D. Avery, pastor emeritus of the Congregational church at Columbia, formerly Lebanon, Conn. [. . .]

Conferring the honorary degree on Lord Dartmouth, Pres. William Jewett Tucker said:

"It was a singular but happy fortune which identified our academic family at the beginning with the ancient and honorable Legge—a family which, a century before the founding of the College, had earned the recognition of the King. The relationship, though involving no corporate responsibilities on either side, has, with us, developed a natural and honorable sentiment, which has always met with an honorable response.

"It is a peculiar pleasure, however, that this relationship can be individualized, and that on fit occasions, members of the family take their place in our academic fellowship. In 1805 Edward Legge, then Dean of Windsor, afterward Bishop of Oxford, received from the College the degree of Doctor of Divinity. In 1860 William Walter Legge, fourth earl of Dartmouth, received from the College the degree of Doctor of Laws. Both of these degrees were conferred *in absentia*. For the first time a member of this family receives a degree from the College in person.

"I bid you, gentlemen of the College, rise and greet our guest as he enters into our academic kinship.

"William Heneage Legge, Sixth Earl of Dartmouth, I have the honor to confer upon you, by direction of the Trustees of Dartmouth College, the degree of Doctor of Laws, the degree through which the colleges and universities of this country express their estimation of men in public life, most fitly conferred upon you in recognition of your active political service, your loyal devotion to public affairs, and your most effective interest in historical researches relating to Great Britain and the American colonies; and no less fitly conferred upon your lordship in recognition of those high personal qualities of integrity, vigor, and honor through which you have maintained the name of Dartmouth."

———————

The corner stone of the new Dartmouth Hall was laid Wednesday afternoon with appropriate ceremonies. A slight rain which had been falling since early in the day necessitated a slight alteration in the printed program. In the College Church, Hon. Samuel Leland Powers '74 presided over the following exercises: Music by the College chorus; address, Charles Frederick Mathewson, Esq., '82; ode, William Dwight Quint '87; music, "Men of Dartmouth," words by Richard Hovey '85, music by Louis Paul Benezet '99; address, Lord Dartmouth. At the close of these exercises, the procession marched to Eleazar Wheelock's grave in the cemetery, where Pres. William Jewett Tucker paid a brief tribute to Dartmouth's founder and first president; thence to the Dartmouth Hall site, where Bishop Ethelbert Talbot, D.D., '70, offered the prayer of dedication and Lord Dartmouth laid the corner-stone. "In the name of the Father, the Son, and the Holy Ghost, I now declare this corner-stone well laid," said Lord Dartmouth, and the Chapel peal was rung. [. . .]

———————

The exercises of the week were brought to a close Wednesday evening, when the President and the trustees tendered a banquet to Lord Dartmouth in College Hall. The magnificent dining-room was elaborately decorated with American and British flags and with pictures of prominent alumni and of Old Dartmouth Hall, and the tables were strewn with autumn leaves tied on streamers of red ribbon. [. . .]

President Tucker opened the ceremonies by proposing toasts to the President of the United States and the King of England, both of which were greeted with enthusiastic cheers. When Lord Dartmouth was called on, the whole assembly arose and gave the distinguished Englishman two powerful "Wah-Hoo-Wahs." Lord Dartmouth expressed appreciation at the enthusiasm with which he had been received in America, especially at Dartmouth, and said in part:

"I can assure you that it is with the deepest feeling of gratefulness that I rise to respond. However long our lives may last, we will always hold the tenderest spot in our hearts for the people on this side of the water. In the press of a certain part of this country I have seen facts about myself and my family. In one little paragraph it has been suggested that as a result of my visit Dartmouth College will begin to drop its 'H's.' If at any time you happen to find one of these H's lying around, just mail it across to me, and we will cherish it as one of the tenderest mementoes of our visit to this wonderful country of yours. I have often been asked to make comparisons between England and America. I do not like comparisons. My impressions are varied, but I am convinced that, however large this country is, there is no room for jealousy, no room for envy, room only for admiration for your wonderful progress. President Tucker is the head of the family of Dartmouth on this side of the water, as I am of the one on the other side. His family is larger than mine, but I do not believe that I envy him in this respect. I do believe, however, that his hope and ambition for his family are identical with mine, that the sons of Dartmouth, whether they be many or few, may be God-fearing men and an honor to the name they bear." [. . .]

⋙ An undergraduate perspective on this interval—and particularly with reference to its guest of honor, Lord Dartmouth—is provided within this letter of October 30, 1904, written by Royal Parkinson 1905 to his father.

DEAR PAPA:— [. . .] The cornerstone celebration was fine. The speeches and tableaux were all fine, but best of all was the spirit of the occasion. The Earl of Dartmouth turned out to be not only an earl but a fine man, and every body, Alumni, faculty and students lent a hand to make it pleasant for him and his family. He appreciated every thing and seemed to be even moved. He was very simple but was always equal to the occasion. He went to foot ball practice. At night he seemed to enjoy the tableaux and the singing and yelling. The next morning in church he made his first speech. He was very nervous and didn't know what to do, but when Pres Tucker announced that he intended to present to the college the letters of Wheelock to his ancestor, in spite of all his nervousness he managed to say in a simple way that after he had received his degree he would not feel that he had lost all connection with the college. That won the whole audience for him and we cheered loud and long.

In the afternoon at the church again. Congressman Powers who presided in fine style called on him unexpectedly. The earl stood for a minute in confusion, then managed to say that he was glad of the opportunity to thank the college for his family and himself. Said that altho he thought it impossible for a man to reach his ideal he believed every man better for trying to. That he hoped to live worthy of the degree that had been given him. "From the time when my illustrious predecessor and your great & beloved founder forged the first link in the chain which connects Dartmouth college with Dartmouth title, as time has gone on other links have been added. But never has there been a more binding or stronger link added to that chain than there was to day when you did me the great honor of conferring on me the degree of LLD. I have no degrees to offer you in return but I will assure you that by no action of mine—and so far as I am able to control the actions of those who may come after me, by no action of any of my descendants—will you have any reason to regret the honor which you did me this morning." When that came from his heart as you could see it did, and as it must have since he was called on unexpectedly, old alumni and guests on the platform jumped up and waved their hats and an alumnus called for a cheer for Lord Dartmouth. We almost had tears in our eyes but we gave the two loudest cheers that ever shook the walls of a building. After that the cornerstone was a small part of the occasion.

At the banquet in the evening his speech was just as simple and appropriate. [. . .]

He stayed over the next day too. [. . .] During the day he went sightseeing. We got up a bonfire and nightshirt parade in the evening [. . .]. It was a big fire and it looked fine to see us all in white. We cheered & marched and presently the earl and Mr Galagher came out and led the parade around the fire once. We sang and cheered. A little group of fellows who had taken part in the tableaux as Indians were out in uniform and appointed themselves bodyguard to the earl. Then the earl made a speech from the senior fence after we all formed in front. He thanked us for the part we had had in making him and his family have so good a time. He ended by saying that when troubles & cares came to him as troubles & cares do come he would think of one of our cheers and take new spirit. Then with tears in his eyes and his voice trembling he said he wished that when he was gone we would think of him not as the recipient of a valuable & honorary degree, but as one of the old boys. I never was more proud of anything than to have had a share in the mighty shout that went up then. Then I thought that we had made him feel that he was a part of the college.

The next morning when he left a quartet of instruments played God save the King and we all bared our heads. Then we gave cheer after cheer for the earl and his family. He stood up in the tallyho and waved his hand and shouted "goodbye, boys". A little farther along and he rose again to call that any Dartmouth man would be welcome in the old country.

Lord Dartmouth seemed to be very simple, always sincere, never going too far, able to rise to every occasion. Both he and the countess and Lady Dorothy were all simple and gentle people, appreciative of everything. They were pleased to hear our songs, to see us rise and take off our hats when we sing the Dartmouth song, to hear us cheer for Pres Tucker, to hear Mr. Powers say that when Pres Tucker called him to substitute for Mr Pierce, he did it just as a subject would obey a king. He was the first one to laugh at the funny things too. When Mr. Powers said that there has been so much rythm between alumni and the college since Pres Tucker came into office, that it was easy for almost anybody to write poetry, and then introduced the odist, he laughed.

We gave them the best in our power. It is one of the few cases where you can't think afterward of any thing that might have been done better. Every body was in it and everyone feels fine that we moved the earl so. But for my part I think the earl moved me and I would like to know him better. I think there are mighty few men that will ever come up to what I think of the earl. When the next Dartmouth comes out I will send you Pres Tucker's Sunday Chapel addresses before and after, and you can see better than I can tell, what kind of a man he is. [. . .]

Extending a Welcome to "the Wheelock Succession"

by WILLIAM JEWETT TUCKER

❯❯❯❯ In the spring of 1907 William Jewett Tucker had, due to ill health, attempted to relinquish the presidency, but was ultimately persuaded by the Board of Trustees to continue in office, with a decidedly limited commitment of activity. (It was during the two-year period which ensued that Ernest Martin Hopkins, then serving as Secretary of the College, took on what he himself later acknowledged to be, through "delegation from both the president and the board," his earliest "major responsibilities" for the overall administration of the College.) In 1909, however, the Trustees elected Ernest Fox Nichols, then Professor of Experimental Physics at Columbia University (but who had been during the years 1898–1903 a member of the Dartmouth Physics Department), as tenth President of the College. Dr. Nichols' inauguration was held on October 14, 1909. At the ceremony, when formally inducted by Trustee Frank S. Streeter 1874, the new President was given custody of the parchment charter granted to the College in 1769 by King George III; and immediately after this had occurred, Dr. Tucker provided, as is recorded within the inauguration's published proceedings, a further and unprecedented feature of the inaugural program.

PRESIDENT NICHOLS, I am permitted by the courtesy of the trustees to introduce you at this point to a somewhat peculiar, because personal, succession, into which each president of the College enters upon his induction into office. The charter of Dartmouth, unlike that of any college of its time so far as I know, was written in personal terms. It recognizes throughout the agency of one man in the events leading up to and including the founding of the College. And in acknowledgment of this unique fact it conferred upon this man—founder and first president—some rather unusual powers, among which was the power to appoint his immediate successor. Of course this power of appointment ceased with its first use, but the idea of a succession in honor of the founder, suggested by the charter, was perpetuated; so that it has come about that the presidents of Dartmouth are known at least to themselves as also the successors of Wheelock, a distinction which I am quite sure that you will appreciate more and more. For Eleazar Wheelock was the type of the man,

45

the impulse of whose life runs on in men, creating as it goes a natural succession: a man whose power of initiative is evidenced by the fact that at sixty he was able to found this College in the wilderness: a scholar by the best standards of his time, the first Berkeley Fellow at Yale: broad and courageous in his mental sympathies, a leader in the progressive movements of his age: and of so high and commanding a devotion of purpose that it brought him to an accomplished end. I do not know in just what ways the impulse of this man's life entered into the life of my predecessors. To me it has been a constant challenge. Whenever I have grown dull of heart as well as of mind, tempted to shirk work or to evade duty, I have found it a most healthful exercise to go over to this man's grave, and read his epitaph—

> "BY THE GOSPEL HE SUBDUED THE FEROCITY OF THE SAVAGE,
>   AND TO THE CIVILIZED HE OPENED NEW PATHS OF SCIENCE.
>   TRAVELLER,
>   GO, IF YOU CAN, AND DESERVE
>   THE SUBLIME REWARD OF SUCH MERIT."

Dartmouth, as you know, has been singularly fortunate in the return into its own life of the fame and service of some of her greater sons, singularly fortunate also in the abounding and unflinching loyalty of all of her sons; but I believe that the greatest possession of the College has been and is still the spirit of Eleazar Wheelock in so far as it has been transmitted through his successors. I think therefore that the term "The Successors of Wheelock" is worthy of public, if not of official recognition. Unwittingly Wheelock himself originated the expression in the very thoughtful provision which he tried to make for those of us who were to come after him. "To my successors," he says in one of the last clauses of his will, not to the trustees nor to the College, but "to my successors in the presidency I give and bequeath my chariot which was given me by my honored friend, John Thornton, Esquire, of London: I also give to my successors my house clock which was a donation made me by my much honored patrons, the Honorable Trust in London."

It is no matter of surprise, as we recall the utter indifference of each generation to those things of its daily handling which are likely to become historic, that these perquisites of the succession have long since disappeared. But happily the intention of Wheelock was caught and held in permanent shape. When John Wentworth, governor of the Province of New Hampshire, returned from the first commencement, he sent back, possibly as a reminder of a deficiency on that occasion, a silver punch bowl bearing this inscription—

"His Excellency John Wentworth, Esquire, Governor of the Province of New Hampshire, and those friends who accompanied him to Dartmouth the first Commencement in 1771, in testimony of their gratitude and good wishes, present this to the Reverend Eleazar Wheelock, D. D., and to his successors in that office."

This bowl, which, as I now produce it, seems so inadequate to the draughts of that time, for this very reason serves us the better as a kind of loving cup.

In the spirit of the original gift, but after the fashion of the later use, I now transfer it to you with the good will of the long succession, and in the personal hope that it may be many, many years before you will have the opportunity to transfer it to your successor.

An Inaugural Chronicle

by MRS. WILLIAM JEWETT TUCKER

❧❧❧ The installation of Ernest Fox Nichols involved a gala academic occasion. The distinguished guests in attendance included a galaxy of presidents from sister institutions, among them both President Lowell and President-Emeritus Eliot from Harvard, Hadley of Yale, Wilson from Princeton, and Butler of Columbia. Seventeen honorary degrees were bestowed—one of them upon Dartmouth's own retiring President, Dr. Tucker. Also attending the exercises, and taking a speaking role at both the inauguration and the dinner that followed it that same evening, was the British Ambassador to the United States, historian-statesman James Bryce (upon whom the College had earlier, during Commencement in 1901, conferred a Doctorate of Laws).

Slightly over a week after the inaugural events, Charlotte Tucker dispatched a long letter, dated October twenty-third, in which she undertook to provide certain of her family members the details of some of what had just occurred in Hanover.

MY DEAR PEOPLE: A rainy night and a quiet morning in bed have helped me collect my scattered wits enough to at least begin the tale of the Inauguration of Pres. Nichols which I should like Margaret and the sisters to see, and then return to me, to put away for Betty and her children to keep. For there are many things about the memorable day which did not get into print, and which I should like to record. First of all was the great *feeling* which underlay all the ceremonies:—sadness, regret, loyalty, admiration, pride and affection for the old order; curiosity, suspicion, anxiety, doubt and uncertainty about the new. It was the knowledge of this which had caused Mr. Streeter to work so anxiously on his short speech of induction. Mrs. Streeter called it the most important thing he had ever done. He is not usually considered to be a man of sentiment. But he has said that Will's influence and the association with him all these years has been the most powerful factor in his life, and it was a great personal grief to him to have to turn the charter over to another man. His voice trembled when he began to speak, and later, when Will delivered his short address, and when he received the degree Mr. Streeter openly shed tears. In this he was not alone. Nelson said there was scarcely a dry eye in his part of the hall. When Prof. Richardson spoke Will's name, in presenting him for the degree of L.L.D. at the

48

end of the long line of Presidents to be so honored, the whole audience, as one person, without pre-arrangement, rose spontaneously and applauded long and loud and then cheered. [. . .] I trembled on my own account and had the greatest difficulty in controlling myself, but I feared still more for the effect on Will. For since Sunday afternoon he had been conscious of his heart all the time, and he had been very uncertain as to whether he could appear at all. He had been dreading the ordeal all the Fall. [. . .] The ovation he received and the knowledge that has come to him in so many ways of the devotion and the loyalty of the multitude whom he has influenced made a fitting crown to his years of unselfish and whole-hearted labor and devotion.

As for the new President, there was nothing but praise as the day went on. His first appearance at prayers, a few weeks before, had been a disappointment; the truth being that when he was confronted by that big crowd of students and faculty he was seized with a sort of stage fright and could hardly read the short address he had prepared. His prayer was only one or two sentences. He is not accustomed to much public speaking and his voice has no special carrying power, though it is agreeable and cultivated. But Thursday all hesitation and nervousness had disappeared. He spoke simply, with feeling, and sincerely, and his English was delightful. The audience hung on his every word. The impression of the whole thing was that of a modest, courageous, independent man, fully conscious of the great responsibilities he was assuming and possessing latent strength to meet them. The ceremonies throughout were most dignified, stately, and interesting in unusual degree. The only false note was struck by Judge Russell, whom some of the New York alumni had [. . .] chosen Pres. of the Alumni Association with the idea that he "might do something handsome" for the College. It was most unwise. He made a mortifying exhibition of his total want of appreciation of the situation, and delivered himself of a trivial, facetious, commonplace kind of impromptu speech such as he might give after dinner at a Dartmouth Club lunch. Fortunately the greater part of it was inaudible. He called the next morning and appeared so queerly that Betty and I decided he was losing his mind. The general comment was that the inauguration was a wonderfully successful and impressive occasion. One of the Columbia Professors told Dr. Smith's brother that he had seen all the important academic functions in America and that this was by far the finest of them all.

I came very near omitting mention of the really remarkable address of Clark Tobin for the undergraduates. In most refreshing contrast to the representative of the Alumni, his brief speech was a model of feeling and form and was delivered in a perfect manner. He came as a poor Catholic boy from South Boston, with no manners or advantages but with the Irish pluck and the "makings" of a gentleman. He is now President of the Senior Class, member of the DKE Society, Captain of the foot-ball team whom the Amherst coach calls the cleanest and most sportsmanlike athlete he ever saw on a football field, and the most influential and popular man in College. He had his mother up from Boston to see the ceremonies, without letting her know that he had anything to do. A plain, homely old woman, with a delightful brogue, and when her boy stepped forward so easily and naturally and delivered himself so splendidly, she was the most "uplifted" person in the crowd,—next to me. [. . .]

Hopkins, the resident member of the Inauguration Committee, had the brunt of all the thousand and one details of the affair, and a large share of the credit is due to him and to Miss Stone. They sat up all Tuesday night, making out the tickets for the delegates and guests, and when Thursday came he looked ready to fade away. Frank was in his element as chairman of the dinner committee and had a most graphic scheme of seating all the distinguished guests as well as the Faculty & alumni—the only difficulty being that at the last moment there were sure to be changes which upset everything. Some of the delegates were unmanageable and one was most discourteous, and it will be many days before the stories die out of the funny and the tragic happenings in the various households. Many of the hostesses had no maids. Mrs. Burton was one of those unfortunates. Pres. Lowell stayed with them and put his boots outside his chamber door. Mrs. Burton fortunately discovered them on her way to the kitchen at 6 A.M. and got them to her husband in season to be blacked and set down again before breakfast. [. . .]

Our guests were delightful, and it was a great help to have Betty at home to assist in entertaining them. She was very thoughtful and ready to take her part everywhere. The Eliots are very simple, *domestic* persons, and are at their best in the home. The only alarming thing about him was his eagle eye for every detail about the house. You know he does the house-keeping altogether in their summer home. Mrs. Eliot spoke incidentally of their beginning the day by singing a hymn. He attends College prayers every day. Mrs. Harris looks a good deal older than when I saw her, as indeed, why shouldn't she, and is a very self-centered person, with the invalid's demands and whines. For example, she carries a little flask of whisky in her hand although she has never needed it. And she wanted to take a back seat Thursday morning in case she should need to slip out. That of course was impossible, as every seat was assigned. But I had the coupé ready to take her home at any time after 11.15, and she stayed through everything, sat up all the afternoon, while the Eliots had naps, and stood the smoke, bad air, heat, and long speeches in the evening better than any of us. [. . .]

It must be confessed that the presence of the women complicated matters in the household. They necessitated our leaving our room for a third-story one, and obliged the housekeeper to take more pains with all the arrangements than she would have given to the men alone. I have registered a vow that this shall be the last occasion when the head of the house is ousted from his chamber and dressing-room. The servants did nobly. Perhaps my plain talk early in the week, when I found rooms very dirty that were supposed to have been cleaned and ready for guests, and the hard work which I put in in supplementing what they should have done had an effect. They are ignorant, inexperienced, awfully *slack* and forgetful. On the other hand, they are willing, interested, grateful for instruction and even for reproof, and fond of the place and the people—and I am having discipline as well as they.

This is the last function connected with Dartmouth College with which we shall have anything to do, and in many ways it has been the hardest. Now Will will settle back and see others "carry forward the work." Grace has been given him to bear in a wonderful manner all the disabilities, the frustration of plans, the disappointments, and the burdens of the past two years and a half, and I hope the years that may come will be filled with peaceful and happy occupations, untinged with regret.

Two from the Class of 1910
Recall Their Student Years

I. by ARTHUR HARDY LORD

≫⇒ "Tenner" Arthur Lord was a native of Hanover, being a son of Prof. John King Lord 1868 and thus a great-grandson of Nathan Lord, the College's sixth President (1828–63). In his retirement, following long association with a Boston publishing firm, Arthur Lord co-authored (with Robert French Leavens 1901) a history of the College during the presidency of William Jewett Tucker, *Dr. Tucker's Dartmouth* (1965). These reminiscences of his own undergraduate period were written by him in the wake of the sixty-fifth reunion of the Class of 1910.

MY ASSOCIATIONS with college life were quite different from those of other classmates because during the first two years of college I lived at home. In the first part of freshman year my relations with Tenners were mostly with those in Wheeler Hall which was the nearest dormitory to our house. I would go over there afternoons or evenings and got to know the classmates who lived there more quickly than I did those living elsewhere. [. . .]

The courses I took in freshman year were those of the regular classical program, Greek, Latin, French, English and Mathematics, continuing the studies I had at Worcester Academy. In sophomore year I dropped Greek and French replacing them with German. I took introductory physics with Gordon Ferry Hull and a semester of chemistry with Bobby Bartlett and though I passed them I realized I was not scientifically minded and dropped the physical sciences. My venture into the biological sciences was still more limited, a course under Prof. Patten, Evolution, a lecture and reading course, but it gave a glimpse of that field which I enjoyed. I majored in Latin, perhaps because of family association or lack of any other field which attracted me. In junior year I had a course with my father in Horace and other Latin poets and found it more stimulating than the prose authors I had studied earlier.

One of the most instructive courses I took was in sophomore year,

European History, under "Eric" Foster. It began with the Middle Ages and his lectures, supplemented by much outside reading, made a strong impression on me and gave me an understanding of that period of history which I have valued ever since. Another course I took that year was Debating, with Craven Laycock. He kept the class on its toes with his brisk observations, but debating was not my metier and I was glad to end it with a passing mark. Mathematics was one of my minors and I found calculus an interesting field which spurred me to take the exam in competition for the Thayer prize, but without success. Courses in economics under George Ray Wicker and Frank Dixon gave me an introduction to those fields, commensurate with those times but not carried far enough to be very useful today. By my senior year I had acquired extra credits beyond what I needed for graduation and at my father's suggestion, in my last semester, I dropped the fifth course and instead I read a list of readings which he gave me in a wide range of English literature and in other classics which I read with diligence and much profit. Also in senior year I took the day long examinations required of applicants for a Rhodes Scholarship. But I got nowhere. I think it was that year in which Joe Worthen, 1909 won the scholarship.

In the sports world of the college my activity was confined to golf. I was on the golf team for three years, most of the time rated fourth. The fall of junior year was our most active and successful one. The team took a trip of nearly two weeks, playing Columbia, Pennsylvania and some private clubs, winning most of our matches and I was fortunate to win most of mine. In our spare time we saw the sights of New York and Philadelphia, watched two football games, all of it quite exciting for a raw country boy. That fall also saw my greatest success, winning the college golf championship by defeating Ray Gorton, Heinie Stucklen and Freddie Martin, all of whom were better players than I but who had poor days. In after years when we lived in Newton, near Gay Gleason, he used to kid me by introducing me as "the man who beat the man who almost beat Bobby Jones."

I also took part in winter sports. I had enjoyed skiing ever since I was a young boy and when Fred Harris initiated the first winter sports meet in February of our senior year I entered. I came in third in the cross country race and also in a 220 yard dash. It was only an intramural event but attracted much attention, going on to become the famous Winter Carnival.

Skating was a favorite sport too. Sometimes Occom Pond would freeze over hard enough to make it skatable before the snows fell. After they came those interested would have to clear a space for any skating and another one for playing hockey. There was the river too but it was rare that it would freeze solid enough before the snow fell to make skating safe. Sometimes during the winter a thaw would be followed by a quick freeze to make some sections useable. But thanks to the mills at Wilder which would close the gates of the dam over week ends, the water would flow back along the edges of the river for a width of 25 feet or so, and when conditions were right it would freeze to give a good skating surface. I remember one unusual such occasion when the New Hampshire side was so fine clear ice that it tempted three of us to go there early in the afternoon. We were able to skate all the way up to Bradford, over twenty miles, taking two hours to get there and not getting back til after dark, which made it not so easy, but we had an exhilarating afternoon. In those days little attention was given to the recreational opportunities in the White Mountains but during the exam period in June of our freshman year Max Stanton and I took advantage of a few days we had free to climb Mt. Moosilaukee. The train from Norwich left us off near the base in late afternoon and we climbed the steep trail up the western slope. We reached the top about sunset, expecting to find the tip top house open but it was shut tight, no sign of life. The prospect of spending the night in the open wasn't pleasant and we were thankful, while we were searching around, to find that there had been other visitors, who had forced open a window and left it so we could get in. It was too dark to look around but we found blankets and quilts under the window which kept us warm sleeping on the floor. We awoke at dawn and went out to see the rosy sunrise. But there was no breakfast to ease our empty stomachs. We were lucky to have saved a few remnants from the picnic we had eaten on the way up and got a little satisfaction from them. We spent a little while enjoying the view then started down the carriage road, reaching Warren, I think it was, in the late morning. There we got a satisfying meal before taking the train which brought us back to Hanover by late afternoon.

Extracurricular activities were numerous, dramatic performances by students or outside companies, music programs by visiting artists, and many smoke talks or lectures by outside speakers on a great range of subjects. One of these outside speakers was Judge Cross of the class of 1841 who was a frequent visitor. His talks were interesting and we especially enjoyed meeting him informally to hear him reminisce on his college days. We were much impressed when he spoke of having known a graduate of ₍. . .₎ the first class to graduate from the College. That we could talk with someone who knew someone connected with the founding of the College made us feel that we had an almost personal link with the events of those times and made them closer to us and more meaningful than when we had read about them in books.

Many events took place in College Hall which was still new in those days. Always popular were the songfests which took place in the large lounge. Often after a meal Harry Wellman, Walter Golds, Les Wiggin or others would sit down to play the piano and a crowd would quickly gather to give vent to their spirits in lusty singing of college songs and the popular tunes of the day. Other social life was limited in those days and the College Prom in May was the gala event.

In my last two years I became active in the Student Christian Association. Karl Skinner 1903, was its graduate Secretary in my junior year, then Wallie Ross, 1909, in senior year. I was chairman of its Employment Committee and a member of the Cabinet and also took part in the services we held in neighboring communities, and I enjoyed friendship with Wallie. ₍. . .₎

In many respects the most memorable and rewarding experiences I had during college years were those working at the College Grant in the summer vacations of my sophomore and junior years. The College Trustees were trying to restore the forest resources which had been destroyed by the companies to which they had sold lumbering rights. In the summer of 1908 Philip Ayres, the forester in charge of the project, engaged Harold Clark, 1908, and myself to join the crew of about a dozen who were working there. An important part of the reforesting process was the care of a nursery of seedlings about an acre in extent. Every two weeks Harold and I had to weed it, taking us two or three days, a dirty, hot, back breaking job on our hands and knees. There was a wide variety of other tasks, trail making, cutting down a stand of tall, old evergreen trees, haymaking, hoeing the potato patch, clearing a field of old pine stumps, and operating a portable saw mill. One special job was to transplant some balsam seedlings in a grove of other trees, a few miles from the main camp. ₍. . .₎

Sundays were days off and Harold and I took advantage of them to explore the woods, to climb mountains, to go swimming or to fish in the streams. It was a totally new experience to live in that world of nature for one who had lived his life in the civilized world. I learned a lot and fully enjoyed those two summers off by ourselves in the still quite primeval woods. In the years since then I have found that the experiences of these summers stand out vividly in memory and that they have influenced my life ever since.

Our graduation exercises on June 29 followed the traditional pattern but one feature of them made a vivid impression on me which has remained in my mind ever since. As we seniors were lined up to let the alumni procession march into the hall I was struck by the appearance of the men of the class of 1860 back for their 50th reunion. To my youthful mind they seemed so old, many walking with faltering steps and slow, seemingly indifferent to what to us was a great occasion, one which would usher us into the new exciting world of the future. [. . .]

II. by WHITNEY HASKINS EASTMAN

⋙ Whitney Eastman came to College from Fort Ann, New York. In the unfolding of his career as a civil engineer, during which he became an officer of a major corporation, he ever maintained close ties to Dartmouth, being a member of its Alumni Council in the years 1932–39. This excerpt of his recollections of undergraduate life is drawn from his typescript autobiography, *The Advantage of Being Born Poor*, written (as is recorded on its title page) "during the summer of 1966 at the age of 78."

M Y OLDER BROTHER Frank was graduating from Dartmouth College in June 1906, and I thought it would be great fun to see him graduate, but I did not have the money to pay my railroad fare. An old friend of the family who was a railroad mail clerk took me as a guest in the mail car as far as Bellows Falls, Vermont. In Bellows Falls I made friends with a brakeman on a B & M train bound for Hanover, New Hampshire, and he took me as a guest in the caboose. I landed in Hanover with twenty-five cents. I thought surely my big brother would pay my fare back home, but like most graduating seniors in those days he was "broke." Frank had worked his way through four years at Dartmouth and knew many of the townspeople for whom he had worked. So he got me a job at 14½c per hour working for Professor Louis Dow, the French professor. I intended to return home as soon as I had saved up enough money. I cut the lawn, pulled every weed out of one of the most beautifully landscaped lawns in Hanover, tended their furnace, washed the walls, floors, ceilings and windows and helped the maids wait on table. The Dow family were very good to me, providing me with a cozy little room and three wonderful meals a day.

They were friends of another professor who needed someone to care for his lawn, so the Dows agreed to share my services with another wonderful family who lived next door to Dean Emerson, then dean of the college. One day when I was mowing the lawn for my new employer, the dean came over to visit with me. He said his wife had heard about my work and wanted me to do some work for her. He asked me if I was going to enter college, and I told him my story. He asked me for the name of my high school principal in Fort Ann High School, Miss Amelia Blaisdell, and he wrote her for my grades. He received such a wonderful letter from her that he approved my academic credentials and awarded me a full scholarship. I have always felt that he did it so I could work for his wife, a charming and wonderful person.

So I entered Dartmouth College in the fall of 1906. My brother Frank was elated and wanted me to take the necessary courses so that I could enter Thayer School, a postgraduate school in Civil Engineering. I discussed my plans with the dean, now one of my several employers, and in order to comply with the college curriculum, I elected to plan for courses during the next four years in physics, chemistry, higher mathematics, graphics, astronomy, analytical geometry, calculus and, of course, English and two modern languages —French and German. I was the only one in my class in Thayer School who elected to take public speaking during college. I felt public speaking was essential because my brother Frank convinced me that there were many brilliant engineers who could not sell a good idea to their superior corporate officers.

Fifty was the passing grade while I was at Dartmouth. I never flunked a course, but I came awfully close. I could not seem to master Physics I, and my professor, Gordon Ferry Hull, called me to his office after my first semester exam and told me that he should flunk me but was giving me a mark of 51, just barely passing. He explained that he knew how hard I was working to get through college, and he wanted to see me enter Thayer School. The good professor was one of my several employers at the time, and his wife liked my work. I think this was the primary reason why he gave me a passing mark. This was a lesson for me. I had high grades in the following three semesters in Physics. [...]

During freshman year I needed a job where I could work for my room as I had not laid by enough money to live in a college dormitory. Dean Emerson found such a job for me. Mrs. Cobb, a doctor's widow, had a fine team of horses which she used to drive around town hitched to a beautiful surrey. Mrs. Cobb lived on South Main Street not far from the campus, a very handy location. She wanted a farm boy familiar with the care of horses, and she felt sure that I qualified for the job.

I had a snug little room in the attic, and it was very comfortable. I had to feed the horses, water them and curry them from head to foot every day and keep the stable spotlessly clean. The going wage in Hanover was 14½c per hour, so that was my rate of pay. She set a price on the room for the college year and made me keep an accurate record of the time spent on each operation down to a quarter of an hour. With all these fractions to deal with it was a full course in arithmetic. She was very pleased with my work and never quibbled over my statements of time spent. She often told me that the horses were never groomed so well, and the surrey was never washed and polished as well before. She gave me many nice handouts from her kitchen which were very welcome.

I also worked for "Deacon" Downing, serving at the soda fountain in his drug store. He always kept telling me to drink as many malted milks as I wanted, and this also helped to cut down my food bills at the College Commons. [...]

The deacon called me "Aphrodites"—why I never knew. Occasionally he would ask me to do some work for Mrs. Downing such as scrubbing floors and washing walls and ceilings. I always seemed to find time to do it—especially because I loved those malted milks, and Mrs. Downing frequently gave me a handout from her kitchen. The Downings were a wonderful family and looked after me as though I were their own son. [...]

For about a year I washed dishes at "The Pillsbury Club", a students' eating club, for my board. There were no limitations on the amount I could eat. Mrs. Pillsbury was a wonderful cook, and being very meticulous, I had to wash the dishes shining clean and scour the baked bean pots and the other pots and pans. My last year in college she appointed me "commissary" in which job I had to keep the tables full and collect the money from the students. We had four tables of eight places each, so I got three fraternities to take a table and guarantee that they would keep them full. One fraternity member waited on each of these "fraternity tables" and got his board for his service. It then became his responsibility to keep his table full. So I only had to round up enough non-fraternity men for the fourth table. My biggest job was collecting the bills for most of the students had to wait for their allowance checks from home, and many of them were slow in coming.

I made quite a bit of money running student dances. I teamed up with "Pa" Chesley, another student who had a three-piece orchestra. We held the dances at the Grange Hall in Hanover and a hall in Norwich, Vermont, across the Connecticut River. I rounded up the students and the girls. There were a substantial number of very fine young ladies, mostly of high school age, living in Hanover. On account of working all over town, I had an acquaintance with most of them. "Pa" took a fee for his orchestra, and I took the overage as my share after paying the rent on the dance hall.

Of all the jobs I had while in college my most pleasant and profitable employment was my association with the Rand Furniture Store. The store was at that time the only new furniture store in Hanover. The Rand family also operated an undertaking establishment.

I worked in the store waiting on students who were buying furniture for their rooms in the college dormitories. I also helped George Rand, Sr., or some other delivery employee deliver the furniture to students' rooms. [. . .] Will Rand, the son, was managing the business. [. . .] Will wanted me to learn the undertaking business and said that his dad would teach me. His dad had learned the trade in the Civil War.

My first assignment was to trim the coffins. The store bought plain pine boxes from a lumber mill near by. Mr. Rand, Sr., taught me how to fit excelsior into the box and cover the excelsior with cheesecloth, fastening the cloth all around the top with carpet tacks. Mr. Rand would put a handful of tacks in his mouth and worked so fast he would meet me before I had finished one side. Then we had to cover the exterior with colored fabric to suit the survivors. Then we attached the fancy handles but always removed them for reuse before lowering the casket into the grave. This was customary practice in those days. After I had served my apprenticeship trimming coffins, my next step was to learn how to embalm a dead person to make him look lifelike. While this might appear to be a gruesome business, I rather enjoyed the experience. The only part of the operation I did not relish was sewing the eyes closed.

The Rands paid me well, far better than the going rate in Hanover. I shall never forget how much I owe to the Rand family for their many kindnesses to me as an employee and as a close family friend. [. . .]

For three summers I worked as a waiter on the S. S. Sagamore on Lake George, New York, running daily on a round trip between Lake George village and Ticonderoga. This was an excursion boat, and I had the pleasure of waiting on some distinguished people, including William Jennings Bryan and President Taft. The tips we received were generous, and I had three prosperous summers. [. . .]

All the people I have mentioned as being my employers were also wonderful friends, and I cannot ever repay them for all they did for me for they are all gone. However, as I returned to Dartmouth many times during the 56 years since I graduated, while they were still living, I always called on them to express my appreciation and to inquire about their families.

The Collegiate Years of
a Movie Magnate

by MATTHEW BERNSTEIN

⋙ Long an eminent motion-picture producer and leading film-world personality, Walter Wanger 1915 is the subject of Matthew Bernstein's 1994 biography *Walter Wanger, Hollywood Independent*, which contains a chapter entitled "The Boy Manager (1911–1914)," the source of this extract.

THROUGHOUT HIS LIFE, Wanger was a devoted alumnus of Dartmouth College. In the mid-1930s, he created the Irving G. Thalberg script library and started a course in screenwriting. He served as president of the college's Alumni Association in the 1940s. Publicity profiles made his attendance there well known.

What is less well known was that Wanger never completed his degree. He was "separated" from Dartmouth for academic delinquency in early 1915 before he could graduate. Wanger's first sustained act of youthful rebellion was to ignore completely his course work and the warnings of the college to pursue his own interests in the drama club, where he uncovered a distinctive approach to theatrical production which involved a tireless pursuit of novelty and marketing it to the faculty.

From the very beginning, Wanger refused to buckle down to the discipline of an ordinary student. As a result he was "admonished" by the college before the December break of his freshman year. The following February, he was separated. An assistant dean explained to Stella Wanger that, even though her son was "a young man of rather unusual ability and promise" and that there "has been no dissatisfaction whatever" with his conduct, Walter had "failed nine semester hours in his work" in math, biology, and even German.

Fortunately for Wanger, a remedy to the embarrassment of dismissal came in the form of another trip with his mother to Europe. During the spring and summer of 1912, between visits with his family in Euis, Wiesbaden, and Marienbad, Wanger attended lectures on

English and German literature and the history of nineteenth-century art at the University of Heidelberg. His sponsor there was Victor Eckert, a drama professor and theater critic, who at summer's end wrote Dartmouth officials that Wanger had "helped" him "with his diligence and interest in every field." Wanger was readmitted on probation the following fall.

Eckert did more than help Wanger recover his place at Dartmouth. He inspired the young theater lover to explore a broad range of contemporary European playwriting and stagecraft techniques, from Stanley Houghton's Repertory Theater in Manchester to Max Reinhardt's productions in Berlin. And in Paris there was Serge Diaghilev's revolutionary Ballets Russes with Leon Bakst's sets and Vaslav Nijinsky's daring choreography for *Afternoon of a Faun.* [. . .]

The knowledge Wanger brought back with him to Dartmouth became the essence of his success on campus, for it encompassed a range of playwrights and production methods that were barely familiar even to the most knowledgeable American theatergoers. George Bernard Shaw, Henrik Ibsen, Maurice Maeterlinck, and August Strindberg by 1911 were well-established names in America. But Wanger also knew the work of less prominent authors such as Houghton and the American Witter Bynner and had become familiar with the innovative New Stagecraft, which he deployed strategically in his first experience as a stage impresario. [. . .]

In early December 1912, Dartmouth announced the gift of $105,000 from Wallace F. Robinson, a financier and head of American Shoe Machinery Company, to build Robinson Hall, a student center including a small auditorium on the second floor. Excitedly, Wanger injected himself into the planning of the hall, persuading Robinson to incorporate the latest stage technology into the three-hundred-seat theater. [. . .]

Wanger coauthored and staged *The Test*, a ten-minute play for the Dramatic Club's vaudeville sketch-writing contest in February 1913. His stage directions read: "Absolute dark stage except for a lighted candle on a rough table. Army cot against back wall in corner. Wireless outfit on table. Two soap-boxes and a chair are lying about." The stark contrast of light and evocative darkness directly echoed the two streams of moonlight that poured over the set of *The Rising of the Moon.* [. . .]

For *The Test*, Wanger and his cowriter were also borrowing the thesis-play aspect of Lady Gregory's work. Just as *The Rising of the Moon* evoked Irish nationalism, *The Test* demonstrated the inherent superiority of Dartmouth over certain other Ivy League Colleges. On stage, a trio of undergraduates each portrayed an alumnus of Yale, Harvard, and Dartmouth, now officers in the American army serving abroad during a future war. The three, seated around a table, are cut off from their comrades. As the play begins, the men await the radio transmission of a decoding key to translate an enemy message. They are grim and tense; an enemy soldier with a machine gun waits for any one of them to step outside.

While the other Ivy Leaguers boastfully discuss the benefits they gained from attending their colleges, the Dartmouth man wistfully alludes to Dartmouth Night—a recently introduced welcoming evening for freshmen, full of speeches about the college's long and illustrious history. When the battery on the soldiers' wireless radio gives out, one of them must venture into the dangerous darkness to retrieve a fresh pack. It is the quiet, self-confident Dartmouth man who makes the essential sacrifice with a smile. The play reaches a rousing climax as he stumbles back into the cabin fatally wounded and dies under the illusion that he is attending a Dartmouth Night.

This crowd-pleaser won the Dramatic Club's "vaudeville sketch" contest and won Wanger the position of assistant manager of the Dramatic Club. Thus honored, he staged a decisively successful "vaudeville" program for the junior prom in May, consisting of a blackface performance, a violin solo, a dramatic rendering of Jack London's *To Kill a Man*, and a performance of *The Rising of the Moon*, complete with balcony-mounted lighting rigs. A noisy crowd of students abruptly rose and left as the Irish play got underway. Yet the remaining audience watched attentively—and with complete surprise—as the Dartmouth Dramatic Club realized its most technically polished and convincingly acted drama in campus memory. Though their attention was exhausted by the lengthy afternoon performance and the stuffy heat that suffused the hall, they applauded the actors enthusiastically.

Two days later, the campus newspaper carried a review by an English professor who noted that "each item of the bill . . . was given in performance a smoothness and finish that we have been educated not to expect in college productions." Those prom participants who had rudely left the performance received a thorough scolding in *The Dart-*

mouth; their casual attitude, reflecting the campus's general view of theatrical activities, was completely inappropriate to the new ambitions of the Dramatic Club. Meanwhile, one Professor Licklider voiced his hope that the reception of these plays "will open the eyes of the College to the brilliant possibilities of the new Robinson Hall."

That summer, a Dartmouth summer administrator appointed Wanger manager of the club's activities. [. . .] From that summer on Wanger—with the help of some talented actors and of the generous budget allocations of the college—transformed Dartmouth's Dramatic Club from a campus afterthought to a polished harbinger of the latest theatrical trends and a worthy competitor to George Baker's famous playwriting workshops at Harvard University. The twelve-hundred-seat theater in Webster Hall was consistently packed with faculty, students, and townspeople. From all accounts, Wanger was responsible for all the major decisions regarding the program: he found the plays, negotiated for performance rights, commissioned set designs and costumes, and sometimes directed the actors. [. . .]

The crowning achievement in Wanger's attempts to make Dartmouth drama equal to, or better than, the professional theater came in January 1914. Wanger obtained from Broadway impresario William Harris the rights to *The Misleading Lady*, a "theatrical crazy quilt" comedy in which an amateur actress, on a bet with a theatrical producer, attempts to obtain a coveted role by persuading its author that she loves him (Paramount Pictures later produced it in 1932 with Claudette Colbert). The Dartmouth production was performed concurrently with the play's Broadway run starring Laurette Taylor, and Wanger used Dramatic Club funds to commission sets from professional designers in Boston and costumes from Parisian clothing designers such as Callot Soeurs and Paul Poiret (the latter being one of the key innovators of orientalist fashion during the teens). Wanger arranged this coup by appealing to author Charles Goddard, a Dartmouth alumnus, and by inviting his coauthor Paul Dickey to give an opening night speech. Dickey was so impressed that he had the players perform two matinees at Manhattan's Fulton Theater [. . .].

The professionalism of the Dartmouth Theater informed not only the standards of the productions, but the operating routines of the club. Beginning in the fall of 1913, Wanger insisted against the advice of students and the administration that the drama group should stage productions during football season. He boldly scheduled the year's first production for the evening of a game against Williams College.

He instituted the policy of refusing to seat late audience members during performances. For tryout sessions. he replaced classic monologues with new plays, and he took over the blocking, rehearsal, and direction of the plays from professional directors, whom the college previously had hired. Financed by the college, Wanger was able to spend money freely: he created a set design department, he produced new shows virtually every month, and he gave the club a more imposing title—the Dartmouth Dramatic Association.

Surveying Wanger's management of the club in early 1914, poet and playwright Bynner told the *New York World*, "The faculty of Dartmouth stand for all this with an equanimity that is certainly a testimonial to the boy manager's genius." The Dartmouth officials accepted his transformation of the club, and his inevitable neglect of his coursework, because his knowledge of contemporary European theater was so clearly innovative and instructive. Indeed, a review of November 1913's *The New Sin* and *Workhouse Ward* noted that the audience was packed with more faculty than students. Their reviews clearly demonstrate that the faculty was overwhelmed by Wanger's shows. One professor in October 1913 praised Wanger's "rare ability and untiring energy. To him, more than to any one person, is due the credit for what seems to be generally acknowledged a complete success." Another wrote that "the nature of [Wanger's work] is warranty against over-praise."

For two years, Dartmouth's administration overlooked his awkward academic derelictions and class scores averaging in the low seventies because of such accolades. With the endorsement of the Dartmouth faculty, which also was learning from his experiments, Wanger was able to "sell" the club activities as a form of extramural education. *The Dartmouth* expressed the hope that "the College will welcome whatever the Dramatic club has to offer it, not only for its mere diversion, but for its upbuilding in the intellectual life." Wanger told the paper that in Europe[:] "the drama is looked upon as part of a young man's education—a necessity if you will—and all boys see the classics and respect the men actively engaged in the work.... America is rich in men of aesthetic taste without the practical side, or on the other hand in men of practical turn of mind without the aesthetic touch. Dartmouth will attempt to educate men who will combine both of these essentials." He spoke from personal ideals, but also with an awareness that his academic standing depended upon it.

Ironically, Wanger barely enjoyed the privilege of staging plays in the new Robinson Hall. For its opening in November 1914, Wanger chose a Dartmouth student's original one-act, consisting of open graves and dead voices in conversation, and a three-act play by Dobbs Milton called *The Burden of Life*. His plans for an elaborate Christmas pageant complete with dwarfs were cut short when the college administration announced his "ineligibility" to continue at Dartmouth. The Christmas show was canceled so that Wanger could satisfy the schools requirements. But Wanger found his old habits hard to shake; in February 1915, he concluded his college career. [. . .]

[. . .] Twenty years later, in June 1934, the Dartmouth Board of Trustees voted to grant Wanger an honorary degree, a decision made on the basis of his work on stage and in Hollywood. It henceforth became a prominent feature in his publicity. [. . .]

Of Educational Policy

Interview with ERNEST FOX NICHOLS

≫⹁ Slightly more than midway of his seven years in office, President Nichols granted this interview, published in the *Boston Evening Transcript* on October 18, 1913.

FOUR YEARS AGO this fall Ernest Fox Nichols became president of Dartmouth College, after the trustees had spent nearly two years searching for a man to fill the position. It is well known that Dr. Nichols was not the first choice of the trustees. They had sought several other men for the position, notably the Honorable Samuel W. McCall, with the hope of securing a Dartmouth man. But none was willing to take up the great work which William Jewett Tucker had laid down, a work which he had made so great that his health could not endure the tax of its administration. Dr. Nichols finally accepted the position, returning after six years to the college where he had been professor of physics. He has now finished with one college generation and this fall begins his work with a second. During those four years many events occurred whose significance showed little from day to day, but which collectively form a policy which is today attracting the attention of educators the country over.

To learn what the future holds for Dartmouth I sought out Dr. Nichols and asked about the broader policies at work in the college. What of individuality would the future Dartmouth possess? What ideal would Dartmouth set before herself to teach her sons? On what kind of an education would emphasis be made?

"Dartmouth seeks to grow only as a college," President Nichols said. He made very definite this emphasis upon the college as distinguished from the university. It is the function of the college, he believes, to teach, and of the university to investigate; of the college to give general culture and of the university to specialize; of the college to interpret and of the university to discover. The college rewards its great teachers; the university rewards its productive scholars. This spirit of teaching rather than investigating exists not only in the college itself, but in its graduate schools. In the Tuck school of business, in the medical school and in the Thayer school of engineering the chief instructors are so busily engaged with instruction that they have but little leisure for research. And they would not have it otherwise, for these schools regard themselves in no sense rivals of university schools, but as supplementary to them.

I asked him what educational ideal Dartmouth has before her. "The purpose of Dartmouth," he said, "is to build the well-rounded man for useful and effective living. The emphasis is not at all on how to make a living, but on how to live."

President Nichols is a believer in the good of a general education, and to obtain exactness he read from manuscript: "The aim of the college is to mould men to judgment, poise, independence, initiative, resourcefulness, endurance, honor, reverence and a large capacity for friendship. A larger proportion of these qualities grow out of faithful drudgery in studies than at first appears, provided broad choice is made among elective subjects; but it cannot be too strongly empha-sized that in study rather than studies lies salvation. Every hour a stu-dent honestly works his head and his heart he extends the reach of his mental and spiritual vision.

"In our day we hear a deal of ill-considered talk about useless stud-ies, time wasted in gaining knowledge one can never use to earn a liv-ing. The chief end of man, to be sure, is not to earn a living, but to live worthily before God and happily with his neighbors; but putting higher motives out of account and descending to the lowest, it may reasonably be doubted if one man in a hundred ever takes from col-lege a single fact which he can turn into money. What he should take from college are well-trained faculties which he can turn into any-thing he chooses.

"The lad who in fresh-baked wisdom refuses to study Greek or Latin for no better reason than that one can no longer earn a living by reciting Homer or Virgil in the marketplace is bedfellow to the boy of undeveloped body who will have nothing to do with outdoor sports because he can see no use in them to one who is training to read proof in a newspaper office.

"The lad who comes to college to learn the details of any of the bread-earning arts is sure to be disappointed, for neither in the class-room nor upon the athletic field will he find the instruction he seeks. Let us then put aside shallow and illusive considerations of practical-ity, and recognize unreservedly in each subject of study what its vigorous pursuit may yield to mind and spirit in giving us a truer sense of lasting values."

An unmistakable trend in Dartmouth today is a reaction against a so-called athleticism. The tendency is not to detract from athletics, however, but to give a greater emphasis to things non-athletic, in an effort to establish equilibrium between them. As some one has said, "there is little at Hanover to attract any but healthy, sensible men," with the result that undergraduate activities receive far more attention than in most institutions, constituting, as they do, a chief means of diversion. The control of non-athletic organizations was recently centralized in a council such as has long managed the athletic interests, and it is expected that with better management and more extended work even more men will participate in these activities.

The future course of Dartmouth, then, is well defined: so to develop as a college that it may in the best way possible develop men and teach them how to live.

But what of the past, particularly the immediate past during which Dr. Nichols has been at the helm? [. . .]

In the past four years, the total assets have increased from $4,200,000 to $5,450,000, an increase of twenty-nine per cent; the endowment funds have grown from $2,800,000 to $3,800,000, or thirty-two per cent; the income from endowment has risen from $115,000 to $152,000, or thirty-one per cent. It is true, however, that Dartmouth is living beyond her income, to the extent of $20,000 last year; and unless additional endowment is forthcoming, retrenchment must follow.

In four years, the great gymnasium has been completed, the Parkhurst administration building erected; Wentworth has been transformed from an old-time dormitory into a modern recitation hall; the chapel has been enlarged; two apartment houses have been provided for the faculty; old Sanborn Hall has given way to Robinson Hall, which, as the home of all non-athletic activities, promises great impetus to intellectual and social life. Although in four years the student body has grown but eight per cent, three new dormitories, North and South Massachusetts and Hitchcock, have been added, sufficient to accommodate one-fifth of all the dormitory residents. Through the old buildings they replaced, and the new marks of excellence which they have set, these halls have given the student body a new standard of dormitory comfort.

While the student body has increased but eight per cent, the faculty has grown four times as fast, or thirty-three per cent, which indicates that the college is approaching an ideal ratio between the number of instructors and students. [. . .]

While Dr. Nichols has been effecting a business reorganization he has not neglected educational work. One of the first problems which he undertook was the definition of the departments of instruction. His methods were quiet and but few knew that efficiency tests were at work; incidentally, he aroused no opposition among the faculty. One of the leading departments now presents a personnel entirely new; others have been changed almost as much. Instruction methods were studied and revised to secure uniformity; subject matter was investigated to avoid unnecessary duplication.

The next step was insistence upon better scholarship. Entrance requirements remain the same, but the college standards have steadily risen. Sifting of the mentally unfit was started in the freshman class by a rule which in its first application separated so many men that a prolonged wail arose among both undergraduates and alumni, and its echoes have not yet disappeared. But in reply to such protests Dr. Nichols says: "The college regards its course as a business investment; and it cannot afford to take a chance on men who show themselves unfit for college in their freshman year. If these men really desire a college education, and are willing to work for it, they can return another year with better preparation." And, strange to say, a considerable number of men do return and make good. [. . .]

The result of these several efforts is a new and very live interest in scholarship. The scholar is receiving more of the honor due him, and the college uses its means to let the scholars be known. One simple device to make men either proud or ashamed of their rank is the list on the administration bulletin board, giving the relative standing of the members of each class. This new interest in scholarship is reflected in comment by Professor Keyes in the August Alumni Magazine: "Some months ago, a well-informed alumnus stated that there was a feeling among some undergraduates that the student body was becoming too studious, and that men were coming too largely to be judged on the basis of their classroom work. There is little likelihood that such a situation will ever endanger the vigorous activity of Dartmouth men. But the statement seems symptomatic of a gradual change which is taking place in the respect paid to the intellect." [. . .]

Robert Frost 1896
Returns to the Campus

➤➤➤ An article in the *Dartmouth Alumni Magazine* for January 1916 began: "Robert Frost, the poet of New England who, by his volume, 'North of Boston', has leaped in the last year from the obscurity of an unknown country school-teacher to the fame of an author widely read both in England and America, is of particular interest to Dartmouth men, because of the fact that he was for one year a student at the College." In the period just preceding the *Magazine*'s publication of this article, a series of letters had been received from the poet by Harold Goddard Rugg 1906, career-long member of the College Library's staff—a correspondence that related in part to arrangements for Robert Frost's coming to Hanover to give a talk and reading.

Littleton N.H.
April 20 1915

DEAR SIR You are correctly informed: I was some part of a year at Hanover with the class of 1896. I lived in Wentworth (top floor, rear, side next to Dartmouth) in a room with a door that had the advantage of opening outward and so of being hard for marauding sophomores to force from the outside. I had to force it once myself from the inside when I was nailed and screwed in. My very dear friend was Preston Shirley (who was so individual that his memory should be still green with you) and he had a door opening inward that was forced so often that it became what you might call *facile* and opened if you looked at it. The only way to secure it against violation was to brace it from behind with the door off the coal closet. I made common cause with Shirley and sometimes helped him hold the fort in his room till we fell out over a wooden washtub bathtub that we owned in partnership but that I was inclined to keep for myself more than my share of the time. I may say that we made up afterward over kerosene. One of us ran out of oil after the stores were closed at night and so far sacrificed his pride as to ask to borrow of the other.

I'm afraid I wasn't much of a college man in your sense of the word. I was getting past the point when I could show any great interest in any task not self-imposed. Much of what I enjoyed at Dart-

71

mouth was acting like an Indian in a college founded for Indians. I mean I liked the rushes a good deal, especially the one in which our class got the salting and afterwards fought it out with the sophomores across pews and everything (it was in the Old Chapel) with old cushions and even footstools for weapons—or rather fought it to a standstill with the dust of ages we raised.

For the rest I wrote a good deal and was off in such places as the Vale of Tempe and on the walk east of the town that I called the Five Mile Round. I wrote one of the poems I still care for at about that time. It is preserved in my first book, "A Boys Will." I wrote while the ashes accumulated on the floor in front of my stove door and would have gone on accumulating to the room door if my mother hadn't sent a friend a hundred miles to shovel up and clean house for me. [. . .]

Franconia N.H.

October 15 1915

DEAR MR. RUGG: [. . .] Go as far as you like in probing my life even to asking me whether at Dartmouth or elsewhere I ever did anything wrong. I never did. And feel free to use anything I have written you. Such indiscretions as I have committed to paper were a necessary part of my inspiration and I must be prepared to stand by them.

It is strange that there is so little to say for my literary life at Dartmouth. I was writing a good deal there. I have ways of knowing that I was as much preoccupied with poetry then as I am now. "My Butterfly" in "A Boy's Will" belongs to those days, though it was not published in The Independent till a year or two later (1894 or 1895 I think), so also "Now Close the Windows" in the same book. I still like as well as anything I ever wrote the eight lines in the former beginning "The grey grass is scarce dappled with the snow."

But beyond a poem or two of my own I have no distinctly literary recollections of the period that are not chiefly interesting for their unaccountability. I remember a line of Shelley (Where music and moonlight an[d] feeling are one) quoted by Prof C. F Richardson in a swift talk on reading; a poem on Lake Memphremagog by ———— Smalley in the Lit; and an elegy on the death of T.W. Parsons by Hovey in The Independent. I doubt if Hovey's poem was one of his best. I have not seen it from that day to this, but I will sware that it talks of "horns of Elfland faintly blowing." So the memory of the past resolves itself into a few bright star points set in darkness—(the sense of the present is diffuse like daylight)

Nothing of mine ever appeared in Dartmouth publications [. . .].

Franconia N.H.
November 10 1915

DEAR MR RUGG: You were just off for something when you wrote and I am just off for something now. I only mention the fact because I am afraid that when I get back from what I am off for it will be some time before I shall be in the mood for any more of the same. You have guessed that I mean talking. It will be altogether at boys' schools this trip and I ought not to mind it any more than so many recitations; but I shall: it is bound to put me off my writing for a while. There is a sort of purturbation that I have my doubts about in this new life I have entered on for the money I can pick up. I believe it would be a mistake for me to think of setting right off for Hanover before I have had time to get well over Boston. I should like December wholly to myself to see if I can't subside and get some work done. I wonder if you sympathise enough to understand. I do want not to seem to fall out with the plans you have taken so much trouble to make for me. But here are two or three all-but-finished poems and here on file are more than as many invitations to print them. They ought to be seen to, dont you say? A matter of a month all to myself ought to settle them one way or the other. What I should like to ask you is to see if you couldnt fit me into your plans for January. Of course if December were going to be my only chance ever to see Dartmouth again I should have nothing to say. I only thought I would tell you how it was with me. I have as yet no fixed dates in January except a reading for Prof Bates of Wellesley on the tenth and the Dartmouth Alumni Dinner ⌈in Boston⌉ on the twenty-seventh.

When you write again will you tell me a little more about your idea? You seem to use the plural "talks" [. . .].

Franconia N.H.
December 2 1915

DEAR MR. RUGG: Mrs Frost has been very ill for some days and is still in a serious condition. You will forgive my having put off writing to you.

January 22 will suit me.

I should like not to get very far from the subject of sound in my talk. How would "Imagination and the Voice" do?—or "New Sounds in Poetry"? I could give you "New Hampshire Gold" which would be a homily on the exceptional in life and poetry. My own preference would be for "New Sounds in Poetry." Something would depend of course on the character of the audience you have in mind for me. I gave this, or virtually this, five times last week. It was most successful with the new poetry society in the Harvard Graduate School and with a group of Cambridge people, professors and their wives.

I should like seventy-five dollars for my pains. [. . .]

Franconia N.H.

December 19 1915

DEAR MR. RUGG: Let's stop right where we are for a moment till I explain. I simply mustn't be put before Dartmouth as standing out for any particular price. I named seventy-five dollars more or less off hand with no very definite idea in mind of what I was going to at Hanover. I thought if it was to be something you charged admission to, you would want me to have as much as you could. It is never for a moment a matter of what I am worth. I am probably worth nothing. Really I ought not to be asked to set a price. I am not in the business and you are—and you ought to [know] what I ought to have. I am getting all sorts of fees. I shall get no more than fifty dollars for what is my chief honor, the Phi Beta Kappa at Harvard in June. So you just straighten the matter out to suit yourself and in the way to make the least noise. Whatever else I may be worth I am certainly worth no noise. Fifty dollars will be all right. [. . .]

>>> Two announcements carried on front pages of *The Dartmouth* provide follow-up documentation relating to the 1916 visit:

December 6, 1915—"That Robert Frost, prominent young American Poet, and author of 'North of Boston' will lecture under the auspices of the Arts January 22 in Robinson Hall was definitely announced at the meeting of that society Saturday afternoon. [. . .]"

January 22, 1916—"Robert Frost, who is to lecture tonight at 8 o'clock on 'New Sounds in Poetry' in the Little Theatre, arrived in Hanover last evening. Mr. Frost is one of the leading exponents of modern verse and is well-fitted to speak on his subject, which deals with the poetry of today. He will probably close his talk by reading selections from North of Boston, the work which has made him famous. An admission fee of 25 cents will be charged. [. . .]"

The January 1916 occasion was the first of what would prove to be, over the years that followed, innumerable returns to Dartmouth by Robert Frost, to read and lecture and teach—including intervals during the period 1943–49 when he held a faculty post as George Ticknor Fellow in the Humanities. The famous poet's last appearance before a Dartmouth audience was on November 27, 1962 (less than two months prior to his death, at age eighty-eight), in Spaulding Auditorium of the College's newly opened Hopkins Center. His presentation, as originally published in the March 1963 *Alumni Magazine*, began:

I THINK THE FIRST THING I ought to speak of is all this luxuriance: all in easy chairs and a beautiful hall—and nothing to do but to listen to me. Pretty soft, I call it. Pretty soft.

I was so made that I—though a Vermonter and all that—never took any stock in the doctrine that "a penny saved is a penny earned." A penny saved is a *mean* thing, and a penny spent is a generous thing and a big thing—like this. (It took more than a penny to do this. There's nothing mean about it.)

And one of the expressions I like best is—in the Bible it is and in poets—they say, "of no mean city am I." That's a great saying, ain't it?—to be "of no mean city," like San Francisco or Boston.

People deprecate our beautiful cities, and I go around thinking how many people living in them must say that: "of no mean city am I." How splendid. And 'of no mean college am I.' (Funny for me to be talking about that.)

And I was thinking—I am going to read to you, of course, principally—I was thinking of the extravagance of the universe. What an *extravagant* universe it is. And the most extravagant thing in it, as far as we know, is man—the most wasteful, spending thing in it—in all his luxuriance.

How stirring it is, the sun and everything. Take a telescope and look as far as you will. How much of a universe was wasted just to produce puny us. It's wonderful . . . , fine.

And poetry is a sort of extravagance, in many ways. It's something that people wonder about. What's the need of it? And the answer is, no need—not particularly. That is, that's the first one.

I've always enjoyed being around colleges, nominally as a professor, you know, and a puzzle to everybody as to what I was doing —whether anything or not. (You'd like to leave that to others. Never would defend myself there.) And people say to me occasionally, "Where *does* poetry come in?" Some of you may be thinking it tonight: what's it all for? "Does it *count*?"

When I catch a man reading my book, red-handed, he usually

looks up cheerfully and says, "My wife is a great fan of yours." Puts it off on the women.

I figured that out lately: that there's an indulgence of poetry, a manly indulgence of poetry, that's a good deal like the manly indulgence of women. We say that women rule the world. That's a nice way to talk. And we say that poetry rules the world.

There's a poem that says:

> We are the music makers,
>   And we are the dreamers of dreams . . .
> World-losers and world-forsakers,

. . . and all that. We are "the makers" of the future. We:

> Built Nineveh with our sighing,
>   And Babel itself with our mirth;
> And o'erthrew them with prophesying
>   To the old of the new world's worth;
> For each age is a dream that is dying,
>   And one that is coming to birth.

That's a big claim, isn't it? An exaggerated claim.

But I look on the universe as a kind of an exaggeration anyway, the whole business. That's the way you think of it: great, great, great expense—everybody trying to make it mean something more than it is.

But all poetry asks is to be accorded the same indulgence that women are accorded. And I think the women, the ladies, are perhaps the go-betweens. They're our ambassadors to the men. They break the poetry to the men.

And it's a strange thing that men write the poetry more than the women; that is, the world's history is full of men poets and very few women. Women are in the dative case. It's to and for them, the poetry. And then for men and the affairs of men through them. (One knows the story that makes an argument that women really run the world in the end, run everything.)

And I'm not defending at all. I just thought one of the figures of poetry—(It's a metaphor, isn't it? You know, various kinds of metaphor.)—but one of the figures you never hear mentioned is just the one extravagance.

This is a little extravaganza, this little poem; and to what extent is it excessive? And can you go with it? Some people can't. And sometimes it's a bitter extravagance, like that passage in Shakespeare that so many make their novels out of: life is "a tale told by an idiot . . . , signifying nothing." That's an extravagance, of course—of bitterness.

People hold you. You say something sad or something pessimistic and something cynical, and they forget to allow for the extravagance of poetry. You're not saying that all the time. That's not a doctrine you're preaching. You loathe anybody that wants you to be either pessimist or optimist. It doesn't belong to it, it doesn't belong at all. Are you happy or are you unhappy? Why are you? You have no right to ask.

The extravagance lies in "it sometimes seems as if." That would be a good name of a book: "it sometimes seems as if." Or it says, "if you only knew." You could put that on the cover of a book. "If only I could tell you," you know. "Beyond participation lie my sorrows and beyond relief"—and yet you're harping on 'em, you see, in that way.

I arrived step by step at these things about it all, myself. I've been thinking lately that politics is an extravagance, again, an extravagance about *grievances*. And poetry is an extravagance about *grief*. And grievances are something that can be remedied, and griefs are irremediable. And there you take 'em with a sort of a happy sadness, that they say drink helps—say it does. ("Make you happy . . . ," the college song goes, "Make you happy, make you sad. . . ." That old thing. How deep those things go.) [. . .]

And then, I could go right on with pretty near everything I've done. There's always this element of extravagance. It's like snapping the whip: Are you there? Are you still on? Are you with it? Or has it snapped you off?

"Hoppy" Becomes President

Reminiscences by ERNEST MARTIN HOPKINS

⋙ Upon his being graduated from the College in 1901 Ernest Martin Hopkins had remained at Dartmouth as private secretary to President Tucker, and over succeeding years he took on an ever-enlarging and wide-ranging sphere of responsibilities. Following Dr. Nichols' succession to the presidency, in 1909, he continued for a year in his post as Secretary of the College; then devoted himself for the next half-dozen years to the business world, becoming a pioneer in the field of personnel administration. Throughout his time away from Hanover, in the period 1910–16, he ongoingly concerned himself with Dartmouth interests, especially within the area of alumni affairs, and he was instrumental in establishing, during 1913, the College's Alumni Council. He was elected President of the College on June 13, 1916, assumed office on August first, and was formally inaugurated on October sixth of that year.

The following excerpts are from *'Hoppy' on His Early Dartmouth Years* and *Ernest Martin Hopkins on His Dartmouth Presidential Years*, published by the College in 1967 and 1987, respectively—both volumes being based on informal reminiscences by Mr. Hopkins, tape-recorded in the period 1958–64.

"I HAD BEEN INTERESTED from 1905 in the various steps necessary to form the Alumni Council, and I was working on that during this time. The Alumni Council eventually got formed, and then the question arose, what were we formed for and what were we supposed to do?

"I had become impressed, in the meanwhile, with the fact that insofar as I knew no Board of Trustees in inviting a President to come had ever known anything about why they were asking him. They had no particular set of specifications: what the College was for or anything. So, I proposed to the Council that we compose an inquiry to the Trustees as to what Dartmouth was all about: why it existed, and what it aimed to do and so forth and so on.

"We worked on that for a couple of years, and I think submitted it to the Trustees either in late '14 or perhaps early '15. (I wouldn't be sure in regard to that.) I wrote the thing, which was a summary of our discussions.

"Well, insofar as I know, it was that document more than anything else that turned the Trustees' attention toward me, and sometime . . .

late in 1915, Mr. Streeter, who was then in the Elliott Hospital in Boston after an eye operation, telephoned me one Sunday morning. (I being a working man, Sunday mornings were very precious to me, and I didn't generally get up very early. But this was before seven o'clock, and there was a sleet storm outside. I was living in Newton.)

"He says, 'I want to see you.' Well, I'd worked very intimately with him in the previous life here at Dartmouth, and so I knew him very well. I said that I would come in as quick as I had had breakfast. He says, 'Hell, I want you to come in now.' So, without any breakfast and without even shaving, I went down and got into the car and skidded into Boston. And skidded is right, too; it was just as slippery as it could be. . . .

"I had no idea, had no faintest idea what he wanted to see me about. I went in, and he said, 'Sit down, sit down.' [. . .] So, I sat down, and he reached out and put his hand on mine, and he says, 'Nichols has resigned.'

"I expressed my surprise. He says, 'Well, you know why I sent for you, don't you?' I says, 'No, I haven't the faintest idea.' He says, 'You're going up there.'

"Well, there were several things to take into consideration. I mean, I knew the local situation pretty well, and I wasn't sure of my welcome. I knew what the outside public would think in regard to it. And, also, there was the very self-centered fact that I was getting about three times as much in income as the presidency paid, and I was on my way to about what I had been aiming at in the AT&T.

"So, I just tried to slow the thing down, and he got very impatient in regard to it. 'Well,' he says, 'fool around; you've probably got to fool around two or three months. That's natural, I guess. But,' he says, 'you're going up there.'

"I confess I began to be convinced I probably was! But then the thing went on—the discussions back and forth—and I became more and more convinced that I didn't want it and more and more convinced that it wasn't the best thing for the College. I held to that pretty definitely.

"And gradually as the word got out, as such things do get out, that the proffer had been made, why various alumni groups began to express reservations in regard to it."

Ironic as it certainly seems in retrospect that there should have been such a degree of opposition to the choice the Trustees had determined upon, opposition there was, including a group within the faculty who protested "that it would be the death knell of Dartmouth academically" if he were made President:

"The whole combination made me very doubtful in regard to the desirability of it from Dartmouth's point of view, and, as I say, I had the perfectly selfish reservations regarding myself. And I had, also, the further factor that Mrs. Hopkins had no desire to return to Hanover. She knew what a college president's wife had to do, and she felt very strongly that we better not.

"Well, there's a lot of goings and comings in there—different Trustees and one thing and another. . . . And finally I definitely made up my mind that I ought not to come back and wasn't going to come back.

"At that time Doctor Tucker came into the picture for the first time. I mean, I had heard nothing from him and hadn't asked him anything, of course, about it. I got this word through Mr. Streeter that Doctor Tucker wanted to see me just as soon as he could. So, I came up.

"Doctor Tucker at that time was bedridden. I went to the house immediately on arriving in Hanover. Doctor Tucker says, 'I understand your situation perfectly well, and I understand the reservations you have. But you and I have worked together a good many years, and we understand some things that we don't have to talk about.' He says, 'I just want to state one thing to you. You're the last Dartmouth man on the list of candidates.'

"I remember at the time, just in order to say something, I said, 'I'm not a candidate.' Doctor Tucker laughed a little. He says, 'Well, we'll use some other word then, but of those that have been under consideration, every Dartmouth man has been eliminated excepting you, and if you don't come the presidency is going to a non-Dartmouth man.' He says, 'Do you think that would be good?' My answer to that is obvious. I said, 'No.'

"Actually, that was the turning point on the thing. I said all right, that I would come if the Trustees still felt after making as definite an investigation as they could that it was a desirable thing to do."

During this interview with the President Emeritus, Mr. Hopkins was told something that startled him greatly:

"I think the strangest thing ever said to me came from a man from

whom I'd least expect it, and that was in the talk with Doctor Tucker.
. . . I don't remember just how I phrased the question, but I really
wanted to know what he thought I had that qualified me for the position. And he says, 'You're a gambler.' He says, 'Dartmouth's at the stage
where it needs gambling.'"

*Over the years that followed President Hopkins often thought back,
reflectively, to this surprising declaration:*

"I never was quite sure whether I was living up to it or over-living
it or what! But—well, regardless of the validity of that judgment on
his part—I think a lot of the colleges suffer from leadership of men
who won't take a chance. I think educational progress *is* a gamble. I
think you've got to gamble. You'll make some mistakes. I mean, I
know perfectly well I made them, and I think anybody would make
them. But I think the net of it all is that if you exclude the element of
chance on the thing, why you're going to lose something. You've got
to take the hazard of that."[. . .]

*With regard to the existence of scattered opposition to his election
within the alumni body, Mr. Hopkins could in later years report:*

"I ought to say there that I think it's some tribute that's due to the
Dartmouth alumni: once the thing was settled there wasn't any disposition, so far as I know, to perpetuate the thing."

*And, too, those on the faculty who opposed his being made President
were also soon won over:*

"Actually, within a couple of years they were among my best
friends. . . .

"But that in brief is the prelude to my coming, and needless to say
I never was sorry I came. I think I had a happier life than probably I
would have had under other circumstances."[. . .]

"I never considered myself as an 'educator.' I was frequently
flattered when people referred to me as an educator. But I never
thought of myself as that. I always thought of myself as an administrator in an educational institution. And I think that's what I was.

"I learned a little about colleges and what they were supposed to do
and what they were about. But I had none of the insignia for the job."

*During the short interval between his election by the Board of Trus-
tees, in June of 1916, and his actually assuming office, on August first, Mr.*

Hopkins made frequent trips to Hanover. ("I was up here weekends pretty constantly."), in order to consult with outgoing-President Ernest Fox Nichols, whom he had come to know well during part of the period (1898–1903) when the latter was a Professor of Physics at Dartmouth and, subsequently, while working under him in the first year (1909–10) of Nichols' own presidency of the College.—

"Doctor Nichols never liked being President. I mean, that was a case where, as a matter of fact, I always thought he was done a good deal of wrong on that thing, because it took him out of the scientific field and he never caught up with it afterwards. And, meanwhile, he never did adapt himself to the presidency.

"I don't think more than a month after he took office, he told me one night, when I was up to the house, he says, 'You know, this thing is all wrong.' He says, 'From the time I can first remember, if I had a problem,' he says, 'I took it into the laboratory and stayed with it, whether it took five minutes or five years.' He says, 'I leave a problem down at the office and come home and think it over, and by the time I get back next morning,' he says, 'there are a dozen more.' He says, 'I just can't work that way; it bothers me to have them there.' . . .

"But personally and socially he was delightful. He hadn't the faintest glimmerings of 'administrative' procedures. I don't think he even knew what the word meant. And I don't think he wanted to. [. . .]

"I was very fond of him, and (which I think he resented) I felt sorry for him. I felt then, and I feel now, that it would have taken very little change in his technique, to have made good as a president. But he didn't want to make a change. . . .

"As I say, I don't think he wanted anybody's pity, but I always think of him, very compassionately, as a man that, quite outside of any responsibility of his own, was thrown into an impossible situation, as far as he was concerned."

In the midst of the various questionings and protests, from faculty and other sources, occasioned by the Trustees' choice of him to head the College, President-elect Hopkins attended Dartmouth's 1916 Commencement exercises.—

"Actually, I was in sort of an anomalous position at that Commencement in 1916. I'd been elected, and yet I wasn't anything. And I've always felt very grateful to the Dartmouth alumni for the courtesy with which they treated me at that period, because they didn't have to do anything."

His formal induction as President was held in Hanover on October sixth, barely a fortnight after the opening of the College for its 1916–17 academic year.—

"I remember the ceremony itself very definitely. . . . I think the general attitude of the attendants that day was one of extreme agnosticism. They'd come from all over the country, and they'd heard something in regard to the faculty attitude here, and they looked over my record and they didn't see much to redeem me in that. But my impressions of the proceedings were that they warmed up, definitely, during the day." [. . .]

The launching of the Hopkins presidency was, in general, far from an easy task. ("I thought for a while there wasn't anything but problems!") And among the difficulties were ones associated with the College's central administrative corps.—

"There was an organization problem which was pretty acute. The Trustees, very early in the game, discovered that Doctor Nichols not only hadn't had any experience in business, but that he didn't want any. (He just hated the business side of the thing.) And they asked me back, at that time, to become business manager of the College, and I wasn't interested. And, then, they elected Homer Eaton Keyes, who was Professor of Art.

"I never knew just how they figured that out! But they made him business manager. And with Doctor Nichols' entire acquiescence, if not enthusiasm, they gave him very large authorities. It was practically coincident with the President's authorities. And they were given without any question. Well, I didn't know how to operate that way."

Thus, from the very beginning, and increasingly, conflict was pronounced and awkward, the Business Director intent on operating, now, with the same independence of the President that he had exercised during the Nichols years.—

"I tried to explain it, but it wasn't easy to explain to him that we weren't going to continue to. And it finally came down to the question of whether there were to be two Presidents or one, and he resigned and left.

"But that was the major organization problem of my early years here—particularly difficult because he'd been a friend of mine. As an undergraduate he'd preceded me as editor of *The Dartmouth*, and we'd roomed together [after graduation] for two years at the Howe Library.

"It isn't pleasant to have to settle those things with your intimate acquaintances and friends."

Also, there was initially considerable awkwardness, or worse, regarding the President's relationships with the Dean, Craven Laycock.—

". . . Craven had of course felt quite definitely, himself, that he would like the presidency. He had been groomed for it. He was very unhappy at the fact that he was passed over on it."

Laycock's disappointment ("He was awfully sensitive in regard to the outcome of the thing.") was manifested partly by his refusal to speak to the man who had been selected instead of him, and by an attempt to conduct his dealings with the President "wholly through memoranda." This was a situation the latter found intolerable; and one stormy night, when he knew other family members were not to be at home, E.M.H. set out for the Laycock house, determined to have a confrontation with the Dean of the College.—

"So, I went up. (And he told me afterwards, one time, that he came nearer dying from shock that night than he ever did before: when he opened the door and saw me.) I explained to him why I had come. And I said, 'I think the time has come for us to have an understanding, because when everything is done and said, I *was* elected President—whether wisely or not—and I'm not going to try to operate with a Dean that won't operate with me.'

"And it was an entirely pleasant party. I discovered that he had wanted to find some way that he felt he could, with dignity, end the feud. And everything went on nicely from then."[. . .]

This selection of passages drawn from Ernest Martin Hopkins' tape-recorded reminiscences might perhaps be brought to a close with one more extract—a story he delighted in telling about himself and Sarah L. Smith, spinster daughter of Dartmouth's seventh President, who lived in the Smith homestead on West Wheelock Street and was affectionately known to the community as "Sally Prex":

"The tradition was that Sally Prex had been disappointed in love. Whether that's so or not I don't know, but she certainly had never married; and she had become the social arbiter of Hanover, which in those days was perfectly possible. . . .

"My freshman year the Dekes were going to give a reception, and the whole question in any fraternity at that time was whether they could get Sally Prex to be the presiding genius or not—that marked you as distinctive or not.

"I was supposed to rustle provisions for this thing. (The freshmen were assigned all the menial jobs.) The chocolate gave out, and I went out to get a pot of chocolate.

"I can see her now, sitting there. I went to put it across the table, somebody joggled my elbow, and I never had the same kind of a feeling and never want one again. The thing just slid off into her lap—a whole potful of hot chocolate.

"She had on a frilled, gray rig that it didn't do any good to. And to make it just as bad as possible, I lapsed into my granite-quarry vocabulary, and said, 'God damn it!' and turned and ran.

"Well, I spent the next two years in avoiding Sally Prex. When I saw her on the street, I'd get on the opposite side of the street. And then came senior year . . . , and Mrs. Proctor, who was a lovely person, a sweet, little old lady . . . , says, 'Hoppy, you ought not to stay away from things just because Sarah Smith's going to be there. She probably doesn't remember you.' So, one day she said there was going to be something, and she says, 'You go with me.' Well, Mrs. Proctor had a position in the town that would give me some respectability, so I went.

"Sally Prex was very gracious, and she showed no signs of ever having seen me before, and that was all right with me—it was fine. From then on I stopped avoiding her and saw a good deal of her. And then during the ten years I was here I was constantly invited to her house and invited to other places where she was—very friendly, in every way.

"When I came back here in 1916, I got this note from her, and she says, 'I belong to the "Wheelock Succession" too, you know.' She says, 'I would like to see you.' So, I went down, and I had a perfectly wonderful afternoon.

"She took me all over the house. She took me up to what had been her bedroom, which was still existent just about as it was, apparently, in the older days. There was a register in it, and she told me that the room underneath had been her father's study. She said as a small girl she periodically would hear what apparently was an animated conversation down below, excepting it was a monologue. She'd get up and listen at the register, and her father would be praying to soften the hearts of the faculty on some discipline case.

"Well, it was a lovely afternoon. I mean, the associations were nice and everything else. (She was a wheelchair patient at the time. I had been pushing her around the house.)

"It came time to go. We got to the front door. I was all ready to go, and she put her hands up. She says, 'I want to kiss you goodbye.' I leaned down, and she put her lips right up against my ear, and she says, 'I hope you'll have a very successful administration. As one of your predecessors, I hope you will.' Then she hesitated a minute, and she says, 'But don't ever try to pass chocolate.'"

The Birth of "The Nugget"

by BILL CUNNINGHAM

>>> Elijah William Cunningham 1919, long a much-celebrated sports writer, editor, and columnist with newspapers in Boston, here tells the story of the coming into being of a special Hanover/Dartmouth institution, the Nugget motion-picture theatre. This text is from a booklet entitled *The Nugget Theatre*, published in commemoration of the Hanover Improvement Society's 1951 opening of its new facility, located on Hanover's Main Street. (The Nugget was acquired in 1922 by the Improvement Society, a local public-service organization; and for a period of years, following the burning in 1944 of the original Nugget building, the theatre's programs were conducted in the College's Webster Hall.)

LIKE MANY ANOTHER alumnus now graying over the ears, I owe my Dartmouth, and all that's happened since, to the unsought help of kind and warm-hearted people who weren't too busy with their own affairs to offer a young fellow a hand when he needed it most. In my case—the case of an awkward, but well meaning, kid strayed up amongst them from the distance of Texas—most of those people were the people of Hanover. I mean the "Town" portion of the community as differentiated from the "Gown." That explains, in part, how the Nugget was born. I said, "in part."

Entering college that autumn of 1915, my financial status was practically illusory. For 30 years since, I've heard of "athletic scholarships" in various institutions of learning from coast-to-coast, but if Dartmouth had any in my campus day and generation, a lot of us were shamefully hornswoggled. The best offered any of us was the chance to work at odd jobs, and scratch as we could for the rest. There was no waiving of room and tuition. You paid that on time, and, in cash, or else.

I attacked the usual run of jobs and hated all of them, but something else was bothering me, too. That was the fact that no movies were available closer than White River Junction. That annoyed me two ways. First of all, I missed the pictures. I was crazy about 'em. But next, and more important, I felt that if Hanover had a movie, I could possibly get a job of the sort I liked, and with which I was thoroughly familiar.

87

For, you see, that was the way I'd worked my way through prep school. [. . .] That had been my summer, after-school, holidays and week-end employment for some three or four years prior to Dartmouth. Hanging around the theaters, I'd learned to write ads, the mechanics of booking, and most of the rest. At least I had a good smattering.

The middle of [. . .] Freshman winter, in some fashion, I heard that the rich man of the town, one F. W. Davison, was about to honor the community with a new building, and that while there'd been a little wild talk about making it into a movie, the probabilities were that it would be a garage. I tore out to locate this Mr. Davison, faster, and with practically as much gall, as a man charging all hell with one bucket of water.

The old gentleman proved very hard to crack. I won't go into the subject of Mr. Davison here because his memory undoubtedly survives. He was, however, the local Croesus, a tall, rheumy-eyed old time Yankee possibly then in his 70's, and considered by all, generations of students included, a very hard man with his money. [. . .]

Old F. W. seemed determined to make the venture a garage. The automobile was beginning to get pretty important up that river road about then. A movie? The reasoning, in general seemed to be that Hanover didn't need a movie because it had never had a movie. When I tried to poll the community to work up some sentiment, that was what I mostly ran into.

I don't recall any active opposition from the college, as such, but there was a lot of undercutting from such things as the Dramatic Association, the Glee Club and such purveyors of standard entertainment. The hard, and open, opposition came from the so-called Dartmouth Christian Association, which was really the college Y.M.C.A. staffed by a professional secretary named Wally Ross—a splendid gentleman, too.

This D.C.A. ran regular free and cultural programs for the students in the Commons, at least once a week, and possibly oftener. This generally consisted of the reading of some poetry, or possibly a few selections on the violin. These were called "6:45's" because that's when they were convened. It knew its goose was cooked if Gloria Swanson and Charlie Chaplin were set up in opposition and it proved to be rather stubborn about the matter.

I weathered all that, however, and kept going back at Mr. Davison. Like the Red Chinese at Kaesong, he wouldn't agree, but he never exactly shut the door. It took me most of the spring to make the sale, and, even then, I'm not so certain he agreed because he smelled possible profits, as because he was thinking of his son.

For the Davisons had one son, Frank, then, possibly, in his 30's. I write this with respect, and with great gratitude to all of them, despite the fact that they all now are long since beyond reach of these words. Frank hadn't found a job that appealed to him. The old man had even bought him a ranch in Montana, and although he'd tried it for awhile, he'd chucked that, too, and was now back in Hanover.

In fact, he was a fairly sensational sight in Hanover because he'd come home equipped with full cowboy regalia and a horse which he rode about town. From anything I ever saw to the contrary, Frank was just an individualist who preferred to do things his way . . . but, to get along, certainly part of his pater's decision to erect a temple to the cinema came from the fact that I finally got Frank on my side. Frank became so enthusiastic, in fact, that he told his dad he felt this was the type of work he really could settle down to.

That did it. The father built the place and gave it to him. I don't know how the papers, if any, were drawn, but, always, in the old man's conversation, at least, the Nugget was "Frank's theater." My dealings, however, were always with the father. He seemed to make the decisions for both of us.

I don't know how I passed my courses that Freshman spring. Most of my time was spent in the Davison office helping draw the plans and studying the price lists of the furnishings and equipment for the original house. I stayed in Hanover that summer, barring some trips to Boston in line of duty, watching it being built and readied for the college year.

In its final form, it was strictly a utility movie. The old man, knowing his students better than I did, wanted nothing in it that wasn't screwed down or otherwise made too secure either to lift or to throw. The floor was of cement. The seats—570 of them as I recall—were of wood and iron securely bolted into the concrete. The walls were of galvanized iron. The rest of the furnishings were a cashier's cage, two machines, a screen and a piano. I was the firm's purchasing agent in all this, subject to the old gentleman's meticulous approval.

When we finally got rolling, Frank was the cashier. I posted the bills and played the piano. I was officially the Manager, and, in self-protection, I strove savagely not to let either know how simple and automatic that was. They sent me regularly to Boston on the highly important mission of booking the films. There really wasn't any booking to do. Since there was no competition in the town, I simply signed up with three companies for two films a week, and took what they sent. You had to do that, anyway.

The films came up nightly from Boston on the milk train, and were tossed off at Norwich. The American Express hauled them up from the depot and deposited them, often in the snow, in front of the Nugget's locked door. Sometime during the forenoon, one of us would go over and move them inside. That's all there was to it.

Many Hanover citizens and thousands of Dartmouth alumni undoubtedly remember the classic pattern the Nugget performances took shortly after we opened with, as I recall it, the college year of 1916. There were three shows a day. The afternoon performance was more or less a dry run for whoever happened to have nothing better to do. From it, however, word generally spread over the campus concerning the class of the fare.

The "first show" right after supper became by gradual custom, "the students' show," where practically anything went, and almost everything did. It was immediately followed by the "last show," which, again, by gradual custom, became the performance for the townspeople, the faculty, guests at the Inn and anybody escorting a lady. These were often completely dignified. They were the ones to which you took your girl.

There was probably never anything in the history of the motion picture industry to compare with the typical "students' show" at the Nugget. Required equipment seemed to be a bag of peanuts, not to eat, but to throw. I used to play the piano in a mackinaw, with the collar turned up over my ears, as I presided at the pianoforte down front in the pit. Occasionally, not even that was sufficient protection, as some dastard would ring in an apple, or even a very wet snowball.

But the big feature was the way the generally jam-packed audience talked to the pictures while they were running. Those were the days of the silents, of course, but the audience was never silent. The skirt of one of the lovelies on the screen would slip up her leg a little and the entire audience would start to yell, "Higher! Higher!" A rooster would crow in the picture—silently, of course—but not in that theater. At least 250 customers would do their generally faulty uttermost to sound like an old dominicker yardmaster at dawn.

Some of this was really very funny. I remember a horrendous villain in some kind of a border melodrama, throwing the virginal heroine all over the cabin in the effort to make her take a drink. After he'd beaten her nearly to death with appropriate coaching from the audience, he finally forced the bottle between her unwilling lips and gave her a draught that seemed in a fair way to choke her to death. There was a moment of deathly silence from the audience behind me, and some peanut propeller shouted, "And now, Babe, what'll you have for a chaser?"

What most of Hanover never knew was that word of this "audience reaction" traveled even to Hollywood, and long before I ever heard the term "preview," some of the big companies occasionally shipped pictures and staff experts on the Nugget, to have them tried out in that critical atmosphere. They never had to wonder about what that audience thought. [. . .]

There's just one other thing. When Old Man Davison and I finally agreed that what Hanover needed was a movie, and came unavoidably to the venal question of what I was going to be so brazen as to expect as compensation, I hit him hard—for $35 a week straight salary! He reeled, and begged me to accept 25 per cent of the business instead.

I was adamant. We argued for two days over the matter, and almost broke off relations at one point. Finally he weakened and gave me the $35, which was my honorarium all the way to the end. I thought I'd licked him. If I'd taken that 25 per cent and could have held on to it until now. . . but shucks! who wants half a million dollars?

Of Freshman Life and Undergraduate Traditions

by CLIFFORD B. ORR

➤➤➤ These excerpts are from letters written home during the academic year 1918–19 (which interval included the closing months of World War I) by Clifford Orr 1922, whose career as writer and editor would include a long association, in the 1930s and '40s, with *The New Yorker* magazine.

[*S eptember 17, 1918*]—This is the end of my second day, and everything is fine. I have no room-mate yet, but think that I may get one tomorrow. There are to be no classes until Friday [. . .].

Delta Alpha (which is another name for hazing) is to start next Monday and last three days. In ordinary times it lasts two weeks, but we must be given time to recuperate before frat initiations which have to be done away with before Oct 1st, instead of February as in former years.

[*September 19*]—Today has been really the first day of college, altho no classes have as yet started. We attended chapel en masse this morning at nine, where we listened to our address of welcome from President Hopkins, and received primary instructions from the Dean. [. . .]

And then tonight the great annual rush came off. The Freshmen were lined up on one side of the campus, with the Sophomores on the other. Then Paleopitus (11 picked Seniors who practically run all non-academical activities), dressed in their white flannels and white sweaters and bearing lighted torches, marched down the center of the campus to the steps of Webster Hall, where they took their stand. A whitewashed football was kicked off, and with wild Indian-like yells, the whole six-hundred of us piled on top of it, and pushed, fought, kicked, bit, tore, punched, and yelled our way the length of the campus, and gave the ball, entirely deflated, into the hands of the waiting Paleopitus. It took almost forty-five minutes of frantic struggling, merciless trampling, and unprecedented howling, but for the first time in *seven* years, the Freshmen won the rush, and the battle was over!

You should have seen the place when everyone had gone! Sweaters, shirts, ties, pieces of trousers and gaiters littered the ground. I *lost* nothing, but ripped my old soft white shirt up the back—the one I brought solely for the purpose.

[*September 27*]—Delta Alpha is over and Freshmen are again happy. Frat initiations begin immediately. I did not make a frat. . . .

⋙ Freshman Orr had in fact missed the three-day Delta Alpha interval because of illness. In his letter of Saturday, September twenty-first, he had written: "Spanish influenza, grippe, and pneumonia have made their appearances here. Several soldiers have the former, and in one dormitory two students have it seriously, while eight or ten others think they are 'coming down' with it. Two fellows in No. Fayerweather have pneumonia. I only hope I can steer clear of it. At present I am O.K."

Striken immediately after writing thus, he was, however, able to report to his parents a swift recovery—although his letter home was reflective of decidedly dire conditions locally.

[*September 26*]—You needn't worry any more, because I'm all right now. The doctor let me go to classes today, and I am feeling almost as well as usual. I still am pretty stuffed up, but coming fine. I surely was lucky not to have been worse. Some fellows who were taken sick before I was are still in bed, and liable to be for some time. I was only in bed for Monday afternoon to Thursday noon, while several right in the same dorm have been there a week. One Freshman has died, and I don't know how many soldiers. Chapel has been cut out, the movies closed, and Dartmouth Night, which was to be held next Monday to celebrate the college's 150th birthday has been cancelled. [. . .] The epidemic has killed what little 'college life' there was.

⋙ As late as mid-January his letters home contained reflections of the continuing subservient nature of the on-campus relationship between freshmen and members of the undergraduate classes senior to them.

[*January 13*]—I may have to cut this short, because I want to send it down town by the Freshman who is on duty tonight. We have to take turns carrying mail and waking the Sophomores in the morning. My dates of duty are Feb. 5 and March 17. But nearly every night I have to do some sort of errand-running for upper classmen. Last night it was for doughnuts and the night before for flash light powder.

All the Freshmen are now wearing their caps. They are not tasseled but are bagged like this . They are absolutely the brightest green you can imagine. They are the same color green as cerise is of red. This week is Freshman "running season" when every Freshman must run out of sight when ordered to do so by an upper classman. So the Campus is covered by bobbing green caps of disappearing Freshmen.

➤➤➤ By spring of the 1918–19 academic year Clifford Orr's letters to his father and mother focused upon yet other aspects of class interrelationships and rivalry on Hanover Plain.

[*May 4*]—These are the happy days. The evenings are so warm and so perfectly delightful that we do our best to get our studying done in the afternoons that we may walk before dark. This afternoon about four o'clock we started out, and having traversed the entire length of the Vale of Tempe, we came out at the river bank a mile or more above town. There we didn't notice the passing time, and so we finally came to with a start realizing that we had just twenty minutes before chapel. Mose and Bing decided to run for it, but Jim and I stayed—we have four chapel cuts a term anyway, and I have only taken one. [. . .]

Have you ever heard of a "hum"? It is a Dartmouth tradition, old as the college, I guess. It happens like this: At quarter of seven the college gathers, the Seniors on their fence at one side of the campus, the Juniors directly across on the steps of Dartmouth Hall, the Sophomores on the steps of Webster, and the Freshmen across from them on Thayer. [. . .]

Then they sing. First the Seniors who are applauded by the other classes, then the Juniors. Then the Sophs, then the Freshmen. Then they go around once more, and then the Seniors sing the special "hum" song and cheer the other three classes. All the other classes cheer. Then all advance into the center of the campus, arm in arm, and form a hollow square around the cheer leaders. Then after cheering the college and the president, they sing the Dartmouth Song and then disperse. It is rather impressive and quite a sight. The campus is lined with spectators and the Inn piazza crowded.

[*May 13*]—Sh - h - h - h - h - h - h. These are the nights of mystery! 'Tis the fatal time. Dirty work is afoot. Listen: Four days are set aside each year, and in those four days the Freshmen have to have a picture taken of the class, the picture to contain 200 members, one officer, *no* upperclassmen, and must be taken within one mile of the campus. It now becomes the duty of the Sophomore class to see that that picture *is not taken,* or, if it is taken, that no officer is in it, or that a Sophomore shows his filthy face when the film is developed. I dare not tell you the plans of our class, for even Freshman mail is intercepted, but tomorrow is the first of the four days, and the fight is on. Already each dormitory is guarded and Freshmen cannot leave in groups. But our plans are well laid.

Last year the picture was taken successfully in the following manner. On Wednesday morning—corresponding to tomorrow,—Freshmen left town by ones and twos, casually and naturally, but before nightfall they were all gathered in a big barn. There they stayed and en masse captured and tied up all attacking parties of Sophomores until the first light of morning allowed the picture to be snapped.

As I say, I cannot tell plans, but it is sufficient to say that I shall probably not sleep after tonight or attend classes for a couple of days at least. But the moon is full.

[*May 17*]—Now that it is all over, and the three most wildly exciting days of my life have slipped by, let me give you a complete but concise account of everything that happened to me. ₍. . .₎

The Freshman plan was as follows: Wednesday morning every Freshman was to leave town in groups of two or three and meet at dusk in bunches of 10 under previously appointed leaders at previously appointed places. Then, as morning approached, these bunches were to move cautiously back into town and take refuge in the gully behind the high school. There they were to wait for the dawn, and take the picture.

So much for the plan. Now for my adventures.

Wednesday morning I arose at 6.45, ate a fair sized breakfast, stuffed a few bars of Baker's chocolate in my pocket, and slipped across the river. I had only about half an hour to wait when three other fellows joined me, and together we hit the trail for the cemetary near West Hartford, Vt. We arrived there soon after half past eight and found a straw filled shed, nicely hidden from the road. There we decided to encamp until dark, when we were to meet the rest of our gang, and slip back across the river by one of the three bridges— Hanover, Wilder or White River Jct. All the morning we stayed by the shed and played cards and read magazines, etc; but just about noon we thought we might as well hike to the river and see if anything was stirring on the other side. We did so, after a hike of about a mile. We arrived at the river bank, just about ¼ mile above Wilder. The sight of the village and the fact that it was dinner time, made us too bold, and casting away all discretion we strode down the main street. We deposited an ice-cream soda inside of each of us, and then started back up the river by way of the railroad track. But when we were in the heart of the village, a car full of sophomores spotted us, and they jumped out and gave chase. Two of us dashed to the right toward the wilderness, but the other two dashed to the left into the middle of the town (I haven't seen them since, but I know they got caught). We ran as fast as we could go for twenty long minutes with the Sophomores at our heels. Over fences, through brooks, across meadows, through groves until it seemed as though we couldn't run another step. And just as we were about to give up, the Sophs turned back; and we dropped right where we were. For an hour we were actually too exhausted to move. All we could do was to lie and pant, and hold onto our hearts to keep them from breaking through with their terrific pounding. Then we dragged ourselves back to our straw shed, burrowed into the straw and rested. It was dark before we moved again. At the cemetary we met three more of our gang—all that showed up, and off we started. At eleven o'clock, after numerous narrow escapes we again reached Wilder. As far as we could see, the town was asleep, and the bridge unguarded, so we began to sneak across. Immediately eight Sophs sprang up at either end, and with wild cries, revolver shots, and club brandishing, rushed upon us. It was then that I felt the cold muzzle of a revolver against my head for the first time in my life. We were bound, the five of us, wrist to wrist, and pushed to the other end of the town. There we were piled into an automobile and with the running boards piled with armed Sophs, we were taken to Hanover. All along the road, the car was repeatedly held up and examined by Sophs.

It was nearly midnight when we reached town. They took us from the car, and conveyed us to the cellar of the Phi Sigma Kappa barn, and there we found that it was used for a jail for captured Freshmen because about sixty captives were there, tied hand and foot, and strewn on the floor. We were thrown down among them, and you can believe that we passed a wretched night, with the cold winds howling through shattered windows, and shrieking through cracks along the damp floor.

At noon came the news that the picture was a failure, as scarcely 160 fellows were in it, so immediately the Sophomores began operations again. All dormitories were guarded and all roads leading out of the village were picketed. Then they began to enter the dorms, grab the Freshmen from their rooms, and tie them up again in their cursed barns. Jim and Bing opened their doors in the response to the frantic pounding and so spent the night freezing in the barn. But Mose and I, merely pulled down the shades, locked the doors, stuffed the letter slot and went to bed, again. At four o'clock P.M. (This was Thursday) I fell asleep and didn't wake until eight o'clock Friday morning. The captives in the barn had been freed again, and whispered reports were circulated that the picture would be attempted again at dawn on Saturday. So once more I ate a breakfast, and once more we sneaked from town. This time there were seven of us, representing the states of Maine, New Hampshire, New York, Indiana, Michigan, Illinois, and Nebraska. From nine a.m. until eleven, we walked directly eastward, and concealed ourselves on the top of a ridge, from which we could watch the roads around. We saw many groups of Freshmen, some of Sophomores, and witnessed several chases and a fight or two. Clubs were not spared, and more than one was knocked unconscious.

We considered ourselves safe, but at three in the afternoon, a crowd of Freshmen-hunting Sophs came up the back of the ridge, and we had to scatter. Jim was caught, but the rest of us got away. A fellow by the name of Morse and I lay down in a hollow at the foot of the ridge for four hours. About seven o'clock we started to move. We found a clump of freshly cut young pines, and by crawling in under them, we managed to keep out of the wind, and for half an hour, I slept.

At ten-thirty we roused ourselves for our night's work. The sky was all overcast and it looked like rain. We were cold and tired, and oh! so hungry, but we were miles from food. In a straight line, we were perhaps only about two miles from the gully where the picture was to be taken, but instead of going in a straight line, we hit the upper end of Mink Brook, that we knew flowed through the gully. Have you ever tried to walk along the edge of a rapid brook in pitch darkness? Don't ever attempt it, especially if you haven't had anything to eat all day, and you are nearly all in anyway. Well, we followed that brook, and that brook went five miles every time it went half a mile, but we dared not leave it because it led directly to our place of meeting, and we were otherwise apt to lose our way, approaching from that direction. We arrived at last, however, in the neighborhood of 1.45 A.M., and had no sooner crawled under some pines to await the gathering of the clan and the dawn when it began to pour. Of course we got drenched.

All over the hollow we could hear whisperings as more Freshmen arrived—or Sophomores, but no one attempted anything in the way of a fight. And then as the distant clock struck four, and the east began to hint at daylight, came three figures ringing cowbells and waving lanterns, calling together the class of 1922. We gathered. It was a funny sight. From out of the darkness on every side, stepped Freshmen, soaking wet, and from the three newcomers learned the astounding news that at four o'clock Friday afternoon (12 hours before), Paleopitus had declared that all picture activities should immediately cease because of "unsportsmanlike actions and excesses" on both sides.

So we crawled home, and at a quarter of five, I once more dropped to sleep in my own bed, and didn't wake until twelve o'clock Saturday noon. Once more I ate—the fourth meal in four days, but I believe I made up for it.

It is now twenty minutes past two of Saturday afternoon, and I haven't been to a recitation since Tuesday morning. But neither has hardly any Freshmen except those who were unlucky enough to get such low ranks last term that they aren't allowed to cut classes at all.

It surely has been a grand and exciting time, and if the whole class doesn't come down with typhoid from drinking streams, and pneumonia from trying to sleep on the grass in a pouring rain, we shall consider ourselves lucky. Thank Heaven, though, it's over.

[*June 9*]—Now I have witnessed two more of the workings out of old Dartmouth traditions. Yesterday was Wet Down, and today was Sing Out.

At 6.45 last evening, all four classes gathered at the sound of a bugle by the Senior Fence. The Freshmen and Sophomores were in old clothes in preparation for coming events. Led by a band, and in column of squads by classes—Freshmen last—we marched up the hill to the stump of the Old Pine, and there eleven of next year's seniors were initiated into Paleopitus. It wasn't very impressive because the crowd was so large and the stump so small. Down the hill we went, cheering each dormitory we passed until we came to Dartholm the president's house. He with his wife and little girl appeared on the piazza and we, gathered on the lawn, cheered each of them. But when Georgianna was cheered, she—about 4 years old—cried and had to be carried into the house. Next we made a circuit of the faculty residences, cheering before the homes of the great, such as President-Emeritus Tucker and Dean-Emeritus Emerson, Dr. Kingsford, Dr. Giles, and the nurses of the Mary Hitchcock Hospital. Then we came back to the campus and found that the whole population of Hanover as well as the rest of the state was lined around the edges.

In the centre stood a big green keg—lemonade. It used to be old New England rum in the days of Daniel Webster. Paleopitus advanced and drank. The Seniors advanced and drank. Then the Juniors. And then the Freshmen and Sophomores, lined on opposite sides, at the crack of a pistol rushed for it, and endeavored to roll it to the opponents' side. If you have never been in a rush, you do not know the feeling of endless pushing, panting, struggling, slipping, fearing every moment that you will be the next to disappear under the feet of the six or seven hundred mad youths and be trampled on until an ever watchful member of Paleopitus pulls you out and hands you to the spectators to be resuscitated if possible. For the first five minutes or so, the keg remained nearly in the middle but soon it slowly began to move toward the east—pushed by the Freshmen. Once I got through the mob to the keg, and was sprawled on top of it with ten on top of me, five hundred and eighty-eight others trying to get on, and one unconscious Freshman *under* the keg. So it went for 30 long minutes, and then the pistol sounded again—and the rush was over with the keg ⅞ of the way to victory for the Freshmen.

Scarcely had we begun to begin to think that someday we might commence to get the beginning of our wind back maybe, when the gauntlet began. The seniors lined up and through them ran the Juniors, being soundly strapped about head, back, and elsewhere with belts, wielded after four years of practice. The Juniors lined up, too, and the Sophomores went through both classes, staggering, falling, fainting and aching from countless blows of the stinging leather. And the Sophomores lined up too. And down the long line of three classes, ran the Freshmen—heads down, ears covered by their hands—blindly, desperately seeking the far distant end—and relief from the pain. For it was pain. Despite Paleopitus, many buckle-ends of belts were used, as was evidenced by gashed and bleeding faces. But taken all in all, nothing very serious happened. Among my acquaintances are two arms out of joint and a broken collar-bone, nothing more.

The crowd then moved to the Senior Fence and the Fence was formally handed down to the Juniors and accepted by them by means of well delivered orations. President Hopkins then presented Pete Gray, pres. of the senior class and Capt. of baseball, as well as a Phi Beta Kappa man, with the annual Barrett prize, a gold medal for greatest all-around achievement in college.

Then a huge bonfire blazed up in the middle of the campus, around which the Freshmen marched with their green caps on their heads. And on a signal from Paleopitus, every green cap flew into the fire. When all were consumed, the entire college sang the Dartmouth song, and Wet Down was over.

But the night was not over, and now the Freshmen—who were no longer Freshmen, but Sophomores appeared again on the campus dressed in white shirts and flannel trousers—those who possessed them—to stroll for the first time *on* the grass, to sing if they pleased, to smoke if they wanted to, *unmolested*! and without caps!! Life is very sweet.

———————————

Sing Out was nothing much. It is merely the traditional name for the last chapel service when the president presides and the Seniors march in and out in their caps and gowns to the slow measures of the March of the War Chiefs. Special music and singing of Men of Dartmouth is the only other thing that distinguishes it from regular chapel—except the large attendance.

Dartmouth in World War I

by LEON BURR RICHARDSON

≫≫⊃ For nearly half a century a member of the College's Chemistry Department and a leading figure within the overall faculty, Leon Burr Richardson 1900 was the author of books of history and biography, as well as works in his own academic field. Here he provides a record of College developments and events associated with the period of the First World War. The extract is from his two-volume *History of Dartmouth College* (1932).

WITH THE OUTBREAK of the World War, the attention of the college was drawn to measures for relief and assistance. In March, 1915, a subscription campaign was organized with the purpose of sending an ambulance unit to France and $2,100 was secured from students and faculty as a result of the movement. Thereby two ambulances were endowed and four undergraduates were enrolled to take charge of them. On December 25, 1915, one of these men, Richard N. Hall, 1915, was killed by a German shell while in the performance of his duty. He seems to have been the first of American college undergraduates to lay down his life in the war. In the year 1915–16 (before the entrance of the United States into the contest) a demand arose among the undergraduates for military training in the college and about 150 of them expressed the desire of entering upon such work. At once, the widest difference of opinion arose concerning that issue, and a controversy, marked by acrimonious discussion in the çollege press and elsewhere, ensued. The trustees decided that such work, as a matter either of compulsion or of elective credit, ought not to form a part of the college course at that time, although they were willing to assist in the formation of a battalion upon a purely voluntary basis. Accordingly, such a company was instituted in February, 1916, under the leadership of Emerson C. Ward, 1917. About 125 were enrolled in it and drill was continued through the spring. The majority of the students, however, seem to have been averse to the movement. The faculty was also divided upon the issue, and a proposal to award college credits for work done in the summer at the military training camp at Plattsburg aroused heated discussion and passed that body only by the narrowest of margins. [...]

The early years of President Hopkins' term were marked by the crisis which confronted the college as a result of the entry of the United States into the World War. Such periods of stress have always been times of trial to educational institutions, as the earlier history of the college has shown, but this upheaval was far more serious than any which had been confronted in previous times. At the beginning of the academic year 1916–17 about 1500 students were enrolled in all branches of the college, the largest attendance which, up to that time, had been attained. Voluntary military training was not resumed in that year and the undergraduate body, as a whole, showed little enthusiasm for the various theories of preparedness, then the subject of such acrimonious debate. With the entrance of the United States into the war in the spring of 1917, as if by magic the entire spirit of the students was changed. The general feeling was that of unrest, academic duties were regarded with impatience, and an intense eagerness to enter active service in the quickest possible way became the one obsession of the undergraduate group. A large portion of them left college within a few weeks of the declaration of war for enrollment in the ambulance service, in officers' training camps and in other forms of activity which gave the most promise of early participation in active hostilities. Those who remained in college united in the demand for an opportunity for military training. At the time it did not seem feasible to place such work under the auspices of the War Department, as a branch of the Reserve Officers' Training Corps, and, accordingly, the trustees undertook the task of providing military training at the expense of the college itself, at first under the direction of Captain Porter Chase, of the First Corps of Cadets at Boston, and later under Captain Louis Keene of the Canadian Expeditionary Forces and Lieutenant John S. Pickett, of the Massachusetts National Guard. Almost at once over 1000 students were enrolled in the new organization, composed of three battalions, with twelve companies, which drilled, at first, two hours, and later four hours a day. [...]

The college year 1917–18 began with a student attendance of less than 1000. Military instruction, still under the auspices of the college and under the direction of Captain Keene, was required of all freshmen, while voluntary sections were organized for upper classmen. The work was not considered to be satisfactory in all respects and those who were required to take it were somewhat doubtful of its effectiveness, but it continued through the year. Nearly all extracurricular activities were diminished or given up entirely, and students were continually leaving the institution to enter active service. Commencement was moved forward to May 27, recalling a similar expedient under the first president of the college during the Revolutionary War, although, in this case, the period of active instruction was not actually shortened, the time gained being at the expense of vacations and holidays.

On June 25, 1918, a Training Detachment of the National Army was placed in Hanover for instruction in telephone work, motor repair, radio, carpentry and cement construction. Drafted men to the number of 272 were assigned to this course, under the command of Captain Max Patterson, with the teachers of the Thayer School in charge of the instruction. Two months later a similar group took the place of the first, and plans had been laid for doubling the number in the third group on October 25; plans which were interfered with by an epidemic of influenza. The men were housed in the gymnasium and opportunities for contact were such that the sweep of the disease, when it attacked the town in September, was alarming, although in no way so serious as was the experience of those herded together in the great military camps. By this time the undergraduate students had returned for the academic year 1918–19, and the authorities adopted vigorous measures, including a cessation of indoor work for two weeks, to combat the epidemic. Conditions in the training detachment were serious and a large proportion of the members of that group took the disease, but, in the end, only ten of them died. Five students also succumbed to the malady.

As the year 1918–19 approached, it seemed doubtful if any college would assemble at all. The national selective service act had resulted in the enrollment in the army of most men of college age, and the work of college education seemed, of necessity, to be about to lapse into abeyance. However, the establishment of the Students' Army Training Corps enabled colleges and universities to continue their activities in a limited way. In September about 750 undergraduates presented themselves, more than half of whom were freshmen, with only 68 seniors in attendance. No lessening of entrance requirements was made by the college to meet this crisis (a policy adopted by many institutions) and all candidates were required to present the usual credentials in full. On October 1, the Students' Army Training Corps was installed. All undergraduates over 18, who were physically fit, were enrolled in the army of the United States and were thenceforth subject to strict military discipline. In this category were 612 men, including 85 in the naval section. Men under eighteen, of whom there were 109, were also subject to military rules, but they were not mustered into the service and received no compensation from the government. Captain Max Patterson, who was already in Hanover in charge of the training detachment and who was later raised to the rank of major, was placed in command of the unit, while from fifteen to eighteen commissioned officers, besides four ensigns for the naval unit, constituted his assistants. The men thus enrolled received the usual pay and subsistence of privates in the army, they ate in the commons, run as an army mess hall, they lived in the dormitories, treated as barracks, they studied during fixed study hours, which were strictly supervised, they drilled for a large portion of the day, and, altogether, they were subjected to a routine as different from the ordinary life of the college undergraduate as can well be imagined. Fraternity houses were closed and fraternity meetings were forbidden. General college "activities" were discontinued, although a mild form of athletics was allowed. The college year was divided into quarters of twelve weeks each. According to the plan which was evolved, men twenty years of age were to be allowed to remain for one quarter only, those of nineteen, two quarters, while those of eighteen could look forward to three quarters. In general, the studies were those usual to the college, although two special military courses were required of all, one on the causes and aims of the war, and the other on military sanitation. These courses were in charge of selected members of the faculty. [. . .]

On the whole, the arrangement, which obviously bristled with opportunities for friction, worked more smoothly than might have been anticipated, and much more smoothly than was the case in many of the institutions to which it was applied. Of course, difficulties and disagreements arose, but they were usually settled in a manner satisfactory to everyone concerned. That this spirit of harmony prevailed was very largely due to the good sense and readiness for cooperation of the commanding officer, Major Patterson, and of his subordinates. The students performed their duties with reasonable cheerfulness, although it cannot be said that they wholly enjoyed the experience. Only after the declaration of the armistice was a distinct feeling of unrest observable, which was soon assuaged by the prompt demobilization of the unit on December 14 and 16. The resumption of the ordinary work of the college was a matter of some difficulty because of the disruption of the normal schedule, and the adjustments which were required to fit the courses taken in the wartime interregnum to the ordinary studies carried during the remainder of the year were troublesome to arrange, although the fact that the institution had not at any time admitted men who did not present the usual entrance credentials in full greatly facilitated the resumption of ordinary college activities. Students who had been enrolled in the military service outside Hanover began to return as soon as hostilities were over. The trustees were liberal in assigning college credits for time actually occupied in military service, and, for the most part, degrees were secured by these men in the same time which would have been demanded had they remained in Hanover.

The faculty, likewise, participated in the activities which were required by the crisis of the war. Fifty-one of them were engaged in work of this kind, most of it in absence from Hanover. From January to September, 1918, President Hopkins was assistant to the Secretary of War in charge of industrial relations. The total number of Dartmouth students and alumni enrolled in the service was 3407, of whom 695 were members of the Students' Army Training Corps. The number of commissioned officers was 1061. Those who died during their term of service were 111, of whom 57 were killed or died of wounds, while 54 died of disease.

The problem of financing the college during the period of rapid decline in student attendance was one of great difficulty and required the most careful management on the part of the trustees, but it was solved with much greater success than had been the case in other emergencies of this type with which the college had been confronted. In looking forward to the college year 1917–18, a deficit of $110,000 was anticipated, but, by careful management, it was found at the close of the year actually to amount to only $50,000. The solution of the problem of meeting this deficiency was in the Tucker Alumni Fund. The maximum yield in any one year from this source had never been much over $20,000. In this crisis, far larger amounts were required. An intensive appeal to the graduates, stressing the obvious emergency with which the college was confronted, brought an immediate response. The amount contributed in 1917–18, $66,412, was more than three times greater than any preceding amount, and was enough, not only to take care of the deficit, but to add somewhat to the principal of the endowment. In the following year, 1918–19, the return received from the government in payment for the services of the colleges in the conduct of the Students' Army Training Corps and the other branches of military activity centering in Hanover made the financial problem less difficult than it otherwise would have been. The sum of these payments was $179,480. From this total, $104,385, expended for subsistence and other expenses of maintenance, was to be deducted, leaving about $75,000 available for the educational expenses of the institution. The deficit at the end of the year was only $19,000, which was also met from the receipts of the Tucker Fund. Provision was also made by capital gifts, largely from Mr. Edward Tuck, for taking care of the rapid rise in the cost of living to members of the faculty resulting from the war, and substantial temporary increases were made in the compensations of all members of the teaching staff who were not already in receipt of the maximum amounts provided by the normal salary scale.

While the number of students in residence in the college at any one time during the two years of the war was always under 1000, the cessation of hostilities exposed all institutions, Dartmouth among others, to an unexpected and embarrassing flow of entering students, which tested facilities to the utmost. In the fall of 1919, 698 members were admitted to the freshman class, while for 100 more, who were property qualified, no room could be found. At the beginning of 1920 the pressure was much worse and on April 30 the entrance lists had to be closed for the year, with more than 1000 applicants, of whom only 624 could finally be accepted. In 1921 it was found necessary to close the lists as early as February 8, when 1200 applications had been received, less than half of whom could be admitted. The total registration of the academic college in 1919–20 was 1678, in the following year it was 1830, and in the next, 1938.

It became very evident to the trustees that some step must be taken to control this inflow of students and to prevent the institution from being overwhelmed by the mere weight of numbers. A more efficient method than mere priority of application was urgently required for proper selection, from the horde who were applying for admission, of the men actually to be received. The trustees determined to solve this problem themselves, without formal consultation with the faculty. As a preliminary step, the policy of expansion established in Dr. Tucker's time was abandoned, and a limitation of the undergraduate college to 2000 students was definitely fixed upon. In determining how that limitation should be made effective, an obvious method was the imposition of entrance examinations upon all candidates, perhaps competitively applied. That proposal was rejected because of the belief of the board that tests of this character are inadequate measures of the attainments and character of the individual, as well as unfortunate in their influence upon the student in his preparatory course, and upon the preparatory school itself. Accordingly, the board determined that the method of admission by certification should be retained. In the fall of 1921 the plan for a selective system of admissions was ready, and after much discussion it was adopted by the trustees on October 28. As a prerequisite to the consideration of any candidate, he was required to present the same credentials of scholarship as those already in vogue. That step, however, was merely the starting point. Information concerning the personality and character of the candidate was also required; this being obtained from various independent sources including among others the report of committees of the alumni, which in various centers interviewed personally each candidate. Upon this basis of information, a careful consideration of the qualifications of the prospective freshmen was undertaken by an officer of the college especially assigned to that work. By him the applicants were divided into preferential classes. In the first class were placed those applicants whose recommendations indicated superior scholarship, and such men were admitted without question and with no further test. In another class came applicants who stood in some special relation to the college, such as residents of New Hampshire or sons of alumni. Students coming from a distance were thought by that very fact to show some degree of initiative and independence, consequently applicants who resided south of the Potomac or west of the Mississippi were given some degree of preference. With the remainder, who seemed to be on practically the same academic level, attention was paid to qualities and interests which were not strictly scholastic, and the boy who could show some decided hobby or indicated individual initiative of various types was given preference over a competitor of the same scholastic rating who could lay claim to no such qualities. The new system went into effect with the class entering in 1922. [. . .]

A Prohibition-Era Murder

>>> The passage by Congress in 1919 of the so-called Volstead Act did not achieve, either on college campuses across the nation or within American society as a whole, anything approaching a total suppression of alcoholic-beverage consumption. The law was widely subverted by bootlegging and other means. Dartmouth experienced during the fourteen-year span of the Prohibition one particularly dramatic—as well as tragic—incident, which occurred on virtually the eve of its 1920 Commencement season. The undergraduate newspaper had suspended daily issuance following the close of second-semester classes. However, immediately upon resuming publication on June twenty-first, *The Dartmouth* carried this account of what had just transpired.

HENRY E. MARONEY '20, of West Medford, Mass., was shot and killed shortly after 1 o'clock Wednesday morning in the Theta Delta Chi house, by Robert T. Meads '21, of La Grange, Illinois. The tragedy was the outcome of a quarrel having its origin in Meads' room in North Massachusetts Hall earlier in the evening where Maroney, in company with J. C. Chilcott '20, H. W. Whitaker '20, and R. W. Hart '21, had gone in search of liquor.

After purchasing a quart from Meads, they retired. Chilcott left the party soon after. An hour later Maroney, Hart and Whitaker returned to Meads' room in quest of more of the liquor. Meads offered to sell them another quart for $20, but as the trio had but $8 between them, they made the alternate offer of buying part of the bottle. This Meads refused to do, and Maroney seized the bottle, passed it to Whitaker with the quick injunction "Beat it." Whitaker, Hart, and Maroney then scrambled through the narrow window—but two feet above the ground.

Meads, incensed, brought forth a 25-calibre automatic which he had been observed shooting several times on previous days, and fired four shots after the fugitives. All of them went wild of the mark, one hitting a tree near the Beta Theta Pi house.

All this happened shortly before midnight. It was not until an hour later that the sequel occurred at the Theta Delta Chi house on West Wheelock Street. Maroney and Whitaker were out of the room when Meads entered the house and made his way stealthily upstairs.

108

Whitaker was the first to catch sight of him sitting at Maroney's desk. Words, practically unintelligible, passed between the two, and then Whitaker took his stand in the doorway, watching Meads. A few moments later Maroney entered by another door, saw Meads across the room, and walked rapidly up to him.

There was no exchange of words between them. Meads suddenly rose to his feet, and shot Maroney through the heart, killing him instantly. He then turned and threatened Whitaker, who dove under a nearby bed. Meads calmly walked down the stairs and out of the house.

He then went to the room of Crile N. Wise '23, in North Fayerweather Hall. He deceived Wise with a trumped-up story, saying that he had hurt a man in a fight, and thought it best to get out of town before action was taken against him. Wise agreed to help him, not suspecting the true state of affairs. Together the two walked nine miles to the Mascoma station at East Lebanon, where Meads took the early morning train for Boston. He was apprehended at Canaan by High Sheriff Claude A. Murray of Franklin, who brought him to Hanover for arraignment Wednesday afternoon.

Wise was captured at Lebanon, en route to Hanover, by County Solicitor John A. Noonan, and held until bail could be secured, as a material witness.

Meads pleaded not guilty to the charge of murder in the first degree when brought before Judge Harry E. Burton of the Hanover Municipal Court. He waived examination on the telegraphed advice of his father, a prominent Chicago corporation counsel, and was committed to the Woodsville County Jail to await action at the September session of the Grand Jury.

The College furnished bail for Chilcott, Hart, and Whitaker, who were bonded over to appear before the Grand Jury as material witnesses in the case. Bail for Wise was furnished by his father from Akron, Ohio. Wise has also to face the Federal Government on a charge of violating the Webb-Kenyon act, prohibiting the illegal transportation of liquor between states.

Subsequent developments in the case indicate clearly that while Maroney had probably been drinking on the night in question, it was by no means to excess, and in no such measure as to affect his faculties in the slightest degree. He was well known and respected by the College as a man who had abstained entirely from the use of liquor during the academic year, and his death brings with it a mighty sense of personal loss to all who knew him during his years in Hanover.

Maroney entered Dartmouth in the fall of 1915 from the Phillips Andover Academy. In spite of his fine athletic record while in preparatory school, he centered his activities in college in the Dramatic Association. He played many leading roles in undergraduate productions during the past few years, chief among them being the lead in the Groves-Markey-Janssen musical comedy success, "Oh Doctor." He was also very proficient in boxing, and was considered the most able man in College in this line by Coach Shevlin. [. . .]

The following statement of the case and its subsequent developments was given out Friday night by President Martin Hopkins:

"I have had no intention of making any public statement concerning the tragedy of Wednesday morning in Hanover unless it should have been necessary to make one to protect the name of an attractive boy of ability and worth, whose sad death has made it incumbent upon others to speak for him.

"In this connection perhaps the most significant thing that I can say is that his degree had been earned and that next week the diploma symbolic of that fact will be forwarded to his parents. We have no purpose of suppressing, nor intention of influencing, publicity upon a matter necessarily of wide public interest. In order that the statement of facts shall not be misinterpreted, however, and in recognition of responsibility to the College collectively and to hundreds of fine boys individually, I wish unqualifiedly to deny that there has been any general system of smuggling in of liquor to Hanover and to say that the College authorities by every device available have kept watch of the situation and checked every known source of supply. To this end officers of the law and the College disciplinary machinery alike have worked. [. . .]

≫> As would of course be expected, the metropolitan press also gave prominent coverage to the Dartmouth murder and the developments that ensued. *The Boston Globe* had on June eighteenth reported, with a Hanover dateline of the previous day:

That Robert T. Meads of La Grange, Ill, confessed slayer of Henry E. Maroney of West Medford, Dartmouth College student, was the central figure in a regular business of liquor smuggling was definitely established here today, according to a statement made by High Sheriff Claude A. Murray of Grafton County.

Furthermore, it is announced by Federal officers that Meads, in company with Crile N. Wise of Akron, O, and an unnamed third person, brought 72 quarts of Canadian whiskey from Montreal to Hanover last Saturday evening.

The liquor smuggled across Saturday night was carried in a Ford car, and on arrival in Hanover was hidden in college property until a disposal of it could be made. [. . .]

Records found today show clearly the nature of Meads' illicit bootlegging. He was accustomed to buy Canadian whisky at $2.75 a quart, and sell it to his fellow students in Hanover at $20. Despite the fact that he has been under suspicion for some months past, last Saturday was the first time that anything definite was obtained against him.

At first it was his custom to bring it over in very small lots, usually in a suitcase or hidden in car ventilators and transoms. Later, however, gaining courage from continued success, he enlarged the scope of his operations [. . .]. It is said that one of his favorite ways of smuggling it across was by strapping the cases to brake beams under the cars, taking them off on arrival in Hanover.

An inspection of Meads' room this afternoon by the sheriffs and newspaper correspondents disclosed empty whisky bottles in all imaginable places. In his bureau drawers were many elaborately-woven silk shirts, and fancy underwear and socks. He was always known as a remarkably good dresser. [. . .]

It was definitely ascertained today that there was very little if any drinking in the Maroney-Hart-Whitaker party Monday night. Several friends of the young men, who saw them shortly before the shooting, testify that they were perfectly sober and all right in every particular. [. . .]

No other instances of bootlegging have occurred at Dartmouth College this year, according to a statement tonight by Pres Ernest Martin Hopkins.

"We have put our finger on the one definite spot," he said. "All has been centered in North Massachusetts Hall and Meads' room has been under suspicion as the source. Any implication that there has been any extensive bootlegging is absolutely false."

≫≫꙳ Following his dash to Hanover, Robert Mead's father was quick to assign to President Hopkins direct personal responsibility for what had occurred, as was recounted in *The Chicago Daily Tribune* on July eighth.

The resignation of President Ernest M. Hopkins of Dartmouth college was demanded last night by Attorney Albert H. Meads of La

Grange on his return from the college, where his son, Robert T. Meads, shot and killed a fellow student, Henry E. Maroney, on June 20.

Attorney Meads said the shooting was the result of a quarrel over whisky smuggled over the Canadian border and that bootlegging by the students was so systematized that hundreds of youths engaged in the practice. He blamed President Hopkins for this condition, and said his resignation would be a fitting sequel to the slaying.

"I went to Hanover, N.H., to help my son the moment I heard of the regrettable affair," said Attorney Meads last night. "What I found out about conditions was so revolting as to be almost unbelievable.

"There are on file in the office of County Solicitor Noonan of Grafton county the depositions of more than 100 students in which they state that they either engaged in or knew about the traffic in booze. To see an intoxicated student on the campus is a common thing. [. . .]

"This slaying should be blamed on the president of Dartmouth and its other officials. If President Hopkins did not know of the whisky traffic the students were engaged in, he was among a very small minority in the town. If he was aware of the bootlegging, it is worse, for he failed in his duty to protect the youths intrusted to his care."

Attorney Meads said he would go to Hanover in September to press an investigation into conditions at the college before the grand jury.

⟫⟫⟩ The trial of Robert Meads was held on September 15, 1920. Found guilty, he was immediately committed to the New Hampshire Insane Asylum at Concord (where he would remain confined until his death in 1964). With the trial concluded, President Hopkins initiated an exchange of correspondence with Grafton County Solicitor John H. Noonan, their letters to one another being dated September eighteenth and twentieth, respectively.

MY DEAR SIR: In the daily papers of Friday, July 10th, there appeared an interview with Mr. Albert H. Meads of Chicago, making certain statements in attack upon the College among which the most sensational was, speaking of the College, "What I found out about conditions was so revolting as to be almost unbelievable. There are on file in the office of County Solicitor Noonan of Grafton County the depositions of more than a hundred students in which they state that they either engaged in or knew about the traffic in booze."

I have not felt it within the proprieties while the case of Robert Meads was before the courts to enter into argument or controversy in regard to any assertion that his father might see fit to make. The statement of the above interview, however, the authenticity of which Mr. Meads has never denied, is one in regard to which the College is anxious to have the facts.

I should be very glad for a statement from you concerning this and any information that you may be willing to give me as to the number of affidavits concerning this matter which have been filed with you and what their purport is [. . .].

MY DEAR PRESIDENT HOPKINS:—I am in receipt of your favor of the 18th, inst., asking for a statement concerning a newspaper publication of Friday, July 10th, last purporting an interview with Albert H. Meads of Chicago wherein certain statements were made attacking conditions at Dartmouth College. I recall very vividly the publication because of the assertion as to the depositions on file in the office of County Solicitor Noonan of Grafton County bearing on the traffic in booze at that institution. I had expected that inquiry might be made as to the correctness of the statements and am pleased that it was delayed until a final disposition of the case had been made as I did not care to inform the public as to just what might be on file in this office.

In answer to your inquiry, which seems quite proper at the time, I will say that I have had on file the depositions of three young men, viz.; Howard W. Whitaker, James C. Chilcott and Crile N. Wise, detailing the circumstances of the shooting of Henry E. Maroney by Robert T. Meads at Hanover on the morning of June 16th, last.

These depositions disclose no system of smuggling nor boot-legging at Dartmouth College, and I have the names of only three men who were engaged in and knew about the traffic in intoxicating liquor at your institution. I mean by this, three men, including Robert T. Meads, who had knowledge of the smuggling for consumption and distribution.

I might say that I had never met Mr. Albert H. Meads until I met him at the Court House at Woodsville last week when Robert was arraigned and pleaded to the indictment, and no information has been given newspaper reporters as to what I had, or did not have, in the way of depositions. [. . .]

The Beginnings of Dr. Seuss

Conversation with THEODOR S. GEISEL

❧❧❧ The *Alumni Magazine* of April 1976, from which the following text has been excerpted, began its presentation of this "Conversation" by noting that "'Dr. Seuss' is of course a pseudonym, one known to millions upon millions of adults and children alike, in the United States and throughout the world," and that indeed the designation "derives from the middle name of author-artist Theodor Seuss Geisel '25." At the outset of his reminiscing (tape-recorded in 1975, shortly before the fiftieth reunion of his Class), the subject of the interview explained that his choice of Dartmouth had been influenced by one of his high-school teachers in Springfield, Massachusetts, who was an alumnus of the College, Edwin A. Smith 1917.

THE REASON so many kids went to Dartmouth at that particular time from the Springfield high school was probably Red Smith, a young English teacher who, rather than being just an English teacher, was one of the gang—a real stimulating guy who probably was responsible for my starting to write.

I think many kids were excited by this fellow. (His family ran a candy factory in White River Junction, Vermont, I remember that.) And I think when time came to go to college we all said, "Let's go where Red Smith went."

Accordingly, in the autumn of 1921, Geisel headed for Hanover, some hundred and thirty miles up the Connecticut River from Springfield.

And what was to prove, as viewed now in retrospect, especially a stimulus to him at Dartmouth?

Well, my big inspiration for writing there was Ben Pressey [W. Benfield Pressey of the Department of English]. He was important to me in college as Smith was in high school.

He seemed to like the stuff I wrote. He was very informal, and he had little seminars at his house (plus a very beautiful wife who served us cocoa). In between sips of cocoa, we students read our trash aloud.

He's the only person I took any creative writing courses from ever, anywhere, and he was very kind and encouraging. [. . .]

From the outset at Dartmouth, Freshman Geisel gravitated toward associations with the humor magazine, Jack O' Lantern*:*

That was an extension of my activities in high school—and a lot less dangerous than doing somersaults off the ski jump.

I think I had something in *Jack O' Lantern* within a couple of months after I got to college.

Jack O' Lantern proved increasingly an object of Geisel's attentions throughout his four years in Hanover, and at the end of his junior year he became editor-in-chief:

Another guy who was a great encouragement was Norman Maclean. He was the editor preceding me. He found that I was a workhorse, so we used to write practically the whole thing ourselves every month.

Norman, at the same time, was writing a novel. And the further he got involved with his novel, the less time he had for his *Jack O' Lantern.* So, pretty soon I was essentially writing the whole thing myself. [. . .]

The general practice of Jack O' Lantern *was that its literary content appeared unsigned, a circumstance which renders it impossible to compile today a comprehensive listing of Geisel's writings for its pages. The author himself has only vague recollections of what he in fact wrote for the publication, although he does remember that certain contributions were written jointly with Maclean, including ones which came about in a singular fashion:*

Norman and I had a rather peculiar method of creating literary gems. Hunched behind his typewriter, he would bang out a line of words.

Sometimes he'd tell me what he'd written, sometimes not. But, then, he'd always say, "The next line's yours." And, always, I'd supply it.

This may have made for rough reading. But it was great sport writing.

The art work included in Jack O' Lantern *was, unlike its "lit," usually signed, and the magazine's issues of 1921–1925 are liberally sprinkled with cartoons bearing explicit evidence of having come from Ted Geisel's pen.*

The 1920s were seemingly "the era of the pun," and many of the individual cartoons are found to have involved puns or currently popular expressions.

Going back, now, over the pages of Jacko *for his undergraduate years, Geisel is rather stern in his judgment of the cartoons that were included, and particularly of those he himself drew.*

In summing up his assessment he says:

You have to look at these things in the perspective of 50 years ago. These things may have been considered funny then, I hope—but today I sort of wonder.

The best I can say about the *Jacko* of this era is that they were doing just as badly on the Harvard *Lampoon*, the Yale *Record*, and the Columbia *Jester*. [. . .]

There were two especially noteworthy aspects of the extensive work Geisel did for Dartmouth's humor magazine.

The first of these emerged during his junior year, and he identifies it as having been in his undergraduate period "the only clue to my future life." It involved a technique of presentation, the approach to a form for combining humorous writing and zany drawings:

This was the year I discovered the excitement of "marrying" words to pictures.

I began to get it through my skull that words and pictures were Yin and Yang. I began thinking that words and pictures, married, might possibly produce a progeny more interesting than either parent.

It took me almost a quarter of a century to find the proper way to get my words and pictures married. At Dartmouth I couldn't even get them engaged.

The other particularly significant feature of Geisel's Jack O' Lantern *career relates to the spring of 1925, when apparently he first used the signature "Seuss." The circumstances that surrounded his employment of the later-famous pseudonym he outlines as follows:*

The night before Easter of my senior year there were ten of us gathered in my room at the Randall Club. We had a pint of gin for ten people, so that proves nobody was *really* drinking.

But Pa Randall, who hated merriment, called Chief Rood, the chief of police, and he himself in person raided us.

We all had to go before the dean, Craven Laycock, and we were all put on probation for defying the laws of Prohibition, and especially on Easter Evening.

The disciplinary action imposed by Dean Laycock meant that the edi-

tor-in-chief of Jack O' Lantern *was relieved forthwith of his official responsibilities for running the magazine. There existed, however, the practical necessity of helping to bring out its succeeding numbers during the remainder of the academic year.*

Articles and jokes presented no problem, since they normally appeared anonymously; thus, anything the deposed editor might do in that area could be completely invisible as to its source.

Cartoons, on the other hand, usually being signed contributions, did present a dilemma; and it was a dilemma Theodor Seuss Geisel resolved by publishing some of his cartoons entirely without signature and by attributing others of them to fictitious sources.

The final four Jacko *issues in the spring of 1925 contained, accordingly, a number of Geisel cartoons anonymously inserted or carrying utterly fanciful cognomens (such as "L. Burbank," "Thos. Mott Osborne '27," and "D. G. Rossetti '25"), and two cartoons, in the number of April twenty-second, had affixed to them his own middle name (in one case "Seuss" alone and in the other "T. Seuss"):*

To what extent this corny subterfuge fooled the dean, I never found out. But that's how "Seuss" first came to be used as my signature. The "Dr." was added later on. [. . .]

In the autumn of 1925 Geisel entered Oxford as a member of Lincoln College:

My tutor was A. J. Carlyle, the nephew of the great, frightening Thomas Carlyle. I was surprised to see him alive. He was surprised to see me in any form.

He was the oldest man I've ever seen riding a bicycle. I was the only man he'd ever seen who never ever should have come to Oxford. [. . .] Patiently, he had me write essays and listened to me read them, in the usual manner of the Oxford tutorial system. But he realized I was getting stultified in English schools.

I was bogged down with old High German and Gothic and stuff of that sort, in which I have no interest whatsoever—and I don't think anybody really should.

Well, he was a great historian, and he quickly discovered that I didn't know *any* history. Somehow or other I got through high school and Dartmouth without taking one history course.

He very correctly told me I was ignorant, and he was the man who suggested that I do what I finally did: just travel around Europe with a bundle of high school history books and visit the places I was read-ing about—go to the museums and look at pictures and read as I went. That's what I finally did. [. . .]

Home once again in Springfield, Geisel lived with his parents and began submitting cartoons to national magazines:

I was trying to become self-sufficient—and my father was hoping I'd become self-sufficient and get out of the house, because I was working at his desk.

Finally, a submission to The Saturday Evening Post *was accepted. It was a cartoon depicting two tourists on a camel, and it appeared in the magazine's issue for July 16, 1927.*
The drawing was signed simply "Seuss" by its draftsman-humorist, resurrecting the pseudonym he had used in the Dartmouth Jack O' Lantern *two years earlier:*

The main reason that I picked "Seuss" professionally is that I still thought I was one day going to write the Great American Novel. I was saving my real name for that—and it looks like I still am.

Actually, the Post *in publishing his cartoon accorded "Seuss" no pseu-donymity whatsoever, for it supplied the identification "Drawn by Theodor Seuss Geisel" in a by-line of type, right along the edge of the drawing itself.*

When the *Post* paid me 25 bucks for that picture, I informed my parents that my future success was assured; I would quickly make my fame and fortune in *The Saturday Evening Post.*
It didn't quite work out that way. It took 37 years before they bought a second Seuss: an article in 1964 called "If At First You Don't Succeed—Quit!"

But success during the summer of 1927 in placing something with The Saturday Evening Post *was a cause for great elation—and, moreover, for a decision on the cartoonist's part to leave Springfield:*

Bubbling over with self-assurance, I told my parents they no longer had to feed or clothe me.
I had a thousand dollars saved up from the *Jack O' Lantern* (in those days college magazines made a profit), and with this I jumped onto the New York, New Haven, and Hartford Railroad; and I invaded

the Big City, where I knew that all the editors would be waiting to buy my wares.

In New York, Geisel moved in with an artist friend from his Dartmouth undergraduate days, John C. Rose, who had a one-room studio in Greenwich Village, upstairs over Don Dickerman's night club called the Pirates Den:

The last thing we used to do at night was to stand on chairs and, with canes we'd bought for that purpose, play polo with the rats, and try to drive them out so they wouldn't nibble us while we slept. God! what a place.

And I wasn't selling any wares. I tried to do sophisticated things for *Vanity Fair*; I tried unsophisticated things for the *Daily Mirror*.

I wasn't getting anywhere at all, until John suddenly said one day, "There's a guy called Beef Vernon, of my class at Dartmouth, who has just landed a job as a salesman to sell advertising for *Judge*.

"His job won't last long, because nobody buys any advertising in *Judge*. But maybe, before Beef gets fired, we can con him into introducing you to Norman Anthony, the editor."

The result of the Geisel-Anthony meeting was the offer of a job as a staff writer-artist for the humor magazine, at a salary of 75 dollars per week. [...]

"Seuss" work in Judge *consisted not only of cartoons:*

I was writing some crazy stories, as well. It was a combination, about fifty-fifty, the articles always tied in with drawings.

Among these combination pieces, extending the type of thing he had begun doing as an undergraduate at Dartmouth, Geisel produced for Judge *a succession of regular contributions signed in a way that brought his pseudonym into the final form of its evolution:*

I started to do a feature called "Boids and Beasties." It was a mock-zoological thing, and I put the "Dr." on the "Seuss" to make me sound more professorial.

At first the self-bestowed "Dr." was accompanied by "Theophrastus" or "Theo." in by-lines and as a signature for drawings, but with the passage of time "Dr. Seuss" was settled on as the standard form of his identification.

"Dr. Seuss" soon found his way into other magazines of the day, besides Judge, *including* Liberty, College Humor, *and* Life. [. . .]

The actual coming into being of a book of his own, the first of what was to be so substantial and celebrated a series of volumes written and illustrated by "Dr. Seuss," derived from a curious stimulus and through decidedly unusual means:

I was on a long, stormy crossing of the Atlantic, and it was too rough to go out on deck. Everybody in the ship just sat in the bar for a week, listening to the engines turn over: da-da-ta-ta, da-da-ta-ta, da-da-ta-ta. . . .

To keep from going nuts, I began reciting silly words to the rhythm of the engines. Out of nowhere I found myself saying, "And that is a story that no one can beat; and to think that I saw it on Mulberry Street."

When I finally got off the ship, this refrain kept going through my head. I couldn't shake it. To therapeutize myself I added more words in the same rhythm.

Six months later I found I had a book on my hands, called *And to Think That I Saw it on Mulberry Street.* So, what to do with it?

I submitted it to 27 publishers. It was turned down by all 27. The main reason they all gave was there was nothing similar on the market, so of course it wouldn't sell.

After the 27th publisher had turned it down, I was taking the book home to my apartment, to burn it in the incinerator, and I bumped into Mike McClintock (Marshall McClintock, Dartmouth 1926) coming down Madison Avenue.

He said, "What's that under your arm?"

I said, "That's a book that no one will publish. I'm lugging it home to burn."

Then I asked Mike, "What are *you* doing?"

He said, "This morning I was appointed juvenile editor of Vanguard Press, and we happen to be standing in front of my office; would you like to come inside?"

So, we went inside, and he looked at the book and he took me to the president of Vanguard Press. Twenty minutes later we were signing contracts.

That's one of the reasons I believe in luck. If I'd been going down the other side of Madison Avenue, I would be in the dry-cleaning business today!

And what reception did the public accord And to Think That I Saw It on Mulberry Street *when the book was released in 1937?*

In those days children's books didn't sell very well, and it became a bestseller at 10,000 copies, believe it or not. (Today, at "Beginner Books," if we're bringing out a *doubtful* book we print 20,000 copies.)

But we were in the Depression era, and *Mulberry Street* cost a dollar, which was then a lot of money.

I remember what a big day it was in my life when Mike McClintock called up and announced, "I just sold a thousand copies of your book to Marshall Field. Congratulations! You *are* an author."

In addition to favorable sales, the comment of one particular reviewer was especially significant in encouraging the fledgling author of children's books toward further effort in this new-to-him field:

Clifton Fadiman, I think, was partially responsible for my going on in children's books. He wrote a review for *The New Yorker*, a one-sentence review.

He said, "They say it's for children, but better get a copy for yourself and marvel at the good Dr. Seuss's impossible pictures and the moral tale of the little boy who exaggerated not wisely but too well."

I remember that impressed me very much: if the great Kip Fadiman likes it I'll have to do another.

On Compulsory Chapel

by HAROLD F. BRAMAN

In a letter to the editor, which was published by the *Alumni Magazine* (under a heading "For Whom the Bell Tolled") in its February 1962 issue, business executive Harold Braman 1921 briefly sketched the history of required attendance at chapel services, through to the time of that regulation's 1925 suspension.

To ABOUT TWO generations of living Dartmouth alumni the ghost of compulsory chapel still remains a weary memory. [. . .] President Tucker looked upon the chapel service as his principal opportunity to fulfill his responsibilities as the moral leader of the College. Although the daily morning exercises were brief and conventional, they did offer the occasion for bringing the College into unison, infusing into the undergraduates a feeling of solidarity.

Voluntary coherence not being a natural attribute of the student body, attendance had to be checked, and rules set up to insure a reasonable observance of the daily chapel routine. As the student body grew in size an orderly means was instituted to record those present. A system of cards was introduced. These were imprinted with the date, and there was a line for the signature of the student, to be written in on the day of his attendance.

To Registrar Howard (Skeets) Tibbetts fell the onerous duty of checking these attendance tickets against the roster of the College, so that at the end of each semester he could report those who had failed to appear the requisite number of times.

In 1901 the Faculty Regulations read that "a student may absent himself from seven chapel services" per semester. In 1917 the requirement was made more positive, but less onerous, with the rule that 65 appearances should be made each semester, with no excuses except to those students who were required to work at eating clubs during the chapel hour. By 1923 this had been reduced to 42 sessions. (Many thought that this was still too many.)

At first, for each excess absence, a deduction of one point was made from the student's general average. When this fell below 50 he was required to take additional work, the amount to be determined by the Committee on Administration. In 1917, with the attendance less restrictive, the penalty for poor turnouts was the deduction of one point and one hour credit for each three overcuts.

To the atheist, the late sleeper, the non-conformist, such a regimen was unpalatable, but the Faculty and Trustees were obdurate until June of 1925, when it was announced that starting that fall chapel attendance would be optional. What a heavenly word—*optional.* It became the synonym of rarely, scarcely, seldom, not often, and not-at-all.

The heralding of the chapel exercise each morning was by an elaborate ceremony of the Rollins bells, which had been donated by William E. Barrett of the Class of 1880 in the year 1903. These comprised a three-bell peal, and the bell of the lowest pitch could also be tolled.

Three college building custodians had the assignment of pulling the bell ropes. These were at a twelve-foot level in the Rollins tower, and were reached by means of an iron ladder and a trap-door. At 8:54 a.m. bell-ringer number one started pealing the highest pitched bell in a somewhat rollicking cadence. At 8:56 he was joined by compatriot number two, and at 8:58 by the third jangler. About thirty seconds before the stroke of [. . . nine] o'clock this tintinnabulation suddenly ceased, and bell number three started to toll twenty times. This had the same effect as the "eight count" of a boxing referee, and immediately reduced the number of potential worshippers to those either inside the edifice, or those within about a 200-yard radius—provided they were fleet of foot and long of breath. If you were in front of the Bookstore or just emerging from College Hall you didn't have a chance. But if you had started across the diagonal duckboards, you might make it.

As the last doleful toll sounded, the chapel monitors slammed the three front doors in your face, and your humble entreaties and vigorous poundings were unheard through the two-inch-thick oak and iron-bound portals.

There were many ruses attempted by potential overcutters. Your roommate might try to hand in two cards on his way out. But these were usually detected by their dual thickness. You might bribe a "brother" who had already fulfilled his total obligation earlier in the year to attend for you and forge your name. This crime had to await detection in Tibbetts' Parkhurst basement. Or you might show up a few seconds after the end of the service and say that you had forgotten to pick up a card from the seat—and could you have one now?

Statistics are not readily available to indicate the relationship between overcuts at chapel and separations from the College. But there must be quite a few non-graduates who squirm a bit when asked, "And why did you leave Dartmouth?" To that will come the candid answer, uttered with bowed but irreverent head, and in distressingly mournful tones, "I went to morning chapel once too few."

≫⁓ Some supplementary testimony on the post-mandatory situation regarding chapel attendance at Dartmouth appeared in a *Boston Herald* news article on January 17, 1926.

Daily chapel at Dartmouth is no more, as far as 97 per cent of the student body is concerned. This is approximately the amount which chapel attendance has dropped off since the installing of voluntary services.

The Rev. Roy Bullard Chamberlain, chapel director, offers estimates that lead closely to this percentage. He says, "Under the old compulsory system the average attendance was around 1000. Now we have from 60 to 75 at the daily services, and from 400 to 1000 on Sunday, depending on the speaker." [. . .]

The reason for the action in abandoning the compulsory basis was to get rid of the irreverent attitude that went with it, becoming more and more pronounced and outspoken in recent years. This aim has been very successful. The old practices of bringing books, papers, conversation, dogs, and other disturbances to chapel stopped automatically. The services are now as truly reverent as could be found anywhere.

Says Mr. Chamberlain, "I feel very happy about the entirely new spirit that has come with the abolition of compulsion. In the recent past, daily services were worse than a joke—blasphemy under the name of religion. The men would cough, read books and magazines, and talk with one another. Even during the Sunday services, when some very excellent musical programs were given, there was always the feeling that the lid might blow off at any minute. This undercurrent of unrest and boredom was by no means peculiar to Dartmouth. The same thing will be found wherever compulsion exists. I would rather have 50 interested men coming here willingly than 1500 coming because they have to and sitting through the services mad." [. . .]

Providing a New Library

by CHARLES E. WIDMAYER

≫﹥ *The Alumni Magazine* in carrying within its April 1977 issue this chapter from the biography *Hopkins of Dartmouth* (1977) by Charles E. Widmayer 1930 (who had been the *Magazine*'s chief editor for three full decades, 1943–73) noted: "The principals in the story of how Baker Library came about were, in addition to President Hopkins, Edward Tuck, 1862, of Paris, Dartmouth's greatest benefactor; Henry B. Thayer, 1879, president of AT&T, Dartmouth Trustee from 1915 to 1936, and chairman of the Trustee committee on the physical plant; and George F. Baker, LL.D. 1927, New York banker and philanthropist, who was a close friend of both Mr. Tuck and Mr. Thayer."

THE VISIT IN 1925 of the Oxford University debaters may have provided some impetus to the decision to go ahead with the building of Dartmouth's new library. One of the Oxford speakers, acknowledging the students' welcome, said that he had a special interest in coming to Dartmouth because he had heard that the College had the largest gymnasium and the smallest library of any college in America. "That burned me up," said Mr. Hopkins.

Without any stimulus from the Oxford debaters, however, the Trustees were on the verge of deciding to go ahead with the construction of a million-dollar library, even though the funds for doing so were neither in hand nor in sight. In order to meet Dartmouth's most pressing need "we were going to borrow the money, or beg it, or steal it," Trustee John R. McLane said later.

The Trustee vote, at the October 1925 meeting of the Board, authorized that measures be taken immediately for the construction of a library, and instructed President Hopkins to appoint a committee to study all questions related to the matter. [. . .]

With the exception of decades of abortive planning for a student social center, no building at Dartmouth had such a long gestation period as did the library. Talk about it began early in the administration of Dr. Tucker, who expressed the hope to live long enough to see three new buildings at Dartmouth—a gymnasium, an administration building, and a library. He saw two of them, and although the library was not built before his death in September 1926, he at least knew that it was assured through the gift of $1 million from George F. Baker. At President Hopkins' inauguration, Mr. Parkhurst said he would be bold enough to prophesy that early in the new administration the College would succeed in building "a college library which shall be the crowning glory of all the buildings we have put up here," and he even went so far as to name it the Tucker Library.

Wilson Hall, erected in 1885 for a student body of 400, was grossly inadequate as a library for 2,000 students, and architecturally it was an unattractive building. It had run out of space, and books were stored in basements and scattered in departments all over the campus. President Hopkins in 1917 had stated that he was opposed to solving the library problem on any minor scale. A cost of $1 million seems to have been in his mind from the very beginning, and although a building of such magnitude delayed things for nearly a decade, his foresight once again was vindicated. Tentative library plans had been sketched over the years by a variety of architects, including Charles A. Rich, John Russell Pope, and Jens Fredrick Larson, the College architect, who did the final design. The Trustees in 1919 had decided to locate the new library "in the center of the square north of the College Green with its principal face to the west." At the time of their 1925 call to action this decision was reaffirmed, but subsequent planning swung the library's principal face to the south and set the building back so there was a large expanse of lawn. [. . .]

Mr. Baker's million dollars was announced as an anonymous gift on May 17, 1926. The story of how it came about is one of the most fascinating of the Hopkins administration, although in its frequent telling apocryphal bits have crept in. The three main characters, aside from the donor, were Mr. Tuck, Mr. Thayer, and Mr. Hopkins, and a very effective team they were. In the sequel, Mr. Hopkins and Mr. Thayer had to move deftly and persuasively to save a $1.6 million bequest of Edwin Webster Sanborn, 1878, who had wanted to give the library in memory of his father and was bitterly disappointed when Mr. Baker's gift killed his dream. Mr. Sanborn had been unwilling to make his gift until he died, and with funds for the library so desperately needed, the President and Trustees decided to go along with Mr. Baker's more timely and more certain offer, come what may.

Mr. Tuck and Mr. Baker were friends of long standing, having first known each other as young men in banking in New York. Both were men of wealth, with an interest in philanthropy, although Mr. Baker as one of the founders of the First National Bank of New York was many times richer than his Paris friend. After his first visit to Mr. Tuck in 1922, President Hopkins mentioned Mr. Baker in a letter to Mr. Tuck, and the latter reported a month or so later that he had written to Baker urging an interest in Dartmouth. In June 1923, Mr. Thayer, another close friend, was in touch with Mr. Baker, who told him that he intended to do something for Dartmouth in memory of his uncle, Fisher Ames Baker, an alumnus of the College, Civil War soldier, and New York lawyer. Baker was devoted to his uncle, who was only three years his senior, and he had walked all the way from his home in Troy, New York, to see him graduated from Dartmouth in 1859. Further discussion of a memorial gift took place when Mr. Baker visited Mr. Tuck in Paris in the summer of 1923. The sum of $50,000 was mentioned and Mr. Tuck, by letter, expressed the hope that he would "double the ante." There was some thought of giving a concert organ for Webster Hall, but by October 1925 Mr. Thayer and Mr. Baker were talking about an endowment fund.

This was the background for the meeting between President Hopkins and Mr. Baker which took place at a Cornell alumni dinner at the Hotel Roosevelt in New York on November 14, 1924. Mr. Hopkins, the principal speaker, sat at the right of President Farrand of Cornell, and Mr. Baker, a trustee and benefactor of the university, sat at Farrand's left. There was not much opportunity for conversation, but after the dinner Mr. Baker invited Mr. Hopkins up to his room, where he brought up the subject of a memorial to his uncle. In his reminiscences late in life, Mr. Hopkins recalled that Mr. Baker asked him what the College could do with $25,000. "Not much," Mr. Hopkins replied. "Why, I thought anyone could use $25,000," said Baker. "Yes, they could," Mr. Hopkins answered, "but that amount wouldn't provide the sort of memorial that would be worthy of your uncle or of you."

The story is told that Mr. Baker sat down the next day and sent Dartmouth College a check for $100,000. The amount is correct, but the fact is that it was a month later, December 16, 1924, when Mr. Baker wrote to President Hopkins saying that he was sending securities worth $100,000 to establish the Fisher Ames Baker Endowment Fund for educational purposes. Mr. Hopkins recalled that in thanking Mr. Baker he decided to press his luck and wrote that he was turning the securities over to the College treasurer "on account." Mr. Baker is reported to have got in touch with Mr. Thayer and asked, "How much is it going to cost me to buy my way out of this situation?"

Mr. Baker now became, in the minds of both Mr. Hopkins and Mr. Thayer, the most promising solution to the problem of how Dartmouth was going to pay for the new library that the Trustees had just authorized. While in London in November 1925, Mr. Thayer wrote to Baker suggesting that he might want to consider giving the library in memory of his uncle. Three months later, President Hopkins wrote to Mr. Tuck, "Mr. Thayer's project, about which I wrote you, moves along gradually, with at least this encouragement, that he hasn't been turned down. . . . If your own influence is exerted and gets time to have effect, I am allowing myself the indulgence of high hope." And three months after that, the good news was made public. The identity of the donor of a million dollars was kept secret until November, when the Boston *Herald* made a good guess as to who he was, and Mr. Hopkins confirmed it. [. . .]

Construction work on the Baker Library began in the late summer of 1926 and partial use of the building began early in 1928, with the official dedication held in June of that year. George F. Baker, because of illness, was unable to be present at the dedication. He had come to Hanover the previous June to receive Dartmouth's honorary Doctorate of Laws, the first trip he had made to the College since his uncle's graduation 68 years before. In September 1928, however, he made a special visit to see the library, and as he was taken through the building in his wheelchair, with President Hopkins and Mr. Thayer as guides, he expressed himself as delighted with it in every detail. In 1930, the year before his death at the age of 92, Mr. Baker asked to see the library again. Baker Library was a benefaction in which he took great satisfaction and pride, and Mr. Hopkins remembered the tears in the financier's eyes as he looked out at the campus from the library colonnade and spoke of the uncle whose name was now perpetuated in the finest undergraduate college library in the country. On that occasion he said, "Dartmouth is a good college. Everybody speaks well of Dartmouth."

As a banker Mr. Baker was pleased that the cost of the library was right on target—$1,132,000, made up of his million-dollar gift, the earlier fund of $100,000, and $32,000 gained in the sale of his securities. Not so happy was his experience at Harvard, where the cost of the business school ran considerably beyond estimate. He therefore felt that Dartmouth was deserving of something more, and when both Mr. Tuck and Mr. Thayer urged him to provide for the proper maintenance of his building, he was quite receptive and gave another million dollars for its endowment. Announcement of this second large gift was made in February 1930.

The happy outcome of the library project, in its planning for the educational work of faculty and students, its design, and its financing, was due to a remarkable group of men, all working together smoothly and as one in their devotion to Dartmouth. In addition to the Tuck-Thayer-Hopkins team, the work of the Faculty Committee on the Library, and especially that of its chairman, Professor Haskins, was superlative. But the leading role of all must be granted to Trustee Henry B. Thayer, 1879, who was of key importance in the relations with Mr. Baker and who, as chairman of the special Committee on the Construction of the Library, spent innumerable days in Hanover overseeing the progress of the work. [. . .]

The solution of Dartmouth's library problem left in its wake the disappointment of Edwin Webster Sanborn of New York, who as early as 1917 had sent a copy of his will to President Hopkins disclosing that he planned to leave his sizable estate to Dartmouth for the purpose of erecting a library in memory of his father, Edwin David Sanborn, 1832, for nearly 50 years a member of the Dartmouth faculty and College Librarian from 1866 to 1874. (Professor Sanborn's wife, Mary Webster Sanborn, was the daughter of Ezekiel Webster, brother of Daniel.) President Hopkins, who had maintained a steady stream of correspondence with Mr. Sanborn from the beginning of his administration, wrote immediately after the Baker gift to inform him that an anonymous donor was providing a million dollars for the library. Mr. Sanborn, angered by what he considered almost a breach of contract on the part of the College, made a tentative offer of $300,000 to preserve the Sanborn name on the library; but Mr. Hopkins replied that the library would have to bear the name of the Dartmouth graduate in whose memory it was being given.

Mr. Sanborn's lawyer, Charles Albert Perkins, was privy to Sanborn's plan to leave his entire estate to Dartmouth, and it was the College's good fortune that he used his influence to bring that about in spite of the library development. Perkins wrote to President Hopkins in June of 1926 that Mr. Sanborn was thinking of changing his will. In this matter, as in his intention to provide Dartmouth with a library,

Sanborn was a man of extreme caution who vacillated and then ended up by postponing action. In Hanover, meanwhile, much thought was being given to the idea of having some part of the library named for Professor Sanborn, but this was finally dropped as being unpalatable to both Baker and Sanborn. Mr. Hopkins wrote to Perkins wondering if a Faculty Club would appeal to Mr. Sanborn. Then Mr. Hopkins and Mr. Thayer got their heads together and came up with the winning idea. A library without books is no library; why couldn't Mr. Sanborn fulfill his dream and appropriately honor his father by endowing the purchase of books for all time? Many meetings with Mr. Sanborn ensued, and in the end he was won over to the idea of a book fund. However, he still wanted a building to bear the Sanborn name. Mr. Thayer, ever resourceful, proposed a building for the Department of English, in which Professor Sanborn had served as Evans Professor and later as Winkley Professor. Mr. Sanborn's reaction was enthusiastic, especially since there would be incorporated into the Sanborn House a replica of the study in which Professor Sanborn had extended hospitality to students at all hours and to men of letters visiting the College.

Mr. Sanborn died March 18, 1928, and left his entire estate to the College, with President Hopkins and Treasurer Halsey Edgerton named as executors. The total amount that came to Dartmouth was $1,655,555. The sum of $10,000 was left to the Dartmouth Outing Club, $344,000 was used to build the Sanborn House, and the remainder went to establish the Sanborn Library Fund. Since the book fund was the principal memorial to his father, Mr. Sanborn left instructions that the English House should be a memorial not only to his father, but also to his mother, Mary Webster Sanborn, and his two sisters, Miss Kate Sanborn and Mrs. Mary Webster (Sanborn) Babcock.

Dr. Tucker had characterized Mr. Hopkins as a gambler, and the whole Baker-Sanborn episode was an example of what he had been wise enough to foresee. President Hopkins took chances, at what seemed to him to be reasonable odds, and the outcome in this case was a magnificent library, a million-dollar fund to maintain it, another endowment fund of approximately $1.3-million for purchasing books, and an attractive home for the English Department. That was an excellent piece of presidential work.

A Senior Fellow Reports

by NELSON A. ROCKEFELLER

≫⟩ On the personal initiative of President Hopkins, the College instituted in 1929 a program under which a small group of students were, in their final undergraduate year, designated Senior Fellows and relieved of all curricular requirements, giving them total independence to pursue educational goals, by means of their own choosing. Statesman-connoisseur-philanthropist Nelson Rockefeller 1930 was among the first group to be selected for such appointment, and this is part of his account—which, entitled "A Gift of Leisure," was published in the June 1930 *Alumni Magazine*—telling of how he occupied himself during his Senior Fellowship period.

DARTMOUTH HAS the honor to be classed with the most progressive colleges in the country. The latest proof that she deserves this ranking is the introduction of the Senior Fellowship, which was first put forth here by President Hopkins. It was received with a good deal of skepticism, but when the plan had been fully explained, the trustees saw its possibilities and gave it their sanction. With the result that five of us have been given the opportunity to spend our senior years in a way that has made them more vital in shaping our lives than any other years we have spent. [. . .]

Last fall found me back at college in precisely the same rut that I had been in the previous year; going on with exactly the same things I'd been doing before. However, all along I had had a desire to study art in the various forms. An interest that had been smoldering in the back of my mind ever since I could remember. This feeling gradually grew stronger and I wondered whether I was really taking advantage of the fellowship. But as the year got under way I found that I had no more leisure that I had had during the first three years.

Finally I realized that it was up to me to make the most of this opportunity and that I wouldn't just drift into it without any effort. [. . .]

So I decided to give up my regular major, keep on with the outside activities, study music and explore in the fields of architecture, painting and sculpture; subjects that I had neglected up to then for those I had considered more important.

I kept on in one course in art last semester after I gave up all other

131

organized class work. It was a seminar course on the "Meaning of Art" and it gave me a general understanding of art in its relation to contemporary civilization and its function in the life of the individual. The course was extremely well handled; it gave me an entirely new point of view and a very good background for my work this semester. It also proved profitable in that it brought me into contact with Professor Packard, with whom, from then on, I did a great deal of work. He possesses the very valuable faculty of being able to stimulate one's interest and make the subject matter seem real and vivid.

With his assistance several of us took up drawing and painting, not with the idea of ever amounting to anything as artists, but in order better to understand what others have done. The work was fascinating. We spent a great deal of time in the new studio in Carpenter and elsewhere, sketching and experimenting in oils. It is unbelievable how such crude attempts can increase one's understanding of paintings.

To guide our efforts, Professor Packard arranged to have Mr. Woodbury, noted Boston painter and teacher, and later Mr. Thomas Benton, exponent of the modern school of painting in New York, come to Hanover to work with us for several days. They both brought examples of their own work which we discussed freely, much to our advantage.

At the same time I was tracing the development of architecture starting with the early Egyptian pyramids. Of course this is a lifetime's undertaking, but I was anxious to become familiar with the outstanding characteristics of the different periods. I have kept going at this during the whole year. This last semester, I have taken one course in Painting and Sculpturing and another in Music.

With this program I have not been tied down to a regular unbending routine, and have been able to spend time on the extra-curricular activities when needed. Of these, I spent most of my time with the Arts, an organization with unlimited possibilities of promoting interest in the various arts among the undergraduates, but one which had dropped into disrepute several years ago as it had come into the hands of a group of lightfooted tea drinkers, at least so rumor has it.

However, it was revived last year, and due to the ability and perseverance of this year's board of governors, with whom I had the privilege of working, the Arts came back into its own on campus stronger than ever. Probably the thing from which I derived the most benefit in connection with the Arts, was the contact I had with the outside speakers. The fellowship enabled me to arrange my work so that I could devote myself to the various lecturers during their stay in Hanover. A day or so spent in the company of such men and women as Harry Emerson Fosdick, Thornton Wilder, Bertrand Russell, and Edna St. Vincent Millay are opportunities that few are fortunate enough to have. And it would be hard to estimate the value derived from such contacts. But there is no question that to talk with and hear Carl Sandburg, for instance, recite his poetry, arouses one's interest and appreciation far more than reading and studying his work in class.

The Arts sponsored a poetry contest in order to stimulate interest among the students. We offered prizes for the three best poems and promised to print them along with the thirty next best poems in an Arts poetry anthology for 1930. There were over four hundred poems handed in by some sixty contributors, and the book just recently went to press. [. . .]

As I mentioned before in Hanover a man studying music, art or drama has a very limited opportunity to hear and see really good things. However, this barrier is broken down by the Fellowships. We, as Fellows, have been able to go to Boston and New York on several occasions to attend the opera or listen to a recital by one of the world famous symphony orchestras; spending the rest of the time visiting museums and galleries. Also several of us attended four of Fritz Lieber's performances of Shakespeare's plays. In this way it has been possible for us to see and hear the best examples of the things we have been studying, thereby giving the work real meaning and greatly enhancing our interest and enthusiasm for it.

Now some may wonder why a year spent in this way is more worth while than one spent in the ordinary manner. Every man that graduates from college must work at least eight hours a day, five and a half days a week from next summer on—that is, if he ever wants to amount to anything. And, of course, the really ambitious ones will work for much longer hours than that. However, these men are going to have a little free time on their hands from the first, and as time goes by they will have more and more, until they finally retire. The big question is, to what use will they put this time? Movies, cards, golf and gossip are all very popular forms of diversion but, when carried to an extreme, they have a decidedly narrowing influence on the individual. And by the time he retires there will be little besides his business to hold his interest. What is the cause? Well, while in college he is forced by popular opinion to spend what spare time he has either in extra-curricular activities or in being a good fellow with the boys. And neither of these pursuits—worthy as they may be—are very conducive to an intelligent use of leisure. There is no time to pursue or even be seriously interested in any of the fields of Arts. Nor does he have much chance to read by himself. If he takes courses in these subjects, the daily assignments, weekly quizzes, long required readings and exams usually stifle his enthusiasm. And the end of the four years when the last exam is passed, he sells all his books and hopes never to see them again. It is the natural reaction and one really can't blame him.

And here is where the Senior Fellowship renders its greatest service. If a man has proved his worth during the first three years at college, and is going to have to keep his nose to the wheel for twenty or thirty years after he graduates, would it not be of infinite value to him if he could spend his last year at college totally free?

And, if you will again pardon the personal reference, this is exactly what I have had the privilege of doing this year. With the result that my whole attitude toward education has changed. It is no longer the old game of just doing enough work to pass the exams and get good marks. There has been no one to check up by giving me a quiz on pages 315 to 375 inclusive. I have been working for the personal joy and satisfaction derived from it. There are new fields to be explored, past histories to unfold, paintings new and old to see and music to hear.

I don't claim to have sprouted wings or to be any kind of an authority as a result of this year spent as a Senior Fellow. But I have developed a growing enthusiasm and appreciation which will stay with me.

Working hours all over the country are continually being reduced and people are beginning to realize the increasing importance of training themselves how to most profitably and enjoyably spend their leisure. And to my mind colleges in the future will have to lay greater stress on training students how to use this freedom, for it isn't something that can be picked up after graduation.

Thanks to this year as a Senior Fellow, I have discovered the key to the door that opens out into a field of interest totally unrelated to the material side of life. And it is now up to me to unlock this door and explore the ground lying beyond.

From a Freshman's Letters

by RICHARD N. CAMPEN

❧ Student life at the beginning of the twentieth century's third decade is reflected in letters written to his parents in Cleveland, Ohio, by Richard Campen 1934 (whose business career would in due course encompass service in various capacities within the chemical industry, as well as active involvement, subsequently, in the fields of both authorship and publishing). The extracts here presented have been chosen by Alexander G. Medlicott Jr. 1950.

September 16, 1930—After getting off at White River we took a Hanover Bus which drove us to school (.50¢). The first thing to do was to get the key to our room so we could rid ourselves of our baggage. (Deposit 50c). The room is a great little room, and capable of comfortably housing us to next summer. [. . .]

The surroundings here are delightful. Beautiful trees, green grass and winding walks surround every section of the college. All the building[s] seem so clean and nice and all are of colonial architecture. [. . .]

I know I'm going to like it.

September 18—This morning we had the opening of college for 1930–31 exercises in Webster Hall. All the professors were donned in their long flowing robes. The professor's degree is discerned by the color of trimming on his robe. President gave a long talk which was too deep to comprehend. The sight of all those intellectuals on the stage was inspiring. [. . .]

I find the fellows here a great bunch. It's not like in High School where a good many are students by compulsion, but everyone is interested and anxious to do well. In other words, sincere. Then too, they are scholastically a picked lot.

September 23—Already in English, French, and Industrial Society I have homework assigned to Christmas.

September 25—Just before our first football game with Norwich (a military academy) the freshmen in every dormitory have to put on a stunt before the rest of the school. The dorm which has the best stunt will be given a couple cheeses and a few crates of crackers. [. . .] In English we are reading a collection of essays which are supposed to be conducive to thought. They are about modern problems such as coeducation, methods of teaching *et cetera*.

October 13—Some big doings here at Hanover today. Admiral Byrd came to town. At twelve o'clock Byrd was received by the reception committee after a long parade down main street, which passed, autos and all, right through the center of the campus. [. . .]

I find it almost impossible to read any deep essay or chemistry in the dorm. There's alway[s] a hundred victrolas going and a lot of yelling. I'll have to find a place where I can really consentrate to the fullest.

October 18—Today's the Columbia game. You ought to see this town. Full of New York swells and collegiates. They sure do manage to get the pretty girls up here for the week ends, and this one is somewhat better than average. [. . .] Lined up in front of the Inn, there are the snappiest lot of cars you ever want to lay your eyes on: Lincoln, convertibles; Packard tourings; Pierce Arrow, sedans. The town has the regular rah! rah! spirit that you read about in magazine stories.

October 28—I'm going to go to more movies than I have been for the past year from now on because I feel that if one goes about it in the right way, he can get equally as much education from a good picture as from a good book.

November 11—This weekend was for a good many of the students an endurance contest because of the house parties. It seemed civilized to see a few girls walking around and I can well venture to say that 550 out of the 553 who were shipped up were very very pretty. [. . .] The girls were not at all bashful about smoking on campus or in downtown Hanover and of course I didn't approve of that. Sat. night, while playing bridge on[e] drunken fellow urinated through our mail slot.

Last Friday night was Dartmouth night. At seven all the students with lighted torches marched 2,000 strong up to President Hopkins' house, where we were given a short talk about Dartmouth spirit etc. Than we came back to the campus and by the light of a huge bonfire sang songs and gave yells in honor of our last home football game, viz; that with Allegheny.

November 19—Last night from 7–9 o'clock, I had a great time. Orv.

Dryfoos and myself got into some real serious conversations about ideals of life and college and a lot of other subjects. We also talked about inferiority complexes, heroism in football etc. It really makes you feel swell to be asserting your own thoughts and to be doing some thinking for yourself, and expressing your own ideas.

December 8—I went skating again Saturday afternoon and decided that I just had to get a hockey stick. There's no harm in just getting into an informal game of it and besides there isn't anything to do but skate around by yourself unless you play. (no music or girls.)

January 11, 1931—Ordered a pair of skiis yesterday and got them last night. [. . .] A fellow I've been very friendly with, taught me all the essentials that he's learned in the ski rec class so far and I actually wasn't too clumsy on skiis considering that it was my first time. [. . .] I learned how to climb hills on skiis—how to turn when tearing downhill and such stuff. We followed some swell trails through pine and hemlock forests and also followed the river for some time. It's a swell sport.

January 25—If I can judge at all what I do I think I did a good job on that exam. Never before have words flown from me so spontaneously, large ones too, I seemed to have all the information on hand and wrote sixteen pages. I hope I did well. You never find out what you do on your exams unless you fail, but I'm going to go to a few of my teachers and ask them what I got, maybe they'll tell. [. . .]

I spent big money on my hair yesterday, had an oil shampoo, but I thought it would be worth while seeing just how they steam the oil in with hot towels and the effect it would have. About a week after I came to [. . .] school my hair did begin to look very thin in the front to me. I don't think its doing well at all in spite of the fact that I rub it most every day. [. . .]

It's been awfully cold here lately. When I walked to breakfast this morning I almost froze my face away and even at noon it was 10 below. It was 30 below at 7 this morning.

February 5—I have passed all my subjects, but as yet haven't received my grades. My teachers this semester are, I think, even better than those I had last and the educational outlook is intelligently sound. [. . .]

[. . .] Tonight Carnival will be officially opened with canon shots, bells ringing etc, and at 7:00 the "Queen of the Snows" will be choosen (admission 50c) [. . .].

The Freshman Green Book came out this week, but it isn't so good, they never are. My picture isn't as bad as usual

February 11—Grades came out yesterday. You no doubt have received them by this time too. I got B in Chemistry; B in French; B in Analytical Geometry; D in English; and C in Industrial Society. The marks aren't as good as I ought to get, that is, I can do better work. [. . .] The B in Chemistry is really pretty good, probably the best mark on the card because Prof. Richardson is rather stingy with his A's & B's. I hope next time to do a good deal better, but there is no assurance of it.

February 21—I like to think that college is worth what one pays for it, but often I can't reconcile myself to that way of thinking. There will be one more bill which will probably come about April of $120 for room rent and that's all to the college. [. . .]
The laundry bag came this morning. Thanks very much for the cakes. The jelly is still going strong. I bought some oranges (a dz. at 25c) this noon. I've haven't been eating half enough fruit lately.

February 24—I never wished to live more in my life. I have some plans which I will expose to you before the year is over. I see that I am at a turning point in my life. My youthful, ignorant happiness is behind me. I am now undergoing a mental transition so that now I am enjoying youthful, intelligent happiness (to some extent.) In a few years I will have completely crossed from the realm of youthful irresponsibility to manly liability.

March 12—Last night I ate supper with some thirteen other fellows from this dorm at Roy Chamberlain's house. He is chaplain of the college and has a good many of the Freshman eat & get together in his house during the year. [. . .]
After the dinner, we all gathered in front of the log fire and started to discuss religion, for the purpose of the gathering was to clear up misconceptions and misunderstandings in religion. He didn't try to force anything down our throats, but said that although college was primarily operated to further us intellectually and physically, we also could advance spiritually and should. [. . .]
After leaving Roy's I went to the Nugget and saw "Hell's Angels", a very entertaining picture. I thought the photography was the outstanding merit, especially the dirigible raid on London. Jean Harlow is very passionate, enticing, luring, impulsive, et cetera. [. . .]

Now to acknowledge Dad's New York phone call. I certainly must have sounded nuts that night. When one of the fellows pounded on the door I was deep asleep and hardly knew what it was all about comme d'habitude. I realized when it was all over that I hadn't even asked about the welfare of Mom & George, nor shall I forget about the new maid. Entering money problems into that friendly conversation was also very tactless, artless, naive, ingenuous, or what you will.

March 16—Had an English exam this afternoon which put me in good spirits. It seems as though after every English exam I think I did well and a week later I get back a D. I enjoy taking an E. Exam though, this afternoon when I was about half done, I stopped for a moment and realized that I was having a lot of fun. [. . .]

[. . .] The hard part about these hour exams is that you have much to write and only an hour to write it in, consequently you've got to hurry.

March 18—The snow is well on its way to a speedy disappearance although a good deal is still on the ground. The past week and I imagine the next to come has been and will be very slushly. The paths on campus are a seething mass of mud and are now covered by board-walks.

March 27— It was just a perfect day in Hanover this morning, clear blue sky, hot penetrating sun, and glorious. Having nothing to do before Chem class at 11:15, I walked over to the Chem building and sat on the portico. An old horse-drawn buggy came by. It was so quaint and New Englandish, and I was so excited about spring coming and going South, and so pleased with everything that I felt like crying for joy.

April 10—*America's Way Out* by Norman Thomas came this morning and I must *sincerely* say that my first glance at it was very enticing. It ought to be a fine summary of Capitalism, Communism, Facisim, & Socialism and I can easily learn something about these governmental systems without confusing that knowledge with any I previously possessed. I'm going to start it as soon as I get this Monday's Chem Exam out of my way. [. . .]

I'm having my black and white shoes made over with rubber soles and heals. Some other fellows have done it with surprising results. They'll make a good pair to wear around here since the whole college is taking to them.

April 21—Last night I heard Will Durant speak on "The Case for India" He gave a splendid account of the Indian's history and a thoroughly good insight into their character. I don't ever remember of enjoying a lecture more. [. . .]

[. . .] (By the way I must recommend a short poem of Keats to you "The Eve of St Agnes." It has a fine sensuous appeal and is famous for its interior description.) [. . .]

This evening a Cleveland boy, Bill Carr, asked me to room with him in 105 Woodward. His room is $160 a year or $80 less than I pay now. His room is great and $160 is real cheap. If it can be arranged 105 Woodward will be my next years address.

April 22—I joined the Hanover Country Club this afternoon and also played my first golf. First I practiced a couple hours and then I played six holes. I think that my form is pretty fair, but I topped most all my drives and did pretty bum with the midiron.

The golf course is a very sporty and picturesque one built on the hills about Hanover. It's really very beautiful and from some of the higher spots on the course you can see the mountains up north.

April 26—Wordsworth ranks high in my estimation also. The other day reading a pastoral poem of his I couldn't stop the tears from continually rolling down my face. The poem is "Michael." I'm sure you both would enjoy it much. I also suggest that you brood over Wordsworth's "The world is too much with us" a sonnet. I enjoy poetry immensely, not so much the music of it, but the thought. [. . .]

Yesterday afternoon I saw Dartmouth beat Cornell in baseball 10–5. It was great fun and the real stuff. Contained some spirit, something almost lacking in professional baseball.

May 19—This past week has been a disastrous one as far as marks are concerned. It isn't that I couldn't have done better, but I let down a bit as the results show. [. . .] I told the instructor that I didn't want to squabble about grades, that I didn't care if my grade wasn't raised, but I did want recognition of what I had done right. [. . .]

A most startling and disturbing fact is that classes end a week from tomorrow. The close of the year has come so speedily that it seems impossible. I[t] seems like only yesterday that I entered college an "unsuspecting freshman."

Today was "Old Timers Day" for the graduating Senior class. You should have seen the outfits, torn and old-fashioned that the fellows had on and some of the things that they did. Among the things put on was a most humorus and rough baseball game. The day reminded me or rather lived up to college life as generally pictured, more than any time this year I can remember.

May 21—I'd hate to come home in June with nothing to do if I am unable to get work from now till the end of the year. (school) I don't think I could endure a summer of country club life and golf, hanging about and doing mostly nothing, nothing constructive anyway. There remains two alternatives for me, either work at some job, or get about the country. [. . .]

Another project which appeals to me and which would use maybe two months, maybe the whole summer is this. That I invest my railroad fare in a Model T Ford June 10 and tour home in it, (latter going places.) I've hitch-hiked lately to the surrounding towns around here and am enough acquainted with the second-hand automobile situation to know of several good M.T Fords at between $25 and $35.

May 27—Well, I've just come from my last lecture of my Freshman year at college. It's all over and I can't believe it. A year which I looked forward to so much and enjoyed so much—gone. [. . .]

At the end of my Freshman year I want to thank you and tell you how much I appreciate your giving me this opportunity of going to college. Of my first year I can say that it might not have helped me to earn dollars or do such and such a thing better but I am sure it will help me to enjoy life more.

Dartmouth from Without

by JAMES WEBER LINN

≫⟫ The *Alumni Magazine*, when it published in January of 1932 the full text from which this extract has been taken, suggested the article—based on a talk that Prof. James Weber Linn, head of the University of Chicago's English Department, had given at a Chicago luncheon of Dartmouth alumni—might well have been titled, alternatively, "How Dartmouth Looks to an Outsider."

As a MIDDLE WESTERNER, a graduate of the University of Chicago before the turn of the century, and one who has never seen Hanover save once and that in midsummer twenty years ago, I may certainly claim to be an "outsider." On the other hand, as a teacher of undergraduates for thirty-three years, in which time I have had some eleven thousand in my various classes in English, I am bound to have been interested in the general subject of undergraduate education. And my feeling is that no one interested in that subject can possibly have failed to develop an interest in Dartmouth, at which undergraduate education seems to have passed through as many phases as anywhere in the country, and to have become, at long last, as vital.

We used to believe, in the Middle West, that Dartmouth was determinedly, not to say crudely, "athletic." We heard, and circulated, stories of young men who rode the rods to White River Junction, swam in blood to Hanover, and appeared before the Dean with the statement that they carried their credentials in large letters on their high-school sweaters; of janitors and night-watchmen from Colorado and Montana, exported to Hanover by zealous alumni, there to be turned by Wallie McCornack into All-Americans; of other freshmen slaughtered like sheep by ferocious sophomores, because they combed their hair and read French. To be sure I was personally acquainted, even in those days, with Henry Hilton, '90, and that most broadly cultured of savants, Professor Frost, who certainly wore clean collars and their learning lightly like a flower. But we knew them to be products of a still older day, when Dartmouth was, like Amherst or Williams, a lit-

142

tle New England college, before blood had become, as we believed, the price of Dartmouth's admiralty. We suspected, nay, we were sure, that Dartmouth from 1900 to 1910 was the stockyards of culture and educational idealism, and thick necks were the red badge of its courage.

However as time went on, it became evident that however rapidly Dartmouth was ceasing to be a little college, there were more and more among her alumni who loved her. More and more young men from Dartmouth were saying, in the course of discussion, "I think," instead of "I'll bet you"; offering evidence rather than five-dollar bills in the settlement of an argument. Though athletic victories continued to be blazoned on her banners, one began to suspect the existence of laboratories, and even of class-rooms, among her dormitories and beside her playing fields. She was still more notable for her interest in winter outdoor sports than for the indoor sport of reading; but it was whispered about that a considerable group of her undergraduates were concerned with the fine arts, and even painted in the open, their heads bloody no doubt with contumely, but unbowed with shame. And then came Hopkins, one of the great college administrators of America, openly placing emphasis on scholarship and intellectual practice—Hopkins, a product of the very time when Dartmouth's reputation for scholarship and intellectual practice had been, among us, at its lowest. Could we have been mistaken, all those years? Its situation among the noble, fierce, yet friendly New Hampshire hills had given it physical prestige; but here was education prestige also in the offing! Dartmouth became interesting. [. . .]

[. . . W]ith the coming of her educational prestige, with her increasing interest in cultural as well as in clear-headed practical education, she has shown no signs of weakening physique. Ten thousand Swedes seem yet to lurk in the weeds of her immaterialism. Her admirably designed system of admissions, the most admirably designed of any college in the country, plus the lure of her formidable but fascinating winter civilization, will take care of that. Only one thing could decay that physique. Booze.

For the charge of excessive indulgence in spirituous liquors is still, out in the Middle West, brought against Dartmouth undergraduates. For one thing, Canada is not far away; for another, when Dartmouth men go in a large body to New York or Boston, they feel themselves free from collegiate responsibility, and are inclined, apparently, to make exceptional whoopee. If this be all, there is no harm done. But an outsider does not know whether this be all. An outsider hears stories that alumni, and the parents of possibly desirable undergraduates, do not like. Even stories of winter-Carnival time at Hanover are more Roman than Greek in their implications. Years ago, I should have believed those stories. Now I do not; because in its educational idealism Dartmouth seems to me to have become Greek; aristocratic; powerful. And in an Olympian civilization there is no place for the decadence of cheap indulgence.

Far be it from a sincere admirer of the Dartmouth of today, however, to end on such a false note. The outsider sees Princeton become a university, Yale become a university. The outsider sees Amherst, Williams, Knox, Grinnell, many others remaining small colleges, beautiful, endearing to the spirit, the gift-shops of culture as the universities are its department-stores. The outsider sees Dartmouth as the great American college; vivid; the one Rubens in our collection.

Nine Deaths by Asphyxiation

❯❯❯ *The Dartmouth* for February 26, 1934, carried across the top of its front page the grim headline "GAS KILLS 9 AT THETA CHI HOUSE," and the paper listed the dead students as Americo S. DeMasi, Class of 1935, from Little Neck, New York; William S. Fullerton 1934, of Cleveland Heights, Ohio; John J. Griffin 1936, Wallingford, Connecticut; brothers Alfred H. Moldenke 1936 and Edward F. Moldenke 1934, from New York City; Wilmot H. Schooley 1935, Middletown, New York; William M. Smith Jr. 1934, Manhasset, New York; Harold B. Watson 1935, Wilton, Maine; and Edward N. Wentworth Jr. 1934, of Mount Dora, Florida.

NINE Dartmouth students were killed early yesterday morning, the victims of carbon monoxide gas escaping from the furnace of the Theta Chi house, where they were sleeping. [. . .]

A furnace explosion early Sunday morning was the cause of the most terrible tragedy to have happened in the hundred and fifty years of Dartmouth College. All nine of the students died in their natural sleeping positions, none having discovered the odorless fumes rising from the basement.

Some time between 12:30, when the last of several visitors left the fraternity house, and early that morning, an improperly banked furnace exploded, knocking off the pipe in the rear which led to the chimney and blowing the front doors open. The explosion was immediately discovered and the doors adjusted properly but the broken pipe was not discovered due to its hidden position behind the furnace. When the fire was banked in the evening it had been completely smothered with coals, instead of allowing a portion of the fire to burn red. As a result the gas accumulated and caused the explosion. The blower in the furnace later blew the carbon monoxide fumes out through the back of the furnace into the sleeping quarters on the second and third floors.

When the janitor, Murtin J. Little, appeared at the house yesterday morning, he adjusted the furnace, which he found burning normally. By that time, the fire had burned red and carbon dioxide replaced the monoxide gas. The janitor then went up to the bedroom where he found the students, who appeared to be sleeping normally. He closed the wide-open windows and left.

Upon returning to the house at 3 p.m. Little found the occupants in the same positions and, becoming alarmed, notified Chief of Police Hallisey, who in turn notified the medical referee of New Hampshire, Dr. Ralph B. Miller, and Dr. John J. Boardman, of the Mary Hitchcock Clinic. The latter immediately informed the administration of the death of the nine students.

Dr. Miller pronounced the occupants dead. Norris Cotton, county solicitor of New Hampshire, accepted this report and approved the identification of the students made by the janitor, Prof. William H. Wood, the faculty adviser, and an undergraduate.

Mr. Cotton also cleared the janitor of neglect or carelessness. There was no defect in the heating plant, it was acknowledged. Improper banking was the cause of the explosion; and since the drafts were not opened correctly, the work was evidently that of someone not experienced in regulating the furnace.

Last Saturday night, a bridge game was being played in the Theta Chi house, and at 12:30 a.m. Sunday morning several who did not live at the house left, and the rest continued to play. This was the last time they were seen alive.

The parents of the deceased were informed by telephone late last night of the tragedy. No decision has been made as yet on the restriction of college activities.

≫᠈ *The Dartmouth*, February 27, 1934:

As over 8,000 telephone calls of inquiry flooded the switchboards of Hanover all Sunday night and yesterday, Dartmouth still remained dazed by the sudden deaths of nine occupants of the Theta Chi fraternity house. Metropolitan newspapers throughout the country gave front-page space to the incident as one of the greatest collegiate disasters on record, while correspondents and photographers, representing the national news services, flocked to a snowbound Hanover.

When the first news of the tragedy reached the campus, it spread with amazing rapidity, giving rise to a maze of conflicting rumors which persisted all yesterday. A garbled report of the affair by the Broadway rumorist, Walter Winchell, in his program over the NBC network, was the first intimation of the news to reach the campus at large, while the nationwide and incomplete description of the calamity led to extreme anxiety on the part of parents and friends of

Dartmouth students. The confusion was heightened by the fact that the early reports made no mention of any specific fraternity. Almost immediately after the broadcast there began the deluge of long-distance telephone calls and telegrams which continued throughout yesterday. [. . .]

Yesterday morning the bodies of the gas victims were removed from the Theta Chi house, which is to remain closed until a further decision is reached. At noon the bodies of Edward and Alfred Moldenke were sent to New York City in accordance with instructions received from their family, and that of William S. Fullerton was shipped to St. Louis accompanied by his brother, Baxter T. Fullerton '36.

Late last evening the body of William M. Smith, Jr. left Hanover for Flushing, N. Y., together with that of Americo S. DeMasi of Little Neck. Under the escort of Ralph Martin '36, a friend of the deceased's family, the body of Wilmot H. Schooley has been transported to Middletown, N. Y. The bodies of Harold B. Watson and John J. Griffin have left for Wilton, Me., and Wallingford, Conn. respectively.

Only one of the victims of the tragedy, Edward N. Wentworth, Jr., will remain in Hanover, pending the arrival of his father, who is coming here from Los Angeles, Cal. [. . .]

It has been pointed out that while carbon monoxide itself is an odorless gas, it is usually accompanied by a strong coal gas smell when produced by a furnace as it was in the Theta Chi house, and it was wondered why the two individuals who were known to have entered the house before the discovery of the deaths had not become suspicious. Interrogation of the undergraduate who delivered Sunday morning papers to the top landing of the Theta Chi stairs revealed that he had often noticed such an odor to be present, and although perceptibly stronger that morning, it did not arouse his suspicions.

In addition to the lives of the occupants, the carbon monoxide also snuffed out the life of a white collie, familiar figure about Hanover, and the pet of Edward Wentworth, one of the nine victims. The dog was found, seemingly asleep, near his master's bed on the third floor of the house. [. . .]

Football in the 1930s

by EARL H. BLAIK

❧ In his book *You Have to Pay the Price* (1960), written in collaboration with Tim Cohane, legendary football coach Earl Blaik tells of his seven years at Dartmouth, just before moving on to West Point for the closing period of his long career in sports. What follows is drawn from his chapter entitled "The Big Green and a Stronger Ivy League."

THE IVY LEAGUE I was part of at Dartmouth, from 1934 through '40, played an all-out football which provided a stern and stimulating challenge to coach and player.

I have stated that in the 'twenties the West, which had originally received its football from the East, was developing it by more advanced thinking. In the 'thirties, I feel there was a swing back to the East. There was better coaching there, on the whole, than was found in other sections. Others may debate this, but I think it is true.

It was in the East that the potential of the single-wing attack, whether behind balanced or unbalanced line, was exploited to the fullest, just before the arrival on the college scene in 1940 of the modern T formation with man-in-motion and flankers. It was in the East that the concept of multiple and ever-shifting defenses, the compensating offenses they demanded, and exhaustive study of films, all combined in forcing coaches to forgo the development of themselves as personalities and characters and to concentrate on being students of the game in a more authentic sense. [. . .]

For the record, our seven seasons at Dartmouth produced forty-five victories, fifteen defeats, four ties. I wish there were room here to salute every single letterman, substitute, and scrub who helped make it possible. I would not pick an All Dartmouth team any more than I would pick an All Army team. It would be unfair. [. . .]

I would say that, as a whole, the Dartmouth players were more interesting as people than the West Point Cadets, because they had more time to lead a normal life. Our players were interested in every-

148

thing and argued about everything. This was the result of the stimulating, inquiring atmosphere of the liberal arts college and the all-per-
meating influence of President Hopkins.

The religious discussions were something. They were usually initiated by Harry Gates, who was called "Heavenly," and had joined The
Holy Ghost and Us, a religious society with a farm near Manchester,
New Hampshire. The sparks set off by Gates were whipped into a
quick flame by [Bob] MacLeod, a Protestant; halfback Phil Conti, a
Catholic; and quarterback Henry (Hank) Whitaker, who said he was
an agnostic.

I recall one argument among this group that carried right into the
locker room at Harvard and right up until it was time to go onto the
field, and the assistants and I had a heck of a time stopping it. However,
the boys didn't let their religious debate prevent them from putting
together a good enough team game to beat Harvard, 26-7. [. . .]

Our '38 record was 7-0 going into the game with Cornell at Ithaca.
Our defeatless string, which began with the Brown game in '36, had
reached twenty-two. But I knew we were up against by far the best
team we would play all year. Our backs could match Cornell's, but we
were overmatched up front. Snavely said afterwards that his team that
day played the game he had been expecting of it all year. Their line
simply dominated us. Nevertheless, the final score was only 14-7 and
MacLeod's running in the last period threatened to tie it up.

A record crowd of 30,486 sat in Schoellkopf Stadium, and the partisan enthusiasm was most intense. The game was only two minutes
old when some Ithacan varlet snipped all the lines connecting our
press-box phones with the bench. [. . .]

The game at Stanford was anticlimactic. The press referred to our
small team as "boy scouts," but we won their respect. We presented
Stanford an angling defense which bothered them for a while. We
trailed, 14-13, going into the last quarter. Then they pushed it up to 23-
13. MacLeod was again outstanding and deserved the All America
honors accorded him.

Despite the downbeat finish in '38, we could look back on solid
progress. Our record from 1935, our second year, through '38 showed
twenty-nine victories, five defeats, and three ties; the Yale jinx slain
and interred; the twenty-two-game defeatless string; Ivy League
championships in 1936 and '37. President Hopkins was happy about
it. So were most Dartmouth people. Yet, even in the Ivy League of

those days, there was a taint of the philosophy that winning regularly somehow connotes a certain lack of respectability. [. . .]

Time and affairs somehow invariably contrive sooner or later to trip up or slow down all football dynasties, large, small, and medium. So it was with our medium-size regime. The freshman classes beginning in 1937 were relatively weaker than those of '34 through '36. This began to show up on the scoreboard in '39, although we tied Navy, 0-0, beat Yale and Harvard again, and were beaten resoundingly only by Snavely's undefeated, untied Cornell team. Cornell that year took good care of Ohio State's Western Conference champions at Columbus and had as good a claim on the national championship as anybody.

In 1940, we slipped a little more. Yale beat us, 13-7, for the first time since 1934. We had lost three other games and had no ranking whatsoever as we approached the next to the last game on our schedule: Cornell, at Memorial Field, November 16. Since midway in 1938, Cornell had won eighteen straight, was ranked No. 1 nationally and was at least a 4-1 favorite over us. [. . .]

We naturally worked at building our men psychologically for a supreme effort. We did not have to sell Cornell's stature. Their record, rank, reputation, and what they had done to us the year before took care of that. There was no problem getting our men keyed up for the game. But as Saturday neared, I thought I detected signs that they might be wound a little too tight. This could be just as harmful as a casual approach. To execute the complex defensive blueprint assigned them and also put on their own offense smoothly, they needed to be dedicated yet relaxed, a finely drawn fusion not always easily attained.

On Friday afternoon, we repaired to our regular pre-game bivouac, the Bonnie Oaks Inn on Lake Fairlee outside Fairlee, Vermont, not too far from Hanover. Saturday morning, we went through our usual routine: an early walk and breakfast. The players were then ordered to rest in their rooms until called by Bevan to have their ankles taped. Any boisterousness was supposed to be out of order. They were supposed to relax.

After breakfast—I guess I had a cup of tea—I went to my room and lay down. I thought about the squad. They looked a little too tight. I thought it over and phoned Captain Lou Young to come up to my room.

When Lou arrived, I tried not to look as white as the bed sheets. I tried to joke with him about the game, but I didn't do a very good job of it. I asked him how he thought the players felt about it. He said he thought they were ready, real ready. I asked him if he understood fully the defensive signals he was to handle, and he said he did.

"Well, Lou," I said, "I think the team is wound a little too tight. Now, there isn't any need for this. We are really a much better team than Cornell expects to meet. We are ready to take them. So, I want the players to relax. After Bevan finishes taping them, I want you to get down in the lobby and turn on the record player. Play some of that hot jazz which seems to be the order of the day. We want to go up to the stadium relaxed."

Lou carried out my instructions and when we boarded the bus, the players seemed to be a little looser. During the ride, I walked up and down the aisle and actually did some clowning, the first time I had done any acting of that type since my role as "Buttons the Bellhop" back at Steele High. Maybe my act wasn't very good, but I believe the players were relaxed the way I wanted them to be when we got to Memorial Field.

I had written in our pre-season football brochure: "the mysterious Indians on one occasion will rise to great play." This was the day. Our defense did the job we wanted. In the first half, we stopped them cold. In the third period, they marched, but we stopped them by an end-zone interception. Then we marched ourselves, and early in the final period we got close enough for end Bob Krieger to place-kick a 27-yard field goal.

With only four and a half minutes to play and the ball on their 48-yard line, Cornell took to the air. Although a light snow had dampened the ball and the field, Scholl was connecting with his receivers. Perhaps they should have begun passing earlier.

One pass was allowed for interference on the 18-yard line, but we were of no mind to complain. It was the "back-diagonal" pass to [Mort] Landsberg. For once, Crego forgot to pick him up right away. Our phone spotters, sensing it immediately, jumped up and yelled, although Crego couldn't possibly have heard them. Crego, however, realized his mistake as the play developed. He saw that Landsberg was sure to get to the ball before he could, and that would likely spell touchdown and the game. But Crego also saw that he had enough of an angle to tackle Landsberg and take the penalty, which he did. It was quick thinking. In light of what followed, it probably saved the game.

From the 18, another pass from Scholl to right halfback Bill Murphy gave Cornell first down on our 5. There was less than a minute to play as Landsberg hit into the line for two. On second down, Scholl drove to the 1. On third down, Landsberg was piled up for scarcely any gain. The ball rested less than a yard away from our goal line. There was time for two more plays at the most.

Now began a series of events which proved to be a weird prelude to an emotional Donnybrook and an aftermath never duplicated in football history.

To stop the clock Snavely called time out, so Cornell was penalized 5 yards for delaying the game. This placed the ball on our 6-yard line.

On fourth down, Scholl passed into the end zone. The ball was batted away from Murphy, the intended receiver. William H. (Red) Friesell, a referee of long-proved excellence, put the ball on the 20-yard line, apparently in our possession.

But then, after a consultation requested by Captain Matuszczak, Friesell changed his mind and returned the ball to our 6. For some reason, according to a subsequent quote from Snavely, Matuszczak and other Cornell players thought there had been a double-offside penalty called on the pass which had been batted down in the end zone.

Captain Young protested vigorously to Friesell that there had been no such penalty, and two of the officials backed him up. But Friesell, apparently confused, continued to allow Cornell possession on the 6-yard line and another down.

There were six seconds left—time for Cornell to get off one play. They huddled and decided to go for a touchdown and victory rather than a field goal and a tie. Two seconds remained on the clock when Scholl passed to Murphy in the end zone, and this time Murphy caught it. Nick Drahos, Cornell tackle, kicked the extra point. The game was over and Cornell had won, 7-3.

The coaches on both sides and the fans thought that was it. But our players, two of the officials, and the writers covering the game knew that Cornell had scored on a fifth down. The writers so reported it. The news swept down from the press box, through the crowd, out onto Memorial Field, into Davis Field House and on through Hanover like wildfire. Students began parading, proclaiming a Dartmouth victory. They paraded throughout the weekend, every hour on the hour. One of the parades ended up in front of our house.

When the situation was brought to the attention of Jim Lynah,

Cornell's athletic director, he stated that if the officials discovered that there had been five downs, the score would be recorded as Dartmouth 3, Cornell 0. Dr. Ezra Day, president of Cornell, concurred.

President Hopkins and I drove Referee Friesell across the Connecticut River to the White River Junction station. He admitted to us he had apparently made a mistake.

On Monday, after Cornell officials had studied the films, which showed five downs and no evidence of a double-offside, they called Asa Bushnell, Executive Secretary of the Eastern Intercollegiate Association, who then forwarded the information to Friesell.

Friesell issued a statement, expressing his regret. Bushnell then stated that no official had jurisdiction to change the outcome of the game and that any further action would have to come from Dartmouth or Cornell.

When this was reported to Cornell, they sent us two wires. One from Jim Lynah read: "IN VIEW OF THE CONCLUSIONS REACHED BY THE OFFICIALS THAT THE CORNELL TOUCHDOWN WAS SCORED ON A FIFTH DOWN, CORNELL RELINQUISHES CLAIM TO THE VICTORY AND EXTENDS CONGRATULATIONS TO DARTMOUTH."

A second from Coach Snavely read: "I ACCEPT THE FINAL CONCLUSIONS OF THE OFFICIALS AND WITHOUT RESERVATION CONCEDE THE VICTORY TO DARTMOUTH WITH HEARTY CONGRATULATIONS TO YOU AND THE GALLANT DARTMOUTH TEAM."

And we wired Cornell: "DARTMOUTH ACCEPTS THE VICTORY AND CONGRATULATES AND SALUTES THE CORNELL TEAM, THE HONORABLE AND HONORED OPPONENT OF HER LONGEST UNBROKEN RIVALRY."

I had been told almost eight years before, by Eddie Dooley and Red Lowden, that a good part of Heaven was right in Hanover, New Hampshire. I believe they were right. It even included the miracle of a game that was won after it was lost. As I look back down the years, maybe it was a sign that I should not leave Dartmouth. [. . .]

Orozco in New England

by LEWIS MUMFORD

‣‣‣ "Orozco in New England" is the title that was used by *The New Republic* of October 10, 1934, for its long article—from which this segment has been taken—wherein cultural historian and critic Lewis Mumford treats of the recently completed frescoes at Dartmouth, done by Mexican artist José Clemente Orozco.

WHO CAN SAY when a tree is dead? After the crown is broken by storms, after blight has attacked the remaining leaves, there may still be strength at the roots. So the chestnuts are coming back; so too, perhaps, our regional cultures, which were blasted by a ruthless and over-rapid industrialization and undermined by attacks of metropolitan "prosperity," may be putting forth fresh stems now from their buried but still vital roots. There are signs of this throughout the country, not least in New England, the oldest and most persistent seat of human culture here. Perhaps the most promising sign at the moment lies in the realm of the spirit—the Orozco frescoes at Dartmouth College.

Six miles up the Connecticut Valley from White River Junction lies Hanover. Here Eleazar Wheelock, dreaming to turn the Indians into rational citizens of Heaven, planted something the New England farmer once valued as much as piety and thrift and hard labor: a college. These people did not wait for prosperity and numbers before they sought the things of the mind. Before the Civil War, according to a sober estimate, there were probably as many bookstores in New England as there are now in the whole country.

Dan'l Webster studied at Dartmouth; so did George Perkins Marsh, a more important alumnus; and to the Dartmouth Medical School, the first of its kind in America, came as a young man the foremost American advocate of birth control, bearing an overripe corpse in his wagon to defray the costs of tuition. On the east side of the rectangular Common stand the austere white buildings of the original college, handsome solely by reason of their clean surfaces and judiciously adjusted proportions, bearing witness to the esthetic sense of

154

the early republic. This sense, of course, was blunted during the nine-teenth century; and can scarcely be said to have been sharpened by the more refined Georgian revivalism—in which construction and expression belong to two non-coöperating systems of thought—that has now taken its place. [. . .]

[. . .] An atmosphere of liberalism had vaguely descended over the place and was duly handed down from President Tucker to President Hopkins. Perhaps the best part of the liberal tradition, its experimen-talism and its faith in the intellect, could be found here. No sweeping change; no sudden announcement of the New Curriculum; no false dawn of the New World. But here the dead wood was lopped off, gen-tly, almost tenderly; there a new plantation was made. Within the modes of the existing society, Dartmouth shows many of its best rather than its worst characteristics. Enough intelligence to accept the responsibilities of intelligence. All this, of course, within the pattern that would provide the world, in sufficient number, with its business executives, its functionaries, its larger professional caste that thinks and feels on the same plane. To ask for more than this before 1930 was to ask for a generation of misfits and martyrs.

The coming of an important revolutionary artist, José Clemente Orozco, to Dartmouth College was the result of the complex tradition whose threads I have been trying to bring together. No single man or event made it possible; or rather, the men and events were themselves shaped by the New England tradition. Thanks to President Hopkins' keen instinct for reality, the art department had been completely refurbished. Here under Professor Artemas Packard was expounded a fresh conception of art—fresh though as old as Herder, Taine, Ruskin —that art is not the empty plaything of the rich and idle, but a neces-sary expression of the emotional and imaginative and ideological life of communities, as important for their existence as their daily bread.

Unostentatiously, without feature write-ups and premature pic-tures in the rotogravure sections, Orozco came to the college in 1932 as a member of the new art department, with the modest salary of an assistant professor and the title of Visiting Lecturer. No hat was passed around among rich donors to bring forth the usual thousands of dollars with their usual visible and invisible strings. The new murals were strictly an intramural project of the art department: a demonstration of the fresco process, and a demonstration of the pos-sibility of creating, even in an environment traditionally hostile to the image, a graphic interpretation of the contemporary world, in a form so permanent that future generations would be able to read, to sympathize and to draw their own conclusions. This happened at a moment when most of the great universities and libraries and cities, wallowing in the depression, were throwing overboard, with cowardly anxiety, every vestige of our cultural life they could remove, leaving behind only their pretentious empty buildings as memorials. Such an act required courage, and, in the best sense of the word, statesmanship. [. . .]

But where was Orozco to work? The answer has more than a touch of irony in it. The one great expanse of wall was in the new Baker Library. On the ground level, the broad base of the building forms a great hall with tall windows: below the ground level, with windows at the top, is an equally long hall. When the builders reached this second room, meant only as a study hall for students taking out books on brief loans, the money had pretty well given out. Fortunately, this room was not "for show": hence it could be left undecorated. The bare wall that so well expresses modern architecture appeared in this Georgian museum-piece by default. For when the money ran out, the superficialities and contradictions of a sterile, imitative, pecuniary culture could be sloughed off—and art came in. Not decoration, not gentility, not Georgian correctness: instead, the realities of human mind and passion, the realities of the world in which we must live and dream and plan and act. In the room where the college confessed poverty it found riches. When Orozco was through painting it, he had not merely produced probably the most impressive mural in North America: he had added a new course to the curriculum. [. . .]

[. . . W]hat have these paintings to do with New England; how do they stand among the white clapboards and the venerable elms? The people who ask this question forget that there are two New Englands. One is the dead and moth-eaten New England that flourishes in the gift shoppes, and that specializes in battered furniture, "ancestors by purchase," imitations of hooked rugs, even replicas of Colonial gardens. The other New England is the same vital regional culture that originally helped nurture Emerson, Thoreau and Hawthorne.

This second New England, conscious of deep roots in its own soil, has never hesitated to go elsewhere for elements that are lacking in its local scene. Its Motley wrote the classic history of the Netherlands; its Longfellow drew upon European folklore from Finland to Spain; its

Prescotts, its Ticknors, its Childses, its Nortons, were aware of their full European heritage, whilst Emerson and Thoreau, seizing on the little library of Eastern classics imported into Concord, so well amalgamated the thought of the East and the West that they are now reckoned in India among the great modern sages. In its more imaginative sons, this New England has always been at home on a world stage, just as its merchants were at home in Hongkong, Singapore and Rio. When their great moments come, these New Englanders call for "wine that never came from the belly of the grape," and they drink it with an unmoved face, as if it were last autumn's cider.

The spiritual vitality of this genuine New England is better embodied in Orozco's murals than in any amount of local history tamely recorded by local artists. A soundly bottomed regionalism can achieve cosmopolitan breadth without fear of losing its integrity or virtue: it is only a sick and puling regionalism that must continually gaze with enamored eyes upon its own face, praising its warts and pimples as beauty marks. For a genuine regional tradition lives by two principles. One is, *cultivate whatever you have*, no matter how poor it is; *it is at least your own*. The other is, *seek elsewhere for what you do not possess*: absorb whatever is good wherever you may find it; *make it your own*. In seeking this distinguished artist from Mexico to paint its first murals, Dartmouth honored the great New England tradition; while by his magnificent painting Orozco has honored that hospitality, even as he has made a precious addition to the tradition itself.

On Falling in Love at Dartmouth

by C. EVERETT KOOP

※≫Ɔ Following his service as Surgeon General of the United States (1981–89), C. Everett Koop 1937 published his autobiographical volume *Koop: The Memoirs of America's Family Doctor* (1991). The book included a chapter on the author's undergraduate years on Hanover Plain, "The Still North, The Hill Winds," from which the following extract has been made.

O N A C L O U D Y September day in 1933, I gazed out the window of the family car with intense excitement as my parents and I drove the narrow road winding through the pine-covered New Hampshire hills to the little village of Hanover. In a way, I was still somewhat surprised that I was headed for Dartmouth College. The family roots went deep in Brooklyn, and most of my relatives and friends expected me to attend college not far from home. My only relative who seemed to know anything about the collegiate world had steered me in the direction of Princeton in nearby New Jersey. But I had chosen Dartmouth mainly because Princeton did not have a medical school and Dartmouth did. It also had a program that covered four years of college and two of medical school in five years. It was the wrong reason for my choice, but it was the right choice. My four years at Dartmouth were among the best of my life; they shaped what happened to me and my family. Much of what I was to accomplish as a surgeon, as Surgeon General, as a person, stems from decisions I made or from what I learned while I was at Dartmouth.

At Dartmouth I fell in love. I fell in love with the rugged hills and serene valleys of New Hampshire. I fell in love with skiing. I fell in love with learning. And I fell in love with Betty.

At first it seemed all so very new, inviting, and yet intimidating. I was a city boy about to settle down in the wilds of New Hampshire. I had graduated from a tiny school with only fifteen youngsters in the senior class, and now I was at a college of more than two thousand young men, among them 670 freshmen, each eager to show what he could do. I would be younger than most, only sixteen when I matriculated. I felt enthusiastic and proud to be part of it all, determined to get the absolute last drop out of this experience away from home. As we drove up the hill to the campus, the stately beauty of the brick Georgian buildings, the elm-ringed green, and the gleaming white buildings of Dartmouth Row gave me a thrill. They still do.

I can't imagine that any incoming Dartmouth freshman prepared with greater enthusiasm than I did. I had spent the summer listening to a ten-inch record that a Hanover store had mailed as an advertising gimmick, and I knew every Dartmouth song as well as those of the other Ivy League schools. My mother heard me sing them so often—sometimes she chimed in with her lovely soprano voice—that she could still get through the words thirty years later when her grandchildren enrolled at Dartmouth.

Right away Dartmouth changed my name. The fellows I met decided that my unusual last name required an appropriate nickname, so I became "Chick" Koop. Years later, when I began my medical career in Philadelphia, I thought an aspiring young surgeon should not be known as "Chick," so I decided to drop my nickname. But the first person I bumped into in Philadelphia happened to be a friend from Dartmouth, who promptly introduced me to everyone as "Chick." That's who I've been ever since.

Dartmouth offered an inviting variety of extracurricular activities, but I decided to concentrate on my studies. And football. I have always said that good surgeons are suspicious people. And I have always said that the field of surgery attracts people who are by nature suspicious and compulsive. But I didn't show any of those tendencies my first week at Dartmouth. Instead of realizing how important it would be not to be late for the first football practice, I went off instead with my mother and father for a drive through the White Mountains, about fifty miles north of Hanover. Our outing took much longer than anticipated and I missed football practice completely. [. . .]

But when spring practice rolled around, something happened that changed my life. In the twenties and thirties, Ivy League football played a much more important role in national sports than people reading the sports pages today might imagine. But Dartmouth had not enjoyed an outstanding season for several years. Therefore, when a new head coach, Earl Blaik, arrived in Hanover from West Point, bringing with him his coterie of assistant coaches, it made quite a stir in the north country and in Ivy League circles in the sports world.

In those days, each player played both offense and defense; offensive centers played defense by stepping into the backfield, the so-called "roving center," where they might intercept passes in the flat, just beyond the line of scrimmage. On the second or third day of spring practice, when Blaik was choosing the first and second squads, I was engaged in an exercise of running at right angles to the trajectory of a short pass and trying to intercept it. A bunch of other guys were trying out for the same position. [. . .]

Later that day, when the first team roster was posted, my name was listed as center. Within twenty minutes after people had a chance to read those typed columns, my life changed. Now, suddenly, there was a certain deference in the way people spoke to me. People who hadn't looked my way as we passed on the stairs of my dormitory now knew my name and seemed anxious to befriend me.

One night during the second week of spring practice I walked down Main Street to get my usual toasted cheese sandwich and chocolate milk shake. As I approached Allen's Drug Store, Blaik and three of his assistant coaches were walking toward me four abreast. I was with my roommate and several friends from the dormitory, and when Blaik's "Hello, Chick!" was echoed by each of the assistant coaches, I was in seventh heaven. I think my friends would have been willing to carry me home on their shoulders if I had asked them.

A few days later we had a scrimmage, the first team against the second team. On defense I was playing roving center, and the opportunity came to intercept a short pass. [. . .] I snagged the pass, found a hole in the line, and must have run about ten yards before I was hit by two very vicious tacklers. I was knocked out cold. I don't really know how long it was, but my friends told me I was on the ground for several minutes. When I tried to walk to the sidelines I realized that my shoulder was extraordinarily sore. More disturbing, something strange had happened to my vision. I was seeing two of everything, a second image superimposed on the first, somewhat to the right and above it.

Nobody seemed too concerned about my double vision or my intense headache. At first Blaik was solicitous. He advised me to come to practice and walk through the plays, but not to suit up and risk further injury. I did this for the rest of the week, receiving the same fawning treatment when I passed the coaches on Main Street. [. . .]

When the weekend came, and my eyes and headache were getting no better, I decided I would go to the Dartmouth Eye Clinic for a consultation with Professor Bielschowsky, perhaps the most knowledgeable person in the world at that time regarding the function of the extraocular muscles of the eye. He addressed me in moderately accented English after a very complete examination.

"What will be your major?" was his first question.

"I'm premed."

"You're premed and you play this foolish game of football? Let me see your hands." I showed them to him, fingers outstretched, palms down and then palms up.

"They're beautiful. They're surgeon's hands. So you not only risk your sight and maybe your life, but your hands and your career. Such foolishness."

He then told me in no uncertain terms and in rather scathing language that being a football hero offered at best a very limited benefit, and I was risking permanent disaster if I suffered another head injury. He explained that I had probably had a tiny hemorrhage in or very close to the nucleus of the fourth cranial nerve that supplied one of the extraocular muscles, that it would probably never improve, but that with eyeglasses I could live with it perfectly well. On the other hand, if the area became more damaged, I would place a surgical career in jeopardy.

He made sense and I knew it. But I had to decide if I were mature enough to give up all that big-man-on-campus attention for the much less glamorous life of an anonymous premedical student. I made the decision and went to see Earl Blaik the next morning in the field house. [. . .]

Blaik tried to change my mind, arguing that many men had played football and then gone on to be doctors. I don't know how I was strong enough to resist his persuasive tactics, but I was. His next comment destroyed the man in my sight forever, no matter how many bronze plaques commemorate his coaching years at Dartmouth and West Point. He looked at me and said, "So, in other words, you're a coward."

That night when I passed the four coaches on Main Street, they looked the other way.

Within a few days, as it became known that I had dropped out of football, the pedestal on which I had been balancing toppled. No longer was I the injured football hero, no longer did people envy my relationship with the new coaching staff, no longer did I eat at the training table, no longer did upperclassmen athletes pay the same attention to me. [. . .]

Giving up football was one of the hardest and wisest choices I made at Dartmouth. Not only had I acted wisely to save my surgical ambitions, but I also moved into a different social world, choosing a quieter path that would bring me close friendships with other premed students. For my last three years I roomed with Mike Petti, another premed student from Brockton, Massachusetts. We became good friends with two other premeds, Ed McGrath, from Milton, Massachusetts, and Dan Barker from Niantic, Connecticut. Two of us came from metropolitan areas, one from a small city, and one from a very small town. Two of us were Protestant and two Roman Catholic. We all shared similar family values, but there was a sufficient diversity to permit arguments long into the night. We couldn't have had more different personalities, but fortunately we all had a good sense of humor.

When I look back on my college years, I bring to mind all the usual hijinks, but most of my time at Dartmouth I studied. There were times it took all the discipline I could muster, as when the shouts and laughter of fellows playing baseball on the green echoed in the chemistry lab where I was fighting quantitative analysis, carefully making sure my experiments came out correctly by using a tiny camel hair brush to remove dust particles from the weights and scales. I had decided early on that recreation did not always fit into the schedule of a premed student or a surgeon.

My zoology major kept me busy, offering me intellectual stimulation and career preparation as well as employment. The college lost interest in giving me a scholarship as soon as I left the football team, so I sought out a variety of jobs to help my father finance my education, although he did not request it. I washed dishes, sold saddle shoes, ran a laundry service, tutored, and finally served as a research assistant in the zoology department. I thrived on work that allowed me to be on the brink of scientific discovery by using not only my mind, but also my hands.

One of my professors, Bill Ballard, was experimenting on lens transplants in the eyes of the *Amblystoma notatum*, a strange little five-inch long amphibious vertebrate. After the professor had taken the infinitesimally small lens from one eye of a newborn (½ inch long) and inserted it into the other, my job was to see that the little creatures maintained their nutrition. [. . .]

When the operating season on *Amblystomae* was over, I found other work to do under Professor Norman Arnold. It was from Norm that I learned embryology, but it was also from Norm that I learned how to teach. In his soft, persuasive, unhurried manner, he went to all lengths to explain the very complicated field of embryology. While he talked to the class, he used modeling clay to make three-dimensional embryology come to life. Although I could not foresee it at that time, my surgical career would be devoted to correcting the defects that occur in the unfolding of embryology in preborn children. What I learned in embryology became so deep a part of my understanding that I have to think it was all part of God's sovereign plan that made me an innovative pediatric surgeon.

Norm was also a true esthete, and it was he who fanned my budding interest in English literature, art, and music. He was the consummate teacher who took great pleasure in introducing me to everything from varieties of Vermont ferns to different types of cheeses. We worked together, we talked together, we skied together, we climbed mountains together. Norm quickly became my closest friend at Dartmouth. By my junior year, I had spent more time with him than with any student friend, and our friendship lasted for decades.

When I first enrolled at Dartmouth, I had planned to take advantage of the special curriculum that allowed certain students to take their first year of medical school as the fourth year of college. But in my junior year I decided against accelerating my education; instead I would use my senior year to gain greater academic and social maturity before entering medical school. I was also attracted to the opportunities zoology presented in my senior year, when I would be able to have my own little lab, my own equipment, and my own projects. This produced the only wavering of my lifelong desire to be a surgeon. I was the recipient of so much of my professors' teaching and convivial largesse that I wondered if perhaps I wouldn't be happy in a similar role. Again, it was Norm Arnold who straightened out my thinking on that. As he so aptly pointed out, if I went on to medical school and surgical training, I could always return to the academic world to do what he did, but if I prepared myself to be what he was, I could never do the other. [. . .]

In another lasting contribution to my life, Dartmouth nourished my love of the outdoors. From my first visit to Dartmouth, I was enchanted by the beauty of the surrounding countryside. In later life, my work would take me all over the globe, to some of the earth's most spectacular scenery, but nothing could replace the special love I developed for the hills and valleys of northern New England.

In the winter I skied. In 1934 skiing in the United States was still in its infancy, and Dartmouth skiers played a major role in the development of the sport. It was while I was in college that the first ski tow in New England began to operate in nearby Woodstock, Vermont. Of course, it was all very new to a boy from Brooklyn.

My first skiing experience was in the light of a waning moon on the hills of the Hanover golf course. One of the greatest thrills of my life was to feel myself start down that very gentle slope with silence all around me, dark spruce trees stark against the white snow, bitter frost in the air, and the unbelievable thrill of gliding with no effort across the hard-packed snow. I became a devotee immediately; every minute that I could spare from my studies went to skiing. I think I skied almost every winter day of my four years at Dartmouth. [. . .]

Perhaps because I had learned how to maintain my balance while roller-skating on cracked Brooklyn sidewalks, I became a fairly decent skier and got to the point where I was at least fearless, if not temperate, and had the temerity to ski the headwall of Tuckerman Ravine, which was in those days a feat usually reserved for experts. Skiing was not only a source of great fun, it was also, at least for me, a risky business. I had more than my share of accidents.

As Dartmouth's famed Winter Carnival approached in my sophomore year, it was bitterly cold and there was plenty of snow—except on top of the tall ski jump, where the wind had blown it away. So a few of us in the Outing Club volunteered to pack snow onto the ramp of the jump. It was hard, slow work: hoisting the snow to the top of the jump with the help of a horse, rope, pulley, and trash can. I waited on the top of the jump to empty the buckets of snow the horse-and-pulley operation had pulled up. It was so cold up there that my hands and feet were numb. I lost my balance, fell, and started down the ski jump on my back, feet first. My screams alerted the crew preparing the lip of the take off at the bottom of the jump, and they caught me. Otherwise, I could have suffered a serious injury, hurtling off the jump onto the landing hill on my back. [. . .]

My enthusiasm for skiing allowed me to get talked into representing my fraternity in the intramural ski-jumping competition. Since I had never jumped on skis, I began to practice. I would get up before my usual hour and attack the smaller practice ski jump at dawn. My routine never varied. I tried the landing hill first to assess its speed and then made three jumps. The limit of that jump was ninety feet, which may not seem much by Olympic standards, but for a boy from Brooklyn who had been on skis but two years, it was the closest thing to flying I would ever do.

On the day of the competition I had a lab and didn't get out until the sun had gone down behind the tall pines at the top of the jump. As soon as that happened, the slushy takeoff hill froze into ice. Because I was late and a little embarrassed to appear timid, I did not test the speed of the landing hill first. That was mistake number one.

Mistake number two was that instead of starting ten or fifteen feet down from the top of the takeoff hill, which was permissible, I went to the top. My third mistake was that instead of standing relatively straight up to brake my speed and slow my takeoff, I crouched. My fourth mistake was to jump when I should have just slipped off the lip of the jump.

All of these mistakes combined to make me rocket off the jump much faster than ever before, and I suddenly realized that I was higher than I had ever been, as high as the top branches of the surrounding pine trees. I had no idea what to do, and I don't pretend to say that I thought it out. But I attempted a kind of somersault to slow my speed and get down as fast as I could. I managed to get halfway around, landed on my back and slid to the base of the hill, feeling as though I had been hit by a truck.

My friends took me on a toboggan to the college infirmary. No one did much for me, and I lay in bed in quiet panic, because I was partially paralyzed. I could move my arms and legs only with great difficulty. No one discussed my condition with me. I plunged into a deep depression, feeling for sure that surgical aspirations and perhaps even a normal life were no longer in my future. Only much later did I figure out that I had suffered a spinal concussion, from which I began to recover after three or four days. This was the first time I had ever been hospitalized. My case was poorly managed, and that made a lasting impression on me. I learned what it was like to lie alone and afraid in a hospital bed, not knowing what the future held, afraid to find out, more afraid not to know. I resolved that when I finally became a doctor, I would not let my own patients lie in fear caused by an inattentive physician. [. . .]

Despite my mishaps, skiing was one of the best things about college. But best of all, Dartmouth brought me Betty.

Before the Christmas break in my junior year, I was chatting with Dan Barker and told him I thought it was a shame that he was now in his senior year and had never invited a girl up for Winter Carnival. I knew that Dan had a longtime steady girlfriend at home, and that it was a foregone conclusion that he would eventually marry her. But I also knew that in the previous summer he had met Betty Flanagan, a girl who planned to enter Vassar in September and whose family summered in the Connecticut shore town where he lived.

I said, "Dan, I feel so strongly about this that I would be delighted to invite you and your girl as my guests at our fraternity, and you will be free to enjoy all the privileges that go with membership in that fraternity for the weekend." I still wonder what was in the depths of my mind as I made this offer.

"That might make a difference. But I don't know which one to ask," he said, looking at two 8 x 10 portraits on either end of his bureau. "Invite that one," I said, pointing to Betty.

We returned from Christmas break, got through the awful month of January, preparing for final exams in the last week of that month, and then there was nothing ahead but Carnival. There was a very special something in the air in Hanover as Carnival approached. Each fraternity and dormitory prepared a snow-and-ice sculpture, and the Dartmouth Outing Club constructed a huge snow statue in the center of the campus. The social events centered around formal dances with white tie and tails on Friday and Saturday nights and a tea dance (so called) after the athletic events on Saturday afternoon. Carnival itself consisted of an outdoor evening on Friday night, a gala affair often featuring an Olympic skating star, stunt skiing, and marvelous fireworks that illuminated the dark pine trees against the sparkling snow. The athletic events featured downhill, slalom, and cross-country skiing races, ski-joring (skiers pulled by horses around a race course), ice hockey, basketball, and ski jumping as the grand finale.

On Friday afternoon, I had just returned to the dorm from a skiing outing and was relaxing in Dan's room, when he walked in and introduced me to Betty. I was dressed only in my skiing long johns. It was an unusual beginning to a long relationship.

My date for the weekend was a girl I had known from home, an attractive, popular girl attending Duke who had little time for me once she saw the other Dartmouth men. After the ski jumping on Saturday afternoon, I returned to the fraternity house and, as was the custom, took off my ski boots so I could be ready to dance, if the occasion arose, in my ski socks. As usual, my date disappeared, but soon the front door opened, and in walked Betty.

"Where's Dan?" I asked.

"He's gone to take a nap," said she, "and he thought I should do the same."

"Do you feel like a nap?"

"Not at all." [. . .]

Although I might not have admitted it at the time, my romance with Betty Flanagan began that afternoon. Our first deep conversation was wide-ranging and fascinating for each of us. Later we often recalled that it had a prophetic quality. Among the many subjects we discussed was the difficulty medical students faced because of the unfair, albeit unspoken, prohibition against marriage for medical students. Little did we realize that afternoon that together we would break that barrier, the first of many. [. . .]

I had no plans to have a date for the Green Key Weekend, Dartmouth's spring house party, in early May. So when one of my fraternity brothers was called home to a funeral, I accepted his invitation to drive to New York City with him. I spent Tuesday evening and all day Wednesday with my family and met my friend to return to Hanover early Thursday morning.

As we drove slowly north through upper Manhattan and the Bronx, I suddenly proposed, "It's a gorgeous day, and we've just driven down the Connecticut Valley. Let's go back to Hanover up the Hudson Valley." I don't think I had a conscious ulterior motive in suggesting the change in route, although Betty insists I did. As we went up the Taconic Parkway, I said, "We have so much time, let's stop off in Poughkeepsie, find Vassar College, and visit Dan Barker's girl for a few minutes."

It took some effort to find Betty Flanagan. We were told she was not in her dormitory, but that she would be along from class if we cared to wait. Betty doesn't like me to describe the way she looked when she arrived from the library. She looked pretty bedraggled in an old polo coat, the lining of which drooped below the hemline on one side. It didn't matter to me.

I don't know why my friend had the good sense to become occupied with some other endeavor, but Betty and I took a stroll around the lake alone, reminiscing on things we had done and talked about during Winter Carnival, and I realized I was developing an unreasonable attachment to this girl, who had already come to mind many times between February and May. When we got halfway around the lake I stopped and said, "This is spring weekend at Dartmouth. Why don't you drive up with us, and Dan and I will squire you around?" A clear invitation, but sufficiently vague.

I have to admit to some immediate trepidation about having made that remark. First of all, I wasn't at all clear about the relationship between Dan and Betty, but I assumed it was tenuous. However, I also knew enough about Dan to know that he would not jump at the opportunity of sharing his girl with me for the weekend. Then there was a histology exam I had to take as soon as I returned. It was very important to my future, but as that thought went through my mind, I shoved it aside.

Betty said she couldn't possibly do it, and I coaxed. She softened a little, I pushed harder, and she accepted. But a problem remained. In those days a Vassar girl needed family permission to visit a men's college campus for the weekend. Betty phoned, finding only her grandmother at home. When her grandmother gave her permission, she unknowingly forged a bond between us that we both cherished for the rest of her life.

My friend reappeared, and the three of us were off, up the Hudson Valley to Rutland, Vermont, and across the Green Mountains to Hanover. I put off thinking about my histology exam. I also put off thinking about how I was going to explain all this to Dan, something that was going to be increasingly difficult because the ride up had convinced me that this was the girl for me. [. . .]

It was Thursday, and since the great influx of Dartmouth dates for the weekend did not begin until Friday, I was able to find a cheap room for Betty up on the third floor of the old Hanover Inn. In was *verboten* for the male students to go upstairs to rooms occupied by young ladies, so I left Betty in the lobby, promising I would be back as soon as I could, after I did some studying for my exam, and that then maybe we could have something to eat. I was nervous about meeting Dan. My attempt at a breezy introduction of the situation to him fell extraordinarily flat. I could tell by the tightening muscles in his jaw that he was angry, and in all fairness to him I have to say that I was so vague he could not possibly have known what my plans were. [. . .]

I was falling in love, and I knew it. I walked back into my room, closed the door, and went through the motions of cramming for the next morning's exam. The pages before me were a blur. I had no interest in the cellular structure of the liver or the microscopic intricacies of striated muscle. After a ridiculous hour, I threw in the towel, faced reality for the first time that day, and decided to go back to the inn and take Betty to dinner.

I called Betty's room from the lobby and got no answer. It never occurred to me that she might have gone out. I told the manager that I had called and gotten no answer and wondered if he could send somebody up to the room to see if she was all right. He looked at me as though I were out of my mind, but nevertheless complied and returned to tell me that the room was indeed empty.

If love is irrational, disappointment in love is more so. I had absolutely no claim on this girl. I knew deep down that even my close friends would not like what I had done. I had told Betty I was bringing her up for a shared weekend with Dan. I had given her no specific plans for the evening. Yet here I not only had an inexplicable emptiness in the middle of my belly, I was unreasonably hurt.

I tore back to my room in the dormitory. I went across the hall and found Ed McGrath, Dan's roommate, sitting at his desk looking very stern. When I inquired where Dan was, Ed said that he had left the room in some anger, muttering something about ". . . at least I'll take her to dinner." Then Ed let me know in no uncertain terms that what I had done was something between highly foolish and unkind. He might have also said insensitive and stupid. He reminded me that in Dartmouth lingo, the definition of someone who took a friend's girl was a "snake." [. . .]

I went across the hall, closed myself in my room, and seethed. Again, the histology text before me was a blur. When I heard Dan come in and close his door, I took off for the inn. Knowing it was against the rules but unreasonably angry with Betty, I walked up the main stairs that left the lobby in full view of the registration desk, found her room on the third floor, and knocked on the door.

When Betty answered, I suppressed all the surging warm and tender emotions that were once again aroused by seeing her. Instead I stepped inside and said in my anger, "Get your clothes packed. I'm driving you to Rutland. You can take a train to Poughkeepsie."

There was never any more sincere consternation than Betty displayed. If I had told her she was responsible for the rumors of the gathering clouds of World War II, she could not have been more startled.

"Why? What did I do?"

"You had dinner with Dan."

"Why shouldn't I? He told me you had sent him to take me to dinner because you had to study."

It was all so very reasonable, so very logical. But I was not. I had foolishly allowed my image of this wonderful girl to crumble over the past hour. I don't recall clearly what turned me back on the right track, but I began to rebuild the image with Betty's reasonable explanation.

As we talked, we rapidly recaptured the magic spirit of our short time together at the Carnival tea dance. We were back to talking about medical students being married. I never asked her to marry me, but I knew she was going to and she knew it, too.

In those few hours, a great many things in my life changed. Couples have been through this experience since the beginning of time. They fall in love, go together for a while, get to know each other, build a base on which to form an abiding faith and love with a lifetime commitment. The unusual thing about us was that we compressed all that into the hours between 10:00 P.M. and dawn. [. . .]

Dawn made its presence known by the light around the window shade. I couldn't believe the speed with which time had passed or the predicament I was in. Not only was I in a forbidden place; I had been there all night. If I had been caught, I could have been expelled. It was another time my medical career hung by a thread.

I said good-bye as though for the last time and started downstairs looking for an alternate route of escape. There was none. When the registration desk came into view, the clerk was obviously asleep. I sat down on the stairs, took off my shoes, and crept out the front door in stocking feet, unnoticed. Once on the porch of the inn, I put my shoes on and, breathing in the crisp New Hampshire dawn, sprinted back to my room. It was about 6:00. I was able to study until about 8:00. I took the exam, proving that from the start life with Betty would be productive. I got an "A."

By the end of Green Key Weekend, Betty and I knew we were headed for life together. [. . .]

Dartmouth shaped my life in ways I am still discovering, and many things that have happened to me and my family can be traced to my decision to attend "the college on the hill." I have already mentioned some: education, close friends, my wife. There would be many green threads woven through my life. My love for the Hanover hills would lead me to spend summers there with my wife and children. That, in turn, would call a second and then a third Koop generation to attend Dartmouth. Our family's attraction to the White Mountains, for both work and play, also reflected my love of Dartmouth. My varied connections with Dartmouth gave me some of my happiest moments, and my greatest sorrow would come with the death of a Dartmouth boy.

There was something very special about Dartmouth. Many of us felt that at an isolated, all-male college, the depth of friendships was greater than on a coed campus, where social success with women can supersede male companionship. (However, having two Dartmouth granddaughters has let me see the Dartmouth experience in a new light.) Over the years, the class of '37 enjoyed what I like to think was a special camaraderie, perhaps because our college years were a brief parenthesis between the worst of the Depression and the war that claimed too many of us. [. . .]

Of F. Scott Fitzgerald and the Movie "Winter Carnival"

by AARON LATHAM

➤➤➤ Aaron Latham's book *Crazy Sundays: F. Scott Fitzgerald in Hollywood* (1971) provides an account of what in 1939 ensued when producer Walter Wanger 1915 engaged the famous novelist to join Budd Schulberg 1936 (later to be much celebrated for his own novels, as well as for his film-writing achievements) in doing the screenplay for a motion picture based on Dartmouth's annual mid-winter festival.

"[A]FTER *Gone with the Wind*] I wanted to quit for a while," Fitzgerald later wrote, "—health bad and I was depressed about the Metro business. But Swanson argued me into a job with Wanger on *Winter Carnival* with a rise to $1500. This was a mistake."

Producer Walter Wanger had hired Fitzgerald to collaborate with a young writer just three years out of Dartmouth named Budd Schulberg. Schulberg had already written a script based on Dartmouth's Winter Carnival, but neither the producer nor the young writer himself thought that it was any good. When Wanger started looking for someone to help doctor his college comedy, he naturally thought of the author of *This Side of Paradise*.

"My meeting with Scott Fitzgerald . . . still holds for me a dream-like, legendary quality," Schulberg later wrote in *Esquire*. "Even while it was happening I felt as if the gods had swooped down and carried me off to serve as a minor player in one of their more extravagant myths." On the day it occurred, Wanger had called the unsuspecting Schulberg into his office and asked casually how he would like to team with F. Scott Fitzgerald. The younger writer shuddered, then wondered if his boss had noticed. "My God," he asked, "isn't Scott Fitzgerald dead?" Wanger answered, "On the contrary, he's in the next office reading your script."

When he was introduced to Fitzgerald, Schulberg saw a figure who seemed to have been drawn with white chalk. He recalls:

"There was no colors in him. The proud, somewhat too handsome

172

profile of his earlier dust jackets was crumpled. To this day I am unable to say exactly what it was that left me with this lasting impression. The fine forehead, the leading man's nose, the matinee-idol set of the gentle, quick-to-smile eyes, the good Scotch-Irish cheekbones, the delicate, almost feminine mouth, the tasteful Eastern (in fact, Brooks Bros.) attire—he had lost none of these. But there seemed to be something physically or psychologically broken in him that had pitched him forward from scintillating youth to shaken old age."

Schulberg had happened to reread *The Great Gatsby* only a few days before, and *Tender Is the Night* had been a favorite of long standing. He remembers, "Scott was flattered and stimulated and, it seemed to me, pathetically pleased to find any product of the Depression thirties who knew, admired, and could talk his books."

Fitzgerald, who was afraid that he had lost touch with the young, had once written in his notebook, "Of course these boys are more serious—this is the generation that saw their mothers drunk." The author who had heralded the speakeasy generation of the twenties was so happy to find a young fan, and Schulberg so pleased to have met a great writer, that they spent days just getting to know one another. *Winter Carnival*, which Scott was being paid three hundred a day to write, waited in a desk drawer. Besides Fitzgerald's fiction, they also talked about politics, the cultural ebb and flow of generations, Hollywood and movie making.

Schulberg was impressed by Fitzgerald's seriousness:

"Scott was not a film snob. In fact he plunged into a study of film making that even included a card file of the plot lines of all the pictures he had seen. Although he thought of himself, naturally, as a novelist first and last, he was not, like so many novelists and playwrights I had known, in film work only for the fat Hollywood checks he needed to get back to his own line. He liked pictures and felt his talent was particularly well-suited to the medium."

Scott was not too good for film work in general, but when it came to *Winter Carnival* he was in no hurry to get started. On the one hand he was used to something better—*Three Comrades*, *Infidelity*, *Madame Curie*, or even *Gone with the Wind*. But on the other hand, since he had had trouble with the big movies he had worked on, now his confidence was crippled and he was not sure if he could handle even a small one.

Schulberg didn't worry. Why should he, with an Immortal helping him to write his script? He supposed that his collaborator was quietly working out the story and would presently interrupt their sprawling conversation to say, "Here's what we're going to do."

Meanwhile, in the quiet of the Valley nights, Sheilah Graham would hear Scott pacing back and forth, as if by moving the body he might trick the mind into motion too, or at least wear out his insomnia. "I was going to sleep every night with a gradually increasing dose of chloral," he wrote, "—three teaspoonfuls—and two pills of Nembutal every night and 48 drops of Digitalin to keep the heart working to the next day. Eventually one begins to feel like a character out of *The Wizard of Oz*. Work becomes meaningless and effort a matter of the medicine closet." One morning he announced, "My TB's flared up." He began to run a low fever and to sweat his bed wet at night. Sheilah would change his sheets two or three times before morning.

The miles he walked within the confines of a single room, and the hours spent with a writing tablet to catch his thoughts as they fell, finally produced something tangible, a ten-page treatment for *Winter Carnival*. It began:

"First, as to the approach: Frankly, I haven't been able to look at this as a group picture in the sense that *Stagecoach* was, or *Grand Hotel*, with its sharp cuts between one melodrama scene and another. A winter carnival simply doesn't have that tense air of destiny that a journey has. It's a spreadout and expansive theme in itself. It has no real trajectory like a boat or stagecoach or a train. In the Dartmouth carnival the election of a queen is the committee's attempt to give it such a climax. So in my opinion this should be more akin to *She Loves Me Not*—it ought to have something of a plot."

The author had studied his movie classics in the same way he had once studied classic novels.

The story Schulberg had written was about a glamour girl named Jill who takes her baby girl and flees her tyrannical husband, only to be stranded in mid-flight at Dartmouth during Winter Carnival when she gets off the train to stretch, and then stands helplessly by as the locomotive pulls off without her. To make matters worse, if Jill's husband catches up with her before she makes it across the border into Canada, he will take her child away from her. Even at a snow carnival with the temperature below zero, Hollywood could still make the old pot boil.

To Schulberg's brew, Fitzgerald wanted to add a villainess, a girl named Florine who in many ways resembled his own daughter Scottie. "She is a freshman at Vassar," he wrote, "and completely dazzled by New York—so much so that she has neglected her work and is on probation in college, a probation which she has broken to come to Dartmouth Winter Carnival, pretending she has been summoned home by the illness of her father. She is wild and feverish—in 1920, she would have been a flapper. At present she thinks she is ahead of the times, but she is really behind them."

Scott also invented a "side-kick" for Florine, a girl known simply as the "little 'blind date' girl." "She never *does* meet her blind date, but goes *without a man* through the carnival," Fitzgerald wrote, "—a staid-faced, unsmiling little girl who might be good for a lot of laughs."

In an effort to give the story some plot, the aging screenwriter suggested that they pit Jill and Florine against one another in the competition for the title of Carnival Queen. "Later in the day the girls are together in a fraternity house," he wrote. "There Jill learns that Florine is going to run for Queen and is sure to win. Jill realizes that if Florine wins, it will be in all the newspapers and she will be summarily kicked out of Vassar for breaking probation. Florine knows it too, but like a little fool is going to run. Jill in a friendly way warns her about this . . . and Florine is snippy, then furious—everything must yield to youth. Out of the way, last year's girl!"

At the Carnival, Jill becomes re-acquainted with Instructor Stuart, who had been smitten by her four years before when she, then a college girl, visited the Carnival for the first time. But when he meets her this time he tells her that "years ago he knew she would never be the girl in his life because she objected to waxing her own skiis." Scott was clearly tired of helpless heroines.

As a snowstorm arises—and Fitzgerald was about to learn just how miserable a Dartmouth snowstorm could be—Jill is crowned Queen. But before she can savor her victory beside a warm log fire, she learns that her child, its nurse, and a driver have been lost in the blizzard. When the car is finally located, it turns out to be on the other side of a swollen stream, and of course the bridge has been washed out. Instructor Stuart straps on a St. Bernard pack and prepares to ski jump the stream to rescue the stranded party. "There is suspense, Jill waxes Stuart's skis, torches blaze in the twilight. Then Climax—he jumps and make it—torch in air."

That was all the script they had, ten sketchy pages, when Wanger suggested that Fitzgerald and Schulberg accompany the camera crew which would shoot background footage at that year's Dartmouth Winter Carnival. Scott protested that he remembered the Carnival well enough from his own college days, but Wanger was going home to his alma mater and he wanted a prize to show off to his old teachers. Unfortunately, Wanger's trophy had dissipated much of its luster by the time the picture people reached Dartmouth. The dissipation began when B. P. Schulberg arrived at the Los Angeles airport to see his son off on his first big assignment and handed over a present, two bottles of vintage Mumm's. As soon as Budd and Scott, sitting next to one another in the plane, were in the air, the younger writer suggested a toast. The alcoholic writer said no at first, but was eventually persuaded.

They talked and toasted their way through the night. Fitzgerald seemed to have the same feeling about the twenties which some people have about their old school: he was chauvinistic about the entire decade. He reminisced about the writers of the twenties: "Bunny" Wilson, Ernest Hemingway, Carl Van Vechten, Gertrude Stein. About the athletes of the twenties: Bobby Jones, Red Grange, Babe Ruth, Jack Dempsey. About the movie stars of the twenties: Mary Pickford, Lillian Gish, Barbara La Marr, Gloria Swanson, Carmel Myers.

The closest they came to working on *Winter Carnival* was to discuss the picture's pipe-smoking Ivy League producer. Scott described him as "Ivy on one side, California palm on the other." The second bottle of champagne followed the first.

They decided to put off working on the script until they got to their hotel in New York; it would be easier to think once they had a room to do it in. But when they had checked into the Hotel Warwick, the four walls didn't help that much. They piled one dismally unworkable idea on top of another, but no progress was evident. Finally Budd decided to go out and look for some old friends. He asked if Fitzgerald minded. Not at all. Scott would take a long bath to relax and then make some notes on what to do about *Winter Carnival*.

When the young writer returned to the Warwick, Scott was missing. Instead of his collaborator, he found a note on his bed. "Pal you shouldn't have left me pal," it said in letters which seemed to stagger across the page, "because I got lonely pal and went down to the bar pal and started drinking pal, and now you may never find me pal. . . ."

As it turned out, Scott was easy to find. Budd rushed down to the street and then began systematically checking every bar he came to. A few doors from the Warwick, there he was, or least there was a part of him, the part the alcohol had not dissolved. The younger man brought the older one back to the hotel and put him through the treatment: black coffees, cold showers. Fitzgerald sobered up enough to apologize and then Schulberg apologized, too. They promised each other to work, *work*, and the rest of the night they tried to. After all, they had a deadline. That morning they were supposed to report to Wanger's suite and tell him their Carnival story.

The two screenwriters really had not been able to appreciate how tired and even shabby they were until they saw how clean and rested the producer was. Wanger looked at them—an old story—and then decided to make the best of the uneasy situation. He asked about the plane trip—Had they seen anyone they knew? Schulberg answered innocently, "Let's see, oh, yes, Sheilah Graham was on the plane." She and Scott had seemed surprised. What a coincidence.

Wanger did what Hollywood calls a "takem." Then he said disapprovingly, "Scott, you son of a bitch."

The story conference went as badly as the preliminaries had. After the disaster was over, Budd found himself apologizing once again.

"Holy God, Scott," he said, "I'm terribly sorry. I never would have mentioned her if I had . . ."

"All my fault," Scott said. "I should have told you. Maybe it's just as well it's out in the open with Walter anyway. I don't know why I feel I have to hide things from him like a schoolboy."

Scott Fitzgerald, the symbol of the younger generation in the 1920s, boarded a train in New York later that day along with carloads of girls who were seventeen, eighteen, nineteen—occasionally there would be a veteran of twenty or twenty-one. They were all going to the Winter Carnival to see several thousand boys who had been marooned on a lonely New Hampshire campus for too long. When the girls came home, they would make their adventures sound like the blurbs on the back of lurid novels. Like them, Fitzgerald too hoped to come home with a story, but one that could be filmed.

Schulberg called it a "wild, surrealist train ride north to Hanover." Fitzgerald started telling the students on the train—many of whom did not believe him—who he was and how much money he made. The students in turn mocked the middle-aged man who was obviously too old to be going to house parties.

The train stopped at a small town; the cars had become a trap to the screenwriters, so they decided to get off, stretch, and have a cup of coffee. They could see the lights of an all-night diner and headed in that direction. Inside the warm shabbiness of the place a radio played tunes dedicated to people who lived nearby, people who would never be more famous than when the disc jockey read their names over the air. The two Hollywood refugees stayed on a little too long listening to the waitress flirt with some truck drivers.

They arrived back at the railroad tracks in time to see the train pulling away without them. The same thing had happened to Jill in Fitzgerald's *Winter Carnival* treatment, but it was too late for the screenwriter to remember that he might have known. They floundered about searching for a plan and then located a taxi, an old Model A which had somehow outlived the F. Scott Fitzgerald era and was still running in 1939. The cabbie agreed to drive them to the next town in the hope that they could get there before the train did. It was so cold that the two men found a blanket and pulled it up over their heads to make a tent, then sipped at the applejack the driver had given them as anti-freeze. Sometime around four in the morning they finally caught up with the trainload of students and moving-picture people. Their careers were saved.

On the train once again, Scott fought back drink and cold and T.B. to come up with an opening shot for *Winter Carnival.* He was so excited about his inspiration that he hustled Schulberg down the corridor to Wanger's Pullman, where at just after five a.m. he hammered at the door until the producer let them in. What the hell did they want? Scott told him. He had a great opening and he had to tell Wanger all about it, cou'n wait, no shir. They would fade in on an Indian school with roomful of young bucks all being solemnly addressed by a Great White Teacher. CUT TO: outside a pack of young squaws rush toward the school on snowshoes. CUT TO: Indian maidens bursting into schoolroom and waltzing around with the braves, bringing the lessons to a fast halt. FADE OUT. FADE IN ON the girls disembarking from train for Dartmouth's Winter Carnival. Get it? Fantashtic, baby, jus' fantashtic. Wanger did not seem to like the opening as much as Scott did. He stared at the author with the unblinking eye of a potato and then went back to bed.

The two writers got no more sleep that night than the night before. They arrived at Dartmouth exhausted, in need of nothing so much as a bed. But there had been a slip-up: the producer had a suite and all of the directors, assistant directors, and cameramen had rooms, but no one had thought to make a reservation for the two men who were supposed to write the picture. Scott insisted on taking the whole thing as a metaphor for Hollywood's opinion of writers. At last the hotel manager found a place for them—a small room with no furniture except a metal two-decker bed up in the attic. This room was even less help than the one back at the Warwick—in fact, it was a positive hindrance. Schulberg remembers the room as a place where "for two days we fumed, labored, drank, suffered icy research, nerve-wracking deadlines and humiliating public receptions."

"One of the things that impressed me most in the course of that arctic weekend hell," says Schulberg, "was the quality of Scott's creative intelligence and the courage of his humor. He was constantly noticing little things that amazed me—details of academic life as exact as the lexicon of O'Hara. . . . At the very moment when the faculty and student onlookers were laughing at him as a drunk and a clown, his accuracy toward them was muffled but deadly."

At a party which one of the movie people gave, a group of professors took it upon themselves to criticize the picture Fitzgerald had come east to make. Scott sank into a chair and listened. From time to time, he would wave his hand and complain, "Lotta nonsense." When he had had enough, he rose and said, "You know, I'd love to be a professor in a university like this with all the security and the smug niceties, instead of having to put up with the things we have to put up with out there in the world. I bid you goodnight, gentlemen." When the author left, the professors said wasn't it too bad about poor Scott.

Schulberg's "other memories of that nightmare weekend" include:

"Scott's trudging through the deep snow to the ski jump in his baggy suit, his wrinkled overcoat and his battered fedora, a gray, grim joke to the young, hearty Carnival couples in their bright-color ski clothes, and of his zombie walk to the door, saying, 'I'm going to Zelda, she needs me. I'm going to Zelda. . . .' This was the first time he had mentioned his wife, whose unfortunate illness had dropped a dark curtain between them. I remember dragging him back from the door and throwing him down on the cot, hard. I remember thinking he had passed out again and beginning to take off his shoes, and his reviving enough to say, 'Oh, you must be enjoying yourself, feeling so strong, so young, so damn sure of yourself. . . .' And I remember losing my patience and temper with him at last and running out to a friendly fraternity bar where I tried to drown our common sorrows, until mysteriously, inescapably, he tracked me down and we went out into the Carnival night laughing and improvising scandalous songs like any other two Carnival celebrants."

In their carnival mood the two screenwriters met Walter Wanger by accident in front of the Hanover Inn. Standing up on the steps, like a Puritan minister looking down on his congregation, the producer fired the two writers and told them to get out of town. They caught the Montrealer back to New York and found that in their condition no New York hotel, not even the shabby ones, would take them in. Once again they had no room. They rode up and down Manhattan in a cab searching fruitlessly until finally Scott whispered "Doctor's Hospital." Scott Fitzgerald's Winter Carnival ended between snowy white hospital sheets.

When he returned to Hollywood, Schulberg was rehired to finish the picture—but not Fitzgerald. "Wanger will never forgive me for this," Scott told Schulberg at one point. "He sees himself as the intellectual producer and he was going to impress Dartmouth by showing them he used real writers, not vulgar hacks, and here I, his real writer, have disgraced him before the whole college."

Malcolm Cowley has called Fitzgerald's Dartmouth Winter Carnival "his biggest, saddest, most desperate spree." Scott himself said, "In retrospect, going east under those circumstances seems one of the silliest mistakes I ever made."

Remembering December 7, 1941

by EDDIE O'BRIEN

Commemorating the fortieth anniversary of the Japanese bombing of Pearl Harbor and America's consequent entry into the Second World War, Edward A. O'Brien Jr. 1943 prepared this reminiscence for publication, under the heading "A record of their fame," in the November 1981 *Alumni Magazine*.

OR MANY people living in Hanover, the day had deeper significance than any other in their lives. Only the moment of birth
would have more effect on the condition of their stay on earth.
For a few, it was the beginning of the end; for nearly all the end of the
beginning. It was, in some ways, an ordinary Sunday in December,
but events 6,000 miles away signaled a complete change in outlook,
an abrupt awakening, a dramatic introduction to realities of conflict.
In the casual, sheltered dormitories and leafy academic surroundings
a way of life was soon to be uprooted. The clean-shaven, short-haired,
lusty young men—cynics or idealists, team players and individual-
ists—would be transported beyond their control or their imagination. Within the next five years they would come to learn the precise
meaning of "the luck of the draw."

Many would eventually bring their experiences back to Hanover.
Some would never return. They would suffer fatal training accidents,
take bullets as they hit the beaches, fall from the sky, or perish in PW
camps. There were many ways to die. Eventually, their names would
be incised on a polished granite plaque, situated on the wall of a
building they never saw, in a place that people seldom visit—the back
porch of the Hopkins Center snack bar.

As the bells of Baker clanged 10:00 a.m., sleepers still occupied
most beds in the dormitories and fraternity houses. Only a few committed students were up and around that overcast morning.
Breakfasters at Thayer Hall numbered fewer than the help. The skies
were slate gray and unappealing. A trace of snow covered the ground,
left over from Saturday's flurries. There was the threat of a little more.
The air was jacket-chilly but not cold enough to produce skateable ice

at Davis Rink, a fact that frustrated Eddie Jeremiah. The hockey coach had been hustling his players from ponds to local prep schools in an effort to get them ready for a season that would include a western trip over Christmas vacation and warm-ups at home against M.I.T. and Norwich. The sophomore line of Riley, Harrison, and Rondeau (all '44) had shown remarkable promise as yearlings. Jeremiah was anxious to see them in varsity league play. But the lack of artificial refrigeration and mild weather was pushing his patience. His captain, Ted Lapres '42, needed work in the nets, and he couldn't get it on Occom Pond.

A scattering of Catholic students were on their way to St. Denis's. They cut through South College, a street that disappeared when Hopkins Center was built, to the church on Lebanon Street where they heard Father Sliney read the gospel according to Saint Matthew and deliver his sermon. There were also services at Rollins Chapel, the White Church, and St. Thomas's Episcopal on West Wheelock. None drew as many students as a Hedy Lamarr movie called *Ecstasy.* [. . .]

Early in the week, Lewis Mumford, the philosopher, was on campus to speak to classes and give an evening lecture. "One of the sad things about America," Mumford told the students, "is that its memory is short—there is a lack of continuity between generations. Many of the men written about in the *American Caravan* were great writers in the 1920s but their importance has vanished—all that is left is memories the editors hold of the men."

And Europe was on fire. Hitler's armies had rolled almost parade fashion through Norway. The Netherlands, Belgium, and France fell as quickly. Now, in December, the Germans were within striking distance of Moscow. At Dartmouth's convocation earlier in the fall, President Hopkins had talked to the students about the menace, saying, with peculiar indirectness, "When preponderantly among the peoples of the earth, might reigns and gives its own perverted definition as to what constitutes right, at such a time right, as defined by the mind and conscience of man through the ages, must oppose with greater might, if it is to survive." This was not exactly a call to arms. The address was entitled "The Probability of the Impossible."

The prevailing mood in Hanover was one of conscious, maybe even nervous, anticipation. Surely, there were both anxiety and a sense of helplessness. For some there was, indeed, an escape hatch showing a little crack of light, a way to chuck it all, with honor. It was vague but not wholly foreboding. A number of seniors and juniors had already registered for the draft but were given time to finish college. Still others had chosen to leave school and enlist, usually in the Army or Naval Air Corps, but some joined the Marine Corps or the Royal Canadian Air Force via Montreal. Dropping out just one or two at a time, these departures were nevertheless widely noted. A few Chi Phis of '42 had joined their '41 classmates, who had already graduated, in what was to be a Dartmouth Naval Air Training Unit at Squantum, Massachusetts.

A Dartmouth student poll, taken in October by *The Dartmouth*, showed that 284, or one-third of the students who responded, favored the United States going immediately to war against Germany. The same question asked in 1940 showed only 75 students with that answer. A Gallup poll, taken in mid-November as an inter-collegiate survey, suggested that Dartmouth students led the nation in "willingness to go to war." The conclusions were somewhat shaky, but the point seems to have been that eastern students were more involved than midwesterners and Dartmouth more aggressively interested than other schools.

But, like students in Ann Arbor or Columbus, undergraduates in Hanover were not wholly preoccupied with the war. On Saturday night, December 6, the Nugget Theater, then located on Wheelock Street behind Casque and Gauntlet, played to a rowdy student house, at 35 cents a head. The show: *Nine Lives are Not Enough*, starring Robert Preston and Ellen Drew.

It was an off-weekend. Many rides had left at noon to go over the mountain to Saratoga Springs and Skidmore or down Route 5 to Northampton, Smith, and Rahar's, the roomy five-cent-hard-boiled-egg and fifteen-cent-beer tavern. Alex Fanelli and Jerry Tallmer, both '42, figured it was to be a quiet weekend so together they rented a car from another student for five dollars and drove to Wellesley where they had late Saturday night dates. Tallmer was editor-in-chief of *The Dartmouth* and Fanelli was editorial chairman.

The hockey game with Norwich was cancelled because the ice was too soft and not enough of it. A concert by the Rochester Philharmonic and Jose Iturbi was delayed, and Slim from Tanzi's delivered a number of kegs to fraternity houses where brothers pooled their resources and chipped in for the beer. There were the usual arm-wrestling matches, bull sessions about women, and guzzling "crew"

184 Miraculously Builded in Our Hearts

races among the mostly male crowd. The late-stayers sang "Bridget O'Flynn," "We'll Build a Bungalow," and "The Fireman's Ball." Two girls in saddleshoes from Colby Junior hung around and tried to teach "Minnie the Mermaid" to a confused sophomore who only wanted to sing "Minnesota, Hats Off to Thee." It was Saturday night.

Sunday was intended as a respite, a time to charge up for the impending exams. A few late risers, some wearing their green 1943 numeral sweaters, unpressed gray flannels, and dirty white buck shoes strolled down to the quiet Main Street. They could buy an ice-cream cone at Allen's or the New York *Times* at Putnam's Drug Store or check out Fletcher's, which was closed. They could peek into the store windows and see skis with steel edges and bindings, complete for $15.50, at Art Bennett's. Button-down Manhattan shirts at Campions sold for $2.50. By noon, it was time for either the stacks in Baker or the radio. [. . .]

At dawn, the voice on the radio said, Japanese planes had come in over the island of Oahu and bombed Pearl Harbor, a Naval installation in the territory of Hawaii. In addition, low-flying Zeros with Japanese markings had strafed and bombed an Army air base called Hickam Field. [. . .] American casualties were said to be high. Word leaped across the campus like news of, well, like news of a war.

Andy Caffrey '43 was in Baker Library studying for a political science exam. Someone said out loud, "The Japs bombed Pearl Harbor." Caffrey's line was repeated so many times across America that it has now become a classic: "Where's Pearl Harbor?"

Bad news has fast legs. The town of Hanover changed its sleepy Sunday afternoon character. Someone with a keen sense of history caused the bells of Baker to ring out patriotic melodies. Flags appeared on the residences as if by decree. Somehow, the stripes of red looked redder, the whites looked more pure, and the 48 stars stood out against the blue field more clearly than ever before. Even the dogs moved cautiously, but quickly, in packs. Steve Flynn '44 and Bill Mitchel '42 rushed to man the newly formed Dartmouth Broadcasting System control room in lower Robinson Hall. It was their first crisis, and they made a gutsy effort to piece together the teletype news and get on the air in some reasonable, logical fashion. They had the audience.

Tallmer and Fanelli had stayed with friends at Harvard overnight but returned to Hanover early that Sunday afternoon. They were in the offices of *The Dartmouth* assembling Monday's issue when they heard the news. Both men had worked on the paper's extra edition at the time of the Dartmouth-Cornell Fifth Down drama in 1940. The thought of another extra occurred to them almost simultaneously. They gathered their forces and went to work. Jim Farley and Craig Kuhn, both '42, pieced together what sketchy information was available. At first, it was thought that the Japanese had bombed Manila along with Honolulu. Joe Palamountain '42 hammered out a thoughtful editorial in line with *The Dartmouth*'s position as outlined by Tallmer. It was a heady evening punctuated with coffee at George Gitsis' Campus Cafe, located a few doors away from the Dartmouth Printing Company on Main Street. There was an extra to get out; moreover, the composition of the Monday, December 8, issue had to be thoroughly revised to adjust to the war facts. No other information was really vital to young men 20 or 21 years old.

By 8:21 p.m. the seasoned staff had the extra on the streets of Hanover. Headline: JAPS DECLARE WAR ON U.S.—SHOOTING BEGINS. It was a single sheet printed on both sides. President Roosevelt's picture was on the front page. Palamountain's editorial was headed "Now It Has Come." Essentially, it expressed relief that the waiting was over. Its final line: "And so, as we enter this fight for our life, we thank the Japanese for enabling us to enter a *united* people."

In his dormitory, Bob Craig '43, a Honolulu resident for 15 years, became a reservoir of information. He described the situation as "inconceivable," adding, "the Navy is supposed to maintain a 200-mile patrol around the harbor."

Takanobu "Knobby" Mitsui '43 lived in Massachusetts Hall. He was a member of one of the leading Japanese families. He talked that evening with Dean Lloyd Neidlinger and decided to remain in school, cabling his parents that he was "in no personal danger and would finish college."

In the basements of fraternities, friends viewed each other with a new sense of evaluation. Decisions were made and remembered. The thought of "soldiering" with this one or that one was often based on past performances on the athletic field, a ready means of measuring physical courage, wit, resourcefulness, and endurance.

By Monday, the chaos of the weekend had begun to be sorted out. President Roosevelt and Congress declared war on both Japan and Germany. The call to arms had sounded. On the following Wednesday, December 10, the editors of *The Dartmouth* demonstrated leadership as good as their word. Both Fanelli and Tallmer left school to enlist. They were two of many.

Others on campus worked things out. They congregated and talked and, together and alone, searched their souls. They called home when they could get to a phone, and sometimes they called girls. They drifted away from Hanover, one by one, or they made deals with the Army and Navy, gaining a little time. By December of 1942 the Navy had commandeered the Dartmouth campus and others as well. Whoever was left went on assignment, in uniform—to Notre Dame, Columbia, Quantico boot camp, Fort Dix, Squantum, Randolph Field.

They would soon enough find themselves among new companions, packed in troop trains and ships, some destinations so foreign as to be completely unknown. Many would fly for the first time in their lives. Months later they would pilot four-engine bombers across the North Atlantic in groups of one hundred. Systematically they would arrive in faraway places with strange sounding names. They would discover red tape, symbolism, volley ball, boredom, steel helmets, raw courage, ingenuity, fire-power, V-mail, and girls who did not speak or understand English. Some ultimately would hear English and be unable to understand it. On occasion they would find each other again in the noisy snake pits and juke-bars of San Francisco, in the grimy pubs of London, on the sun-baked coral runways of tiny Pacific atolls, in freezing Quonset huts in the Aleutians, on the busy decks of massive gray carriers. They would come to know the sights and sounds of *kamikaze* and the shattering blast of Browning Automatic Rifles. They would bellow "Dartmouth's In Town Again" in cafés of the Montmartre, and pray to Michael the Archangel as they were dropped across the Rhine. And some would shout "wah-hoo-wah" on the intercom, 18,000 feet above the Ruhr Valley. Still others would do white-collar clerical work, struggling at cryptography or statistical profiles in little offices around Washington, at Brooklyn Navy Yard, or in Dayton, Ohio. It was the game of American roulette, and there were losers and winners. With it all there was a euphoric sense of adventure, a taste of vertical and horizontal travel, even though the price of the tickets was high.

The momentous events of the next few years would bring death and sorrow, love and joy, honor and glory. The memories of what happened before and after that fateful Sunday are in sharp focus because the men of the time fulfilled a tradition that cannot be denied. They signed up and took their chances.

People had, reasonably, predicted that the promising political science major, Stubbie Pearson, would some day be governor of Minnesota—at least. He died piloting a dive bomber in an attack on a Japanese cruiser off the Palau Islands. Both Stan Wright '42 and Ambie Broughton '43, of the hockey team without December ice, died in the sweltering Pacific. Wright was a Marine, shot moving in on Tarawa, Broughton, co-pilot in a B-24, on a bomb run. Jack Nunnemacher, with the 10th Mountain Division, was mortally wounded in the mountains of Italy. John Smith '43 was killed in action, on December 7, 1944, in the Philippines. There were many others.

At graduation, Pearson had said in his valedictory to the class of 1942: "This is the war for the future. Man must replace the importance of material gain. We must humanize ourselves. Man is man and that is all that is important. . . . Do not feel sorry for us. We are not sorry for ourselves. Today we are happy. We have a duty to perform and we are proud to perform it."

World War II on Hanover Plain

by RAY NASH

⋙ Long a member of the College's Art Department and an internationally known authority in the field of printing and graphic art, Ray Nash in his book *Navy at Dartmouth* (1946) chronicles on-campus developments centering upon America's preparation for, and then active participation in, the Second World War.

T HE BEAT of war drums, muffled and distant at the opening of 1940, continually grew more distinct through the nation and in New England their rat-a-tat was loudest. Student Opinion Surveys of America, as published in *The Dartmouth*, early in November reported a small majority of American college students still thinking it more important for the United States to keep out of war than to aid Britain, but in New England, a full year before the Japanese attack, the poll indicated that one and a fraction out of three college men was ready to volunteer immediately for armed service in event of war against Germany, Italy or Japan. The actual figure was thirty-six per cent, as compared with twenty-three and a half per cent for the country at large. As the year drew to a close these surveys revealed that during twelve months five per cent of American college students had lost faith in the ability of the United States to keep out of the European war: the percentage dropped from sixty-eight to sixty-three, although a dwindling majority of fifty-three per cent remained "isolationist". [. . . .]

Through 1941 the drumbeat tempo quickened and its volume swelled to a heady roll. President Roosevelt in January called President Hopkins to the Iron and Steel Priorities Board, beginning the exodus which was to draw nearly half the official family into national service. [. . . .] Dartmouth definitely faced the war issue in the spring of 1941. The gap had closed: "interventionist" student leaders were crowding the president and the American Defense Dartmouth Group. Their generosity was stirred profoundly and their sense of justice outraged by each new Axis conquest. They could no longer feel free to lie in the sun and to picnic on the Pompanoosuc. On April 24 their spokesman, Charles Guy Bolté, printed on the front page of *The Dartmouth* a "Letter to the President of the United States" beginning "Now we have waited long enough" and appealing for American pilots, mechanics, soldiers and sailors to be sent at once where they were needed: "We cannot win without fighting. . . . We can lose without fighting. . . . We can win if we fight now." Immediately after graduation the author, with a number of companions, joined the King's Royal Rifles—the old Royal Americans—and went overseas to seek out the enemy.

The class day exercises showed that the decision had been taken, reluctantly but irrevocably. Said the class poet, Thomson H. Littlefield[:] "We'll be going to the war, for the war [/] Needs us. It finds us prepared. [. . .]" and Charles B. McLane in the customary address to the College included the following credo:

"Today our world is 'powerless to be born'. But it will not always be so. I cannot imagine our being forever in this state of confusion and uncertainty. If we are wise we will not destroy those preparations we have already made for the birth we are expecting. We must have faith—faith in the particular, uncomplicated things we know and believe in today, that we can get our hands on quickly. . . ." [. . .]

The address to the Old Pine by Jack Brister was brief, sober and eloquent. The closing words, from a man who could not wait for American entry into the war and fell while leading his Tommies in battle, are memorable:

"There is no need to justify our love for Dartmouth, just as there is no need to justify our love for our country. And yet remember that this love means trying to understand, it means forgiving, it means fighting what we know to be wrong.

"Loyalty is not an easy thing. It's not a promise to pay or the paying of club dues. It's not something we can here create by swearing or pledging to. Loyalty is something we can't help. The loyalty is in us. As the grain is in the wood, the loyalty has grown in us. We must be worthy of the grain we bear."

The tide had turned and was running toward war. The mood in the Bema, where a few uniforms already shone among the black gowns of the graduating class, was one of sober resignation. [. . .]

Under governmental direction the nation was transforming into a mighty machine to produce the necessaries of war. In its sphere the College kept pace. In April—while *The Dartmouth* aired its conversion to all-out, short-of-nothing aid to the Allies and the National Youth Committee Against War fought a student poll on the question of war entry—the president announced the new official Committee on Defense Instruction, following a report late in the winter on planning courses with a view to "defense" work or service in the armed forces. This ten-man board was set up to advise students, standing as arbiter between undergraduates and their draft boards, and generally to supervise the adjustment of College courses and procedures to the national emergency. [...]

The Committee on Defense Instruction pondered early and long the proposal that properly qualified students be given the opportunity to complete their full college program in three years instead of the normal four. In midsummer of 1941 there was indication that Dartmouth was prepared to take this step if it should become necessary, but no definite decision was announced when College opened. "Pearl Harbor" settled the question and the middle of December at a special convocation President Hopkins told students that the accelerated program had been adopted. [...]

The marching began in Hanover in the summer of 1942 when a Naval Training School (Indoctrination) opened at the College on July 14. [...]

From July until the following June 4, 1943 when the Naval Training School (Indoctrination) closed to make way for the Dartmouth V-12 unit, more than five thousand men, most of them lately commissioned lieutenants in the Naval Reserve, from all walks of life and every part of the country, passed through this eight weeks' preparatory course. [...]

When America entered the war the Navy moved promptly to supplement the program for training volunteer reserve officers authorized by the Officer Reserve Act of 1938, under which many college men were already heading toward the midshipmen's schools. [...]

The V-12 program, designed as the comprehensive plan for all naval officer procurement through the colleges—except aviation cadets—was outlined by the Naval Advisory Council on Education in August of 1942, following initiative taken in the matter by the training division of the Bureau of Naval Personnel. In November it came through in recommended form to President Roosevelt who approved it December 1. [...]

Although the general scheme of V-12 had been announced in the middle of December 1942, the men of Dartmouth, as late as Washington's birthday following, were still asking themselves what part the College was going to have in the plan. Of the total enrollment in college of twelve hundred fifty, about half normal strength, more than five hundred were aspiring sailors and marines already accepted and sworn in who awaited the word from Washington with what patience they could muster. [. . .] February passed, then March, and finally, on April 5, flashed the message so long looked for: Dartmouth would have a V-12 unit. Thirteen hundred trainees—then a possible twenty-four hundred according to a rumored quota revision ten days later—would be on the campus July 1.

Dartmouth already had received more than a sprinkling of salt. For one thing, the Naval Training School (Indoctrination) had pretty thoroughly indoctrinated the College and community. For another, a proportion of undergraduates swelling toward half the campus population were already "in" and recognized the Bureau of Naval Personnel as well as the College as boss. In January these sailors-and-marines-to-be had totaled five hundred twelve [. . .]. Less than half as many Dartmouth undergraduates had signed up for the army.

Nothing so far was said about marines, although a broad hint had been dropped in April when the authorities of the First Naval District, asked if Dartmouth students in the Marine Corps Reserve would be reassigned to the College on July 1, answered with a flat yes. It was near the end of May before the grapevine began buzzing with news on the subject. An unidentified College spokesman was quoted by *The Dartmouth* as saying the matter was under consideration and at the same time the Harvard *Crimson* scooped its esteemed contemporary by announcing that "all marine reservists in eastern colleges may go to Dartmouth where there will be a unit of about six hundred." Captain Briggs, who was winding up his indoctrination school, capped these stories with his assertion that Major (later Lieutenant Colonel) John Howland USMCR, was about to arrive in Hanover. On June 9 the major actually turned up at the College and began preparing to receive a quota of six hundred sixty marine privates for training as an integral part of the V-12 Dartmouth unit.

Commander William F. Bullis USNR was the first commanding officer of the unit, although he remained in that capacity for less than one term. [. . .]

The first V-12 class at Dartmouth had been on the campus three months when the new commanding officer, Captain Damon E. Cummings u s n arrived in Hanover on October 4. [. . .] His first unit order dated October 16, 1943 contained the following paragraph which in itself constituted a sort of Dartmouth V-12 charter: "In the performance of their duties, officers shall cooperate closely with the appropriate College authorities, and shall be careful not to assume authority in matters which are the responsibility of the College." [. . .]

The College was in charge in the classroom as the Navy was in the gym. Under the V-12 curricular scheme, prescribed first year instruction focussed principally in five departments: mathematics, physics, English, graphics and history. In each one of them President Hopkins appointed a professor as director of V-12 work.

In addition a large new "department" was set up for teaching the courses in naval organization required of all trainees. It was established under the directorship of Professor Richard H. Goddard in the spring of 1943. A faculty group of more than a score recruited from various departments of the College was prepared for their venture into an entirely new field through a course conducted by Lieutenant C. K. Wallace of the seamanship department in the Naval Training School (Indoctrination) just then closing to make way for V-12. [. . .]

All the foregoing adjustments within the College were made to accommodate only the unspecialized, fully prescribed first and second term courses, and at the beginning that was all there were to worry about. By the opening of the March term, 1944, however, a considerable proportion of the trainees had advanced to the stage where specialized courses were demanded. There were many enrolled, for example, in the engineering courses such as elementary heat power and electrical engineering, in chemistry and psychology; more were taken care of at the Thayer School in civil engineering and at the Tuck School in pre-supply specialties. The Medical School had been included from the beginning in the V-12 scheme, operating as a distinct unit under the same commanding officer. The pre-medical curricula included work in chemistry, physics, mathematics, foreign language, naval organization and physical training. [. . .]

The problem of accommodation to all of this unaccustomed emphasis was not simplified by the continued presence on the campus of "irregulars" or students who had begun their college career before entering V-12 and were permitted wider latitude in election of courses than the "regulars", though their choice had to constitute an approach to the prescribed curriculum followed by the "regulars". And finally the College felt duty bound to the couple of hundred civilian students, either too young for military service or for other reasons excluded, to give them the very best opportunity to pursue the ancient search for truth and wisdom without the sense of being lost in an armed camp.

In the process of becoming the largest V-12 college in America almost overnight, Dartmouth was pushed out in some places and pulled in at others and all this caused inevitable strains and confusion. But what surprised everyone was the facility of adjustment. The transition from liberal college to training school was rapid and effectual owing to the same kind of administrative forehandedness already seen in the psychological preparation of the College for war. And it was everywhere lubricated by the eagerness and ability of faculty and staff to be of help in the national crisis. [. . .]

When the draft reached down to take eighteen-year-olds some campus cassandras gave the College only a few months to live, but the president recalled that in all five previous wars Dartmouth had participated in the national effort to such effect that its doors had never been allowed to close, and he expected the same would be true this time. [. . .]

The story of the Dartmouth V-12 unit rose to a climax at the end of winter term 1945. Instead of the rather impromptu, breathless graduation exercises which had marked the despatch of previous classes, the College on Sunday, February 11 contrived to hold a ceremony reminiscent of commencements in more favorable times, complete with printed programs and the faculty in full regalia on the Webster Hall platform.

The guest of honor and principal speaker on this occasion was Captain D. L. Madeira usn, director of training in the Bureau of Naval Personnel. [. . .] Captain Madeira soon had his audience in blue and green perched tensely on the edge of their seats. As everyone knew, he said, Congress had just acted favorably on the Navy's program for permanent naval reserve officer training courses in fifty colleges besides Annapolis. Of course nothing could be said officially, he observed slyly, because the legislation had yet to be finally approved by President Roosevelt, who was at the moment in the Crimea, but assuming the signature would be secured, the new plan had immediate interest for men in V-12. For instance, it would mean none of the members of the student audience would be in V-12 more than another term or so because V-12 was practically washed up, finished.

A dropped pin would have clattered on the floor of Webster as the speaker paused for his matter-of-factly spoken words to sink in. In place of V-12, he went on, there would be the Naval Reserve Officers' Training Corps, expanded by means of the addition of twenty-three new college units as yet unspecified—this time the sly glance was directed at President Hopkins nearby on the platform—to bring the total to fifty throughout the country. [. . .] The NROTC would, of course, call for a four year course of study, and commissions were to be granted only to those satisfactorily completing requirements for the degree. "The fact that Dartmouth hasn't sent two senators and twenty-five representatives to see us about getting a unit can be attributed either to Dartmouth's commendable faith in the Bureau of Personnel or, perhaps, to the fact that New Hampshire doesn't have twenty-five representatives," said Captain Madeira.

Under date of May 3, 1945 Vice Admiral Randall Jacobs, chief of naval personnel, wrote to President Hopkins:

"I take great pleasure in informing you that Dartmouth College has been selected as the location of one of the new units of the Naval Reserve Officers' Training Corps in accordance with the terms of your application. It is planned to commission the unit on or about 1 November 1945. [. . .]

The College forthwith proceeded with the business of winding up the affairs of its associated school, the Naval Training School (V-12)— of which the last four-month term opened on the second anniversary of its installation—and to establish a Department of Naval Science staffed by a faculty of officers provided by the Navy. As steps in the transition, the College faculty voted a special degree, bachelor of naval science, to be awarded trainees caught in the in-between stage who, by an inconsiderable margin, could not qualify for the regular B.A., and Dr. E. Gordon Bill, dean of the faculty, turned the "navy courses" over to the jurisdiction of the usual departments of the College in whose field they belonged, after dismissing the course directors with a benefaction for their valuable services. In this process an official delegation sent by Admiral Jacobs was of substantial assistance to the College authorities. [. . .]

Brotherly Advice
on Choosing a College

by PHILIP ALVAN SHRIBMAN

»»̀ Writing on February 18, 1942, from aboard the U.S. Navy transport ship *Crescent City*, somewhere in the Pacific, Philip Shribman 1941 both transmits counsel to his younger brother, Richard, and provides a testament of his own devotion to Dartmouth. Ensign Shribman died less than a year later, off Guadalcanal. His brother, Richard M. Shribman, did in due course follow him to Hanover, as a member of the Class of 1947. The letter has been lightly edited, for publication here, by his nephew, David M. Shribman 1976.

DEAR DICK: It's not very often of late that I get a chance to write you, but I feel like writing now, so might just as well go ahead. It's growing on me with increasing rapidity that you're about set to go to college—and tho' I'm one hell of a guy to talk—and tho' I hate preaching—let me just write this & we'll call it quits.

I'm quite sure that this letter won't do much good—not because you won't heed it—but because I know, from my own experience and observations both, that a person only learns by personal experience—by doing.

I don't much care where you go to college—any top school is as good as the next—but this I know: No matter where it is, you'll hardly begin to appreciate it till it's all over. It's sad but true. Today I wouldn't trade my four years at Dartmouth for any & everything in the world. I got to truly love that school. [. . .]

If you went to a trade school you'd have one thing you could do & know—& you'd miss the whole world of beauty. In a liberal[-arts] school you know "nothing"—& are "fitted for nothing" when you get out. Yet, you'll have a fortune of broad outlook—of appreciation for people and beauty that money won't buy. You can always learn to be a mechanic or pill mixer etc., but it's only when you're of college age that you can learn that life has beauty & fineness. Afterwards it's all struggle, war: economic if not actual. Don't give up the idea & ideals of a liberal[-arts] school. They're too precious, too rare, too important.

195

As for your studies, yes, they're important—not because they teach you something concretely, but because it's thru them that ultimately you'll pick up the things you'll later find valuable. And you'll enjoy, after a time, the comparative ease with which a well trained mind absorbs. [. . .]

Dick, the more I'm away from Dartmouth the more it means to me. I'd take a janitor's job there now just to be there; not that I'm afraid to be out here, or afraid I'm liable to get it: not at all. I'm happy here & doing just what I want—what's right—but—well, it's hard to put "love" into any concrete terms, & if you ask Mom and Dad they'll tell you I really "loved" Dartmouth as much as any fellow can "love" an institution. Any college will be just a jumble of stones, cement, land, & men till you add yourself to them & give to the school as well as receive from it.

You'll do O.K. I think, cause if you just get off your fanny I know you've got the stuff. Mostly: Look around you—keep your eyes open—try to see what's what—hold onto the things that you know to be right. They'll shake your faith in a lot of the things you now think are right. That's good—& part of education—but look around & try to make up your own ideas on life & its values. [. . .]

Read what you want, do what you want. I'm far from a moralist. I think only one person can tell you if you're doing the right thing— that's yourself. By that I don't mean don't listen to advice—just remember that you ultimately live with yourself & you pay for any mistakes *yourself*, not the people who gave you the punk advice. Condemnation is easy to get, praise the opposite, Dad always says. A guy can be good all his life, but if he makes one slip near the end, no one remembers all the good things.

But I'm getting off the track. I really haven't much point in writing this—just an old alum beginning to envy a prospective freshman—& hoping that you get as much if not more out of college as I did. [. . .]

And if at the end of college—if there are still people in the world around who'd like to deny experiences like it to others—why I hope that you, like me, think it's all worth while to get in & fight for. One always has to protect the valuable in this world before he can enjoy it. Good luck to you—and make the most of what you've got.

Most sincerely, always,
PHIL

A Joyful Spirit

by JOHN SLOAN DICKEY

➤➤ On August 29, 1945, the Board of Trustees made concurrent announcement of the intended retirement of Ernest Martin Hopkins (after twenty-nine years in the presidency) and their election of his successor, attorney John Sloan Dickey 1929, then serving in Washington, D.C., as Director of the U.S. State Department's Office of Public Affairs. The new President's first address to the College community was on Dartmouth Night, November 9, 1945, just eight days after his having taken office. The talk, which he entitled "A Joyful Spirit," is here reprinted from President Dickey's volume entitled *The Dartmouth Experience* (1977).

TWENTY-NINE years ago President Hopkins concluded his inaugural day, and began his great leadership, with a Dartmouth Night celebration.

You've all heard about the man who spent three years, instead of one, as a freshman—not, as you might think, because he was a little slow, but rather, as his mother explained, only because he was so very thorough. Well, I'm one of those thorough fellows. My inauguration began a week ago yesterday, but for me it won't be over until tonight's celebration is on the books. For Dartmouth Night is certainly one of the moments—and there are many others—when the Dartmouth spirit walks abroad. And whether a man be freshman or President, his induction to Dartmouth is not complete until he and that spirit have walked abroad together.

Tonight's gathering marks the fifty-first anniversary of the institution of Dartmouth Night. President Tucker founded it in 1895 for the purpose both of bringing the freshmen into the Dartmouth family and of bringing the entire College together—to use Hovey's words— in a "pledge of fellowship." Today, this Night is set aside by men of Dartmouth the world around as a time when worldly masks are laid aside, to share again the joys of a common fellowship and to pledge a new and ever-greater devotion to the College and its cause.

No man, I think, is entitled or is able to tell you just what Dartmouth is and what is its cause. But each man of us, I also think, owes it to himself, and perhaps to others in the fellowship, to have some

197

notion of what he expects of the College and what he wants for himself. I do believe that as we know these things we will better understand Dartmouth and her cause.

From the first, Dartmouth has been a liberal-arts college. It has been often said that the historic college is more concerned with men's lives than their livelihoods. And as far as I am concerned that is well, so long as we do not lose sight of the fact that there is some relationship, both backwards as well as forwards, between leading a good life and the way a man keeps alive.

The historic college has always insisted on its right and its duty to pursue the truth, without let or hindrance from prejudice or any other interest, and to make that truth known. And again, as far as I am concerned that is well, so long as we are sufficiently humble to grant to providence, and the next generation, the possibility that the truth of the day for us may not be an eternal verity—and, also, so long as this spirit of humility is not, in practice, carried clear across the spectrum of tolerance, to the point where men of knowledge and good will become incapable of action and leave the world's doing either to those who don't know or who don't care or, as in all-too-recent times, to those who do evil gladly.

This is not the occasion to speak too seriously too long, but because there is so little time and because we meet too infrequently these days, let me say just this much more on this point. As you gradually discover for yourselves the things you care most about—and I hope for you they may be the right things—don't take them for granted. In all your learning get not only wisdom, but also build the will and acquire the capacity for doing something about those things which need doing.

I personally care not very much whether your doing be in the public service or in the ranks of the citizenry. I do want very much that this generation of educated men of Dartmouth should "be ye doers of the word, and not hearers only, deceiving your own selves." And remember this: there is so little time.

But I have spoken of understanding Dartmouth, and that is not just understanding the basic liberal-arts objectives to which Dartmouth College, as one of the great historic colleges, subscribes.

Some have said that Dartmouth is not a college—that it is a religion. I take it that what is meant by this is that men who have lived together on Hanover Plain *believe* in Dartmouth. And whatever else may be said, surely that is true and surely that must be good. There are few things, or so it seems to me, which give as much satisfaction to a man as belonging to something in which he really believes.

Some may (and often do) ask, Why do men feel that way about Dartmouth? Is there really any such thing as the Dartmouth spirit? I doubt for my part that there is any one answer to those questions, unless it be that these men who feel that way about Dartmouth lived together on Hanover Plain and that ever since the days of Eleazar Wheelock this plain has also been the dwelling place of the spirits of the men who over the years built this College. As any good country-man will tell you, you cannot live with a spirit but that spirit gets inside you. However else the Dartmouth spirit may manifest itself, it does give rise to a sense of family, to a sense of belonging to some-thing together. Hovey has done a better job than anyone else in putting it into words. A time comes to almost every man who has lived on this campus, when he sings those words "as brother stands by brother" he suddenly realizes that he belongs to a larger family—and is the better for it.

A week ago the Trustees of Dartmouth College took an action which characterizes as well as any single thing I know that sense of family which exists among Dartmouth men and between the College and her sons. The evening before President Hopkins retired the Trustees voted to establish the Ernest Martin Hopkins Scholarships for the benefit of the sons of Dartmouth men who gave their lives in military service during World War II. The holders of such scholar-ships will receive tuition, room, and board and be known as "Hopkins Scholars." This means that during the next twenty years there will be men on Hanover Plain who bear the proud title of Hopkins Scholars in honored memory of their own fathers who, as members of a gen-eration of Dartmouth men coming under the influence and concern of Dartmouth's great and beloved Hopkins, gave their lives that Dartmouth and its causes might live. I can imagine no greater honor to any college than that it should so honor and so tangibly perpetuate the spirit of its sons who died to keep men free.

Having spoken somewhat more seriously this Night than I proba-bly shall on future Dartmouth Nights, I especially want to remind you that, above all, the Dartmouth spirit is a joyful spirit. Twenty-nine years ago President Hopkins, on this occasion, concluded his inau-gural day with Stevenson's words at the end of his tale "The Lantern

Bearers": "But those who miss the joy miss all." I doubt that I can ever tell you more of the spirit of the great man who led Dartmouth through these past thirty years than by telling you that in his closing words to the faculty and Trustees, at last Thursday morning's ceremony, he came back once again to those same words: "those who miss the joy miss all."

Gentlemen, thanks to Ernest Martin Hopkins, in greater measure than men can express, you and the oncoming generations of Dartmouth men will not miss the joy. It is yours for the keeping.

My Life Was Lived in Robinson Hall

by FRANK D. GILROY

⋙⊃ Pulitzer Prize-dramatist Frank Gilroy 1950 here reminisces about certain elements of his undergraduate years, in an essay that extends from his contribution (the source from which the title here used has been taken) to the College's 1991 publication *Mentors*—a celebration of some of Dartmouth's great teachers of the past—the volume being comprised of tributes by alumni to "the teachers who changed their lives."

THERE WAS A constant excitement in Robinson Hall I never encountered in any other building at Dartmouth. Home base for varied extra-curricular activities, it pulsed with that special energy and ambition when all dreams seem possible. The motley group that inhabited Robinson seemed to walk faster and with greater purpose than most.

Lodged in the basement was *The Quarterly*, a literary magazine where poets, essayists and short story writers tried their wings. There was also a bathroom labeled MEN, with no complementary facility for women. This in pre-coed days.

The first floor housed *The Dartmouth* ("America's oldest college newspaper"); The Dartmouth Outing Club where all those healthy looking guys, called 'Chubbers' I believe, circulated; an office where *The Aegis* was assembled and edited; an office which memory can't fill—did it have something to do with Travel?; the offices of COSO, which organized concerts and the like, presided over by Warner Bentley; and an office where dear Wally Roach, ever smiling, avuncular, produced all the silk-screen posters advertising whatever events were taking place.

Second floor was headquarters for *The Jacko*, the humor magazine. Also the theatre where Warner Bentley, Henry Williams and George Schoenhut each year presented several full-length plays, Experimental Theatre productions and the Inter-Fraternity Play Competition whereby so many students enjoyed the once-in-a-lifetime experience of appearing before that beast of many eyes called AUDIENCE.

The third floor provided the offices and studio from which WDBS, the college radio station, broadcast.

Somewhere in that happy warren was the German Club. Who can forget Professor Stephan Schlossmacher, white mane and black cape flowing, as he forever dashed and bubbled?

And didn't the Dartmouth Christian Union have digs in Robinson? I recall George Kalbfleish, head of the DCU, a former Marine chaplain, frequently in the building.

Fearing I've left someone out, I checked the archives. Unfortunately, no record of tenants circa 1950 exists.

———

Robinson Hall's heartbeat, the Associated Press ticker in *The Dartmouth* office, which clattered incessantly, was audible the moment you entered. The cadence occasionally punctuated by a bell heralding news of local significance. The night Truman upset Dewey we watched the miraculous story unfold letter by letter on the ticker till morning.

It was *The Dartmouth* that introduced me to Robinson Hall when I heeled (is that term for apprenticeship still in use?) as a Freshman. It was a six-day-a-week paper in pre-TV days, serving an area well beyond the college. Veterans, returned from World War II, invested the paper with worldly concerns and viewpoints that often gave the administration fits.

Because it published six days a week, you spent a large part of every day but Saturday in Robinson—plus most of a night, every two weeks, when it was your turn to help "put the paper to bed". Exiting Robinson and crossing the campus at dawn, the paper safely tucked in, flushed with fatigue and a sense of accomplishment, remains a treasured memory.

———

As I climbed the masthead, *The Dartmouth*, and therefore Robinson, demanded more and more time.

It's three a.m. My turn to write the editorial. Mind a void.

The Night Editor, at the printing plant on Allen Street (Foley's, I believe) informs that the linotypists (Al and a gnomish man given to the bottle) have run out of copy. Only the editorial is missing. He says this calmly, but there is a hint of panic in his voice that compounds my own.

Will I be the first editor in the history of the "oldest college paper" to come up empty—the paper printed with a blank space trumpeting my failure?

NEVER!

———————

But it's not just the paper that binds me to Robinson Hall.

In Junior year I began to write plays. Have two full-length and numerous one-acts produced in that theatre on the second floor.

How did Warner, Henry and George accomplish all they did in that confined space? Their production of *Glass Menagerie* (Tom O'Connell '50, Alan Tarr '50, Mrs. Marion Folger, Louise Rapf; inspired set by John Wulp '50) remains vivid across almost fifty years.

I had a story or two published in *The Quarterly,* which meant time in the basement.

Occasionally I took part in radio panels on WDBS, acquainting me with the third floor.

And so it went for four years. No time to ski or do almost anything that didn't take place in Robinson.

I didn't read as much as I'd have liked. Often wish I could have done a fifth year with Robinson behind me.

How vital was Robinson Hall to Dartmouth at that time? Imagine today's campus absent Hopkins Center.

When I return to Hanover, I rarely visit dormitories where I was domiciled. But Robinson Hall, where I *really* lived, is a must.

An Attack Launched
from the "Chicago Tribune"

by EUGENE GRIFFIN

≫≫⁊ In its November 1, 1948, number *Time* magazine reported of *Chicago Tribune* correspondent Eugene Griffin and that newspaper's publisher, Col. Robert R. McCormick: "Last winter, when the Colonel heard that an un-American blight was mottling the Ivy League, Griffin toured the Harvard, Yale and Princeton campuses. [. . .] This fall the *Trib* got around to Dartmouth." Following Griffin's Hanover arrival (characterized by *Time* as being "with notebook in hand and hatchet up his sleeve"), he encountered in Baker Library an exhibition, "Quality in Newspapers," mounted in connection with the College's newly instituted Great Issues Course, which had been created through the initiative of President John Sloan Dickey himself and was required of all Seniors. "The exhibit," *Time* went on to report, "pained Griffin. It gave examples of how news is distorted. Its examples were marked clippings from the *Trib* and from the Communist *Daily Worker*, contrasted with clips from the New York *Times* and *Herald Tribune*."

The Chicago paper's assault on Dartmouth—presumably providing further evidence that Ivy institutions were, as it had earlier proclaimed, "infested with the pedagogic termites of communism"—consisted of a series of five articles. Here is the lead-off salvo, published on October 18, 1948, which had as its main headline "NEW DEALISM FORCED ON DARTMOUTH."

D ARTMOUTH COLLEGE, founded as an Indian mission in the foothill forests of New Hampshire, is no longer the little school described by Daniel Webster before the United States Supreme court in 1818, when he said, "It is a small college but there are those who love it."

It is one of America's great privately endowed schools, and among those who love it are the 22,000 alumni. The roots set down in the Hanover campus are long and enduring. They are nourished by traditions of a unique undergraduate life.

Students at Dartmouth seem to carry themselves with a bit more of a swagger and dress more informally than do the undergraduates at Harvard, Princeton, and some other Ivy league schools. The Dartmouth men are more at home in the outdoors, in the woods and hills not far from the Canadian border. Their annual Winter Carnival is nationally famous. Everybody at Dartmouth skis, or tries to.

Dartmouth athletic teams and tribes of cheering students sometimes seem to be fired with the marauding spirit of the Goths and Visigoths when they invade the campus of a more refined eastern school. A few years ago New York's Times Square was thrown into confusion when the Dartmouth Indians emerged unexpectedly from a subway and stopped traffic on Broadway while the Dartmouth band played the school song. [. . .]

Daniel Webster successfully defended the independence of Dartmouth in 1818 against an attempt of the New Hampshire legislature to expropriate the school as a state university, and a spirit of rugged independence always has been the mark of a Dartmouth man.

Now, however, under the leadership of President John Sloan Dickey, who came here three years ago directly from a state department propaganda job, Dartmouth college has become the eastern seaboard's newest seat of higher indoctrination in the New Deal cult of America-Last internationalism.

Every Dartmouth senior must take a course called "Great Issues in the Modern World," which Dickey imposed upon the curriculum last year. The course has placed Dartmouth alongside Harvard in the front rank of New Dealish schools. Great Issues has received rave notices in pro-British sections of the New York press, and other colleges have sent scouts to Hanover to copy it.

Its prophet is Archibald MacLeish, poet and former assistant secretary of state. Dickey was a MacLeish disciple in Washington, and remains faithful in Hanover. On Dickey's list of guest lecturers, MacLeish is the keynoter, the man who tackles the question, "What Is a Great Issue?"

Dickey told THE TRIBUNE that he could understand MacLeish's definition, which is to the effect that a great issue is one that has been a headache to the human race for ages past, probably will be for ages to come, and having a moral core.

Prof. Robert E. Riegel of the history department is one of the many who do not share Dickey's talent for understanding MacLeish. "No understandable answer (to the question: What is a great issue?) was ever given," Riegel wrote to the Dartmouth Alumni magazine.

Altho it has been announced to Dartmouth alumni that Dickey's proposal to introduce the Great Issues course was approved unanimously by the faculty, there is scornful opposition to it today among both faculty members and students. One professor merely held his nose when a reporter asked him what he thought of the academic value of the course.

Chief objection to it on the campus is that Dickey has made it a required course for graduation from Dartmouth. Guest lecturers are common at all colleges, where students are free to listen or stay away, but Dartmouth seniors must listen to the speakers Dickey brings in and write term papers on what is said. Prof. Riegel has pointed out that practically everything talked about by the Great Issues lecturers is presented one or many times elsewhere in the Dartmouth curriculum.

Most serious indictment of Great Issues is the belief held by many students and professors that the course is slanted to sway the senior class in accordance with Dickey's own internationalist bias.

"John (Dickey) is so hepped on his own utopian dream of One World that he probably would be surprised to hear that his course is a one-sided mess of propaganda," another faculty member commented.

A Tribune reporter found Dickey indeed protesting that his own prejudices did not protrude into the Great Issues program.

"We tell the students that the lecturers' convictions are not doctrine," Dickey said. "It's just like a ride on the subway: The man who sits next to you this morning will argue one side of an issue, but maybe tomorrow you will hear the other side."

Who are the lecturers invited to sit next to Dartmouth seniors on Dickey's subway?

Scheduled for the first semester this year are: President Dickey; Joseph Barnes, former foreign editor of the arch-British New York Herald Tribune and presently editor of the New York Star (the reborn PM); Barnes and Archibald MacLeish in a discussion, "Context of Our Times"; MacLeish again; MacLeish again; John M. Clark, editor of the Claremont (N.H.) Eagle, on "The Use of Newspapers."

With the course launched by the above speakers, it moves into a second phase under the chapter title of "Science and the Quality of Progress," and lecture topics include "Some Immediate Problems in Atomic Energy," "Biology as Applied to Human Affairs," "Is Man in the Ecological Circle?" and "Technology, Trouble-Maker or Trouble-Shooter?"

If the course follows last year's routine, it will include groups of lectures on such themes as "Modern Man's Political Loyalties," "International Aspects of World Peace," and "What Values for Modern Man?"

In addition to Dartmouth and visiting professors and a few representatives of industry, the speakers included Lewis Mumford, author; Rep. Christian A. Herter (R. Mass.); Edward U. Condon, director of the bureau of standards, who was accused by an un-American activities committee of having associated with suspected Russian spies; Harry W. Baehr, editorial writer for the New York Herald Tribune; Thomas K. Finletter, former assistant to the secretary of state who spoke on world government; Dean Acheson, former undersecretary of state; Nelson Rockefeller, former assistant secretary of state; Llewellyn White, who was assistant director of the Hutchins commission to investigate the freedom of the press, and Archibald MacLeish, again and again.

Down in the basement of Dartmouth's Baker library is brewed the real poison of America-Last propaganda, in a room called the Public Affairs laboratory. Here the seniors are taught that what the Herald Tribune says is gospel, and that what appears in THE CHICAGO TRIBUNE is prejudice. Attacks against THE TRIBUNE and its Americanism are handled by two professors, one a zoologist and the other a friend and protector of ghosts.

The Dartmouth senior class is taught that it is sophisticated and intellectual to swallow everything served up by the internationalists, and that it is smart to sneer at news reported in the interests of America.

A Tribune reporter went down into the America-Last laboratory to see what was cooking. He found it in charge of Prof. W. W. Ballard of the zoology department and Prof. Alexander Laing, assistant librarian. Before he took over his role in Great Issues, Ballard conducted a class in human anatomy.

Dartmouth Years of
"A Third World Citizen"

by HENRY S. ROBINSON

≫≫ Henry Robinson 1951 in his 1986 *Autobiography of A Third World Citizen* tells of his childhood in racially segregated Washington, D.C.; of going to college and, then, to graduate school; and of his long career as a teacher of history, both at the secondary-school and collegiate levels. What follow are some of the author's memories of and reflections upon his four years on Hanover Plain.

THE SUMMER OF 1947 was exciting, not only from the viewpoint of entering a prestigious college, but from the vantage point of participating in anti-segregation protests. The 15th Street Presbyterian Church held its annual summer vacation bible school in which I assisted. There one hot, summer day I and two female colleagues decided to test the rigid color bar in several places of public accommodation. Our selected targets were the Tivoli theatre on northwest Fourteenth Street, several five-and-dime lunch counters, as well as the tearoom of the Woodward and Lothrop department store. Reactions on the part of the segregationist establishments were varied. [. . .]

[. . .] Two years later sit-ins at local lunch counters and restaurants would officially begin. We three teenagers were probably pathfinders, setting out on a difficult and unchartered course. I will never forget the reaction from one of my close relatives who, when apprised of the sit-ins, remarked: "You should not associate with those radical girls. You might have been shot. Furthermore, you are soon going off to college." Frankly, my colleagues and I were proud of our "radical" protests. I will never regret confronting an unjust, anti-democratic system. World War II was over and foreign anti-democratic coalitions had been defeated, but segregation and discrimination, racism, and bigotry daily reared their ugly heads in the Nation's Capital.

Bitter memories of an undemocratic social and economic system were partially muted by my leaving Washington for the stimulating environment of northern New England and Dartmouth College. Sep-

208

tember, 1947 was in a sense the beginning of a new chapter in my short life. I was now on my own, free to make my own decisions, to pick and choose college courses, to set out on new adventures, and to conquer new horizons. On a brisk, cool September morning my parents and I set out via automobile to distant Hanover, New Hampshire. We motored past the then-segregated campus of the University of Maryland in College Park. Later in the day we interrupted our journey to spend the night at a downtown hotel in Manhattan, New York. The "Big City" was fascinating: elegantly attired ladies in below knee-length dresses, sophisticated gentlemen in ties and jackets, brightly flashing neon lights at Times Square. Contemporary Manhattan in no way resembles the Manhattan of 1947.

On arrival on the campus of historic Dartmouth College, founded in 1769, and the last of the colonial colleges, I was promptly registered and enrolled in the Class of 1951. My parents supervised my moving into a single room in south Massachusetts Hall and bought me the necessary furniture. On their departure I nostalgically waved good-bye. For the first time in my life I was a free agent.

My adjustment to college life required about a month. I met many friendly people during my freshman year and remember the football games, an enormous bonfire on the Commons in front of Baker Library, participating in strenuous physical education courses in the spacious gymnasium, and burning the midnight oil. Freshman studies were very demanding; I was a pre-med student my freshman year and the numerous science courses which were required took a tremendous amount of the student's time. I will never forget the rigors of freshman English. Each week we freshmen were required to write a theme on any subject. My first semester's teacher was a stern and demanding man of Scottish descent—Professor McCallum—who was notorious for his low grades—D and F. But I mastered the intricacies of theme writing and obtained a B grade at the end of the first semester. I feel that I benefited enormously from the rigorous demands of our stringent professor. My second semester English professor was a fledgling teacher, Mr. Bond, a Harvard Ph.D., who was nervous but efficient. I recollect reading Chaucer's *Canterbury Tales* in Middle English and Melville's *Moby Dick* in that first year. Another teacher I will never forget was Mr. Washburn, a colorful and sultry New Englander who taught French literature. We youths did not learn much French literature from Professor Washburn, but we were exposed to the ribald jokes and anecdotes of the elderly Yankee. One of my classmates and fellow "sufferers" in the French literature class was Mike Monroney, son of the then Oklahoma congressman and later senator, A. S. Mike Monroney. Mike was a veteran of the Second World War. He is one of the few majority Americans I have met who is relatively free of racial prejudice. I well remember babysitting for the young veteran and his wife.

Northern New England was frigidly cold and noted for its long, dreary winters. The winter of 1947–48 was no exception. Temperatures dropped to -30 degrees Fahrenheit and the snow fall measured 108 inches. [. . .] I kept warm, dressed comfortably in a sheepskin coat, cap, earmuffs and furlined gloves.

At the end of my freshman year in May, 1948 I returned to Washington, D.C. where I obtained summer employment as a messenger in the advertising office of the *Washington Post*. I carried copy proofs to various businesses—department stores, theatres, etc. That summer was extremely hot and walking in the above 100 degrees Fahrenheit temperatures was a very unpleasant experience. But the job gave me valuable insights into the problems of working people who were not as fortunate as I. On one occasion I remember riding on an elevator with the owner of the *Washington Post*, Eugene Meyer, an elderly patriarchal figure. On another occasion I defied the color bar by using the "white" men's restroom in Kann's department store. I also recollect the ominous headlines in the local press regarding the explosive and dangerous Berlin blockade.

My sophomore year was in a sense one of crisis—I no longer was a pre-med major. Science courses were not my "thing." Since we students had to select a major in our sophomore year, I chose history with a minor in international relations. I in no way regret this change in my college career. On the contrary, my later life style and world outlook would have been radically different had I followed in the footsteps of my father and grandfather. Had I become a medical doctor I more than likely would have practiced in Washington, settled on the pretentious "Gold Coast" of upper Sixteenth Street in Northwest, and led a prosaic life with the vapid and phony black bourgeoisie.

The author joined the Dartmouth Outing Club and in that autumn—1948—I and several other members of the Club set out to climb New England's highest peak, Mt. Washington, which majestically rose over 6,000 feet in the Presidential range of northern New

Hampshire. We journeyed via auto to the base of the lofty peak. We spent our first night camped out in comfortable sleeping bags. I can still remember drinking our leader's hastily prepared coffee on the morning of our ascent. The ascent was arduous and exciting, and as we climbed the treacherous peak we could look far down into a deep ravine which was perilously close to the narrow hiker's trail. Though it was October the weather was delightful at lower altitudes; at high altitudes there was some snow. Years later, while skiing and hiking on lofty peaks in Europe, I would recall my early initiation into the intricacies of mountain climbing in picturesque New Hampshire.

At this time in my college reminiscences I would like to mention my Third World fellow classmates. Darker faces were not too common on Dartmouth's campus. In the era before affirmative action scarcely a dozen Afro-American students were enrolled. Other non-whites included a few Orientals, one Kenyan-Indian and one or two Native Americans. Ironically, Dartmouth had been founded for the education of Native Americans. In 1824 the first Afro-American student was admitted to the College. Our faculty was all-white, with the exception of a Chinese professor. The majority of the students were WASPs, a few were Jewish and members of other non-WASP white ethnic groups. However, the majority of the students and faculty were cordial and a few, genuinely color-blind. The last bastion of lily-whiteism was the fraternity row. A few of the fraternities were non-discriminatory; most were segregated. But this aspect of racism was gradually eliminated on the part of the administration and progressiveness among the faculty and student body.

Among my Third World classmates I recall my classmate from Dunbar High School, Orlando Hobbs, who, in his senior year, was a senior fellow and graduated Phi Beta Kappa; Thomas Fraser, an affable youth whose father would in later years be chosen as an interim president of Morgan State University; a nephew of Lester Granger, the director of the Urban League; at least two other graduates of Dunbar High School; Samuel Chu, now a distinguished professor at Ohio State University; Robert Wilkinson, now a medical doctor; Abdul Sheikh of Nairobi, Kenya; Eddie Williams, an outstanding football player of the Dartmouth varsity team; and a Mohawk Indian who, in his weaker moments, would revile "Whitey."

After completing my sophomore year I returned to Washington to spend the hot summer unemployed. 1949 was a recession year. Like thousands of American college students I failed to find employment. The vagaries of the capitalist system closely affect our lives. For young, idealistic persons as myself, an element of cynicism muted an otherwise optimistic outlook. Even the personal intervention of a U. S. Senator did not open the doors of economic opportunity. So I spent the long, hot summer reading and looking forward to better days. [. . .]

Junior year at Dartmouth was probably the most rewarding. Intellectually, new horizons appeared. Philosophy and medieval history occupied much of my academic pursuits. One of the most brilliant and stimulating professors at Dartmouth was the late philosopher Philip Wheelwright. Professor Wheelwright was old-line American, a Princeton University graduate, endowed with a razor-sharp, inquiring mind. I spent many pleasant and profitable days in intellectual "rap" sessions with Professor and Mrs. Wheelwright. He was one of the few Dartmouth professors who permitted his students to challenge him in the classroom. Most of our professors held the opinion that students should be seen and not heard. In reality, we were a captive audience. Professor Wheelwright admitted candidly that he never knew whose examination he was reading since he always turned over the cover sheet showing the student's name. As a young teacher years later, I would adopt this policy.

Another course which fascinated me was entitled "Renaissance and Reformation," taught by Professor Williams, whose lectures gave remarkable insights into the panoply of European monarchs, popes, artists, and religious leaders of the Protestant Reformation and medieval Renaissance. Late medieval and early modern Europe still command my interest and avid attention.

One of the most outstanding teachers and lecturers at Dartmouth was Professor Adams whose dynamic lectures in European diplomatic history were both fascinating and informative. Eccentric, kinky-haired, and suggestively resembling a mulatto, Professor Adams commanded our undivided attention and respect. He unconsciously instilled in me a healthy respect for diplomatic history which I would earnestly and energetically pursue as a graduate student and professor.

As an undergraduate I was strongly influenced by several challenging books. One was More's *Utopia* in which the ideal society of the martyred statesman was outlined; another was Plato's *Republic*; others were Chaucer's *Canterbury Tales*, the Holy Bible, selections from the nineteenth century French symbolist poets—Verlaine, Rimbaud, Baudelaire, a biography of the abolitionist statesman, Frederick Douglass, and another of the Haitian revolutionary and liberator, Toussaint Louverture. Like no other literary works these selections played no small role in shaping and molding my intellect. [. . .]

In my junior year I left the Presbyterian Church of my paternal ancestors for the Episcopal Church. Though I had been received into the Presbyterian Church at the age of ten, my interests were never firmly rooted in Calvinism. While pursuing the college course "Renaissance and Reformation" I acquired an insight into Roman Catholicism, but I considered entry into the Catholic Church, at that time, premature. Confirmation classes were given by an affable Anglo-American priest, Father Hodder, whose church was the center of religious and social life for Hanover's Episcopal students. Sometime in 1950 I was officially received into the Episcopal Church. I remember my paternal grandmother, a staunch Presbyterian, sending me a thoughtful confirmation card. [. . .]

The summer of 1950 was an improvement economically over the previous summer. I worked several weeks with the Bureau of the Census in one of the First World War temporary buildings near the Tidal Basin and Constitution Avenue. The decennial federal census offered gainful employment for multitudes of Americans.

The international scene worsened, and in June, 1950 war broke out in Korea. For a few weeks it seemed that the conflict might widen, especially after the Chinese intervened in December. We college students were very much affected since we were eligible for military service. However, the government was generous and most of us were classified "2-A," a student deferment. The author clearly remembers remonstrating with a hard-boiled, female Selective Service official in December, 1950 regarding the importance of deferring college students in good academic standing so that upon graduation they might be better able to serve the country. Surprisingly, she concurred with the outspoken twenty-year old student, who was awarded a coveted student deferment until July, 1954.

My senior year passed rapidly. I remember holding a senior position on the staff of the College newspaper—*The Daily Dartmouth*, the oldest college daily in the U.S.A. Since sophomore year I had been a diligent worker on the staff of the newspaper. On graduating, we staff members received a modest remuneration for our services. On one occasion while working for the campus paper I recall knocking politely on the door of some residents in one of the dormitories. One of the residents was Rodman Rockefeller, who smiled at me while sitting on his bed and tying his shoe.

Graduation in June, 1951 was a memorable event. Senior week was extremely active, and we graduates were too busy to be nostalgic about leaving our beloved Alma Mater after four years of intellectual and social maturation. My parents, grandmother, and sister motored to the Hanover Plain from Washington, D.C. They were accommodated in neighboring Vermont at the cozy rural home of a female relative of the renowned inventor Thomas A. Edison. I will never forget us seniors assembling on the Common on a clear, warm day for one of the major events of our lives. Unfortunately, I no longer remember the name of the commencement speaker or his theme.

After the graduation my family returned separately to Washington. I travelled alone, reflecting on my future as one now legally of age and about to enroll as a graduate student in a prestigious university.

College Life, Expulsion
—and a New Beginning

by JUDSON D. HALE SR.

≫> The editor of *Yankee* magazine, Judson Hale 1955, in his autobiography, *The Edu-cation of a Yankee* (1987), candidly portrays a decidedly bibulous time he spent at Dartmouth and tells what in his Senior year resulted from that life-style—although, as proved to be the case, the full story would not have, by any means, a totally grim conclusion.

REACHING PUBERTY during my freshman year at Dartmouth launched me toward a series of typical adolescent milestones that most other boys my age had already experienced years before. At one moment I was a little boy, shouting desperately into my pillow each morning and particularly dreading my freshman Navy R.O.T.C. class on Wednesdays because that was my day to call the roll. And then, in a flash, I was, in sound and appearance, a young man. At long last.

Unfortunately, my sudden physical maturity didn't eliminate my little-boy insecurities. I still wanted to be thought of as wild, funny, daring, someone with a devil-may-care attitude. Only now, with the appearance and sound of normalcy, my capability for doing so was increased a hundred times over.

The first two milestones were innocuous and routine, though each had a large potential for trouble. They were, in order, my first drink (followed on the same occasion by my second, third, fourth, and fifth) and my first kiss. Both occurred on the same evening, with the latter being sort of forced upon me. As a Green Mountain College girl I'd known for ten minutes and I sat side by side on a couch in my dor-mitory room, my roommate playfully snapped off the lights and left. We were both too immature not to feel compelled to attempt a tenta-tive kiss. It was awkward, closed-mouthed, dry—even embarrassing —but it *was* the first!

The drinks were exclusively my own doing. Shortly after the kiss, they caused me to abandon the Green Mountain girl in order to throw up on the door of the bathroom down the hall, the first of many college episodes in which, sad to say, alcohol played a major role.

Even my memories of first love and, shortly thereafter, first sex, if indeed that's what it was, are dimmed by the alcoholic haze surrounding them. The "love" entailed drinking premixed whiskey sours with her in the black 1946 coupe I called the Crow ("just caws," I delighted in saying when someone asked me about the name) somewhere on the Middlebury College campus. Then there'd be the long drive back to Dartmouth as the sun was rising and waking up in my Economics 1 class with my professor's angry, somewhat contorted mouth yelling at me from one foot away. There was something about my sleeping in his class that grated on his nerves.

Sometimes she'd come to Dartmouth, and it was during one such visit that *the* first occurred, or if not, a reasonable facsimile. We were parked in the Crow on the Dartmouth golf course, there were the usual whiskey sours and hours of silent fumbling around, but as dawn was breaking and hundreds of birds began singing like crazy, we crossed over that mysterious line between pretend and real for perhaps two minutes. Or maybe I just *thought* we did.

At the bourbon-and-milk-punch party at my Phi Kappa Psi fraternity house the following noon, after I'd put her on the bus going back to Middlebury, I stood apart from my friends and attempted to strike a pose that would appear as mature, wise, and worldly as I felt. Later that afternoon, I joined a few others in sailing 78-r.p.m. records across the living room at the stuffed moosehead hanging over the fireplace. Parts of records remained imbedded in the plaster there for many years.

I know today that my Dartmouth years, overflowing as they were in a sea of beer, milk punch, and, yes, those whiskey sours, were a waste of precious time. In fact, the pace of my education slowed to a crawl just as I was exposed to everything one of the finest educational institutions in country had to offer. [. . .]

During the winter of my senior year at Dartmouth, my sister, by this time a Bennington graduate, married a prep-school teacher in Lake Placid, while I had several dates with a pretty brown-haired Skidmore sophomore with a reputation for being unwilling even to hold hands. Her strict adherence to her Catholic religion did not, however, preclude her willingness to heartily join my friends and me in the steady intake of alcohol that seemed to be the basic prerequisite to any sort of "fun" during my Dartmouth days. Her name was Sally Huberlie, she was from Rochester, and when we kissed in front of her dormitory in Saratoga Springs one cold evening after we'd attempted to have a drink in as many of the town's ninety-nine bars as possible, I felt complimented. She didn't just hand out kisses as a matter of routine. Also, my recently acquired "Peck's Bad Boy" reputation seemed somehow to balance easily with her reputed "straitlacedness," and we had felt mysteriously comfortable with each other from the moment we were introduced by our respective college roommates.

There were a few more dates, a few more kisses, an exchange of letters; but then the series of silly events leading to my expulsion from Dartmouth, two months prior to graduation, swept me off in a different direction. I wouldn't see Sally Huberlie for another four years, but by then the timing would be as right as the relationship.

"Is it true you were thrown out of Dartmouth for vomiting on the dean of the college?" is a question I'm often asked these days. I used to refer to the incident humorously in speeches to various organizations around New England. I stopped doing so after a 1975 live television talk show in New Haven, in which the host up and asked me whether or not I had had an alcohol problem at Dartmouth. That somehow didn't seem so funny.

Yes, it's true I was expelled for throwing up on Dean Joseph McDonald. But that was only part of the problem. I threw up on Mrs. McDonald, too. And over fifty other people, I'm told. All in about thirty seconds.

The real blame lies in exactly ten "if only I hadn'ts" . . .

1. If only I hadn't driven the Crow over the lawn in front of the dean's office after a heavy spring rain and become stuck there (the Crow had no reverse gear, so I couldn't back out of my parking place), Dean McDonald would not have demanded I turn over the Crow's keys to him for a period of two weeks.

2. If only I hadn't given Dean McDonald the keys to the secret meeting room in my fraternity basement and kept the keys to the Crow, I would not have been arrested for speeding on the road to White River Junction two days later and so been listed in the local newspaper that Dean McDonald read every day.

3. If only I hadn't consumed a countless number of whiskey sours

at the fraternity cocktail party prior to the annual variety show put on in Webster Hall every spring, and

4. if only I hadn't decided to go to the variety show anyway, despite my general condition, in a friend's black hearse (Dean McDonald having by then appropriated the Crow).

5. If only I hadn't parked the hearse on the front steps of Webster Hall, having failed to have found a convenient, more acceptable parking place, and

6. if only I hadn't been a friend of the two ushers who thought it would be funny to allow me inside.

7. If only they hadn't given me a seat down front, and

8. if only I hadn't almost immediately gone to sleep and awakened a half hour later knowing I was about to be sick.

9. If only I hadn't decided to try for the men's room in the back of the hall, running up the full length of the aisle, my hand over my mouth, spraying secondhand whiskey sours in both directions.

10. If only Mr. and Mrs. McDonald hadn't been sitting in aisle seats that evening.

When I called my mother in New York to inform her and my father that I've been expelled from Dartmouth and would be home the next day, she was furious—at Dartmouth.

"I knew you should have gone to Harvard," she said. She had never understood why I'd chosen Dartmouth over my father's alma mater. At the time I had explained to her that I wanted a country college where everyone hiked in the mountains, went on canoe trips, fished, and that sort of thing. She said no one did those things in college, and as it turned out for me, she was right.

She was also angry at Dartmouth for allowing me to be "drummed out of the United States Navy for cowardice" during my sophomore year. It's true I'd been dropped from the Navy R.O.T.C. program for flunking the written gunnery exam that year—but then, to give my friends a laugh, I'd ripped the buttons off my uniform and painted a yellow stripe down the back of my navy overcoat. She came across the coat in my closet during Christmas vacation and so I laughingly told her I'd been literally drummed out of the navy in an elaborate ceremony performed in front of the entire student body. When it was obvious she believed me, there was no undoing it. She was convinced it had happened.

"How could you allow one of your sensitive young boys to be subjected to such a mortifying experience?" I heard her demand on the telephone the evening I returned home. It turned out she was speaking with the president of Dartmouth College, John Sloan Dickey. President Dickey had accompanied my father on fishing trips to the St. Bernard Fish & Game Club in Quebec on several occasions, along with former Dartmouth president Ernest Hopkins, but her tone on the telephone that evening was anything but friendly. She wanted him to reinstate me at the college "immediately," saying Dartmouth and not her "Butch"—somewhere along the line she'd acquired that private name for me (which she still uses today)—was solely responsible for "everything." Whatever minor transgressions I may have committed, she told him, were simply a reaction to being drummed out of the navy in front of the entire college!

Evidently President Dickey investigated "the incident," because a friend of mine told me later that a Navy R.O.T.C. professor announced to his senior class during the last week of their final term that "contrary to a silly rumor instigated two years ago by some joker," the United States Navy had *not* "drummed" anyone out or painted a yellow stripe down anyone's back since the days of John Paul Jones! President Dickey's investigation must also have convinced him that Dartmouth College was, indeed, better off without Judson Hale. My expulsion stood. [. . .]

My mother and father sailed for Europe in late June 1955, leaving me to mow the lawns at their current country home in Weston, Connecticut, until I received my army draft notice, expected momentarily. Of course, I was also free to visit their penthouse apartment on New York's Central Park South on occasion. They were barely past the Statue of Liberty before I'd made up my mind to make a *permanent* visit to the penthouse apartment. When they returned in September, they found a note pinned onto the apartment door. It said simply, "I'm in the Army now. Love, Jud." They had to call the Pentagon to learn my whereabouts. Out at their eighteenth-century farmhouse in Weston, purchased from singer Jimmy Melton the year before, the lawns had turned into pasture.

Waiting for almost two months to be drafted into the U.S. Army while living in a penthouse apartment in New York turned out to be a delightful experience—I think. It consisted mostly of drinking martinis out on the balcony and watching the glittering lights of Central Park while discussing the problems of love and the world (90 percent love, 10 percent the world) with my Dartmouth friends who stopped by. [. . .] My draft notice came none too soon.

Tuberculosis came my way [two years later, in 1957,] during bitterly cold winter tank maneuvers on the Czechoslovakian border. The donor was my skinny platoon sergeant, who was so sick with what he thought was the flu that he could barely smoke down his daily three packs of cigarettes. Perhaps I shouldn't have borrowed his water canteen or used his radio headset during days he remained bundled up in his tent. [. . .]

As I entered a doctor's office at the hospital, he was placing a white gauze mask on his face. Another scary signal!

"According to the blood test you received last week, Hale," he said, "you have tuberculosis. You were the only one besides your platoon sergeant to test positive." He went on to tell me I'd be kept in Frankfurt for a few weeks and then flown to the army hospital in Valley Forge, Pennsylvania.

"How long will I be there, sir?" I asked, and his answer was somewhat numbing. "It could be as long as seven years." he said. [. . .]

For the first week, my only activity was being taken downstairs for x-rays, over and over again. I guess someone just wasn't doing them right. Otherwise, I was pretty much left alone to write "brave letters," which I very much enjoyed doing. "Don't bother trying to get me reinstated at Dartmouth," I wrote Dean Joseph McDonald. Several months before I'd written to ask if I could return for my final term following my discharge from the army, and he'd replied that, although he'd look into it, he thought my chances were "slim."

"Just forget it," I wrote him from the Frankfurt hospital, absolutely reveling in the self-pity of it all. "I have tuberculosis and probably won't recover for seven years, if I ever do." It was deliciously dramatic. He wrote back a sympathetic, friendly note saying he'd personally see to it I was reinstated "no matter how many years from now that must necessarily be." At long last Dartmouth was on my side again, though, to be sure, the method utilized was not the sort to be widely recommended to others.

My letter breaking the news to my mother and father, I decided, ought to be more upbeat. I felt the kindest approach would be an attempt at humor, so I described the hilarious way some of the nurses held their breath whenever they came near me, how my "luxurious private suite" was the deserted fourth floor of the hospital, that my only treatment was to be "zapped by x-rays all day long," and that at least it appeared I would "get a good rest" over the next seven years. Needless to say, my mother and father were not even slightly amused by the letter. The very morning they received it, my father telephoned Robert Cutler at the White House. An old friend of my father's from the Boston days, "Bobby" Cutler had been openly ambitious over the years, even considered somewhat "pushy" by some of his more staid friends, and was then an aide to President Eisenhower. [. . .]

Everything changed overnight. I was moved down to a large corner room on the third floor, I was provided with snacks as well as almost-gourmet meals, several doctors came to see me twice a day, and I was started on a brand-new antitubercular medication, taken in pill form, that would miraculously eliminate tuberculosis sanitariums all over the world within a few years and cure a mild case such as mine within months.

A week later, I was lying, masked, on one of dozens of stretchers, mostly occupied by men with broken limbs or accidental wounds, in an army plane droning its way across the Atlantic toward home. [. . .]

My eleven months in the tuberculosis ward of the Valley Forge Army Hospital consisted of becoming proficient at bumper pool and shooting rubber bands at the ceiling in such a way as to have them land within a painted circle on my chest, an activity resurrected from childhood "rest periods" in Chestnut Hill and Vanceboro. We also watched Sugar Ray Robinson's career fade away on the Friday and Wednesday night fights, flirted with the masked high school girls who came every afternoon to teach us how to hook rugs and make leather wallets, and after lights out, consumed the Dewars White Label my Dartmouth friends from New York and New Jersey smuggled in to me every weekend.

I also wrote Dean McDonald that, thanks to the brand-new tuberculosis medication, I'd be ready to return to Dartmouth the following winter. He confided to me later that several college officials were reluctant to go along. My recovery following so quickly after my "I'll-probably-die" letter seemed to indicate a continuation of my erstwhile college shenanigans, but Dean McDonald, true to his word, helped me *in* every bit as much as he'd helped me *out* three years before. (We corresponded as friends off and on until his death in 1983.)

When I was released from the hospital in December 1957 and

retired on 50 percent disability pay, I returned to my mother and father's home in Weston and, of course, to the penthouse in New York. (How my father managed financially to support all of this plus the trips to Europe would not become apparent for another five years.) It was at Central Park South, while cleaning out the desk I'd occasionally used during vacations from college, that my hand felt the edges of a crumpled piece of paper that had become partially wedged behind one of the drawers. I pulled it out in several pieces. It was a four-year-old handwritten letter from Sally Huberlie, that cute-but-strict Catholic girl from Rochester I'd dated a few times at Dartmouth. The one my friends predicted would never kiss me—but who did. The one I never thought could match me drink for drink throughout a bar-hopping evening in Saratoga Springs—but who did. While I sat there placing the pieces of the letter together, I wondered what in the world had ever happened to that girl. Probably married, I thought, with two or three children already.

The desk drawer still didn't operate smoothly. Reaching even farther back, I pulled forth a crumpled envelope with her address on it, and it was then, on a sudden, perhaps mysterious, impulse, I picked up pen and paper and wrote her a note. [. . .]

Three months and several dates-with-Sally-at-Dartmouth later, I found myself driving to Rochester for a three-day weekend in order to conduct a serious, even profound, conversation with her—perhaps with her parents too—on the subject of the possibility of our undertaking a mixed-religion marriage. Once one was finally a mature, responsible individual, I thought, one didn't leap impulsively into anything. One analyzed all the pros, cons, pitfalls, and advantages of, for instance, joining her supposedly strict Catholicism to my odd, convoluted mixture of skepticism, New England Puritanism, mysticism, anthroposophy, and guardian angels. How would it all affect our children? After three days of thoughtful discussion, perhaps then we could intelligently sort out our individual priorities and make whatever plans seemed appropriate according to the conclusions we'd arrived at through the orderly analytical process.

Our discussion lasted less than a minute. "The fact our religions are different doesn't really matter to me," I said. "Does it to you?" "No," she answered. We were sitting next to each other on the couch in her parents' summer cottage on Lake Canandaigua, a few miles west of Rochester. Her mother and father had just gone to bed, and we were prepared for a long night and the most important conversation of our young lives.

"It doesn't?" I said, surprised at her simple answer. "No, it doesn't," she said firmly. "Oh," I said. We looked at each other for perhaps a full minute. Finally I broke the silence by saying, "Well, let's get married." "Yes," she said without hesitation, and we kissed. It was done. A few minutes later she ran into her parents' room to tell her mother. My excitement matched hers exactly, and for the next three hours we chatted happily about pure love, emotion, instincts springing from the subconscious, and how the quickest method of smothering all three was through intellectual analysis!

The next morning, her father, a genial, loving, self-made man who'd just turned his fuel-oil business over to Sally's brother, put his arm around my shoulder with the casual, midwestern ease I so admired but could never duplicate, and said, "Welcome aboard!" It all felt very, very right.

Following my Dartmouth graduation in June 1958—seven years after first arriving there as a squeaky-voiced little boy who spent much of his time shouting into his pillow—I began looking for work in New York City. The wedding day was set for September 6, and surely it would be awkward not to have found a job by then.

"What can you do?" was the age-old question put to me by the people who interviewed me at advertising agencies and publishing houses. I would laughingly reply that, well, I could drive a tank and had majored in English at Dartmouth. Few laughed in return. I said I had worked on my high school newspaper. At that piece of news, their eyes would glaze over.

"My brother is putting out a little magazine he calls *Yankee*," my mother remarked to me as I was seeing her off on the *Ile de France* one evening in July. She was sailing to Europe to see Drake again, scheduled to return just before the wedding. "He may know people in publishing. Why don't you write him? But don't say I suggested it."

I'd met my Uncle Robb Sagendorph only twice before. The Sagendorph family was not the sort to favor get-togethers. [. . .]

Uncle Robb's four-page, handwritten reply to mine began, "It is interesting to hear you want to go into the 'publishing' business" and went on to describe no less than "eighteen subdivisions" within the industry. [. . .]

As I was to learn over the next twelve years, my Uncle Robb, bless him, the man who would be a more profound influence on my life than any other, was at his worst when giving personal advice. However, it didn't matter. I couldn't fathom what he was talking about in that first letter, anyway—until I reached the bottom of page three.

"I have an interesting little opening here at the moment," he wrote. That I understood. "The pay wouldn't be too hot—$55 a week . . . there'd be a lot of proofreading, layout and detail work . . . but you'd be in a focal spot where you could familiarize yourself with just about all the angles."

Perfect, I thought. Six months or perhaps a year with Uncle Robb's little New England magazine and I'd return to the big city able to say I could do a few things besides drive a tank! [. . .]

Incidentally, Uncle Robb paid me slightly less than $50 a week and denied offering $55. I did not, however, resort to showing him his letter (which I now have framed on my office wall). Like my mother and all the Sagendorphs, Uncle Robb never responded particularly well to proof.

My Dog Likes It Here

by COREY FORD

⋙⁊ Humorist Corey Ford wrote "My Dog Likes It Here" for the October 1953 number of *Ford Times*. A note accompanying the magazine's publication of the text identified it as part of a series on the theme "My Favorite Town" and explained, regarding the articles, "Traditionally, they have been on the human side, detailing the town's claims to distinction, not in statistics, but in the author's experience." However, the editors added, "Here's one with a reverse twist: Hanover is not only the author's, but also the author's dog's favorite town."

MY DOG made up my mind to live in Hanover. My dog is a large English setter, who acquired me when he was about six months old, and who has been making up my mind for him ever since. When we go out on a leash together he decides whether to run or walk or halt abruptly at the corner lamppost to mail a letter. He decides what time I get up in the morning, and which chair I can sit in (except the overstuffed chair in the livingroom, which is his). Naturally, when the time came to choose a place in which to live, I left the whole decision to my dog.

He picked Hanover because he says it is a very good town for dogs. A lot of dogs seem to feel the same way, because the town is full of them. I don't know how the word gets around; maybe the resident dogs leave secret signs on trees for other dogs to read, the way tramps do:

"This is a good jungle, no cops to chase you, and plenty of food to eat."

Hanover is the kind of town where dogs wander unescorted up and down the street, and the butchers save meat-bones to give them, and when you eat at the Hanover Inn, which is one of the best eating places in all New England, the waitress wraps up your tablescraps in a paper napkin so you can take them out to your dog in the car.

A good dog-town is a friendly town, small enough to call up when a neighbor's dog strays from home, and easy-going enough to stop the car if a dog is crossing the street. Hanover is like that.

Maybe it's because it is a college town: dogs prefer students, be-

225

cause they're the same age. You'll always see a dozen or so dogs on the Dartmouth campus, dashing between the legs of undergraduates playing softball, or lolling on the grass beside a group of collegians with shirts peeled off, sun-bathing on a warm spring afternoon. Stray dogs are always running out on the football field and getting in the players' way, and once an English setter named Bucky, who owns the Secretary of the College, fell in love with the captain of the baseball team and held up the Dartmouth-Harvard game for ten minutes because he insisted on lying on the pitcher's mound at his hero's feet.

A lot of Dartmouth people are owned by dogs. President John Sloan Dickey belongs to a big golden retriever, who sits beside the President's desk in the Administration Building all day and walks him home every night on a leash, to make sure that Dr. Dickey doesn't run away. During a fraternity initiation one of the pledges had to survey all the Hanover dogs, to determine which was the largest; he measured fifty-seven dogs, and Dr. Dickey's was second. (The winner was an elderly St. Bernard who is associated with the English Department.)

The town stands above the Connecticut River, on the broad Hanover plain which Eleazar Wheelock cleared almost two centuries ago to found a missionary school for the Indians. Its center is the Dartmouth green, a level rectangle of grass bordered by fine old elms and surrounded by the green-shuttered Georgian brick buildings of the college. I happen to think it is the most beautiful college commons in America. Baker Library dominates the campus, and indeed the town itself. Its lighted white spire is the first thing you see, as you drive toward Hanover; and from morning to evening its chimes ring their cadences on the hour, echoing over the campus and sounding through the business district and filtering into all the private dwellings, becoming a subconscious part of every life, linking the college and the town into one community together.

Hanover is a small town—its population is only about four thousand—and it is unspoiled by progress. No railroad scatters its soot over the neat white frame houses; no great cement highway bisects it. It's still a small town. When you pick up the phone, you ask the operator for a name instead of a number. The stores along its Main Street are as up-to-date as those of any big city; but shopkeepers call you by your first name. It has a fine modern hospital and efficient schools and post office and movie theater; but on the edge of town the fields are being plowed for corn, and the pine-covered hills are loud with grouse in the fall, and every December men in boots and checkered shirts, with hunting licenses pinned to their caps, lounge in the doorway of Campion's store and discuss the ten-point buck that Joe seen last night up to Moose Mowntin.

A college town is not like other towns. Its life changes with the college year. All summer long, when Dartmouth is in recess, Hanover lazes about its local business, and the stores are half-empty, and there is room to park on Main Street; but the place seems empty, a little older and even a little lonely. The townspeople say to each other: "It's certainly nice to have a little peace and quiet for a change!" But the words echo hollowly, as in a house without furniture.

Then in the early fall, when the air quickens with the first cool nights and the katydids predict frost in six more weeks, the town suddenly stirs to life. Warm new blood gushes through its veins, and it is twenty years old again. Two thousand handpicked young men, the best of America's new generation, pour into town by train and plane and private car to start another school year. They stroll down Main Street in dungarees and T-shirts and battered white bucks, they jam into the flick—it's the New Nugget now—and howl insults at the lovers on the screen, they crowd along the lunch counters, their heels locked around the rungs of the stools, gulping milk-shakes and poring over the *Daily D.*

Sometimes the town burghers shudder, when the boom of a football rally shakes the night air, or when a swarm of out-of-towners and uninvited guests invades Dartmouth's traditional Winter Carnival and turns the village streets into bedlam. Sometimes there are brushes with the local gendarmes, when youth erupts violently after a siege of exams.

Once, a few years ago, the town fathers made the tactical mistake of passing a law requiring the students at Dartmouth to pay a poll-tax in order to vote. The students paid the tax. Then, in March, they moved in on the annual town-meeting, outnumbering the local residents two to one, and within an hour they had voted for such long-needed improvements as a beer-bubbler in the center of the campus and a new Town Hall five hundred feet high and six feet square. The poll-tax was revoked.

The college is deeply conscious of its obligation to the town; President Dickey states over and over that the duty of a liberal arts college is to share its cultural treasures and its spirit with the community where it lives. Its lectures and concerts are open to the towns-people. When a heavy winter snowfall cripples transportation, students and faculty turn out to aid in shoveling the streets clear. If a forest-fire threatens, the undergraduates make the supreme sacrifice of cutting classes for the day in order to help.

Every Christmas the fraternities at Dartmouth give elaborate parties for the children of Hanover, complete with ice cream and cookies and a bagful of presents distributed by the football tackle dressed up as Santa Claus.

I like Hanover in the winter, when ski-boots squeak on the hard-packed snow and ski-racks are fastened to the tops of cars headed for Balch Hill.

I like it in the spring, when the duckboards are down for students to cross the muddy green, and northbound geese honk overhead, and the opening day of trout season is only a couple of weeks away.

Best of all I like it in October, when the tang of wood-smoke is in the air and the gold and crimson hills that surround the town are like folded Persian carpets, and on a fine fall afternoon, when classes are over, Dartmouth students and townspeople alike shoulder their shot-guns and take off for the grouse and woodcock covers, with a setter or a pointer or a spaniel tagging at their heels.

Which is why my bird dog would rather live here in Hanover than any other place in the world. I'm glad that he decided as he did. I feel the same way.

"Don't join the book-burners."

by DWIGHT D. EISENHOWER

❧❧❧ Although the principal guest and the recipient of an honorary Doctor of Laws degree at the College's 1953 Commencement, the President of the United States was not scheduled to address the throng that attended the June-thirteenth ceremony. (Lester B. Pearson, Canada's Secretary of State for External Affairs, delivered the "Commencement Address.") He did, however, undertake to make, toward the very close of the exercises, some informal remarks—remarks which served to produce headlines in newspapers all across the land, because of their inclusion of an admonition that began, "Don't join the book-burners." The journalistic stir that resulted from the President's words on this occasion was associated with the then-current campaign of Wisconsin's junior United States Senator, Joseph R. McCarthy, to have the State Department remove "unAmerican" or "objectionable" books from its U.S. Information Agency libraries abroad. The dramatic pronouncement at Dartmouth represented, as one historian later observed, "President Eisenhower's taking public issue, at last, with Senator McCarthy's anti-Communist witch hunt." The full presidential text is here reproduced from the *Alumni Magazine* of July 1953.

YOUR PRESIDENT POSSESSES a brash bravery approaching foolhardiness when he gives to me this platform in front of such an audience with no other admonition except to say, "speak informally"—and giving me no limits of any other kind.

He has forgotten, I think, that old soldiers love to reminisce, and that they are in addition notoriously garrulous. But I have certain limitations of my own, learned throughout these many years, and I think they will serve to keep me from offending too deeply.

But even if I do offend, I beg in advance the pardon of those families and friends and sweethearts that are waiting to greet these new graduates (with a chaste handshake of congratulation) and assure you that any overstaying of my time was unintentional, and just merely a product of my past upbringing.

First, I could not pass this occasion without the traditional congratulations to this class on the completion of four years of arduous work at a college of such standing as Dartmouth, and of which there is no higher.

Next, I think I may be pardoned if I congratulate you on the quality of the addresses you have heard today up to this moment. I think that your commencement address and the two valedictory addresses established a standard that could well be one to be emulated even here in the future.

Now, with your permission, I want to talk about two points—two qualities—that are purely personal. I am not going to be an exhorter, as Secretary Pearson has said. I want to talk about these two things, and merely suggest to you certain ideas concerning them.

I am going to talk about fun—joy—happiness: just fun in life. And I am going to talk a little about courage.

Now, as to fun, to get myself straight at once, for fear that in my garrulous way I might stray from my point, I shall say this:

Unless each day can be looked back upon by an individual as one in which he has had some fun, some joy, some real satisfaction, that day is a loss. It is un-Christian and wicked, in my opinion, to allow such a thing to occur.

Now, there are many, many different things and thoughts and ideas that will contribute—many acts of your own that will contribute—to the fun you have out of life. You go along a bank—a stream bank—in the tropics, and there is a crocodile lying in the sun. He looks the picture of contentment. They tell me that often they live to be a great age—a hundred years and more—still lying in the sun, and that is all they do.

Now, by going to Dartmouth, by coming this far along the road, you have achieved certain standards, and one of those standards is, it is no longer so easy for you to have fun. You can't be like a crocodile and sleep away your life and be satisfied. You must do something, and normally it must involve others—something you do for them. The satisfaction—it's trite, but it's true—the satisfaction of a clear conscience, no matter what happens.

You get a lot of fun out of shooting a good game of golf. But you wouldn't have the slightest fun out of it if you knew to achieve that first 79—you broke 80 today—if you did it by teeing up in the rough or taking the slightest advantage anywhere, and no one else in the world but you knew it. That game would never be a 79 to you. And so it wasn't worth while because you had no fun doing it.

Whatever you do—a little help to someone along the road, something you've achieved because you've worked hard for it, like your graduation diploma today—those things [that] have become worth while in your own estimation will contribute to your happiness. They will measure up to your standards, because your standards have become those that only you know. But they have become very high, and if you do those things they are the kind of things that will satisfy you, and make life something that is joyous, that will cause your face to spread out a little, instead of drawing up this way ⌜indicating a long face⌝—and there's too much of that in the world anyway.

You are leaders. You are bound to be leaders; you have had advantages that will make you leaders to someone, whether you know it or not. There will be tough problems to solve. You've heard about them. You can't solve them with long faces. They don't solve problems—not when they deal with humans. Humans have to have confidence. You've got to help give it to them.

This brings me to my second little topic, which is courage. I forget the author, but one many years ago, you know, uttered that famous saying, "The coward dies a thousand deaths but the brave man dies but once."

In other words, you can live happily if you have courage, because you are not fearing something that you can't help. You must have courage to look at all about you with honest eyes—above all, yourself—and we go back to our standards.

Have you actually measured up? If you have, it's that courage to look at yourself and say, "Well, I failed miserably there, I hurt someone's feelings needlessly, I lost my temper"—which you must never do except deliberately—you didn't measure up to your own standards.

Now, if you have the courage to look at yourself, soon you begin to achieve a code, or a pattern, that is closer to your own standards. By the same token, look at all that is dear to you, your own family—of course, your own children are going to be the greatest and most extraordinary that ever lived, but also look at them as they are, occasionally.

Look at your country. Here is a country of which we are proud, as you are proud of Dartmouth and all about you and the family to which you belong.

But this country is a long way from perfection—a long way. We have the disgrace of racial discrimination. We have prejudice against people because of their religion. We have crime on the docks. We have not had the courage to uproot these things although we know they are wrong. And we, with our standards—the standards given us at places like Dartmouth—we know they are wrong.

Now that courage is not going to be satisfied, your sense of satisfaction is not going to be satisfied, if you haven't the courage to look at these things and do your best to help correct them—because that is the contribution you shall make to this beloved country in your time. Each of us as he passes along should strive to add something.

It isn't enough merely to say, "I love America," and to salute the flag and take off your hat as it goes by, and to help sing *The Star Spangled Banner*. Wonderful—we love to do them, and our hearts swell with pride, because those who went before you worked to give to us today standing here, this pride. And this is a pride in an institution that we think has brought great happiness and we know has brought great contentment and freedom of soul to many people.

But it is not yet done. You must add to it.

Don't join the book burners. Don't think you are going to conceal faults by concealing evidence that they ever existed. Don't be afraid to go in your library and read every book as long as any document does not offend our own ideas of decency. That should be the only censorship.

How will we defeat communism unless we know what it is, what it teaches? Why does it have such an appeal for men? Why are so many people swearing allegiance to it? It's almost a religion, albeit one of the nether regions.

We have got to fight it with something better, not try to conceal the thinking of our own people. They are part of America, and even if they think ideas that are contrary to ours, their right to say them, their right to record them and their right to have them in places where they are accessible to others is unquestioned, or it is not America.

I fear that I have already violated my promise not to stay too long and not to exhort. I could not, though, go back to my chair without saying that my sense of distinction in Dartmouth's honorary doctorate, in the overgenerous—the extravagantly overgenerous—remarks of your president in awarding me that doctorate, and the present of this cane from the young men of the graduating class—all of these things are very precious to me.

I have been fortunate in that my life has been spent with America's young men, probably one of the finest things that has happened to me in a very long life.   I thank you again for this award.

What Makes a College New?

by BANCROFT H. BROWN

≫⌐ This was originally presented by Bancroft Brown, Dartmouth's Benjamin Pierce Cheney Professor of Mathematics, as a talk during June of 1957 at the twenty-fifth reunion of the Class of 1932. When publishing the text in Feburary 1958, the *Alumni Magazine* characterized it as "a remarkably astute and instructive analysis of the teaching side of the College."

T HE CLASS OF 1932 was a fortunate class. It came to Dartmouth at a very good time. Let me summarize the accomplishments of the half-dozen years before the class arrived in the fall of 1928: (1) A selective system for admission had been put into operation, a system that really worked; (2) there was a new curriculum, with reasonable distribution, reasonable freedom of election, and a strong major; (3) there was a new library which was, and still is, about the best of its kind; (4) there had been built up for this new and larger Dartmouth a solid core of young, enthusiastic assistant professors and instructors.

It was a new college that the Class of 1932 came to: old in traditions, but very new in spirit.

What makes a college new? This is the question I want to examine and try to answer. Why was Dartmouth old in 1890 and new in 1895? Why was she new in 1928? What is she today? What makes a college new?

It isn't the students. They respond, they reflect a change, but they do not cause it.

It isn't the alumni that make a college new—although they can mightily help, and under the wrong conditions, mightily hinder.

Leadership you must have. An outstanding president, backed by a competent and understanding board of trustees. This is necessary, but it is not enough.

For a college to be new, you must have a good faculty. That *may* work. It will work if you have a great faculty.

From which you may gather that I am going to say a lot about the faculty of Dartmouth College. You are very right. As responsible alumni you know a good deal about many aspects of the College. Possibly the phase you know least about is the faculty. In addition to undergraduate contacts, some of which have become blunted, and some of which have become sharpened over the years, you have three pieces of positive information: (a) it is a funny, funny faculty; (b) it sleeps in trundle beds; (c) it indulges in unmentionable orgies in Leb and the Junction.

Certainly it is funny. As for the trundle beds, Rand's Furniture Store reports that their sale has fallen off the last few years—apparently another old tradition failing. But I do want to enter a mild protest against the orgies in Leb and the Junction. Perhaps I don't know how to go about this business of organizing orgies. The most desperate thing I have ever succeeded in doing is to buy a bottle of Scotch for home consumption.

Dartmouth has been old much more of the time than she has been new. She was born old. Eleazar Wheelock brought an old, old college to Hanover. The faculty was old, the *Gradus ad Parnassum* was old, the Bible was old, the drum was old, even the whole curriculum was old. The faculty in particular remained old. It is true that there were a few great teachers, and a very few scholars; and in all charity I must say that was purely accidental. The average was mediocre, and the depths were abysmal. In conservatism and orthodoxy, the Dartmouth faculty exceeded the faculty of any other college in New England.

Dartmouth was never new until William Jewett Tucker assumed the presidency in 1893. He caught the imagination of the student body, fused the alumni into a loyal unit, and expanded every phase of the College. Every one talked about the "new" Dartmouth; she was new. He did one more thing: he brought into the faculty William Patten, John Poor, Charles Darwin Adams, David Wells, Frank Dixon, Fred Emery, Craven Laycock, Ashley (Dutch) Hardy, Herbert (Eric the Red) Foster, Ernest Fox Nichols, Louis Dow, Gordon Ferrie Hull, and Leon Burr (Cheerless) Richardson.

That was not merely a good faculty; that was a great faculty. Give Dr. Tucker all credit for seeing that a great college must have a great faculty. Give him credit for his ability to go out and assemble such a faculty. There is still much room for credit for a great faculty which realized Dr. Tucker's dream.

New things don't stay new—not without a lot of effort. The newness had worn off when Ernest Martin Hopkins took over in 1916.

And before he could do much, there was a World War on our hands. Once that was over, things started to click.

The College grew amazingly, outrageously. Some completely new system of admission had to be developed, and was. The faculty had to be expanded, enormously. But teachers must have some assurance that this is a good place to come to. At that time a Department had a permanent head, and rather incredible powers were delegated to him. He could hire and fire and, within limits, set all salaries. He arranged all schedules, planned the courses, picked the textbooks. That's not a good set-up for an ambitious young instructor with ideas. Further, there were two or three Departments where the autocracy of the head made conditions quite intolerable. So the Trustees, at the instigation of their young president, abolished the system, installed a rotating system of chairmen, and gave the humblest instructor the same voting rights as the most august professor. This plan was more liberal than that which obtained at most of the comparable institutions. As a result of this, from 1919 to 1928, Dartmouth skimmed off a good deal of the cream from the Eastern graduate schools, and a vigorous, competent, young faculty with only a sprinkling of veterans greeted the entering Class of 1932 in September 1928.

That faculty stuck. Statistics are the last thing you want to listen to: but when I say that faculty stuck, I could back it with an impressive array of figures. Teachers went to Amherst, shifted to Brown, shifted to Harvard, shifted to Chicago. Teachers came to Dartmouth and stayed. A liberal policy of promotion and tenure, freedom so genuine you didn't have to talk about it all the time; these and other factors made Dartmouth an attractive prospect for a teacher at the start of his career. This Hanover Plain is a curious thing once it gets its hooks into you. You damn the climate, damn the B & M, triply damn the month of March—and stay.

All of this in retrospect had its good and its bad points.

A job on the Dartmouth faculty was safe and secure. That was good. But it was too safe and too secure, and that was not so good. During the period 1920–1945, it was unusual for an instructor or assistant professor to be refused a reappointment, and if he stayed on, as most of them did, he was eventually promoted to a full professorship. Although the Trustees have the final authority in all such matters, it is the older members of the faculty who have the real responsibility; and it was we who made the mistakes. [. . .]

A little too much we followed the line of least resistance. There were times when we paid just a little too high a price for harmony.

And so the new faculty of the 1920's stayed on, and were promoted. Mind you, it was not a mediocre faculty; it was a good faculty; and yet somehow it missed being a great faculty. It had lost just a touch of the fresh, new feeling of 1928. And the main reason for this brings us into a very difficult question—the question of teaching and research. This is tricky, and you don't get a mathematical answer to this question.

A community of scholars must do two things: it must teach and it must create. Every scholar in the community must teach, or create, or both. The community is judged by the sum of their achievements.

Now it is silly and wrong oversimplification to say that colleges should teach, and graduate schools should do research. Both must do both. The problem is one of shading and balance. [. . .]

For many scholars, research is the biggest thing in life. Teaching is incidental, if that. The two greatest mathematicians who ever lived were hopeless flops as teachers. Sir Isaac Newton, required to give lectures at Cambridge, delivered them to empty halls. Karl Friedrich Gauss simply refused to have any pupils, claiming (and with some justice) that no one could profit from his instruction. For the great big men, research is the whole story. They grudge the time and effort spent in teaching [. . .].

At the other extreme is the man whose life is one long devotion to teaching. He himself, he likes to tell you, was once tempted by the siren of research; but since no man can serve two masters, he chose the greater, the nobler career of teacher. He explains that no one is worthy the name of teacher if he squanders his energy on creative writing. He himself devotes all his time to planning his teaching. He devotes so much energy to planning that he has precious little left when he finally enters the classroom. He prides himself on his carefulness and objectivity, and spends untold hours correcting hour examinations, and considering whether a split infinitive should cost the culprit 2 or 2½ points. Every college department loves a guy like this because he will take on all the tedious jobs that no one else wants. It is human nature to keep him and even promote him—but he is not an asset to a community of scholars, and you know it. [. . .]

Now in the 1930's we made a very honest mistake. We knew that the universities gave an exaggerated emphasis to research. We knew that some colleges aped them. We knew that was wrong. But we swung just a little too far the other way. What we said to our young instructors was this: "First of all, Dartmouth asks you to give your best efforts to teach and inspire your students." That is not enough. We should have asked more. And so in the thirties there was a subtle slackening of the creative urge at Dartmouth. We were content with too little. [. . .]

Statistics have no meaning here; we can only judge trends, and try to judge fairly. Personally I would say that we were content with too little, that we did not demand quite enough of ourselves and of each other, and that the Dartmouth faculty in those years never quite realized its full potential. The world of pugilism has an expression for this. In speaking of a fighter who has gone a long way, but has missed the top, they say, "He wasn't hungry enough."

So the faculty of the 1920's was here in 1940, older, more urbane, dedicated to teaching, full professors with tenure, much more tolerant than the faculty you knew, but definitely overloaded at the top. "What's wrong," you ask, "with having a top-heavy professorial group? Won't the instruction be better, and isn't that what we want?" Here at last is a question to which I think I know the answers.

The first answer is that it costs too much. You have to pay professors more than instructors.

The second answer is allied to the first. You pay them more, and also you get much less out of them. You have no idea what a low minimum of actual teaching an established oldtimer can get away with. [. . .]

My third reason is that even if a departmental group of professors is young, they aren't going to stay young, and they will almost certainly stagnate unless new blood is brought in.

If that doesn't seem to you at first thought a good reason, I'd like to enlarge on it. I give you my own Mathematics Department. In 1928 the Department consisted of five professors, four assistant professors, and two instructors. In 1945, seventeen years later, three of these eleven had died—the other eight were full professors. The important thing (and the bad thing) is that during those seventeen years, there had been no new blood added to the group.

Now let me make clear why that is a very bad thing. You may think of mathematics as a static thing invented by Euclid, unchanged and unchangeable. That isn't so; in the last thirty years the very foundations of mathematics have changed; symbolic logic has acquired an imposing structure; entirely new disciplines such as game-theory and linear programming have appeared from nowhere. Three of my younger colleagues have recently written a book on *Finite Mathematics* which is used in a course taken by 200 freshmen. In my considered judgment I am not competent to teach this course; and with this judgment I am quite sure my very competent young colleagues would concur, although they are too much the gentlemen to say so. The survivors of the old group have of course heard of these new developments. What we have never had until quite recently is a succession of young enthusiasts who would tell us that these things are good, and that a considerable amount of the traditional analytic geometry—calculus sequence is now archaic. It's hard to make changes unless you are prodded; and for years we didn't have any prodders. [. . .]

No, a college faculty must not be static; it must continually draw in younger men, trained in different schools and in different disciplines. There must be constant flow: in and out.

I have detailed some of the sins of omission of the faculty in the 30's and early 40's. The Second World War found us with a solid core of full professors, and not much else. What there was of the younger group immediately girdled the earth. The older group stayed on and put in some exhausting work on the V-12 contingent. This was necessary; but it was dull plodding, and there was very little opportunity for creative work. When it was over, we were a tired lot, and we weren't any younger either. We remembered the old days, and we wanted to get right back to them. In this nostalgia there was a touch of staleness. In 1945 Dartmouth wasn't "new," as she had been in 1893 and in 1928. President Hopkins, a great leader who had brought the College even beyond the vision of Dr. Tucker, and who had seen the College through two World Wars, wanted a new man, a young man on the job. The faculty hated to see him go. We were just tired enough so that we were a little afraid of change, and we were afraid there would be changes.

There have been. Now I am not going to embarrass anyone on the scene by singing praises for jobs that are still not finished; and this will have to be in generalities. That tired old faculty bounced back. There has been remarkable and quite unexpected creativity. There has been added a brand-new younger group of impressive size, and slightly terrifying ability. The friction between the two groups has been remarkably little. Somewhat to their surprise, young instructors coming here have been immediately given considerable responsibilities, and urged to recommend and then put into effect rather sweeping changes. The word has gone out that Dartmouth is a good place for a young instructor with ideas. The methods by which this younger group have been recruited come as a bit of a shock to those of us who knew the old days when you boarded the noon train for Boston and picked up an instructor the way you would pick up a hat at Raymond's.

The simple fact is that today we have a good faculty which is on the verge of becoming a great faculty.

What do you do with a faculty after you have it; or more exactly, how does a faculty operate to achieve its greatest potential? [. . .]

I think I can make a point here only if I am specific. And I very much want to make the point. So I apologize only in a perfunctory way for talking about mathematics and myself. When I came to Dartmouth as an instructor, I was given five freshman sections of 24 men each. [. . .] It was slightly stultifying for me to give the same lecture five times in a row—and I really liked teaching—but it must have been deadly for the students who heard my fifth phonographic recording. Still and all I did earn my keep, although it was not the best way to do it. 120 students a semester is a pretty fair load for a beginner. Every time I got a promotion the number of sections was reduced, and by the time I had been here ten years, I was teaching two or three classes, with an overall of something like thirty students a semester. There is something fundamentally wrong about that way of operating.

I won't detail all the experiments and changes; but I would like to tell you how we do it today. An experienced man in the Department lectures three times a week to a group of 125; then we supplement this with one hour of conference, handled by instructors or teaching fellows, in small groups of about 15.

That is what we do for the large freshman and sophomore courses. Advanced courses and Honors courses are all in very small groups. Honors courses, by the way, begin the very first semester of freshman year.

I know that 125 may sound pretty conservative to some of you. I've tried much larger, but they don't seem to work as well. I am a blackboard and chalk man; I know only the technique of the theatre; a flesh-and-blood actor in constant touch with his audience—responsive to their cheers, doubts, and hisses. Now if you have 400 students, there seems to be a loss of contact; and for another thing you have to write with the chalk sideways. I'm pretty conservative, and will settle for 125. An experienced man can handle two such groups; that's only one lecture a day, plus organizational details. It's much better to have these groups in different subjects. If you repeat, you don't do as well the second time. But 250 students is a good fair teaching load. You feel that you are pulling your weight in the boat. Of course, if one had a really modern lecture room, and projectors, and all kinds of gadgets, it *would* be sort of fun to take on the whole freshman class. [. . .]

Finally, I am not going to describe in detail the new three-course three-term program. As responsible alumni of the College you are supposed to know about such things. Since I had nothing to do with it, I have no hesitation in saying that I think it is the greatest step forward in curriculum and organization that the College has ever taken. [. . .] The 1957 curriculum seems to me to be in a very real sense a dynamic thing, whereas the others were static. If any one thinks he can heave a sigh of relief and say, "Well, that's over for the next thirty years, let posterity worry about the next change," if any member of the Dartmouth family has that kind of an idea, he is very much mistaken.

Not that a new curriculum, or a new reading course, or a new anything else ushers in the millennium. Undergraduates are going to continue to be undergraduates; sophomores will continue to be sophomores; the month of March will not be abolished. But there will be big changes.

Now, please, I am no prophet. I am not defining College policy; and I am not sending up any trial balloons.

But a lot of things are being talked about. We talk about a five-day week. We talk about a grading system confined to Honor-Credit-Fail. We talk about an Honor System. We talk about fewer courses, large lectures, and a much greater use of teaching fellows and assistants. That means a smaller faculty. We talk about summer sessions. For juniors and seniors, we talk about two terms in residence, one term of independent study anywhere, and one term free. Brash upstarts, forgetting the traditions of 188 years, talk about co-education.

For once again, Dartmouth is new. By the same standards which showed her newness in 1893, and again in 1928, she is new.

What is newness? Newness is the assurance that you can do your job, plus a positive hunger for making the job bigger, and doing it better. Newness is second wind. Newness is that surge of power under which the dynamo gives out more than it takes in; under which the whole is greater than the sum of its parts. It is I, a professional mathematician, who tell you that this can happen. [. . .]

The Computer at Dartmouth

by JOHN G. KEMENY

※》ꝋ Four years before he became, in 1970, the College's thirteenth President, and while Dartmouth's widely celebrated work in the realm of computer science was still in its infancy, John Kemeny made this presentation to guests of the College who were attending a "Dartmouth Horizons" program—its text subsequently revised by him for publication in the February 1966 number of the *Alumni Magazine*.

D URING THE PAST YEAR we saw the twentieth anniversary of the first dropping of the atomic bomb. I am not going to discuss the bomb, but I am going to tell you a little story about some computing that went into the bomb.

When I was sent to Los Alamos, they assigned me to what was then called "the computing center," which really consisted of some rather primitive IBM bookkeeping machines. There were seventeen of them in a large room. A staff of between fifteen and twenty of us who worked in three shifts—24 hours a day, six days a week—tried to solve some mathematical problems going into the construction and dropping of the bomb. A typical problem took us about three weeks to do, working 24 hours a day, six days a week, and we worked about a year and a half on various kinds of problems.

I recently made an estimate as to what this would mean in terms of the present Dartmouth Computation Center. I have come to the conclusion that any sophomore at Dartmouth College starting from scratch—this is, where he has to start writing instructions for the machine—could do all the work that was done in a year and a half at Los Alamos in one afternoon. And he can do it in one afternoon at a time when there may be thirty other people using the same computer. This is the system that I would like to tell you about.

I shall start with a word of motivation. When the new Computing Center was proposed to the Trustees of Dartmouth College, our major argument was the following. Computers are beginning to have an increasing effect on the lives of all of us. Almost all large businesses today are influenced by computers. Twenty years from now all busi-

241

ness, and most private lives, will be influenced by computers. Whether this is going to be a fully favorable effect, as it could be, or a very harmful one will depend on whether the people who make the policy decisions know what computers can do and what they can't do, or whether they blindly trust the people who run the machines. An institution like Dartmouth College that trains many of the leaders of the nation in business, in government, and in research, has an obligation to make sure that our liberal arts graduates understand one of the most significant factors that will influence their lives. Therefore, we have made it a requirement that everyone who takes at least a year of mathematics at Dartmouth (which includes 80% of each freshman class) must learn something about using the computer. Not just indirectly, but must actually use the computer and show that he understands how to put it to good use.

Now this raises a very serious problem. Computers are very expensive, and human beings, especially when they first try using a computer, tend to be very slow. So the problem is: "How do you enable hundreds of students to use the same computer?" The answer is what is called a *time-sharing system*—a system under which many different people can all use the same machine at the same time.

With this system each user sits at a teletype machine, which is a pretty ordinary typewriter except that it can send what it types over telephone lines. It is connected by a telephone line to the computer. There are 40 teletypes hooked to our present computer. A number of them are at the Computing Center. A few of them are at departments that make heavy use of computing, some at the Associated Schools, and some of them are at remote locations. People have called in to our Computing Center from all over the country. Dean Tribus gave a demonstration in Scotland: he fed in problems there, had them solved in Hanover, and the answers were typed out seconds later in Scotland.

With any teletype, by calling in, you have complete control of the computer and absolute freedom to work with it as if you were the only person using the machine. You don't ever have to see the machine. You don't have to know how it works. All you have to understand is an extremely simple language, called BASIC, that we have constructed for this purpose. It is something our students typically learn in three hours. And then you can sit down and have one of the most powerful research and educational tools at your complete disposal.

At the moment, the heart of the computing equipment is located in an ugly basement in College Hall. But the new Peter Kiewit Computation Center is already under construction, on the corner of Elm and Main Streets. This will provide the kind of elegant surroundings such a magnificent system deserves.

There is a famous story about the trouble with computers. Twenty years ago the difficulty was that they never did what you told them to do. The trouble with computers these days is that they do exactly what you tell them to do, not what you meant to tell them to do.

As this story indicates, the major problem in computer usage is learning how to instruct the machine—or *programming*. The human user must in a few instructions explain to the machine what he would like it to do. This requires that he anticipate all the difficulties that may arise in thousands or even millions of computations. And since the machine has no "common sense," the instructions must be absolutely precise and complete. It is to this skill that we want to introduce our students.

We are currently putting about 650 freshmen through the training program each year. During the second semester of their mathematics sequence they have to write four programs having to do with mathematics and they must work on them until they get the right answer. Now this is not an enormous chore. It is a small part of their course. On the other hand, it makes all the difference in the world whether you have ever used the machine or not used the machine. Once they have passed this requirement, they never, if they wish, have to touch a machine again in their entire lives.

On the other hand, if they want to, the machine is there any time they can get their hands on one of the typewriters, day or night. So a student can go there and do his homework in a physics course, or do a research project in an engineering course. There is a statistics course for psychologists which is built around computers. The student may be a research assistant for a faculty member and solve a significant research problem. All these things have happened during the past year and should happen with increasing frequency in the future.

Of course the Computing Center is even more important for the faculty. All of a sudden we have, literally at our fingertips, a tremendously powerful computer. In the past, if you had a big research project, it was worth while going through all the labor of writing programs, punching up cards, submitting them, and going back a dozen times until you got it to work. Now we are at the stage where, with most research projects that require numerical work, you can sit down at the typewriter and not get up from that typewriter until you have your problem solved.

This is a common experience. And I assure you that if this sounds fantastic to laymen it sounds much more fantastic to people who are experts on computers. For example, we had a consultant visit us last summer. Very fortunately he was here for two weeks, because for the first week we could not get him away from the typewriter. And he had been working with computers for years! Our time-sharing system was a revolutionary new experience for him.

How does this marvelous system that allows 40 different people to use the machine at the same time work? The Computation Center uses equipment manufactured by the General Electric Company. The heart of the system is not one, but two computers. The "computer" in the ordinary sense is a GE-235, which is a nice high-speed computer. It can do about one million multiplications a minute. Its memory is large enough to hold 8000 nine-digit numbers, or 16,000 instructions. While this is quite remarkable, it is far from the fastest or largest machine now available. We are proud of the fact that our system works without needing a multi-million-dollar computer.

The second machine is the Datanet 30. Its availability was one major reason why we bought General Electric equipment. It handles for us all the communication with teletypes, and makes all the key decisions. In effect, it is the boss, and the GE-235 is its slave. It talks back and forth to you. And it is a very special machine that can talk to all 40 teletypes at the same time in such a way that it could be typing out 40 different sets of answers on 40 different teletypes, some of them in California, all at full speed.

There is also a very large memory which is connected to both computers. This memory looks like a gigantic jukebox, and works somewhat on that principle. It can store a few million numbers (or instructions) and find any block of 1000 of these in a quarter of a second. These magnetic disks are a tremendous improvement over magnetic tapes, since it does not matter whether we want information from the "beginning" or the "end."

Let us now follow a typical program through the system. A student sits down at a teletype and types a short list of instructions. These enter into the Datanet, simultaneously with everyone else's program. The Datanet deciphers the teletype signals, and collects them on one of the disks. When the student types RUN, the Datanet signals to the GE-235 and tells it to go get the program from the disk and work on it. Let us suppose that the work is complete within five seconds, as most requests are. Then the computer places the answer (or an error-message) on one of the disks and goes on to the next problem. While the Datanet types the answer on the student's teletype, the GE-235 may be solving a dozen other problems.

Let us suppose that there were errors in the original program (and there usually are). Then the student simply retypes those lines that had mistakes in them, or types a couple of new lines, and types RUN again. His old program is still on the disk and will remain there as long as he sits at the teletype, so that corrections can be entered simply and quickly. An experienced person may be able to get a dozen runs in a quarter of an hour—usually enough to make all necessary adjustments in his programs.

But what if his program requires more than five seconds? Then the Datanet signals "time is up," and the GE-235 moves all its computations to the disk. Each customer waiting in line gets a shot at the machine and then the student is allocated further computing time. His problem will still be done, but he is not allowed to hold up the bulk of requests, which require only seconds of computing. Our experience is that if we need a quick run we get service within ten seconds. And a long problem, requiring a minute of computation, will be completed within five minutes.

The disk memory is also used for saving programs. This has many important applications. For example, a student who is unable to complete his work in a single session may save his program and return to it at his leisure. A faculty member may develop a program that he wants to use repeatedly for a research project. He can save it on the disk, and retrieve it in seconds any time he needs it. Altogether between five and ten thousand programs can be saved. Among these are the so-called "library programs." These are programs of general interest, written by experts, available to anyone. For example, there is a program for computing correlation coefficients. A social scientist needs to know practically nothing about computers to use this. He simply calls the program from the "library," types in his data, types RUN, and within a few seconds he has his correlation.

What we have learned is that we have been asking the wrong questions about computers in the past. We used to ask, "Is man better at doing this or is the machine better at doing this?" Usually, if the machine could do it at all the machine was better. But this is the wrong question to ask. The right question to ask is, "What is the best way of getting a given result when man and machine work together?" And what we have found out is that man and machine form a team that is of course much faster than the human being alone but much smarter than the machine left to its own devices.

So instead of trying to write an enormous program and let the machine calculate for hours—and heaven only knows what happens in between—you let it work for a while, look at it, and make a suggestion to the machine, and let it go on. This gives a new feeling to computing. Many of the leaders in computing feel today that this kind of time-sharing is the future of all computing, not just because many more people can use it, but because of this tremendous new feeling of man working together with a device that magnifies his own mental resources.

If you think this physical equipment is fabulous—and it is—what you really should appreciate are the students who wrote 90% of the instructions for the machines. [. . .]

We have some of the most fantastically able undergraduate students in the country. And if our system is better—and as we think it is—than the systems of other institutions, it is not because the equipment is better, but because the brainpower of a small number of faculty members and a large number of hard-working students has made the difference for Dartmouth College.

Undergraduate Disc Jockey

by PAUL GAMBACCINI

>>> Following his graduation from Dartmouth in 1970 and two years as a Keasbey Scholar at Oxford, Paul M. Gambaccini entered upon a professional career in radio. Settling in England, he became a widely known and highly popular figure in British broadcasting. Within his 1986 autobiography, *Radio Boy*, from which this excerpt has been taken, he reminisces about his experiences as a member of the staff of the College's student-operated station, WDCR.

AFTER PRESENTING *Sounds for the Tri-Town* during the summers of 1967 and 1968 I began regular work on the programme in the 1968/69 academic year. [. . .]

I feel fortunate that my greatest day-to-day contact with new releases occurred in the period 1966–70. The last half of the sixties was a peak for pop with the Beatles and Rolling Stones leading the way on the rock front and the Atlantic acts and Motown family pacing the r&b field. The second string of that era—Simon and Garfunkel, Creedence Clearwater Revival, the Lovin' Spoonful, the Mamas and Papas —would be stand-outs any other time.

What is most mind-boggling now is that these artists usually had a new release every three months. Nowadays singles are timed to coincide with the sale of new albums, which are more profitable for record companies. Consequently, few American stars have more than three singles per year. In those days the flow of material was steady, and the excitement on the airwaves was palpable.

The Beatles did more than anyone else to make disc jockeying a thrill in the sixties. Thank heaven we were on Capitol Records' Air Mail service from Los Angeles. To have to wait a few days for a new Fab Four release would have made us dreadfully behind our competitors in the eyes of Beatlemaniacs who wanted to hear and, in many cases, buy new product immediately. Capitol got the records out so quickly I once received a new Beatle single without being aware one was due. I held the disc, 'All You Need Is Love', and wondered if it was some sort of jest. Playing it and discovering it was for real was one of the most pleasant surprises of the decade.

247

When a new Beatles 45 came in everyone wanted to hear it. What may have seemed like just another excellent pop record to a jaded jockey in Britain was for Americans the latest memo from cultural Mission Control. The Beatles shaped the fashions and social attitudes of the sixties, sometimes because they themselves were innovators and other occasions because they were the first to publicize and popularize esoteric habits they themselves tried out. Bob Dylan may have turned them on to marijuana, but it was their 'A Day in the Life' from *Sgt. Pepper's Lonely Hearts Club Band* that did more to tempt Dartmouth students to smoke pot than any other influence. 'I'd love to turn you on,' John Lennon sang, and the Big Greeners let him do just that. The change in campus consumption from booze to weed in 1967 was not just definite, it was dramatic. It was as if over half the meat-eating population had become vegetarian overnight.

The visual influence of the Beatles' *Sgt. Pepper* image was also apparent. As the Liverpudlians sported facial hair, so did students who would never previously have considered growing a moustache. The colourful bandleader costumes also caught on, and John 'Straight Nait' Naitove's Sgt. Pepper suit was the envy of his Gamma Delta Chi fraternity brothers.

None of this would have happened had the music not been of vital importance to our everyday lives. I and countless others have speculated elsewhere as to why the Beatles not only entertained but mattered. Suffice it to say here that they did. When a Claremont radio station somehow got a copy of *Abbey Road* before we did we sent someone down the interstate to hustle a taped copy to Hanover for immediate broadcast. When we received pirate tapes of the *Get Back* sessions, ultimately issued as *Let It Be*, we gave several airings to the song 'Let It Be', even though our copy was not of normal broadcast quality. We simply had to share the excitement of new Beatle material with our listeners, who agreed that in the extraordinary case of this act hearing something was better than hearing nothing.

Langdon Winner wrote in 1968 that 'The closest Western civilization has come to unity since the Congress of Vienna in 1815 was the week the *Sgt. Pepper* album was released. In every city in Europe and America the stereo systems and the radio played [it]...'

I cannot speak for Austria or Alabama but I can talk about Dartmouth. The week that record came out the Dartmouth Bookstore, Modern Records and every other conceivable outlet were under siege.

Walking across the college campus was like living inside a tape loop of *Sgt. Pepper* tracks mixed at random. No sooner would 'With a Little Help From My Friends' fade out as you walked by South Mass than 'She's Leaving Home' would fade in from Mass Hall. Wait a minute, there's 'Lucy in the Sky With Diamonds' coming from North Mass and now, yes, someone else is playing it in Gile and I do wish they'd either play it in synchronization or take the speakers out of the windows and *Good Lord* does that guy in Hitchcock have 'A Day in the Life' on loud. Now he's on the orchestral bit and he's turned it up full blast and *it sounds as if the world is ending*.

Playing records loudly in dormitories was not an innovation of the late sixties. Irritated neighbours were probably complaining about overly audible wind-up gramophones between World Wars. But there may have been a new brazenness in placing them in open windows on sunny days. Turning a record all the way up for the whole world to hear was a statement of rebellion that dovetailed perfectly with the political and social mood of the times. This is what I want to hear, the noise polluter was saying, and it is what you should want to hear, too. If you don't, tough.

Oh for the time when it was not technologically possible to make a record so loud! Unless the disc was something most people were genuinely interested in, such as a new Beatle album, this over-amplification was an antisocial act. In the psychedelic era, with electric guitars blaring away noisily, it could be downright offensive. Spring weekends, when loud music got adrenalin pumping as sure as the sap was running through the trees, could be cacophonous.

The only time I can recall a speaker in a window actually enhancing the effect of a record was when I returned to Gile after my afternoon show in time to hear the end of Isaac Hayes' eighteen-minute version of 'By the Time I Get to Phoenix' screaming out of North Mass. The writer-turned-monologist Hayes' extended version of Jim Webb's classic had a lengthy instrumental passage at its conclusion, complete with a repeated brass riff and drum roll that seemed to be dramatically announcing 'And now, *sunset*'.

The fundamental relationship in pop, as in any musical form, is between the artist and the listener. Naturally enough, while at Dartmouth, I was most often moved by music when alone in Gile Hall. There, my emotional defences down, and the pressures associated with broadcasting them removed, records could hit me hard. [. . .]

My 406 Gile roommates shared my preference for rhythm & blues. One day Larry DeVan got the news his beloved grandfather had died. 'Gambo, "Cover Me",' he requested, and I knew he wanted to hear the Percy Sledge ballad of that name. This soul stirrer was a slow and mournful plea for emotional support in a time of stress. As I saw Larry take comfort and strength from the recorded performance I wondered if Sledge himself ever knew the positive effect his work had on people he would never meet.

DeVan was a walking contradiction. 'The Pear', as he was nick-named because of his unusual shape, held rather disturbing views on racial issues, claiming to prefer George Wallace to Hubert Humphrey or Richard Nixon in the 1968 Presidential election. Yet he was a fervent r&b buff, consistently preferring black music to the rock so popular in the sixties. He saw no contradiction in these positions. In the dorm room we shared with Mike 'Thunder' Thorman during our second and third years at Dartmouth my desk was situated in an alcove, underneath the stereo. If Larry barked '"Everlasting Love", Gambo' from the lounge chair on the other side of the room, I knew he was ordering me to play Robert Knight's crossover hit, not promising eternal friendship.

Thorman was also an r&b fan, though his musical tastes were wider. A student government officer, he had to decide who our class should sponsor in concert at the college's largest venue, the Nathaniel Leverone Field House. I suggested that the '70s present Ray Charles. His live show, complete with orchestra and female vocal group the Raelettes, was superb, and his historic string of hits was still current enough to have big box-office appeal. A major promotion should go with a proven great, not a possibly off-the-wall psychedelic act. Thorman agreed, so did the class government, and Charles put on one of his customarily magnificent performances. He stomped through 'Hit the Road Jack', soothed us with 'Georgia On My Mind' and satisfied sweethearts present with 'I Can't Stop Loving You'.

All through the show I looked forward to my scheduled interview with the star. I had been too young to know Ray Charles' work during his years as an important jazz artist, and I did not hear this part of his output until years later. But I had loved his rock era hits, especially 'What'd I Say', and appreciated many of his country and western covers, especially 'Busted'.

After the show, which ended in a mighty ovation, I went backstage for my appointed meeting, accompanied by my guest Kathy Shap-leigh. Oddly, the dressing room had no door, but I realized that Leverone's architects had probably not thought privacy a priority in an all-male college. Kathy and I knocked on the wall, the nearest thing to a door available, and strolled in. Never have I so regretted such a casual entrance.

'Don't you have any consideration?' bellowed an unidentified aide. I could see his problem. There was a world-famous artiste, the brilliant Ray Charles, sitting in his underpants, and here I was trooping in with a teenage girl who, even though she was no naive ninny, was not accustomed to seeing nearly naked superstars.

'Couldn't you knock?' the handler blasted. He needn't have used such volume to make a point which had already impressed us. The sole and ironic result of his outburst was to draw the attention of The Genius himself who, being blind, had not noticed the presence of a silent young woman on the other side of the room. If he was embarrassed by our thoughtlessness, it was only at that point.

Kathy and I briefly retired to the other side of the dividing wall. Moments later we returned for a delightful twenty-minute session with Charles, whose love of music and mankind was equally evident. Particularly touching was his appreciation of Aretha Franklin.

'I *love* Aretha,' he purred, referring to the newly-crowned Queen of Soul. 'She has so much *feeling*.' I have never heard a word imbued with as much of its own literal meaning as 'feeling' was by Ray Charles at that moment. It seemed inevitable that he and Miss Franklin would have to seek each other out for a duet, as they indeed subsequently did for a live recording. [. . .]

Teenagers will do almost anything for charity. They are so naive and well-intentioned they believe they can change the world by going door-to-door selling fruitcakes or organizing massive jumble sales. I was no different, except that instead of selling fruitcakes I stayed awake for a thirty-nine-hour radio marathon. That made me the fruitcake.

The cause was the 1968 WDCR Let's Help campaign. Let's Help had been a two-month charity campaign launched the previous year to benefit the Save the Children Fund. Now the beneficiary was A Better Chance, better known as ABC, a scheme for the education of minority children. [. . .]

General Manager Jeff Kelley had the bright idea of holding a radio marathon, a pictureless version of the telethons that regularly raised millions. Listeners would phone in pledges in order to hear their favourite records. I would be the disc jockey and he would be the newsman, reading the reports at the usually scheduled times. This seemed an inventive scheme, but it was even cleverer than listeners realized. Kelley scheduled the fund-raiser to coincide with The Harvard Weekend, the time of the annual Dartmouth-Harvard game when virtually the entire student body drove down to Massachusetts for three days of dating, drinking and an incidental football match. WDCR always experienced staffing problems during this exodus. To require only two on-air personnel for the entire weekend was a stroke of logistical legerdemain. [. . .]

I looked forward to our own marathon, scheduled to last from 6.30pm Friday evening until 8.30am Sunday morning. I tried to train for it not by staying up nights but by storing up sleep. I somehow thought that if I wasn't tired to begin with I could somehow sail on into Sunday without fatigue. The one thing I did that probably was genuinely helpful was to take a nap three hours before the show began. At 4.45pm, wide awake, I left my dormitory to go to the radio station. [. . .]

I walked the two hundred yards or so from Gile Hall to Robinson more attentively than usual. After all, I wouldn't be covering this stretch for nearly two days [. . .].

My contemplation ended abruptly as I reached the back door of Robinson Hall. My mission was to go where no WDCR deejay had gone before: thirty-eight hours into the future. Naive and nineteen as I was, I felt no fear. If I fell asleep while a record was on, Kelley or a worker would wake me.

Workers there were. Even though it was the Harvard Weekend and the massive undergraduate flight had already occurred, WDCR had attracted some of its most loyal men to the cause. There were volunteers to man the phones, taking pledged donations in return for the play of a favourite record. There were volunteers to find the discs in the Record Library and bring them to the studio. And, bless him, there was a volunteer to get our food from the Red Door delicatessen, which was supplying our grub for the weekend in exchange for a few well-timed though necessarily subtle on-air plugs.

The marathon began at 6.30. It was easy. I was given a pile of records with names and amounts of pledges attached and started breezing my way through them. This was less work than the usual disc jockey programme in which the announcer has to think of something to say between each record. Here the subject matter was provided in the form of the donations and the donors. All I had to do was throw in the occasional explanation of what we were doing, the Let's Help phone number, the always-changing but always-there time and temperature, and I was laughing for thirty-eight, thirty-nine, heck, fifty hours. Bring on the night, I challenged the gods.

And then it happened. Unexpectedly, unthinkably, a plane headed for Lebanon Airport crashed into Moose Mountain only a few miles from Hanover. I first learned something was amiss half an hour into the marathon when Dave Prentice came into the studio to warn me that Kelley was on the phone about an air accident. We didn't yet know if anyone had died. We didn't even know if it was a passenger plane.

Seconds later Kelley rushed in, hurried in gait but calm in voice, to tell me that when the current record finished I should announce he had a bulletin to read. Yes, he told, a plane had crashed into the mountain. Yes, he confirmed, it was a passenger flight. Without warning the whole nature of our project was about to change.

I have often marvelled at the selfless service students at WDCR perform without thought of compensation. On that evening they gave special reason to be thought of with love. Immediately upon hearing of the disaster everyone with a car and a few without volunteered to go to the crash site, even though hardly anybody knew where it was. Moose Mountain was approached circuitously on an unpaved road suitable in winter for four-wheel drive vehicles only. No one was fazed: Prentice knew the way and others would follow. Armed with tape recorders and paper pad, the makeshift WDCR news team sped into the night.

Anyone who has ever listened to a radio station when news unexpectedly breaks knows that air product instantly assumes a schizophrenic nature. Frequent flashes of news are interspersed with regular programming, which must continue if only because there isn't enough news to fill the available time. Complicating our quandary was that our marathon had been heavily promoted in advance and that many listeners tuning in, oblivious to the events in Etna, would still be expecting to hear the charity broadcast. The result was that for the next eighteen hours the Beatles, Simon and Garfunkel, and whoever else someone wanted to pay good money to hear alternated with Jeff Kelley's updates on the crash. [. . .]

For myself that evening was a peculiarly disjointed experience. I had to keep the marathon moving, aware that the tragedy had taken place but not sounding overwhelmed by grief. A sizable portion of any community takes cues from its broadcasters, and if a familiar figure goes to pieces on the air the mood of the masses can be negatively affected. I was writing down donations and dedications in spare seconds between starting one record and cuing up the next, but sometimes calls relating to the crash came through on my line. Moose Mountain was topic A on the world's wires for a couple of hours, and if only by default WDCR found itself the focal point of the planet's enquiries. [. . .]

For Jeff Kelley the evening was the greatest test of professionalism he ever faced. What had started as an exercise in staying awake had turned into overseeing a news-gathering operation unlike any DCR had ever run. Usually one could incorporate wire service copy into one's story. This time Associated Press and United Press International knew less than we and our makeshift news team had to provide all our information.

Kelley had to collate the staff's submissions and to read them in an authoritative but calm tone. He also had to make sure every report was tasteful. Any lapse in discretion, no matter how unintended or impromptu, would be remembered for years by a disappointed and perhaps unforgiving community. [. . .]

Not only did Jeff and his make-do staff, most of whom had never previously been newsmen, have to gather the facts with the utmost accuracy, they had to field compassionately telephone enquiries from friends and relatives of passengers desperate to know if their loved ones were among the survivors or the dead. This was a particularly sensitive occasion because we had announced that not all on board had perished, and any party could logically have the highest hopes for good news. [. . .]

To make the breaking of bad news even more difficult, the *Valley News* appeared on the newsstands Saturday morning with the preliminary list of dead. The airline had issued a supplementary list of more fatalities after the paper had gone to press. Breakfasters sat baffled at their kitchen tables as they read of one number dead and then heard of a higher toll. Had they heard properly? Had more really died?

And, more to the point from Dartmouth's perspective, had Professor of Music Milton Gill really perished? It wasn't in the paper, yet Jeff Kelley just said so on the radio. One of Gill's greatest friends, a member of the English faculty, called WDCR, puzzled and worried. I had to field his query. To this day I remember my rather formal pronouncement: 'I hate to say that he was among the victims.'

The Moose Mountain tragedy galvanized the Tri-Town area. Jeff Kelley and I would have been naive not to realize that some of the pledges that Saturday were made by listeners who might not have donated had not the plane crash given them cause to reflect on their own good fortune. Whether the incident aroused feelings of guilt or native charity, many members of the community gave generously, and we surpassed our goal. Gil Tanis, assistant to the President of the College, pilgrimaged personally to our third floor studio. 'You boys have done a terrific job through all of this,' he said, fighting back his tears and wordlessly leaving a generous cash donation on the console.

By midday Saturday, when the turmoil over the tragedy had begun to abate, Jeff and I were mentally if not physically exhausted. Fuelled by adrenalin all night long, we now found ourselves in the situation many performers running on nerves are in after a performance: we wanted to collapse. Jeff didn't fall. I did, right on to the sofa in the second floor COSO (Council on Student Organizations) office. This sounds like a premature end to our marathon, but it wasn't. We were merely switching to Cambridge for coverage of the Harvard game. Knowing I wouldn't be needed for two hours or so, I conked out. Kelley went for a stroll downtown. I was awakened in time to resume our marathon later that afternoon. No one listening knew that I had slightly cheated. [...]

The final sixty minutes of the marathon were captured on tape. They proceed as I remember them, with the battle being not so much to stay awake as to pronounce words distinctly. No matter how long one is on the air one's attention is kept from wavering by the number of technical tasks always at hand. It must have been far easier for me to stay awake than my beleaguered newsman, who had twenty-five-minute gaps between engagements. But though the mind be willing the tongue may be weak, and slight slurrings of words characterized the conclusion of our superstint. At one point Kelley slipped and referred to me as his usual morning colleague Bob Shellard.

'Jeff, are they making minutes longer these days?' I enquired.

'No, but they're making more of them, Bob,' he replied.

Honestly—after thirty-eight hours in the same studio complex he still didn't know my name!

I ended the marathon at 8.27 with the aptly-titled 'Urge for Going' by Tom Rush. Somehow I got back to my dorm. Unlike my reflective stroll to Robinson Friday evening, this journey was completely forgettable. I have no recollection of anything between the finish of the Tom Rush record and waking up back in 406 Gile at five in the afternoon. [. . .]

Records are made to be broken, and our thirty-nine hour spread was comfortably eclipsed in the early seventies by another team of DCR masochists. I had no regrets about being bested in mere number of hours. I dare say our weekend was one of the most memorable ever spent at the radio station. [. . .]

The Parkhurst Hall Take-over

by STEVEN E. TOZER

⋙⋗ The most dramatic manifestation at Dartmouth of the student militancy that in the 1960s and '70s was experienced on campuses all across the United States was the forcible occupancy in the spring of 1969, during the Vietnam War, of the College's main administration building, Parkhurst Hall. A decade later, Steven Tozer 1972 (who would ultimately have a career involving, first, administration and, subsequently, a university professorship) provided a detailed account of the occasion, in an article entitled "When They Resisted," featured in the *Alumni Magazine* for May 1979.

I N 1968, like many high-school students who had received letters of acceptance from Dartmouth, I was basking in the sunshine of my senior year. I had been captain of the football and wrestling teams, had been selected to spend the previous summer in Europe as an American Field Service student, and had received such awards as "Scholar Athlete" and "Representative Student" at my high school in Springfield, Illinois. I reveled in my good fortune and future. I was 18. Exactly a year later, I was in Rockingham County Jail, serving a 30-day sentence for my participation in the occupation of Dartmouth's Parkhurst Hall.

To the folks at home, the events of May 1969 were clear evidence that I had changed dramatically from the boy they knew. Undoubtedly, the SDS ⌈Students for a Democratic Society⌉ had warped another young, impressionable mind.

But for me and for many others of that time, political conviction did not arrive suddenly; it had been growing quietly for years. Mario Savio and the Berkeley free-speech movement had come into our Midwest home in *Life* magazine; Martin Luther King had marched, and blacks had been beaten on home television; and Bob Dylan sang "Masters of War" and "The Times, They Are a Changin'" on the radio. And they all spoke of ideals that home and school taught me to respect: freedom, justice, and equality among people.

The war in Vietnam loomed large for many working-class high-school friends who were not college-bound. My friend Brad and I talked about the war while working as lifeguards in the evenings at the

257

YMCA. We declared, almost as if making a pact, that we would not kill anyone for reasons that were not our own. [. . .]

Discussions of the war and of U.S. military policy continued from my first weeks at Dartmouth. Most of my friends seemed more sophisticated than I in the political issues at hand. Henry articulated his interpretation of the violence of the 1968 Chicago convention. Fred and I discussed U.S. foreign policy and the role of our military in supporting dictatorships in Southeast Asia and Latin America. And Sandy, my roommate, agonized with me over the relationship of Dartmouth's ROTC program to U.S. military organization. He had reason to agonize; he was at Dartmouth on an ROTC scholarship. [. . .]

Current events and much current political literature supported the radical view. Together with Michael, we were five freshmen from the same dormitory, and although none of us had "radical" backgrounds, we reinforced one another in our views. On the other side were the arguments of our dormmates. The common line of debate they most often presented was that we had no right to interfere with the rights of others to choose military training at Dartmouth. Our common response was this: If our military force were shelling villages and killing thousands of Vietnamese men, women, and children, then good cause had to be shown; if none were forthcoming, then we could respect no one's right to join and aid such an organization. In fact, it was our obligation to interfere.

The effort to divest Dartmouth of its ROTC involvement developed out of a growing national perception that we were engaged in an irrational, immoral war and that there were no significant legal actions that one could take to stop it. The campaign developed slowly and tentatively; and although I was only a freshman, I found that my suggestions were considered as seriously as were those of professors and older students. Everyone had opportunity to be heard.

We were all new to this sort of thing, and our campaign proceeded like any other: We distributed home-made leaflets, made posters, set up information booths, canvassed, carried signs, and initiated a Take-a-Professor-to-Lunch program of dialogues with faculty members. We argued that if a major institution such as Dartmouth refused to participate in the U.S. military program, it would add significantly to the growing swell of sentiment against the war.

The faculty, however, adopted a compromise proposal which did, in fact, phase out ROTC over the next few years. That the resolution included plans to consider re-institution of ROTC in four years—after we had graduated from Dartmouth—appeared to reflect not a moral stand, but an effort to appease the student body. Not only was the option to maintain ROTC included in the resolution, but all military programs would continue to operate for the benefit of those students already engaged in military training. The College would reduce its commitment to the military effort, then, but only temporarily.

A meeting of anti-ROTC students had been scheduled in College Hall for May 6, and I attended. I was on my way to give a guitar lesson to a Hanover boy, so I had my guitar. I had no plans to do anything political after the meeting, as we had lost the faculty vote and I was very discouraged. I did not see how one more meeting could have any effect.

I remember seeing Jonathan, a dormmate, outside College Hall. He asked me if I planned to participate if a demonstration followed the meeting. I said no, that I had something to do afterward. He said, "We *all* have other things to do."

I was late, and the meeting inside was short. It was the biggest crowd I ever saw at anti-ROTC meetings, numbering perhaps 250 people. Dave Green was on the stage saying that the time for talking was over; it was time for action. He said *he* was going over to the administration building; anyone else was welcome. There was no haranguing, no rationalizing. He strode down from the stage and out the door.

Only a sophomore, Dave Green had uncanny timing; it was good strategy and effective leadership. He felt, I think, that one more democratic meeting of suggestions and resolutions was a futile prospect. He was angry, he wanted support, and he got it. Most of the crowd streamed over to Parkhurst Hall. We had staged one sit-in meeting there before, and it was not clear what this new action would be.

I followed with ambivalence. I had engaged in a series of discussions with Dean of Freshmen Albert I. Dickerson '30, and we had reviewed at length the arguments of the anti-ROTC campaign. He represented to me the best possible source for the conservative view. The subject of a Parkhurst take-over had come up because it was, in view of the events at Harvard, Columbia, and other campuses, a "natural" option for students who saw themselves as part of a larger movement. It was also the symbolic and functional center of the College; the offices of the President and the deans were there.

During my conversations with Dickerson, I had said I doubted that such a take-over would occur, but that if it did, I expected to participate. Dean Dickerson said he hoped I would not, and I genuinely respected his concern. He always seemed fair to me and took a sincere interest in my progress. I knew he would be disappointed in my militant activity, but I felt a greater responsibility to the issue. The more of us who participated, I reasoned, the less easily this gesture of indignation could be dismissed by the faculty, alumni, and general public.

I did, however, tell the dean that I expected to be a moderating influence if the occupation became violent. Campus violence between students and police had become familiar through the headlines, and I felt it served no purpose. It was not naive to suppose, as facts later confirmed, that non-violence would have to be defended in the midst of a militant action. It *was* naive to think that if students behaved non-violently, then police would necessarily follow suit.

At least a hundred of us—perhaps many more—entered the building at first, and to my knowledge the plan of action was not fully communicated to many people. I first became aware of what some demonstrators had in mind when I saw building employees leaving the building in a hurry. I went straight to Dean Dickerson's office. I don't know if I had already seen Dean Thad Seymour pushed and pulled down the stairs and out the door by the surging students, or if I saw that only later, but I tried to persuade Dickerson to leave under his own power. He would have none of it, and he was eventually carried out in his office chair. Because of his age, I feared for his safety on the stairway and helped him keep his balance until he was outside. He treated the entire episode as a kind of prank, smiling and admonishing throughout.

By the time I got back into the building, nearly all of the employees were out, with the exception of a faculty member in a basement office who was said to have heart trouble. Word spread that he was to be left alone; there seemed to be an unspoken agreement that our action should cause no injury. To my knowledge, it caused none.

At this time people began milling throughout the building, taking stock of the situation and talking over strategy. It was certainly not clear what we could accomplish by occupying the building. [. . .]

I telephoned the boy whose guitar lesson I was supposed to give, telling him I would have to miss this afternoon.

Through the years, almost countless memories from the hours inside the building have drifted vividly back. There are some I don't want to forget.

While it was still light, for example, I wandered through the President's office, where students were occupied watching the crowd gathering outside. Climbing a narrow stairway and a ladder to the roof, I found my roommate and Bill Geller, a wild-haired, pink-shirted, indomitable sophomore busily hanging a crimson banner on the flagstaff. Many in the crowd were incensed by this, and yelled obscenities and threats up at us. I clearly remember several who chanted "Hang the commies!"

I could see signs protesting the action and some supporting it. Students were running from all directions, and the crowd was already more than the yard could hold. The street was blocked with the curious, the sympathetic, and the vociferously hostile. I recall my extreme puzzlement that these students could become so upset over the temporary occupation of property and yet remain calm in the face of hundreds of thousands of dead and mutilated bodies less than a day's jet-ride away. I was shaken by what seemed an impossibly wide gulf between that group and those in the building.

Returning to the group on the main stairway, I found them discussing the next steps to be taken. Early in the occupation, there had been no need to identify oneself as "there to stay" or "only there for a while." It wasn't clear that anyone was going to stay for very long. Various ideas were now considered, and some decided to stay until forcibly ejected. It would, even if the ROTC issue was lost, demonstrate that this issue was not just student whim; it was a principle that we were willing to risk our college careers to defend.

It was at that time that many students began leaving; some unobtrusively, others with no little regret and apology. One student, Jim, said, "Look, you guys, I'd like to stay, but my dad would kill me." There was no pressure to have these people stay.

I don't think anyone seriously expected our action would persuade the faculty to reverse their decision; but neither did we, as a group, ever relinquish that hope. College demonstrations had already changed policy at other schools. [. . .]

Soon we were down to 56 students, former students, and sympathetic community members. All five of us who were freshmen dorm-mates remained, along with three other first-year students.

At one point, a student began to remove the U.S. flag from the main hallway flagstaff, but he was stopped. It was agreed to let the flag remain there because our action was not intended to undermine, but to reinforce, the principles for which it was supposed to stand. It remained throughout the occupation.

Don, who had been in Chicago during the 1968 Democratic Convention riots, was afraid that we would encounter the same kind of police brutality that he had encountered there. He argued against a passive surrender to the inevitable arrest, stating that our chances would be better if we used table legs and trash-can lids for our defense and escape. Non-violent argument prevailed, and it was agreed that we would employ passive resistance in the tradition of the civil-rights arrests that had taken place for years in the South.

My guitar was passed around as the hour grew later and the crowd outside thinned. Different people played and sang while we intermittently communicated with school officials through handwritten notes. Food was passed in through a window, and an air of camaraderie began to develop.

That mood recalls for me the frequent criticisms of student activism of that era, that it was motivated not by political conviction but by "adventurism." It was true that we felt adventurous; we were sharing a new experience in resistance to an illegal and immoral national administration, and it created excitement in all of us. But there were simpler ways to have adventures; we were there because we believed in the rightness of our resistance. [. . .]

The details of the arrival of the troopers, the dogs, the riot-gear, and the vehicles are interesting, perhaps, but they belong in another account. *Time* magazine did as good a job as any. *Time* did omit, however, the fact that we had overdone the barricading of the huge double-doors of the administration building early in the day. After the troopers' futile banging away showed that the doors would have to be destroyed for them to gain entry, we removed some of the benches and tables so the doors would give way more handily. We forgot to notify the troopers of our cooperation and on their next heave, they burst through with unexpected ease and tumbled into a heap on the floor. We were not there for combat and we allowed ourselves to be carried away to the waiting buses.

In all but a few cases, the police were civil enough. Don, who had feared police violence, was maced heavily as he was carried struggling from the building. In the process, an over-zealous trooper first delivered a full stream of the excruciating chemical squarely into the face of his commanding officer. Finally, we were all loaded and driven to a nearby armory until our removal to jail.

Our temporary release and subsequent hearing were marked by a number of legal maneuvers most conspicuous for the lack of defense we received from a local law firm. I had occasion to meet with our lawyers at various times, as a part of our group and as a representative of our group, and I do not regret their incompetence; we expected to be found guilty. I do regret that we and the Hanover community paid them several thousand dollars. We soon found ourselves serving 30-day jail sentences for criminal contempt of court, and if the lawyers had a hand in shortening it by three days, it has been a well-kept secret.

Memories of our time in jail are still vivid. I don't know the basis for the particular groupings of students, unless they were random, but we were divided among several county jails throughout New Hampshire. I was in the largest group; the 14 of us spent our hours at Rockingham County Jail talking politics and resistance and doing course work for the spring term. We were allowed, depending upon the particular professors, to finish class assignments from our cells. Some of our group were seniors or graduates and were politically more sophisticated than others; they often led discussion. New ways of resisting the war were debated, as were new lifestyles for those who would graduate or might be dismissed from school. The occupation of Parkhurst was discussed, but it was generally considered over and done.

My journal from those 27 days contains a record of the disturbing hours I spent in these discussions. Such books as Oglesby's *Containment and Change*, Dumhoff's *Who Rules America?* and Marcuse's *One Dimensional Man* were made available to us through faculty members and sympathizers. Clearly, our country was guilty of the imperialism and underhanded dealings of which our State Department accused other nations. And clearly, too, our military policy was often formulated to benefit select financial interests. Even conservatives conceded these things, but they were quick to protest that such exploitation of others was a necessary part of Cold War policy. It is only recently that the undeniably corrupt and illegal activities of government agencies during that time have become public news items.

Those who didn't believe it was happening then don't believe it is happening now.

Finally, we returned to campus, and our College Committee on Standing and Conduct hearings began. Some students were suspended because of their radicalism in general and their Parkhurst roles in particular. All of us who were freshmen were given one or two semesters' probation but were allowed to continue schooling. Sandy was dismissed from ROTC, and I was not allowed to return to the football team in the fall. (When I went to talk with Coach Bob Blackman about the turn of events, he showed sincere concern for my judgment. "Don't you realize," he asked, "that if you are ever working for a big corporation—say IBM—if you don't conform to their rules, they'll just fire you?" I agreed that yes, they probably would; and I think that as Bob and I looked across his big desk at one another, each realized that the other was operating out of an entirely different playbook. I never played football at Dartmouth again.)

The suspensions of some students had led to the general advice that we plead contrition to the CCSC if we cared to stay in school, but that seemed to me to abdicate a position we were trying to strengthen. I therefore went in with rhetoric blazing, attacking the faculty for "their commitment not to conscience, but to contract." The committee listened patiently, tolerantly, and then asked me if I had anything more to say. I was almost speechless at the lack of concern over my indignation; the meeting was adjourned.

I attribute the committee's benign aspect to the just-concluded testimony of Dean Dickerson, who spoke on my behalf. It was emotionally difficult for him to do so, because his position was radically against that of the demonstrators', and he wanted no confusion about that point. I was not allowed to hear him speak, but his words to the committee carried weight; he ordinarily presided over it. He and I had formed a friendship that lasted, I think, until our last meeting in his office the day before he died in my senior year.

I have never regretted the episode that was Parkhurst '69. Part of who I am now is whatever small courage or abandon it took to join my fellows in that protest against Dartmouth's military cooperation. I have remained active in social and environmental issues and am now pursuing a Ph.D. in education, doing another kind of homework that helps in knowing one's country. [...]

The Black Student at Dartmouth

by WALLY FORD

⋙⋗ In this article, written during his Sophomore year and published in the June 1968 *Alumni Magazine*, Wallace L. Ford II 1970 (who would ultimately enter the law as his profession) treats mainly of the Dartmouth Afro-American Society and the goals of its members in working for "a new awareness" of their contribution to life at the College.

AN OBSERVER OF the campus situation at Dartmouth College may say with considerable certainty that the strongest and most influential agent of social change and awareness at the College is the Dartmouth Afro-American Society. With a membership consisting of almost every black student at Dartmouth (although membership is not closed) the Society within a few short years has accomplished a great deal in terms of recognition of black students in Hanover, and of black people in this country and around the world. [...]

In the late winter and early spring of 1966 a group of black students at the College, mostly freshmen and sophomores, met many times to discuss their respective experiences and feelings. To a man, they decided that there were certain basic aspects of the Dartmouth Experience which were or could be injurious to the black student. Among these points was the fact that there was a consistent, almost systematic, exclusion of black students from the college activities, thinking in terms of a black student's being able to retain his own identity. Due to a situation not at all peculiar to this school, the black student was (and to a definite extent still is) excluded from having a sense of really participating in activities on campus while being consistent with his own feelings. [...]

It was just too easy while being in Hanover for a black student to lose all sense of identity with, or relevance to, black people in this country. This stemmed from the fact that black students were consistently ignored as black students, while simultaneously there was very little at the College that related to the Black Experience. Consequently, because of the very human desire to feel "a part of things," many black students in the past had renounced their identification with black people, adopting all the values of white people without question, offering little if anything of their own experience. Therefore, through no fault of their own, many black students at all-white campuses such as Dartmouth were forced, in order psychologically to survive, to become as white as their skin would permit (*i.e.* as much like white people as possible).

These Dartmouth students who met in 1966 decided that it was imperative to react against this compulsory whitewashing by banding together at Dartmouth in order to make the Dartmouth Experience relevant to black people. They were most aware of the very persistent phenomenon in the American tradition which involved the black college student: those who could provide the skills which would lead to the betterment of black communities, which would lead to an acceleration of the progress of black people towards political and economic freedom, were coopted out of black society and into white society. Those who could do tremendous good were indoctrinated with the concept that whatever is connected with black people is inherently inferior, and as a result, black people characteristically left the black community when they became professionals. [. . .]

During [Governor of Alabama George] Wallace's visit to the campus, there were a certain number of demonstrations and intentionally disruptive activities initiated by black students in protest over what DAAS members felt were the racist and oppressive policies and practices of Wallace in relation to black people.

The activities caused quite a campus controversy as to their legitimacy. Although a great deal of tension was created by what has been termed the "Wallace Incident," most members of the Society did not regret the incident because Dartmouth students finally were forced to recognize the fact that there were certain grievances which the black students, indeed all black people, had, and there was a consequent cognizance of the Dartmouth Afro-American Society as a significant organization.

Quite coincidentally, when Wallace was in Hanover there was national press coverage via radio, television, newspapers, and magazines. As a result, many people who "never knew there were any up there" were made aware of the existence of black students at Dartmouth. Moreover, many people recognized the fact that perhaps there were some students at Dartmouth who were definitely willing to make their experience relevant to black people during the course of their formal training at an institution of higher learning. [. . .]

Conveying Bicentennial Greetings

by THE EARL OF DARTMOUTH

❧❧ꝫ In June 1969 the opening of the College's two-hundredth-anniversary observance had as one of its special features the presence in Hanover of Lord Dartmouth—the Ninth Earl—and his Countess. On the day before Commencement (at which exercises both Lord and Lady Dartmouth would be awarded honorary doctoral degrees) a special ceremony was held, wherein formal greetings were accorded the Earl and Countess (by speakers representing the Trustees, faculty, students, and alumni) and His Lordship was given a gold exemplar of the newly created Dartmouth Bicentennial Medal. The text that follows, transcribed from a voice recording preserved within the College Archives, is part of what Lord Dartmouth said to the assembled audience on that occasion.

W E ARE VERY HAPPY to be here at the inauguration of the bicentennial celebrations. I have always heard that Dartmouth is famous for its fine buildings and for the beauty of the surrounding countryside. Both of these have far exceeded our expectations. We are enjoying our visit, particularly because of the warm and friendly welcome which we have received on all sides.

I am very touched that after two hundred years Dartmouth College should wish to maintain the connection with my family. This began when my ancestor the Second Earl acted as sponsor, and the new College took its name from him. The connection has always been greatly cherished on our part.

In 1904 my grandfather came here to lay the cornerstone of the new Dartmouth Hall. When I was a little boy I remember him telling me of his visit and of the wonderful reception which was given to him. "It was," he said, "a reunion between Dartmouth and Dartmouth."

My aunt, Lady Dorothy Meynell, who is now eighty-five, came with him on that occasion sixty-five years ago. She is very fit and well and still has a vivid recollection of the College. A short time ago I had tea with her and told her of our proposed visit. She showed me her diary and fascinating photographs in her album, taken here in 1904. She has written me a special message which I would like to read to you. This is the message:

"I am so delighted to hear that you and Raine are going to Dartmouth College for the inauguration of the bi-centenary of the granting of the charter in 1769.

"My visit there in 1904 is still fresh in my memory, and I shall never forget the wonderful welcome we received when I went there with my father and mother. I still have some of the lovely maple leaves, in their autumn coloring, which I brought back, and still ringing in my ears is 'Wah-Hoo-Wah, Wah-Hoo-Wah, Da-Diddy-Dartmouth, Wah-Hoo-Wah.'[. . .]

"I cannot wish you more delight and enjoyment of your visit than we had so many years ago, and I hope you will convey my heartiest congratulations and good wishes to all at Dartmouth. [. . .]"

There are probably not many people still alive who were on the campus at that time, although it is quite obvious that the Class of 1904 is still very active.

I do want to thank the College most sincerely for this special casting in gold of the Dartmouth bicentennial medal. It is a wonderful and historic present, and a very great honor for me to receive it. It will always be treasured by me and my family. I know that this special medal has been authorized by Act of Congress, approved by the then President of the United States, and struck at the United States Mint. I much admire the design, which is another triumph for Mr. Rudolph Ruzicka.

The medal bears two mottoes. One is "VOX CLAMANTIS IN DESERTO," which clearly illustrates the main purpose of Eleazar Wheelock and the other founders of Dartmouth. This intention, over the years, has been broadened to meet the requirements of modern life, but remains as vital today as it was then. The other is my family motto, "GAUDET TENTAMINE VIRTUS," which I translate as "Virtue rejoices in travail." This could very well also have been adopted by the other Dartmouth, especially in its earlier years. But in spite of many problems, both legal and financial, and much travail, Dartmouth flourishes today and rejoices on its two-hundredth birthday. Long may it continue to rejoice.

This great College is acknowledged all the world over as an important seat of learning. It is perhaps even more important that, in addition, the moral principles and the integrity and the high ideals and ambitions of its founders should remain alive here at Dartmouth, now and for another two hundred years. I am sure they will.

As Retirement Approached

Interview with JOHN SLOAN DICKEY

➤➤➤ At the close of his Convocation address in the autumn of 1968, President Dickey revealed to the College community that he had informed the Board of Trustees he wished to conclude, during the 1969–70 academic year, his incumbency in what he characterized as "one of the world's wonderful jobs." Some nine months later *Yankee* magazine's June 1969 number featured a long interview entitled "A Candid Conversation with Dartmouth's John Sloan Dickey," from which these excerpts are drawn.

S hortly after his announcement of retirement, we asked President Dickey to grant us time to question him in behalf of Yankee *readers about his quarter century as Dartmouth's president, as well as about the contemporary issues facing most of today's college presidents. He most kindly assented, and so it was that on a gray winter afternoon last February we began the recorded interview in his office on the Dartmouth campus by asking him what he considered his most important accomplishment during his 25-year tenure . . .*

Well, I think that would probably be in the area of upgrading the quality of our faculty, or faculties—we actually have four faculties here: the faculty of arts and sciences, the faculty of medicine, the faculty of engineering, and the faculty of business administration. It is important, I believe, that we have been able to more than hold our own in the highly competitive market for teacher-scholars. That hyphen is something we look for—we want men who have outstanding abilities as teachers, who can teach with competence, but we also want them to show some scholarly interest, to have that kind of creative urge which will keep them on-going learners for the next 20 or 30 years. If a man is not interested in teaching, if he is trying to run away from teaching and wants to spend his life primarily in research, then he shouldn't come here, because we are an institution that has always placed first priority on a first-rate undergraduate education. On the other hand, we don't think a man can be a good teacher if all he is going to do is retail other people's knowledge—he is not going to set the example of being a learner, which is probably the most basic thing that a good teacher teaches. Rarely do we promote a man to tenure who doesn't have strong credentials both as a classroom teacher and a scholarly, creative person. [. . .]

In addition to the strengthening of the faculty, what other changes have occurred during your administration that you would point to with pride?

I don't think I want to single any one thing out, but there are two or three things I'm proud to have had a hand in. However, my greatest satisfaction is the overall vitality and strength of Dartmouth today, and the preservation of the strengths I inherited—and I inherited a lot of them. For example, the president's office is operated today much as it has been through the years—an open-door policy is still maintained as it always has been. More people come to see me without appointments than do with appointments—faculty, students, alumni. These are the practices and the style of a small college. Well, today Dartmouth is not a small college, but a relatively small university complex with three graduate professional schools and a growing graduate program in Arts and Sciences. We have, I think, been able to grow strong in today's terms without losing the basic qualities I inherited. To give a more concrete answer to your question, however, I am proud to have been associated with the building of the Hopkins Center and the realization of an educational concept which brings the creative arts into the center of the community and has made art, music, theater, and the craft arts part of the daily life of everyone here.

The Hopkins Center has achieved recognition far beyond the Dartmouth Campus, Mr. Dickey, and I understand it was an important factor in bringing to you one or two of your more creative faculty members . . .

Yes, well, this wasn't the sort of development, or achievement, if you want to call it that, that was universally applauded before we got it. It didn't have general faculty interest or support, except for those who would be directly involved in it. There was indifference on the part of many, even antagonism. Many of the alumni couldn't see why there should be any more attention paid to the arts than when they were here. And we had the inevitable controversy over the proposal to erect a modern building. The whole business of raising money for a project in the eight-million-dollar area, of winning support from the trustees, the faculty, and the alumni was a long, strenuous business.

Yet today I suppose there is no single facility which has played such a vital part and had such a broad influence in the life of the college or in strengthening the relationship of the college with the larger community, regionally, nationally, even internationally.

As I said earlier, however, it is difficult to single out any one development. Other fundamental developments have been critically important to the institution: the "re-founding" of the Medical School and the Thayer School of Engineering, the extensive strengthening of the Tuck School of Business Administration, and the establishment of the Kiewit Computation Center that plays such a large role in the daily life of the College and in its service to the region. And I would not want to leave the record on this question of accomplishments without mentioning the William Jewett Tucker Foundation created to further the moral and spiritual work of the Dartmouth Community. In Project ABC (A Better Chance) and in a variety of other imaginative ways, the Tucker Foundation has been the cutting edge of Dartmouth's response to the "concerns of conscience" for both students and our society.

What do you think are the greatest challenges facing your successor?

Well, I have mentioned several things I think I'm leaving "undone," so to speak. But I think his greatest challenge will be to find a viable role in relationship to the whole institution. These enterprises of higher education are going through a crisis in internal government today, with the healthy demands of students, faculty, and everybody else for a more active role in their government. *Authority* is dispersed throughout literally hundreds of student and faculty committees, but the ultimate *responsibility* is traditionally concentrated in the president's office. And that is the central problem today facing the president of any large and complex American educational institution; he bears the ultimate responsibility, but in order for him to act he must work through hundreds of channels, talk with dozens of people. It is very difficult to get anything done.

Do you think a college president should be primarily an educator or an administrator?

He most certainly has to be both, particularly in an institution such as Dartmouth. If he isn't an educator at heart, I don't think he is going to be a good college administrator. But being a good educator, in the sense of being a good scholar, is far from enough. Some men have the capacity for being an administrator, but they don't have the taste for it, they don't have a taste for the daily troubles which are the normal fare of administration. If a man doesn't really enjoy seeing sick people and he's a doctor, he's in the wrong profession. If a man can't stand a daily fare of imperfections, of poor "fits" that he's got to try doing something about, then he ought not to be in administration. [. . .]

What do you think has helped you the most as a college president, your experience as a lawyer or your experience in public affairs?

That is something I have never thought about, but I do rate highly the experience I had in the State Department, in organizing and creating programs that had to be manned and developed within a big and growing organization, and having to convince Congress and the public about them and the money that had to be provided for them. I gained a breadth of outlook from being in charge of our international cultural affairs, our educational and information programs. It was almost a postgraduate course in the affairs of the world. During the last couple of years in the State Department, I was also teaching in The School of Advanced International Studies. I don't think that the law helped me as much, though it does teach you to be careful of facts.

How far do you think a college president should go in responding to the demands of a minority group who may be causing quite a little trouble on the campus?

This is a classical example of what I mean by judgment. There's no point beyond which he probably shouldn't go, and there are lots of points beyond which he should go. I've had to go along with quite a few things here I thought were unwise, but I haven't gone along with anything that I thought was destructive to the institution. I think the line of judgment has to be: which is the more destructive to the long-range interests of the institution, to respond although not yourself convinced or not to respond? The "extremist" groups remain small groups on almost every campus unless and until the college is forced into or trapped into some action which seems to the larger group of students or faculty to be wrong, or which draws a lot of people in on some issue other than the one which the extremists originally created.

These extremist groups can do outrageous things, and they do outrageous things, and my contempt for their outrages is as great as any other person's in the country. But I think in so far as anyone can be wise about these things—and nobody can be wholly wise about them—I would rather err in trying to be reasonable and responsive up to the point where it would be destructive to the institution than to adopt a rigid position at the outset and thereby invite a lot more people to join the extremists. I try also to distinguish between destructive "extremism" and pressure for positive ends often "unreasonably stated"—granted that each of us has his private definition of that much-abused term—or, to put it another way, between those groups whose purposes are ultimately destructive of the institution and others whose rhetoric may be provocative but who are seeking to improve the College and society. Implicit here is that educational institutions have a great capacity for correcting their own foolishness, and there is inevitably a great deal of foolishness inherent in a community of young men passing through the four years that separate boyhood from manhood. Mistaken ideas ultimately get very harsh treatment in a free marketplace of ideas, and unsound movements are usually self-limiting.

I have been following this turmoil, this turbulence on the campuses, more closely than I have followed any other problem since I've been on this job. I began to realize more than a year ago that the problem isn't just a generation gap, though God knows there is a generation gap and it is terribly wide. What is going on is world-wide, not only in schools, but in the church, in the military, and in business institutions: there is a basic re-examination of the role of authority in all institutions everywhere, even in the family. It isn't only youth that is questioning authority, as witness the upheaval in the Catholic church, but it is the nature of youth in this as in other things to be impulsive and more violent in both speech and action. The young are impatient and want to fix up the world in twenty minutes. What I'm saying is that you cannot understand or deal with such a complex situation by thinking you are dealing with a bunch of unruly children who can be put in their place by rapping their knuckles. There's no question that when you get people trying to get their own way by the use of force, they may have to be dealt with by the use of force; but I think it's the last thing in the world you ought to turn to. That is why so many educational institutions, so many faculties and administrators have been tried to the limit of human patience by people who act outrageously. College presidents have felt that they just had to explore every alternative, exhaust every possible resource, before calling in the constabulary.

And now we get back to that question of the college president's responsibility to act without his having the actual authority to do it. The democratic ideal is so thoroughly ingrained in the American culture that a college president, or dean, or other administrative officer usually finds himself involved with several student and faculty committees before any action is possible. That is a difficult way to govern anything anywhere. A serious aspect of the whole thing when it comes to dealing with outrageous behavior is the dispersal of authority in a college. It's easy to say, "Why doesn't the president do this, or the dean do that?" But if asserting authority merely means closing the school down because he can't carry the faculty with him, or because three-fourths of the student body supports two dozen extremists, it may be less destructive to the institution if the president, or the dean, recognizes the limitations of his actual authority and take the longer way home via a very difficult and uncertain democratic process. It's often a hard choice.

Even though there is this world-wide revolt against authority, most of these extremist groups are making quite specific demands, aren't they? Are any of these demands reasonable and just?

The extreme element, the SDS [Students for a Democratic Society], for example, wants all of the fundamentals changed, as far as I can make out. They just don't accept the possibility that there is anything about society as it is today that is good. Other groups shade from that position on up to those groups who simply want authority spread around the place rather than concentrated in the hands of a few. The militants among the black students want what the militants in the black community throughout the country want: immediate social justice; and anybody who has as good a claim on social justice as they have is likely to be pretty "unreasonable" as to when he wants it. In the main they are not identified with the SDS kind of reaction against all organized society.

Then there are those who feel that young people haven't been treated as adults. Frequently they haven't, and frequently they haven't *been* adults. At some institutions we are also beginning to get students who are militant against the militants; they are tired of the demonstrations they have to walk through, tired of the strikes that make life intolerable for all students. Where it is all going to end, I don't know. People get emotional and start cracking at each other and then someone gets hurt. When someone gets hurt the public authorities move in—once the police or the National Guard moves in, it's a different ballgame, and a hard one to keep playing by normal academic rules. [. . .]

Are you in favor of instituting co-education at Dartmouth?

We are unquestionably in the middle of a movement towards co-education at the moment in this country. It has a fairly long and an honorable history, and has worked elsewhere, as far as I know. But I believe that any institution that is not co-educational should plan a careful and concrete program before going ahead. I don't believe that co-education here is inevitable, nor is it necessarily wrong. I do urge that it should be examined in relation to all other commitments Dartmouth sees ahead for the next decade. I think we must have concrete answers as to whether Dartmouth's limited resources and limited energies, if directed towards the education of women, would create a stronger institution than if they were directed to other new programs. I think the study now being undertaken will decide this. [. . .]

Do you believe that a good football team is essential today in a college such as Dartmouth?

No, it is not essential, but I'll tell you that the ups and downs of the athletic program are reflected in the happiness of the college community more than those who have no time for athletics realize. A good football season seems to create a climate of happiness for reasons I don't pretend to understand entirely. [. . .]

What do you plan to do after you retire as president of Dartmouth?

Give more attention to the field of foreign affairs, which is my field of professional interest along with education, and particularly I want to do some special work in the area of U.S.-Canadian relationships. I may do a little consulting, possibly some writing. We're building a house in Hanover. I wouldn't want to get too far away from Dartmouth, even in retirement. In all ways it's home for me.

Dartmouth Buys A 'Lemon'

by WILLIAM LOEB

≫≫ This was the heading of the front-page editorial that appeared on May 8, 1970, in the Manchester, New Hampshire, *Union Leader*—a newspaper whose publisher, William Loeb, had long been acutely critical of the College. What occasioned this particular journalistic assault was newly installed President John G. Kemeny's having undertaken (successfully, as it would prove) to calm student reaction and avoid potential violence at Dartmouth, within the highly volatile climate that existed on campuses nationally, in the wake of the tragic anti-war riot at Kent State University.

I T S E E M S to this newspaper that Dartmouth has bought another lemon for president and has gone from bad to worse.

To what OTHER conclusion can any reasonable person come after listening to President John G. Kemeny's announcement that he is suspending classes for all the rest of this week, beginning last Tuesday, so that students can spend time in conferences on what he calls the "constitutional crisis" facing the nation?

It is also to be noted that, in his monthly broadcast, President Kemeny called for a day of mourning for the four students shot and killed at Kent State University in Ohio.

THIS NEWSPAPER HAS NO RECORD, HOWEVER, OF THE DARTMOUTH PRESIDENT CONDEMNING THE RIOTS ON COLLEGE CAMPUSES ACROSS THE COUNTRY.

It is also interesting to note that President Kemeny has joined a number of other college presidents in sending a letter to President Nixon, asking him to meet with them to discuss the problems being faced in Indochina and on college campuses at home.

To discuss the problems on college campuses might be helpful, but just what do these college presidents think they are going to tell the President of the United States about Indochina? Just what experience do they have that qualifies them as current foreign affairs experts with knowledge that is unavailable to the President? This is absurd!

It seems to this newspaper that what has happened at Dartmouth has happened at many other colleges and universities. A small clique of left-wingers among the alumni, individuals with some sort of guilt

276

complex over their wealth, take control of university affairs and disregard the vast number of sensible, patriotic alumni. These cliques select a president, such as the new president of Dartmouth, and then the university is stuck with him.

The only remedy to this situation is for the sensible, patriotic alumni of these universities to take a more active role if they want their university to be rescued from the hands of left-wingers. They must take an active interest in university affairs, select candidates for the boards of trustees and see to it that they are placed on the board of trustees. Gradually—it will be a long, slow process—the control of our universities can be rescued from the present left-wing domination.

In the meantime, the world is not waiting with bated breath for the decisions which will result from that week of "contemplation" of our so-called "constitutional crisis" in national affairs.

What unmitigated nonsense to assume that these theory-filled professors and these students, most of whom have never made a dollar in their lives but who are the products of the charity of their parents and the taxpayers, will come up with any really significant contribution to solving any national crisis!

AS MORE OF THEIR LOOTING, THEIR BURNING, AND THEIR VANDALISM IS EXPOSED TO THE VIEW OF THE GENERAL PUBLIC, IT IS BECOMING VERY CLEAR TO MOST AMERICANS THAT A LARGE SECTION OF OUR ACADEMIC COMMUNITY IS INTELLECTUALLY AND MORALLY BANKRUPT!

As Congressman Louis Wyman pointed out in his statement on the "constitutional crisis," it is time that college presidents assumed rational leadership of THEIR communities and defined the offenses for which students should be summarily dismissed.

Until some sort of rational order is re-established on our college campuses, we can expect more nonsense such as we are seeing at Dartmouth where, as far as this newspaper can determine, the deterioration of the great university which Daniel Webster so dearly loved is rapidly progressing.

The Coming of Coeducation
and "the Dartmouth Plan"

by JOHN G. KEMENY

›››› Dartmouth was the last of the Ivy institutions to adopt coeducation. Thomas W. Braden 1940, then a member of the Board, wrote in his nationally syndicated newspaper column for November 26, 1971, an account reflective of deliberations by the Trustees that had taken place the previous weekend at Hanover, saying in part:

"So here we are, 16 Dartmouth men of various classes sitting around a long polished table in the trustees' room, trying to decide whether to admit women to Dartmouth, and hold classes the year around, partly so as to make room for women. [. . . .]

"We behaved like men asked to adopt a new mother. 'My gut feeling is it's wrong,' somebody remarked. 'It's only my brains that make me do this.'

"We did it. [. . . .] Our brains told us that the college owed a duty to society and that barring some catastrophe, which would once again make physical strength the test of survival, society was going to become less and less the sole possession of the male. Our brains told us it was pointless to continue the college as a unique institution if the only way it could be unique was as a relic. But our hearts cried. We liked the mother the way she was."

Dartmouth's transition to coeducation and the College's adoption of year-round operation were treated of by President Kemeny in his report entitled "The First Five Years," published in the April 1975 *Alumni Magazine*.

COEDUCATION WAS an issue on which men of good will who deeply loved the College could hold diametrically opposite views and firmly believe that they were right. They could—and they did.

We know more about the attitudes of the various constituencies on coeducation than on any other subject. A professional survey by the late Oliver Quayle '42, taken of a carefully selected cross-section of the alumni, revealed the following facts. A majority of the alumni favored the education of women at Dartmouth *in some form*. On the other hand, no specific plan could come close to mustering majority support. Of the 40 per cent of the alumni who were opposed to any form of coeducation, more than half had extremely strong feelings on the subject. Furthermore, the alumni classes were split according to when they graduated from the College. The classes in the '20s were

278

firmly opposed, the classes of the '60s were strongly in favor, and there were all gradations between. Although many tried to question the accuracy of Ollie Quayle's poll, various samplings I was able to make myself reassured me that he accurately reflected the opinions of the alumni body.

The constituency most strongly in favor of coeducation was the faculty, which came out nearly 10 to 1 in favor. The student body was also strongly in favor, but with a vocal minority in opposition. One of the perplexities of the debate was illustrated by the student who claimed, "Everybody I know is opposed to coeducation" and another student who claimed, "Everybody I know favors coeducation"—and they were both right. Friends tend to think alike, and having spent a great deal of time discussing this controversial issue they reached the same conclusion. Similarly, groups of alumni with identical opinions found it difficult to believe that other alumni thought quite differently about the question. In short, this was potentially the most divisive issue facing the College.

The controversy started before I became President of Dartmouth. The Trustees had established a committee on coeducation co-chaired by the senior Trustee, Dudley Orr '29, and Leonard Rieser, then provost of the College. Three faculty members had been chosen to represent Arts and Sciences; I happened to be one of them. Our committee was hard at work throughout 1969, and we were ready to make the first public presentation of our tentative findings late that year.

December of 1969 will be remembered by many members of the Dartmouth family for the truly memorable Charter Day celebration. The Alumni Council rescheduled its meeting so that the members could participate in this historic event. By that time I knew that I was one of several serious candidates to succeed John Dickey in office, but I had no way of estimating my chances. I was therefore surprised when the president of the Alumni Council requested that I give the major report on coeducation to the council. I remember thinking that I had only two options: I could alienate half of the Alumni Council, or all of it. I told my wife that whatever chances I might have had to be chosen as the next President would evaporate after I gave that report.

I was to learn an extremely important lesson on that day in mid-December. I would never again judge the alumni so unfairly; I learned that if one faces a group of alumni and tells them honestly and frankly what the issues are, and why people feel one way or the other about the merits of the issues, one gains respect even from those who totally disagree.

The following month, I was elected the 13th President of the College and my role changed dramatically. As one of the majority of the Trustee committee who favored coeducation, I faced a major challenge to come up with plans that would be in the best interests of the College, that would lead to as little bitterness as possible in the alumni body, and that could be approved by the Board of Trustees—without jeopardizing the financial well-being of the institution.

From my discussions with the Alumni Council it became clear that even alumni who favored the admission of women would not accept a large reduction in male students. Yet I was reluctant to follow the examples of Yale and Princeton in enlarging the student body significantly. A thousand more students on campus would require the construction of very expensive facilities and would result in a degree of crowding that would have a highly negative effect on the educational process. I therefore began to think seriously about the idea that we increase the total student body without increasing the number on campus at a given time. The idea was to add a fourth term to the academic calendar and spread a larger student body out among four terms. While I had no more than the germ of an idea, and two separate faculty committees would eventually have to put in enormous amounts of work to design a practical plan, I do not believe that the Trustees would have voted in favor of coeducation if it had not been coupled with the Dartmouth Plan.

I would like to acknowledge that I was wrong on another major issue confronting the Trustee committee—the form of coeducation to be adopted. A variety of options were explored ranging from building a women's college near Dartmouth, through some form of an "associated school," to full coeducation. On this issue I was prepared to compromise because I felt that an associated school would provide almost all of the educational advantages of coeducation and would gain much wider acceptance from the alumni. The faculty voted overwhelmingly against that plan. In view of our experience in the past three years, it is clear that the faculty was right!

After all the arguments had been mustered on both sides, and all the constituencies had been heard from, the decision was up to the Board of Trustees. A special meeting of the Board was called for Saturday and Sunday, November 20–21, 1971. This was the most remarkable meeting of the Board of Trustees I have had the privilege to attend, and I deeply regret that we did not tape-record the session to make it available to future Dartmouth historians.

Besides all the material prepared by the Trustee committee, the Board had requested a variety of additional information. An important role was played by the consulting firm of Cresap, McCormick and Paget. They presented their review of the combined financial impact of coeducation and year-round operation, both short-range and long-range. They estimated that after transitional costs, and after the costs of some facilities modifications, the College could roughly break even, with the possibility of a modest additional expense or a very small net profit. Our experience has proven these estimates accurate; we have had a small addition to the net budget of the College, within the range predicted, and have reduced significantly the cost per student at Dartmouth.

The consultants also prepared, with the kind cooperation of Yale and Princeton, a confidential report on the experiences at those two newly coeducational institutions. The Trustees also had a survey of high school students indicating that our plan for year-round operation would meet with considerable acceptance, a prediction that has been borne out by the large increase in applications.

Two other developments might have had an effect on the Board's decision. The possibility had been raised that new federal legislation would make it mandatory for the College to become coeducational, and there was a fear that applications to Dartmouth might start declining as they had at other private single-sex colleges. The Board was informed that neither of these two events had occurred, and therefore it was under no *compulsion* to act in favor of coeducation.

Dean Carroll Brewster had been requested by the Board to consider alternative administrative arrangements, particularly as might be used to implement the "associated school" idea. He reported that following that route would mean substantial additional administrative costs and would significantly reduce the educational benefits of coeducation.

The most fascinating part of the Board's discussion centered on the question of the role of women in future American society. Several Trustees expressed the conviction that women would play an increasingly important role in leadership positions in the country. Therefore, they argued, Dartmouth, which had traditionally prided itself on the training of leaders, should train women as well as men for leadership roles. It was also argued that if, in the future, our male graduates would work side by side with women, we would be providing an unreal learning atmosphere in an all-male college. The argument that we prepare our students for "a man's world" may once have been accurate and persuasive, but it was no longer true.

The Board recessed late Saturday afternoon to give its members a chance to reflect overnight. I believe that none of us had much sleep that night. The Sunday morning session was a solemn one. All the arguments were over, and it was up to the Board of Trustees to decide the future of the College. Under the leadership of its chairman, Charles Zimmerman '23, the Board passed two key votes. It voted unanimously to put the College on year-round operation. It then voted—by a substantial majority but not unanimously—to matriculate women as undergraduate students starting in the fall of 1972.

The Board then turned to various implementing actions. Most important was the approval of the blueprint for year-round operation prepared by the Faculty of Arts and Sciences. Next was the question of the number of women students to be admitted to the College. The Board limited itself to setting a general guideline for the first four coed classes: the male student body should be set at 3,000 and as many women should be admitted as the Dartmouth Plan would allow. My estimate at the time was that this number could be as low as 900 or as high as 1,100. As it has turned out, we will have roughly 3,000 men and 1,000 women enrolled in the College next year.

Finally, the Board of Trustees voted to authorize the President to attract to Dartmouth a distinguished woman educator to help with the transition to coeducation. One of the academic administrators I had grown to like and respect most was Ruth Adams, president of Wellesley College. Dr. Adams had announced in September of 1971 that she would retire from Wellesley at the conclusion of that academic year. I was most fortunate in being able to persuade her to accept the position of vice president at Dartmouth. We agreed that she would serve full-time for three years, and part-time for an additional two years, to help us with the problem of transition. Her long experience, her quiet advice behind the scenes, and her unshakeable good humor were invaluable assets to a group of male administrators, none of whom had ever had any experience at a coeducational institution.

Our women students, faculty, and administrators are more in her debt than they will ever realize.

We had nine short months to get ready for both year-round operation and coeducation. It was an extremely hectic and very happy period in the lives of many of us. There was great excitement and anticipation on campus following the very lengthy debate. It is a good feeling to know that all of the arguments are behind you and you can finally go into action. During this period, we were mentally preparing ourselves for an endless number of problems that would no doubt arise from the major changes. [. . .] But most of the anticipated problems with coeducation never materialized. I still find it difficult to believe just how smooth the transition has been. [. . .]

I have noticed increasingly that those who objected to coeducation in the abstract have found it very difficult to object to the women of Dartmouth. The male student body at Dartmouth had always had a distinctive character. We have discovered that women students come to Dartmouth for very much the same reasons that have made it so attractive for two centuries, and they are in a very real sense the natural counterparts of the men of Dartmouth. Their love for the College and their loyalty to the institution are—if possible—even greater than that traditionally shown by our male students.

I am confident that future historians will record that Dartmouth made the great change at the right time, and that it became a better educational institution for having done so.

One of the most common indictments of the efficiency of academic institutions has been the fact that a very expensive plant stands idle for three months of the year. The difficulty has been to devise a plan that would permit institutions to break out of the straight-jacket of the nine-month academic year. Although Dartmouth was not the first school to go on year-round operation, I believe that the Dartmouth Plan is the most attractive such option yet adopted by any college.

Using the physical plant for 12 months rather than 9 has advantages *only* when the student body is increased. Otherwise, expenses increase slightly without any gain in revenues. But if in moving to year-round operation, one accomplishes a significant increase in the student body even though one must add proportionately to the faculty and the administration, the fixed costs of the institution remain unchanged and one achieves an overall lowering of the cost of education *per student.* At the time we adopted the Dartmouth Plan, every Dartmouth student was receiving a subsidy of roughly $3,000 because the annual cost of each student's education was that much greater than the tuition charged. We succeeded in achieving a substantial increase in the student body at an average subsidy of about $300 per added student, thus significantly lowering the average cost per student.

We can accommodate 3,200 undergraduate students at Dartmouth using a combination of dormitories, fraternities, and some living quarters in Hanover and surrounding towns. Expanded opportunities for off-campus study, particularly in our language-study-abroad program, add about 200 students per term. Thanks to the Dartmouth Plan, our goal of 4,000 undergraduate students will soon be achieved.

In adopting the plan the faculty voted to bring our graduation requirements more in line with those of other colleges. Reducing the number of terms from 12 to 11, we set a graduation requirement of 33 courses—the most common academic requirement at comparable institutions is 32 courses. In addition each student is required to elect a summer term as part of his or her attendance pattern. If each student spends only 10 terms on campus during fall, winter and spring instead of the traditional 12, it is possible to increase the student body by 20 per cent without increasing the number of students on campus in any given term.

While accommodating a larger student body to implement coeducation may have been the chief goal of the Faculty of Arts and Sciences, the plan was also recommended for its important educational advantages. The Dartmouth Plan provides a new degree of flexibility for students to design their own academic calendar. In addition to choosing exactly which terms they wish to attend, they have the option of finishing in three years if they are in a hurry (and very few of our students are) or gaining additional time for reflection by spreading their education over five years. But the most important opportunity presented by the Dartmouth Plan is the holding of significant jobs during leave terms. While summer jobs have long been traditional for students, many challenging jobs are not available in the summer. In addition it is now easy for our students to arrange to be on leave for six months at a time, thus making them candidates for more interesting jobs. At a time when so many students have serious doubts about what they wish to do with their lives, the chance to try out a future profession while they are still undergraduates is a very valuable opportunity.

Dartmouth students, with their customary ingenuity, have also used their leave terms for a wide variety of experiences. It is common for students enrolled in foreign study to spend an extra term traveling. One student managed to stretch an overseas job into a round-the-world trip. The Dartmouth Plan has also provided new opportunities for athletes to be members of national or Olympic teams by scheduling their leave terms appropriately. The record so far is held by a student who is a member of a national team both in the summer and in the winter and yet will graduate with his class. At a time when young people clamor for freedom of choice, the flexibility of the Dartmouth Plan is proving highly attractive.

The Dartmouth Plan can also be a boon for faculty research. Since faculty members have considerable choice as to which three out of four terms they will teach, it is easy to combine a one-term sabbatical with summer teaching and spend half a year at another institution. Even without a sabbatical, many faculty members have opted to teach four terms one year and two the next year to provide a six-month break that can be invaluable for completing a scholarly project.

A not insignificant by-product of the Dartmouth Plan is the fact that we have been expanding our faculty in a most favorable job market. As I have noted previously, this should have a major impact on the quality of the faculty.

After two-and-a-half years' experience we may safely conclude that the plan works and that it has proved enormously attractive to applicants to the College. That does not mean that the plan is perfect; as with any radically new idea, there is room for improvement. [. . .]

It is my judgment that the great freedom and flexibility that students have gained, and their opportunity for significant off-campus experiences, far outweigh the few problems that were caused by the Dartmouth Plan. I am also convinced that the remaining problems can be solved as we gain more experience and find better ways of administering the plan. During the last two years, we have received many inquiries from other institutions as to how our plan works. Given the financial plight of higher education and the necessity to operate institutions more efficiently, I would not be surprised if the Dartmouth Plan—today a radical experiment—were someday to become the pattern for higher education in the United States.

A Letter to Parents

by ALBERT I. DICKERSON

≫≫⊃ While Dean of Freshmen, in an incumbency that spanned the period 1956–72, Albert I. Dickerson 1930 adopted the practice of dispatching several "Parents Letters" annually—sent to provide fathers and mothers with information, as well as gentle reassurance, about what was being experienced by their sons during their first year as Dartmouth students. This is the text of Dean Dickerson's "Parents Letter #4" in the academic year 1971–72. It was dated December twenty-second.

D EAR PARENTS OF '75: First, let me wish to you, and to your '75 sons who are our bond of mutual interest and concern, a Merry Christmas and a very good New Year. Most of you will still be together when this letter reaches you—unless something unexpected happens between this writing and the scheduled mailing date, or in the vagaries of the mails thereafter.

FIRST TERM GRADE REPORTS

Since this letter is written to accompany the grade reports of your sons (his copy of his grade report is being sent to him at his campus mail address), we should say something about first-term grades. Very likely there is in your home at this moment too intense a concern about *grades*: too intense for a variety of reasons in a variety of situations, but, speaking more generally, because (a) grades are never a precise measure of learning and (b) grades for the first ten weeks of a student's college career are often a very imperfect measure of his intellectual potential or his effort.

Perhaps the enclosed grade reports won't mean much to you without some frame of reference. (I discovered this when I got an IBM grade report like the enclosed for one of my sons who went to another college, without any explanation: this is one of the reasons why these Parents Letters have been concocted.) Based on the experience of recent years, the breakpoint between the quarters of the Class of 1975 on the basis of point average will be: top quarter: 5.0-4.0; second quarter: 4.0-3.7; third quarter: 3.7-3.0; lowest quarter: 3.0 and below.

286

In a "Happy New Year" letter like this one, it would be nice if all these reports could be straight A's, but there will be only about a dozen or two of these.

If your son has always up to now been in the highest quarter in school (as most of them have) and now appears in one of the lower quarters (as three quarters of them do), I can only remind you that he is working now as a member of a rather carefully selected group of students whose range of ability is much higher and narrower than the range of abilities of students in almost any secondary school; and only one-fourth of them can be in the top quarter! Some of us do our sons little justice by holding up to them unreasonable standards of achievement: sometimes, perhaps, because we achieved at that level ourselves; often because we didn't and are looking to him to realize our unrealized ambitions. The compassion of college counselors and deans is spent in largest measure on the student who is pushing himself as hard as he can and being pressured by parents for higher grades than he is earning.

Many of us who make up American society pay little daily heed in the family circle to the life of the mind and to excellence in its exercise. If your sons and daughters combine qualities of competitiveness and competence, they may "compete" themselves into selective colleges and arrive on the campuses without any real understanding of why they are there. If this happens and they get to college without any real feeling of the importance of intellectual exercise for its own sake, this is not their fault, but ours. Certainly the colleges contain more students whose motivations are either of the wrong kind or are insufficient in degree than society can afford. (The undermotivated ones are affectionately known as "loose hangers" in the undergraduate vernacular.)

THE JANUARY SYNDROME

As you receive this, your son will be thinking about his return to Hanover and may indeed be on his way. This is therefore an appropriate time for description of what I call the January Wish-I-Were-Somewhere-Else Syndrome, to which I alluded in the November letter. This is a phenomenon which will be manifesting itself in residential colleges all over the country during the next few weeks. Happily for Dartmouth, the calendar of our three-term, three-course program removes one of the main elements of the syndrome. Your son came home for the holidays with his first college finals under his belt. They weren't anywhere near as traumatic an experience as the sophomores had made him believe. The fact that these first finals are now behind him, for better or for worse, gives the Dartmouth freshman a welcome feeling of relief and of belonging.

But speaking generally, the campus-bound freshman as January approaches is not a happy man. Home had never looked so good to him. You were never so liberal with the keys to the car. The brothers and sister, if any, were never so indulgent. As for the girl, either (a) *she* never looked so good, or (b) they broke off, or (c) the worst happened and *both* of these things occurred. (The latter is known as being "shot down.") None of these three eventualities tends to cheer the student in January as he sets off to return to his college campus. The sense of adventure and discovery which dominated the September departure is missing. In its place is a sort of delayed homesickness. So . . . the freshman, having vastly enjoyed the all-too-brief hometown exhilaration of being The Returned College Man, goes back to college to face, under most college calendars, the culmination of all his academic insecurities as the dreaded finals approach. Even the Dartmouth freshman, with that particular ordeal behind him, turns his face toward Hanover with a sobering sense of still having his way to make as a college man.

So in January in residential colleges everywhere, freshman deans are talking to freshmen who come in to say they think they should quit college, or transfer; go to work, or join the army, or travel. They talk about their health, their sinuses, the climate; about your health or business problems, or the illness of aunts or grandparents; they yearn for the life of the big city (whether or not they have ever lived in one); they have suddenly discovered that a college nearer home (where possibly a particular girl happens to be attending or planning to enroll) offers courses especially well adapted to their suddenly discovered needs; etc., etc. Things they never mention are (a) homesickness and (b) worry over finals.

For this description of the January Wish-I-Were-Somewhere-Else Syndrome, I have drawn on various colleagues at other colleges. It's a comfort to all of us to realize how universal this experience is.

HAVE THEY BEEN HAPPY HOLIDAYS?

Our calendar provides a Christmas recess of generous length, but even so you probably will not need all your fingers to count up all your son's evenings at home. Indeed, I surmise you would not find it mathematically too difficult to compute the total of waking hours spent under the family roof, especially if you eliminate those spent at the table and around the refrigerator.

With your sons perhaps at home to read over your shoulders, I hope to sound not too flippant about the foibles of freshmanism. However, one of the many fine qualities of the typical freshman is his honesty and candor, and I am sure he will not mind a few general observations concerning characteristics of his age group that may irritate or amuse his elders. After all, parents are People and they are entitled to a Point of View. The main purpose of these letters, beyond the transmission of grades and other essential information, is to make a modest effort at strengthening the insights and the understanding between home and campus; and in this effort I try never to say to a parent anything I would not be prepared to say to the son, or vice versa.

So let's face it: a college freshman is likely to be a pretty self-centered fellow. At the freshman's age and in this once-in-a-lifetime situation of feeling that one must make his place quickly in a new peer group of substantial size and of high and varied abilities, there is a great deal of self-questioning; of self-evaluation in relation to academic challenges, in relation to fellow-students, in relation to girls, in relation to everything. In simple fact, freshmen spend a lot of time thinking about themselves. It is understandable if parents, in the face of this sometimes massive self-preoccupation, occasionally feel rebuffed. It is an odd but widely recognized fact that it never occurs to young men of this age, who are themselves extremely sensitive to criticism from their families, that parents also have feelings, and can also be sensitive about being "wanted" or being treated with bare toleration.

Some of you have observed, usually with more amusement than irritation, exaggerated assertions of independence by word or deed by these young men who know as well as you do (hence the instinct to assertiveness) their degree of continuing dependence in more than just the financial sense. If some of your freshman sons seem to have all the answers, I can only warn: wait until they are sophomores!

Occasionally tensions build up during the first long vacation and threaten a serious break between the student and his family. "How would *you* feel," I asked a freshman in one of these situations, "if *your* son, after having spent only five evenings at home in a three-week vacation, disappeared entirely from the family ken for his last days—including New Year's Eve—and dashed home from the Rose Bowl with just enough time to pick up his suitcase and add a few final touches to the chaos of his room before rushing off with friends to the airport?"

Well, things usually work out a little better than that and leave a tolerant afterglow of loving amusement behind them. Take as an example this letter which a mother wrote me during a recent January in response to that year's version of this Parents Letter:

"Yes, indeed, the College Man returned! He visited his high school making sure to wear his 'Dartmouth' jacket although the weather called for the winter coat; and from his talk I later gathered that he made quite an impression. He visited his former French teacher, giving her suggestions which she appreciated, of course. My own ego is only beginning to inflate since his departure. My grammar has been corrected; world events have been explained to me with great patience; and in simple language I have been psychoanalyzed daily. How I ever managed to get through college and hold down a fairly responsible job is still a mystery to me but much more so to him! Yes, it's amazing how much they learn in four short months of college.

"However, I noted a change in him. Living with eight boys has made him more considerate. He waits on himself without complaint and is much nicer to live with . . . [. . .]"

THANKS TO YOU

I want to thank many of you for your letters, some of which are still on my desk awaiting reply. The "form letter" is probably the least satisfactory medium of human communication, and it is a tribute to your fine understanding that some of you have responded in such warmly friendly and personal ways to these letters. [. . .]

Working with John Kemeny

by A. ALEXANDER FANELLI

❧❧❧ Alexander Fanelli 1942 served, as he himself here indicates, in the capacity of an Assistant to the President of the College during three successive administrations. In this reminiscence he concentrates on a few memories associated with the Kemeny years, 1970–81.

THE ELEVEN YEARS that I worked with John Kemeny as his Executive Assistant were for me the most enjoyable and the most instructive of a thirty-five-year career that included college/university teaching, ten years in the Foreign Service (five in Rome and five in Washington, D.C.), and sixteen years as assistant to three Dartmouth Presidents—John Dickey, John Kemeny, and David McLaughlin—before I retired in June 1983.

John Kemeny inherited me from John Dickey, for whom I had served as a Special Assistant from 1967 to 1970 for Dartmouth's yearlong bicentennial celebration in 1969. But I had gotten to know and admire John Dickey much earlier, in the late 1940s, when I worked in the Public Affairs Laboratory of the Great Issues Course.

While I knew that when John Kemeny was elected President he was highly regarded as a gifted teacher and a skillful rebuilder of the math department, I knew very little else about him. Looking back nearly thirty years, I remember that I liked him immediately, when we first met.

Within the first few months after John Kemeny's inauguration an incident happened that could easily have terminated our relationship—and my employment! JGK had agreed to be interviewed by John H. Fitzhugh of *The Connecticut Valley Reporter*. Being a competent reporter, Fitzhugh asked JGK some rather delicate questions about coeducation, the Trustees, relations with alumni, Dartmouth finances, et cetera. Being an honest and forthright person, alone in the room with the questioner, JGK answered all of these queries with candor and in some depth.

A few days later the newspaper crossed my desk, and I read with increasing alarm Fitzhugh's account and his direct quotation of JGK's answers. The question in my mind was: Should I let this pass and hope for the best, or should I alert the President to the dangers that could arise from his overly candid replies to such questions in this instance and in the future? I finally decided to write JGK a two-page memo focusing on the negative consequences that might ensue from four of the direct quotations attributed to him in the Fitzhugh article, prefacing my remarks with a declaration of my assumption that the President "would not be well-served by an assistant who was less than frank." At the end of my remarks I suggested an office procedure that would, hopefully, minimize or eliminate the dangers in such interview situations. When my memo was returned to me I was greatly relieved to find JGK's bold "OK" penned in the margin of that paragraph.

JGK's acceptance of my criticism in this instance wasn't the only indication that our relationship would develop cordially over the years. Thanks to a generous alumnus in Denver, an extremely comfortable Cadillac (bearing "VOX-1" registration plates) was available to transport the President, with a College chauffeur, to special events in New Hampshire, Vermont, New York, and elsewhere. At some point in—I believe 1971—JGK asked me if I would mind accompanying him on one of these trips, and serving as driver, so he could discuss various items of College business with me. I accepted with pleasure and enjoyed this and subsequent similar occasions very much. JGK would sit in the back, with his work papers spread out on the seat.

On one such trip we had a blowout of the right rear tire, fortunately not at high speed. Although I had had a great deal of experience changing tires on the first car my wife, Betty, and I ever owned (a 1929 Model A Ford, bought from a local farmer for one hundred fifty dollars), I had never worked on a Cadillac before, and was having some difficulty because this particular one had partial wheel-covers on the back wheels. As soon as he became aware of my distress, John Kemeny came out to help, and the two of us managed to wrestle the bad tire off and install the spare.

Perhaps the most memorable of such trips for both of us was one to Albany, where JGK was to speak at the alumni club dinner. Governor Nelson Rockefeller, who unfortunately had to be out of town that evening, had very generously offered to have a pre-dinner reception at the Governor's Mansion, and he insisted that JGK and I stay there overnight. When we arrived at the mansion we were greeted cordially by the major-domo and shown to our respective rooms. As I looked with amazement at the walls of my bedroom, I realized I had never seen such impressive paintings outside of, perhaps, the Uffizi in Florence. "JGK has to see this," I said to myself, and walked briskly toward his room, only to meet him halfway there. "Alex," he said excitedly, "you have to come and see the marvelous paintings in my room!"

Because there were so many important changes in the College in the years between 1970 and 1981, the volume of incoming mail to the President increased dramatically over that period. During the first few weeks of his presidency JGK said (wisely) that he wanted to see *all* the incoming mail, and of course we complied with his request. Later, after an especially sharp upturn in mail from alumni, JGK said, "OK, now we shift to a different system."

Eventually, the procedure adopted was that after the mail was opened by Ruth LaBombard, some was routed directly to various administrative officers for a direct reply. The rest of the President's mail came to me, and I would then type a draft reply, which would be passed on to JGK, attached to the incoming letter. Because I had been fortunate in earlier years to serve as special assistant to a fairly important officer in the Department of State, I had become rather adept at this ghost-writing task. In my job at Dartmouth it was easy to tell how close I had come to sounding like JGK, since my "success" was inversely proportional to the number of changes he would make in each draft.

Over a period of months, my drafts sounded more and more like John Kemeny, and most of the thousands of drafts I wrote were in the "zero or one-change" category. But in the beginning it was not all that easy to pass the test. As I write this, I have in front of me a three-by-five card I have saved for nearly twenty-eight years. In JGK's handwriting the message reads: "Alex: These are very good drafts, but could you translate them into Hungarian? Or at least into the style of a certain Hungarian? Thanks, John"

One of the many things I liked about John Kemeny was his sense of humor. However, I discovered that it wasn't always limitless. The reception room to the President's office contained, in addition to the secretaries' desk and cabinets, a couch with a low coffee-table in front of it. On that table was the largest solid glass ashtray I have ever seen. When the first report of the Surgeon General on the dangers of smoking arrived in the mail, I placed it where I thought it would do the most good: directly under the reception area's glass ashtray. One morning when JGK noticed it there he came into my office and asked me if I was aware of the location of the report. "Yes," I said, "I put it there." "Do you think that's a good idea?" he asked. "Well, I thought it was," I replied. "But it doesn't have to be there, of course." I promptly removed the report to another location.

I myself had smoked rather heavily for about fifteen years, but fortunately I stopped in 1953. JGK knew that I didn't like anyone to smoke in my office. When he wanted to talk to me about something he rarely phoned me and asked me to walk the forty feet to his office, perhaps because he didn't want me to suffer his smoky environment. Almost invariably he would walk to my office. That was very thoughtful, but the trouble was that nine times out of ten he would arrive totally unaware of the smoking cigarette in his fingers. Eventually he would realize he was smoking, and he would search frantically for an ashtray (which, of course, I didn't have available). Then he would retreat to the reception room and put out his cigarette there, before returning to my office. What a *nice* Hungarian!

One final memory that I will not soon forget: Shortly after JGK had told me that he wanted to keep me in his office as his Executive Assistant, and after I had told him that nothing would please me more, I was stunned to receive a phone call from Prof. John Rassias (deservedly known as the high priest of foreign-language study at Dartmouth), offering me the opportunity of supervising and teaching a group of students in the Italian program at Florence for the fall term of 1971. However, this would have involved, among other things, my going to Florence a few weeks before the beginning of that term, to arrange segments of the program there concerning the arts.

I went immediately to see John Rassias and told him that I would have loved to do this, but that I couldn't imagine leaving John Kemeny in the lurch for that length of time, at this point in our relationship, to say nothing of the near-zero probability that JGK would even consider letting me go to Florence. Rassias, who must have learned hypnotism at some point in his formative years, just looked at me fixedly and said, "Please, just go and ask him."

When I went to see the President and related the above, he was silent for a moment and then asked me, "Do you enjoy teaching?" I said, "Yes, I do. Very much." He asked, "Are you a good teacher?" Without hesitation I said, "Yes. Enough people whose judgment I respect have told me I am." JGK was silent. Then he smiled and said, "OK, you can go." Then before leaving for Florence I scribbled a note to JGK thanking him for several things, and I closed with this sentence: "I realize that 12 weeks in Florence will be pleasant under almost any conditions—and I thank you for letting me go—but I must beg you not to describe it as a 'vacation' lest the Romance Languages Dept should refuse to pay my salary!" As usual, JGK had the last word: "I assume that any other job, compared to your present one [that is, being his assistant] will be a vacation!"

As an "equal opportunity" assistant, I am happy to express my special thanks to Jean Kemeny for her friendship during those eleven years when she served as JGK's full-time partner in the presidency. Jean made me feel like a member of the family on the many formal and informal occasions for Trustees, faculty, alumni, and honorary-degree recipients at the President's House and the Outing Club. I also want to give special recognition to Ruth LaBombard for her years of devoted service in the President's office during JGK's tenure. Often it was her quiet competence and wisdom that enabled the rest of us—including the President—to work more effectively in the interest of the College.

A Sister and Brother
Talk about Dartmouth

by GAIL and ROBERT SULLIVAN

>>> Business woman Gail F. Sullivan 1982 (Tuck School 1987) had been preceded at Dartmouth by her journalist brother, Robert B. Sullivan 1975. In 1997 the two engaged in a light-hearted colloquy titled "Sluggo's Sister Chooses Dartmouth," which was featured in the March number of the *Alumni Magazine*—as part of a special section, "Women of Dartmouth: An Unabashed Celebration," marking the rounding out of a full quarter-century of coeducation at the College.

B*ob Speaking:* I got out in '75, on schedule, having had a ball. Gail got in in '77 and I said to her, "That's great! Congratulations!!!" [. . .]

Ours—mine and Gail's and our brother Kevin's—was one of those first-generation-to-go-away-to-college families, and so we knew nothing of other schools. But I, at least, knew about Dartmouth—big time. And I knew about women at Dartmouth. Or so I thought. Or so I feared.

Mine had been the transitional class—the forgotten, unequivocally non-historic class. Admitted all-male, we spent freshman year with one-another guys, and with the term-transfer gals from the Seven Sisters, whom we liked for liking Dartmouth. [. . .]

Gail was the brains in the family. (Like *that's* hard to believe!) And so, sure, of course she would want Dartmouth, and Dartmouth her. But Harvard wanted her too. Why, then, this unreasonable early-decision decision for Big Greenerhood?

Let's ask her.

Gail Speaking: Well, it was your fault. You know that. Don't put it on me, like it was some failing.

I'll explain to the others. . . . My introduction to Dartmouth came in 1971 when my brother started his freshman year. I immediately wanted to go there too, mainly because, at 11 years old, I still wanted to copy almost everything my brothers were doing, and because I had come to the conclusion, having visited Bobby, that Dartmouth had to be the most beautiful college in the country.

Now back in 1971, I realized there were obstacles. Primarily, Dartmouth wasn't accepting women. But that didn't change my mind about wanting to attend. Nor did anything else I learned about the place during the seven years between my brother's matriculation and my own.

After the women-eligible question had been wisely rectified by the powers-that-were in Hanover, I watched closely to see if this, indeed, was the place for me. I heard about "all-nighters," and came to know that the finals schedules were, at best, painful. I watched as ₍. . .₎ Bob struggled through *Ulysses* over Thanksgiving holiday. But I figured tribulations such as these would not, could not be unique to Dartmouth. As to things more exclusively Green, I was introduced, as an observer, to beer pong, and even to Heorot's Medieval Banquet ₍. . .₎.

I saw all this stuff at a not-too-distant remove, but still wanted to attend college in Hanover. First of all, I wanted to experience some academic rigor—I really did. And seeing Bob sweat as he did indicated there were rigors to be found in the Upper Valley. And then, the fraternities didn't seem all that bad; the people in them seemed, in fact, very nice. And finally there lingered that beauty thing, that intangible. I had fallen in love with Mt. Moosilauke, the Dartmouth Skiway, and homecoming bonfires.

I'm a little embarrassed to admit that my reasoning for wanting to attend Dartmouth didn't go much deeper than that. I was reflecting on this shallowness recently after I spoke with a high school senior—a guy—who was trying to decide between Dartmouth and the University of Pennsylvania. He rightly had given a lot of thought as to how the two experiences would differ, how each would impact his career, his life. He asked many good, detailed questions. I compared his well-developed inquiry to my own, by-gone decision-making process. I think, in retrospect, that I should have at least considered the fact that I would be attending a school that was in only its seventh year of coeducation and was still 75 percent male. ₍. . .₎ But I don't remember wondering at all how "the ratio" might impact me, except perhaps in a few positive ways, such as how easy it would be to make the swim team. I mean, how many good swimmers could there possibly be in a class with just 316 women?

Bob Speaking: [. . .] It seems to me, the Dartmouth that we saw during our cumulative decade wandering the Hanover Plain was a community in vigorous, forced evolution. [. . .] Dartmouth wanted to time-travel epochs in a trimester. Impossible? Dartmouth thought not. And Dartmouth was, I think in retrospect, right to go about the evolution of its singular species this way.

It created some tension when I was there, and some stupidity. I remember the hazing of women. I recall resentment at what they were doing to the bell curve. I even believe, looking back, that there was pressure on them to be "Dartmouth men." One Saturday afternoon I played in a game of mixed, full-tackle rugby, during which a small woman got her back broken; read into that whatever you will. A lot of us in the original class of '75 drank too much, so we thought a cool woman was one who drank too much too. A bunch of guys [. . .] got blitzed one night and wreaked some pretty serious havoc in the halls of Woodward. Bad stuff. And this was the stuff I was worried about when young Gail started telling Mom and Dad about how she'd like to go to Dartmouth some day too, just like Bobby.

But it seems to me—and I aver that this is not colored by the murky gray haze of reminiscence—that all of this nonsense changed pretty quickly. Kemeny let it be known that poor behavior was unacceptable, and Dartmouth people are, after all, pretty smart. By the time I graduated, the men and the increasing numbers of women were brothers and sisters, by and large—*we're all in this together, up here in the woods, clamantising in deserto unitas. And while we're at it, Let's Beat Harvard!* My dorm, Hitchcock, was one of those hyper-liberal room-by-room dorms: Your neighbor was of the other sex, no matter which sex you were. And by Junior year I found myself pals with a lot of my neighbors. [. . .]

Gail Speaking: [. . .] And I found a good, safe place. I found things I expected—the rigor, the aesthetic—and things that surprised me, too.

What I found at Dartmouth right off the bat was a bunch of good women swimmers. In fact, there were a lot of talented women in just about every field. Although I'm sure I experienced my share of freshman jitters, they were not female freshman jitters. I never felt outnumbered by men. It seemed that all around there were women leaders: president of the Dartmouth Outing Club, managing editor of The Dartmouth, all the usual résumé items that lead to a C&G tap. Perhaps women were succeeding because they were striving that much harder to excel, in the way minorities often do to prove their worth. For me, if that was a motivating factor, it was subconscious. In fact, I remember early on at Dartmouth I took a lot of math and science classes, the kind of intro courses many students took during their freshman year. [. . .]

In any event, in those freshman classes on those high-stress tests days, I was clearly just another student, another walking ID number, another breathing Hinman box address. It was simply impossible to feel I was suffering any discrimination.

A couple of concessions: Maybe my experiences within an all-woman dorm—Woodward, Bob!—and on a women's sports team colored my perceptions on equality and inequality somewhat. And maybe it was that times had already changed. I have heard reports that it was not as easy for women in earlier classes to fit in, and I don't doubt the reports. But I can only speak for myself, and in 1978 I immediately felt an equal member of my freshman class. [. . .]

Of course, there was room for improvement. I would have liked more women professors. Fraternities were great fun, but also had a dark side. Social alternatives were limited.

Bob Speaking: Not as limited as they had been.

Gail Speaking: Really?

Bob Speaking: Yeah, in retrospect I would say so. Basically, we had the frats. Dorm parties and the frats. The things at the Hop were okay freshman year, but they seemed hopelessly old-fashioned—like a mixer out of Fitzgerald or something. They were boys'-school remnants.

So there were those things. And then, of course, we road-tripped. That was an alternative, and it was fun—no question. But would we have done it if there had been more choices in Hanover? No.

The road-tripping is an interesting thing to look at. You see, we formed these frat-guy habits, and that was part of the reason for the early tension. It's senior year, and we're still road-tripping to Colby, because it is our habit and because we have old friends there. Well, what did this look like to others on campus—to the women, and to some in the underclasses? Insulting and hidebound behavior, that's what it looked like.

Remember that Winter Carnival when I visited you? [. . .] Entirely different from ours. Ours were somehow more . . . desperate. Yours were more airy. Yours were brighter. We ate in Thayer or took our dates out for a big meal at the Bull's Eye. That spaghetti-fest you guys had—it was a healthier thing, a vibrant communal scene. Yours was a friendlier Carnival, I thought. Ours were almost entirely nocturnal. I never would have entered that Carnival cross-country ski race that you and I entered that year. No way, no how.

Gail Speaking: But we were still playing beer pong.

Bob Speaking: Well, that's what evolution's about. You retain your most advanced traits. You hold on to your classics. Beer pong just may be the opposable thumb of a Dartmouth education.

Gail Speaking: How did you feel, visiting our Carnival?

Bob Speaking: Elated, frankly. Confident for you, confident for the College. [. . .]

Gail Speaking: Do you think the place has continued to change?

Bob Speaking: Yeah, from what I've seen. I mean, the people still seem larger than people at other colleges, and healthier. Not that there's ever been a Dartmouth type exactly, but . . . we always used to resist that notion, even in the pre-intellectual-loner era . . . but there's something intrinsic that the most blatant and forceful alterations of ethos and student-body composition can't seem to chip away at.

Gail Speaking: Which is good, I think. You can change greatly, and greatly remain the same. An institution that can do that is a pretty soulful institution.

It's strange . . . I know my Dartmouth was far different from yours, and from today's. I mean, yours was all-male at first, and today's is half female—that's a difference, no doubt about it. But to me, Dartmouth, when I got there, did not seem a different Dartmouth than Bobby's. . . .

Bob Speaking: Hey!

Gail Speaking: Than the OLD Dartmouth. Nineteen seventy-one, 1978, today, tomorrow—a beautiful college filled with talented people.

Bob Speaking, Nothing more.   *Gail Speaking:* Nothing less.

"Cohog"

by SUSAN ESTRICH

⋙ A law professor at the University of Southern California and the first woman to have served as manager of a presidential campaign (that of Michael S. Dukakis, in 1988), Susan R. Estrich (Wellesley Class of 1974) spent her junior year at Dartmouth —encountering an institution that was, to put it euphemistically, in transition.

"COHOG."—It was not a word I knew. It wasn't even what I was. But it was who I became, at least for a year, the first year of coeducation at Dartmouth.

My grandfather went to Dartmouth, on a scholarship from Salem High, where he played football for the Witches. But it was the Dartmouth Indian banner that would hang in his hospital room 50 years later. Mo Freedberg—Class of '09. He was the first member of his immigrant family to go to college, the one whose experience was the totem for the rest of us. After him, college became the rule and not the exception, for the men anyway. And not just college, but Dartmouth. My Uncle Bob, my mother's brother, went to Dartmouth, and so did my Cousin Irwin. My mother didn't go to college—she went to work—but she was a Dartmouth daughter, and a Dartmouth sister, as loyal as any alum.

Dartmouth wasn't accepting women when I applied to college, and Radcliffe didn't want me, so off I went to Wellesley, which was precisely where I belonged. Still, there were times sophomore year when the janitor was the only man we'd seen in weeks and the merits of single sex education seemed to be outweighed by the miseries of bridge on Saturday night. Wellesley, like Dartmouth, was a member of something called the "Twelve College Exchange," which allowed men and women from the remaining single sex schools to spend a year at the opposite extreme. My grandfather died that January, which sealed it. Not only did I apply to spend my junior year at Dartmouth, but I convinced three friends from my dorm to apply with me. None of us focused very much on the fact that Dartmouth would be accepting women students for the first time that fall; we were going as juniors, not as freshmen, as visitors, not coeds. We thought we would be welcome.

My roommate from Wellesley and I had a triple on the third floor of South Mass; our friends were downstairs. The first day, the four of us sat at the big window in our room watching as everyone headed to the dining hall, staring with our mouths open. Men. So many of them, streaming by our windows, literally thousands of men, and so few of us. Among juniors, the ratio of men to women was something on the order of 14 to 1. The four of us walked into the dining hall that first night and literally hundreds of heads turned. Is this heaven or what, we said to each other. No bridge in pjs for us on Saturday night anymore, we promised each other.

We were wrong. Dartmouth was many things but it was not heaven, at least for women in 1972.

The freshmen and the transfers, whom we met on our first days, didn't know that they weren't supposed to like us. They learned. By the end of the first week, when the upperclassmen had come back, the cohog jokes began in earnest. Real men didn't date cohogs. Cohogs were worse than dogs. Cohogs would blow the curve, ruin the football team, and force everyone into summer school. Being nice to a cohog was a sign of weakness.

In retrospect, it seems clear that there must have been some men, even then, who understood that women would strengthen Dartmouth and not destroy it. But the loudest voices belonged to those who opposed coeducation, and the distinction between a matriculating coed and a visiting Twelve College exchanger involved a level of attention to detail that tended to get lost with the first keg.

I was the only woman in most of my classes. I blew the curve. My first semester I got straight As, and citations in all three classes, without ever having uttered a word in class. I bought a keg at Bones Gate, the fraternity where I had stood up (translate: outdrank) Norman Mailer, along with the Dean who called us cohogs, and countless freshmen, but it didn't really matter. I never got a grade less than a straight A at Dartmouth, and never felt sure that I belonged. I couldn't wait to get back to Wellesley, if only to disappear in the crowd. By spring term, I was hanging out in the 1902 room in the library, which was a somewhat safer place for a cohog.

Not long ago, I ran into a man I knew at Dartmouth, now a successful investment banker, who told me that he remembered me dancing on a ping pong table at Bones Gate. I'm sure it's true, but it's not what I remember, not what I learned. What I learned at Dartmouth was that I could stand up to the best of them. I learned that I was just as good as they, that I could succeed even when the odds seemed to be totally stacked against me. I also learned about loyalty and fraternity, in the best sense of the word, about the ties of identity and experience that bind us, that turn us into who we are. I learned what my grandfather learned, nearly a hundred years ago. The sexes change; Dartmouth is without question a stronger, better place because of the presence of women. But the lessons—and the spirit—endure. Women may have blown the curve, but they have not blown the tradition. Women of Dartmouth stand proud.

Mater Dearest

by REGINA BARRECA

≫> Essayist and English professor Regina Barreca 1979, who may be said to exhibit here equal parts feminist and humorist, was guest editor for the *Alumni Magazine*'s issue (March 1997) celebrating twenty-five years of coeducation at Dartmouth, and she herself provided its opening piece, "Mater Dearest."

ONE OF MY STRONGEST MEMORIES from my first few weeks at Dartmouth is that sinking feeling of being unsure where I was headed. I never knew whether I was in the right classroom, the right building—often I felt as though I wasn't even at the right college. (One of my aunts in Brooklyn wasn't so sure either. "You're going to school in New Hampshire?" she asked me. "You're pregnant, right?")

But then came the moment after I had been on campus for awhile, when another poor, dazed, lost soul actually asked me for directions. She thought I knew what I was doing, and when I could answer her questions about the location of the reserve reading room I realized that, in fact, I *did* know what I was doing. It just didn't feel like it until then.

I get the same feeling reading this issue called the Dartmouth Alumnae Magazine, which brings a distinctively female voice to the cry in the wilderness. The boundaries of "The Dartmouth Experience" are inevitably revised and refigured when they are experienced by newcomers to the northern territories. New People come and give directions.

Still, we need to be reminded now and then that women have actually colonized the joint. The masculine experience tends to be considered universal, which is why women need to get their stories out. Early in the coeducational era, the tales we heard as students about the history and character of the College were ones, necessarily, about men.

This is not a big shock. For a couple of centuries the College had prided itself on making men out of boys. It certainly made a woman out of me. It also made a feminist out of me, which is to say that I subscribe to the radical belief that women are human beings. It was at Dartmouth that I came across one of my favorite passages by the essayist and novelist Virginia Woolf, concerning the way she was barred from entering even the libraries at Oxford and Cambridge, let alone the classrooms. Here was one of the century's greatest authors and she was kept out of the library because the male students and scholars couldn't bear to be disturbed by a woman—and they found women essentially disturbing. Woolf wrote how dreadful it was to be locked out. But then it occurred to her that it is "far more dreadful to be locked in."

At mid-seventies Dartmouth I wasn't always sure whether men should be let out. I was introduced to "Dartmouth's in Town Again, Run, Girls, Run" on my freshman trip. We were voted an "eight" as my friends and I walked past Mass Hall on the way to Thayer; collectively, we accepted this as a reasonable, if not generous, score. It didn't occur to us to offer our own signs and numbers as we slid over these established thresholds or to do anything but ignore the guys who shouted out phrases encouraging us (how can I put this politely?) to have their children. This is not necessarily a useful oratorical skill in late-twentieth-century America; to the extent that women no longer get public ratings on campus, men have benefited from the change as well.

Before such an enlightened time, I was learning a thing or two myself. "When our fathers were here there were no women," the men used to tell me.

"When your grandfathers were here there were no electric lights," I told them back. "Things get better."

And so they have. In my mind I carry a reminder of this: an image of us women as we walked to Thayer on an uncharacteristically warm March evening in 1976. Laughing, we seem to be pushing past our predecessors—the men in wigs, the boys in tight trousers, the returning G.I.'s still awkward in their civilian clothes. We "coeds" were not asking to be let in. That was Dartmouth's decision. Having come in through a once-locked door, we were helping to show the way out. The students who came after us are doing the same thing. [. . .]

Founding "The Dartmouth Review"

by BENJAMIN HART

≫⊃ In his book *Poisoned Ivy* (1984) Benjamin J. Hart 1981 tells, within a chapter entitled "All the Truth That's Fit to Print," of how *The Dartmouth Review* was brought into being, as an undergraduate newspaper and vehicle of conservative expression—one that would often be, over the years that followed, at the center of controversy, both on campus and off. The narrative here excerpted begins with conversation between the author and his friend Michael Keenan Jones 1982, in the setting of the faculty home where Benjamin Hart was then living.

"Dᴵᴰ ʏᴏᴜ ʜᴇᴀʀ what happened to Greg Fossedal?" Jones asked. Greg Fossedal was editor of *The Dartmouth*. We never understood how he got to be editor, because he was known to be conservative, while the rest of his staff ranged from moderate to extreme left. As a result, he was having a terrible time at the paper; his proposals and ideas were usually ridiculed and voted down by other staff members. He wanted to make *The Dartmouth* a first-rate paper, but his staff wouldn't even let him write editorials. Greg had been editor for six months and by now must have been a miserable young man.

"He was just fired as editor of the paper," said Jones. [. . .]

"That's outrageous," I said.

"No big campus outrage," said Jones. "If he'd been fired for being a Trotskyite, we'd never hear the end of it. You know, I was thinking that this campus needs another student publication, and in a bad way."

"If we had a paper, we could print your columns," I said.

"Can you imagine? The newspaper would feature columns by me." Jones laughed. "We could make an all-out assault on the *ethos*."

"We could combine news, culture, and opinion," I said. "People would have to read us. [. . .] I'll bet Greg Fossedal would be interested in our publication."

"He can be the editor," Jones said. "We'll need money for the first issue."

"We'll worry about that later," I said. "First let's get our staff together."

306

"The most important thing is to be completely independent from college authorities. It's the only way to maintain credibility," said Jones.

"Absolutely."

"What are we going to call it?" Jones asked.

"We'll have to give that some thought."

"Let's get Fossedal in on this thing right away," said Jones.

"I'll call him," I said. [. . .]

I called South Massachusetts dormitory. The phone rang maybe fifteen times before Greg finally answered. Like an owl, Greg was a nocturnal animal.

"What is it?" he asked in a groggy and slightly irritated tone.

"Greg," I said, "this is Ben Hart calling. Can you meet me and Keeney Jones in five minutes in the Segal house? I think you'll be interested in what we're doing."

"What is it?" he asked again.

"We're starting a newspaper. You're going to be the editor."

"What newspaper?"

"It doesn't have a name yet. The first issue will come out in two weeks. It'll be the graduation issue."

After I explained the idea to him, Greg got excited.

"I've been waiting for something like this for a long time," he said. "I've always wanted to start my own paper."

"Here's your chance. You can now write your columns endorsing unapproved candidates. Jones can write unapproved ideas. This will be a completely *unofficial* publication."

"I'll be right over," said Greg and hung up. [. . .]

Within minutes we heard Greg Fossedal enter the house, slamming the door behind him. [. . .]

Fossedal's skills as a reporter were unmatched by any other under-graduate, and his expertise in the mechanics of putting together a publication was invaluable to us. After he was fired at *The Dartmouth*, there was an immediate drop in subscriptions, advertising revenue, and the quality of news coverage, as the "D" declined from being a poor newspaper to one that was almost painful to read.

"How's it going, boys?" asked Greg as he stepped into the room.

"Sit down," said Jones [. . .].

"Let's think of a name," said Greg.

"I've already thought of one," said Jones. "*The Dartmouth Review.*"

"Sounds fine to me," said Greg.

"Who can we get to work with us?" I asked.

"I think we can get cartoonist Steve Kelley," answered Greg.

Kelley was a junior. For two years running, he received an award as the top college cartoonist in the country. *The Dartmouth*'s editorial editor, however, often canceled Kelley's daily cartoon slot if he judged the material "insensitive," or offensive to special interest groups on campus. In disgust, Steve stopped submitting his stuff. Kelley was a conservative, and his cartoons often showed an irreverence toward the local pieties. During my years at Dartmouth I discovered that, generally, guardians of the *ethos* do not like cartoonists, satirists, or jokers of any kind. Its true believers tended to be grim. These people saw nothing funny in Steve Kelley. And to their lasting chagrin, he found lots that was funny about them.

"I'm sure we can get Dinesh D'Souza to work for us," Fossedal went on.

"What does he do?" I asked.

"He's a dark-skinned fellow from Bombay. Dinesh D'Souza, or Distort D'Newsa, as he is called by his critics. He's only a freshman, but he's already won awards for reporting. He also quit working for the 'D' recently. He's now sending his stuff to outside publications."

During Dinesh's four years as an undergraduate I'm sure he published more material than any student his age in the country. He was a regular reporter for the *Manchester Union Leader* and the *National Catholic Register*. His stuff has been in *National Review, Policy Review, Reader's Digest, Conservative Digest*, and countless others. He later became editor-in-chief of the *Review*. By age twenty-two, he had written two books. "Even though I happen to be from India," he liked to tell newsmen, "I take great delight in slaughtering the sacred cows around this place." While at Dartmouth he maintained a 3.8 grade point average and was admitted to Harvard Business School.

"I'd like to meet this guy," I said.

"I'll get him on the phone right now," said Greg.

"See if you can get Kelley over here too," said Jones, "and what about that girl friend of yours?"

"Rachel?" asked Greg.

"Let's get her selling advertising," said Jones.

"I'll try," said Greg. "I'll also see if I can convince Gordon Haff to jump on board. He's invaluable to *The Dartmouth*. I don't think he likes it over there, and he's an expert photographer and layout man." [. . .]

The Dartmouth Review was launched. It was a tabloid newspaper, only twelve pages, with a mix of humorous and serious content. In its portrayal of the antics of Dartmouth's administration, the *Review* has been described as the *National Lampoon* of the Right. It was, in a way, but there were also think pieces by such people as Milton Friedman, Thomas Sowell, Walter Williams, George Will, the student editors, and others. [. . .]

Greg Fossedal funded our first issue by cashing his student loan check, with which we paid the printer. In addition, Greg wrote most of the copy, during the week before finals. Not only was Greg able to put out a top-quality newspaper during final exam week, on almost no advance notice, he also got straight A's in his courses and scored 796 out of a possible 800 on his Law School Aptitude Test. He would later turn down admission to Harvard, Yale, and Stanford law schools to go into journalism full time. At age twenty-four, he would take a job on the *Wall Street Journal* as the youngest editorial writer in their history. It is no overstatement to say there would have been no *Dartmouth Review* without the talents of Greg Fossedal. [. . .]

A First Lady's Observations

by JEAN ALEXANDER KEMENY

✧✧✧ These reflections by Mrs. John G. Kemeny are from her book *It's Different at Dartmouth* (1979), which provides a view of the College and of various Dartmouth-associated matters as seen by one who came to Hanover a faculty wife in 1954 and, then, was at her husband's side throughout the eleven years (1970–81) of his presidency.

"IT IS, SIR, as I have said, a small college. And yet there are those who love it. . . ."

Words learned by every high-school student. A major case argued before Chief Justice Marshall and the Supreme Court of the United States in 1818. The College was Dartmouth, and her advocate was Daniel Webster, class of 1801. The College is still small, and still loved—sometimes fiercely—by her alumni, faculty, students, staff, Presidents and first ladies.

And Dartmouth *is* different. Is it the place? The lack of formality and pompousness? Is it the direction the President takes? Is it the basic stuff of the College—her students and faculty? Is it all of these plus a special enthusiasm which sets the College apart and makes her a distinct, very different institution?

Dartmouth in another setting wouldn't be the same. Here there's a freedom beyond the campus bounded only by hills and streams; here there's still a quality of life unspoiled by urban haste and hassle.

The President makes a difference. The College has one who listens, who still pioneers, who unravels complexities and creates imaginative solutions, who will look and plan for the future beyond his own tenure.

Dartmouth is chauvinistic; it is not pompous. It can laugh at itself. Too many institutions take themselves so seriously; if *it* didn't happen on their campus, *it* didn't happen.

The College is comfortable with informality. A President's wife can disrupt traditions and not be classed an interloper who stepped out of bounds. A student is uninhibited about ringing our doorbell and asking to see the President, for the President is likely to be available.

310

Faculty and administrators are comfortable with friends outside their own departments, outside the academic community. Town and gown communicate.

Dartmouth is not a perfect paradise. Most of her imperfections are quite visible. But a vitality exists here, an optimism that when change is needed, change is possible.

There is no typical Dartmouth student. They come in all colors from all classes from every state and abroad. I know the daughter of a New York television star and the son of a Beirut taxidriver. Most are happy here, many are ecstatic, some bitch. Peer pressure is a force for good and bad. Isolation breeds fellowship, spirit and loyalty. It shapes admirable attitudes which last along with some obnoxious macho types which are disappearing. (I will be delighted when the last passes away and is interred.) [. . .]

Seven out of ten undergraduates come from public schools. Half of all students are on financial aid. Dartmouth is one of the few colleges that admits *first* and *then* looks at the family's income. And the College feels it has an obligation to make sure that the student does not have to drop out for financial reasons.

Students are listened to. The administration often adopts suggestions from undergraduates—simple ideas for improving the operation of the College which no one else had thought of.

Students have been told that the faculty are accessible, and they expect them to be. (Many write when they are away at graduate school, or off for a term, how hard it is to see or know a professor.)

Most undergraduates live on or near campus. After a brief era when communing with nature out of town was in, they found that nature was unkind—delivering 35-below temperatures in sparsely heated, rundown farm houses. [. . .]

The attitude of the faculty is different at Dartmouth. Teaching an excited freshman, still open to ideas and not yet veneered with cynicism, is a challenge, not a chore. Excitement is fragile; it needs to be nurtured, not turned off and withered by a bored graduate-student teacher. Most of the nation's universities use graduate students heavily. Cheap labor.

The outstanding researcher who wouldn't know an undergraduate if he bumped into one—who has nightmares about teaching—doesn't belong here. Neither does the teacher whose only piece of research was a Ph.D. thesis.

Putting together a faculty composed of stimulating teachers who also continue doing original work in their field is not easy. The combination is uncommon. Finding professors who feel that an hour spent helping a confused, lost student is not a waste of precious research time, whose first commitment is to their classes, who spend most of their time *on* campus, not *off* touting their achievements and toting up the number of outside consulting jobs, makes recruiting much more difficult. But it can be done.

A faculty member will not get rich on salary. There are children to educate, mortgages to pay off and unbearable property taxes to dig up. Many of the students these professors educate, will, five years out of Dartmouth, be making twice as much as their teachers.

A country that rewards glamour with million-dollar contracts still whines about the modest salary of a professor. "Two courses a term; eight hours of teaching per week! What do they do with all their free time?!"

Dartmouth faculty members spend hours preparing one lecture, they make up and grade their own exams, they read hundreds of papers, they hold office hours for students (and are usually in!), they invite students home, are freshman advisers, serve on College committees and write scholarly books and papers.

And then, if they have free time, they are involved in the region. They are selectmen and Town Meeting moderators, they serve on school boards and recreation councils, they study the environmental impact of industry on the area and they serve in the legislatures of Vermont and New Hampshire.

They are sports fans and sportsmen. They are opera lovers and cellists. They can build a pipe organ or a log cabin. Some live on farms, tend livestock and mammoth gardens, raise their own food and write significant papers on feeding the world.

In 1969 a new kind of chair was established—*not* for research, but to recognize excellence and encourage innovation in teaching. (John was the first recipient.) Dartmouth is primarily an undergraduate institution. Teaching is what it's all about. Sticking out the slow rise to full professor (and only four out of ten assistant professors will make tenure), working hard and saving little, takes a dedicated person. Dartmouth has five hundred. [. . .]

Holidays are ignored by the College. The service staff takes off, but everyone else functions. Classes are held, most offices are humming and John generally has a series of meetings. Even his birthday was not sacrosanct; he was scheduled to chair a meeting of the CAP which is held every two weeks in the President's office. The Committee Advisory to the President discusses matters of promotion and tenure. Their debates are serious, in-depth and *very* time consuming. They begin the middle of the afternoon and *never* end before 6 PM. An earlier adjournment would be certified a miracle.

Before John left that morning I reminded him: It was his birthday, it was the end of May and as usual he was exhausted, he needed some fun. I had planned a modest celebration and they could damn well stop pontificating by 6!

"I can't promise—exactly, but I swear faithfully to be home by 6:30."

He wasn't. He wasn't back at 7. I called the Office. No answer. A ringing phone *could* be heard but was ignored. He wasn't back at 7:30. Fed up and fuming, I gunned my Jeep down Webster Avenue louder and faster than any Porsche. I raced up two flights of stairs, stormed into the meeting, and, quite of breath, spit out an ultimatum. "You've got five minutes. If you haven't finished by then, you'll have to do without the chairman!"

Mouths dropped. Dead silence. One professor stood up, politely. A lady had entered the room. But I was no lady. I was an avenger who strode haughtily into an outer office and made sure to slam the door.

Four minutes later, the meeting adjourned, all business completed. [. . .]

In 1971 a stir began on campus, grew into a rumpus and ended in a great debate dubbed—unofficially—"The Mrs. Kemeny Case." Why? I had gone to a faculty meeting.

I went to learn, not to unhinge the faculty. I wasn't a feminist trying to crash an almost exclusively men's club; I went as the President's wife who had become a nationwide spokesman for the College. I needed to know Dartmouth's problems and the direction she was taking. I went to save my husband valuable time. Why should he have to regurgitate a three-hour meeting when I could brief myself?

Attendance at these meetings was confined to the Arts and Sciences faculty, senior administrators (who felt free to send a *very* junior administrator in their place) and representatives from the student newspaper and radio station. Wasn't I as necessary to the College as some administrators? Shouldn't I have as much access as the student media? I poured out these arguments to John who agreed, "Why don't you come." I did. I sat quietly in the back, absorbed, and didn't even interrupt.

I was not unnoticed. A delegation of senior faculty soon confronted John with an enormous problem: "Unauthorized persons are attending faculty meetings!" My name was not mentioned. John didn't bristle; he listened calmly and then informed the group that the "problem" would be brought before the Executive Committee.

Was there anything in the Faculty Handbook to cover this situation? John couldn't find a definitive statement. Although the rules were explicit about who could *vote* in faculty meetings, nowhere did they state who could *attend*. The Executive Committee chewed on the "problem," trying to find some guidance in the rules. They failed, so the matter was sent on to the Committee on Organization and Policy. And here the debate ended. For the elected chairman that year was a populist social scientist who took a very far-out position. Not only should Mrs. Kemeny have the right to attend meetings of the faculty —meetings should be open to *all* members of the Dartmouth community (even students!). And this view carried.

Now, in the Observer Section (marked by a handsome card), sit faculty spouses, students, staff, townspeople and me—all "unauthorized persons" a few years ago. No one checks our credentials. Fifty to a hundred will come if the agenda is likely to be controversial; more often there are only ten. The visitors listen politely. There are no demonstrations or giggles.

And probably most of the faculty don't even remember the time when they were whispering, "My God! The President's wife! It isn't done!"

Three Commencement Messages
—Emphasizing a "Sustaining Bond"

by DAVID T. McLAUGHLIN

◈◈◈ David McLaughlin 1954 succeeded John Kemeny as President in late-June 1981, beginning an incumbency that would extend over a period of the next half-dozen years. As had been true of his modern-era predecessors in office, President McLaughlin annually drew the College's Commencement exercises toward their close by addressing a brief personal valediction to the members of the Senior Class. In doing so he, like President Kemeny before him, adopted a practice initiated by John Sloan Dickey: of ending his text each year in essentially the same way. He cited ". . . the sustaining bond that will forever exist between you and your College." (Mr. Dickey had invariably concluded his remarks by declaring, "And now the word is 'so long,' because in the Dartmouth fellowship there is no parting.") Here quoted, as initially published at the time of their delivery, are three of President McLaughlin's valedictory addresses: his first, from June of 1982; that of 1983; and the one given in the final year of his presidency, 1987.

MEN AND WOMEN of the Class of 1982—and I salute you thus with a very special regard that can only be associated with a freshman President addressing a Senior Class:

This moment is one of leave-taking, but it is an occasion calling for words of farewell that involve no finality of parting.

You who have completed this phase in your lifetime of learning are "rounding out" your undergraduate relationship to Dartmouth, and you must move forward to meet new challenges, in different arenas and in different roles. Those of us who have been charged, here on the Hanover Plain, with guiding your growth and development as students and as citizens must now see you go forth.

At Commencement exercises it is customary, in viewing the global scene, to dwell upon the problems facing the graduating class: the imbalance of national wealth and power, the recessed condition of the economy, the insecurity associated with the existence of nuclear arsenals, the plight of the oppressed. . . . These circumstances are real, and they constitute challenges awaiting a generation of men and women who have been schooled in critical thinking and moral consciousness. I do not take these matters lightly—nor should you. But neither should we be overwhelmed by their enormity.

Exactly fifty years ago, when this nation was reeling under the weight of the great depression, President Ernest Martin Hopkins emphasized to the graduates of 1932, in making his Baccalaureate remarks to them: "Those who . . . formerly went forth were not supermen compared with the men of today, nor were they men in whom the College had greater pride, nor to the promise of whose lives did the College look forward with greater assurance than to your own lives."

And twenty-five years ago when President John Sloan Dickey addressed the seniors of the Class of 1957, who were also entering into a troubled world, he declared: "Caring is a precious thing. Its intensity is personal to all creatures. . . . Human caring has an added dimension. It goes to the quality of a life, as well as to its mere existence. The quality of caring is what Dartmouth is all about."

Both of these valedictories were messages of optimism, stressing the importance of both human and institutional concern. And so it should be today. You of the class of 1982 enter a world of troubles and uncertainty; but you do so possessing the educational foundation for substantial further growth, the ability—and, I trust, the determination—to contribute positively to society, and the capacity to achieve personal fulfillment within your lives. None of these, however, can be realized without compassion for and responsibility toward your fellow human beings.

Moral judgment is the essential companion to technical literacy; and in moving onward from this College you will necessarily face many critical things that all of us must confront in our lives. You will need to make decisions with courage, with compassion, and with the confidence that comes only from having discovered the truth of issues and of yourselves. Your worthy acts and good deeds will nourish not only you and society, but they will help assure that this institution will always purposefully be—for you and for others—"Dartmouth undying."

As you now depart from "the gleaming, dreaming walls of Dartmouth," know that you take with you our confidence, our affection, and our abiding faith in the sustaining bond that will forever exist between you and your College.   Good luck—we wish you well.

M EN AND WOMEN of the Class of 1983: You were matriculated into this College as impressionable, anxious, and thoroughly "pea-green" freshmen; and, through a remarkable transformation, you now go forth as men and women who are enriched and broadened in intellect; more worldly in experience; confident in yourselves; and (one would also very much hope) less absolute in your opinions.

At the College's Convocation ceremony in the fall of 1979, President John G. Kemeny directed this special message to the members of the Class of 1983: "As you go through your college years, . . . you will find the College will challenge your basic beliefs. I hope it will challenge your prejudices, and I hope that many of them will crumble. I hope that you will make use of what the College offers, to build a new body of beliefs which you have carefully examined . . . , that you will do a job of synthesis, in addition to the job of analysis. . . ."

You of the graduating class have, on this occasion, the opportunity to look back upon and to assess that which President Kemeny urged you to undertake. For those who did not during these past four years totally fulfill his charge to you in this regard—and I suspect there just may be a few such standing here before me now—you should find both encouragement and reassurance in the realization that the formulation of one's convictions and of the body of one's beliefs is an ongoing process. Within the liberal arts, indeed, it is never-ending.

You, as graduates in 1983, are entering a world that is uncertain, except for the certainty that human condition will never remain in a constant state. And this circumstance requires that those who relate and contribute positively to this ever-changing condition, those who have had the privilege of being educated toward that purpose, shall be involved in an "evergreen" learning experience: always questioning, forever growing, perennially renewing one's sense of self and extending one's personal development in a world that cries out for leadership and for understanding.

On this day of Commencement, the measure of the role the College has played in your development and, through you, in society's well-being will be gauged as you leave this special place—as you go forth, variously, to pursue your individual careers; to contribute to greater causes than those careers alone; and to continue, very particularly, your lifetime of liberal learning.

But just as this leave-taking is a natural and a necessary element of the Dartmouth experience, may I stress that so is returning.

Until we meet again, know that you take with you our pride in your accomplishments, our affection for you, and our confidence in you. We wish you luck—this within the embrace of the sustaining bond that will forever exist between you and your College.

M EN AND WOMEN of the Class of 1987: We now stand together, preparing to take leave of this very special place. You, this morning, and I to follow in just five weeks' time.

During your four years on the Hanover Plain you have been given the opportunity to grow, intellectually and morally, and to do so within the context of a realization that understanding is achieved through study and critical assessment, and that differences are best resolved by reasoning and tolerant discussion, rather than confrontation and violence. What you have learned here, both through formal instruction and through positive lessons outside the classroom, can serve you well as you assume the roles of productive and involved citizens in a society searching for new truths, and as you engage your responsibility to others and to yourselves from this day forward.

Thirty-three years ago, almost to the day, President John Sloan Dickey, in delivering his valedictory to the Dartmouth class with which I was graduated, said: ". . . there is no yonder point in any human venture beyond the reach of Dartmouth's teaching, if you will but return to it and have it so." As is true of all worthwhile associations, we have returned to it and have it so.

It is irrefutably true that, regardless of age or position, we all play the roles of both teacher and student in our relationships with others. And, with that realization, we must always conduct ourselves accordingly: with mutual respect, with humility, with courage, and with utmost integrity.

The Class of 1987 will ever be special to me, as the last class to be graduated during my Dartmouth presidency.

Until we meet again, know that you take with you our pride in your accomplishments, our affection for you, and our abiding confidence in you. We wish you success—this within the embrace of the sustaining bond that will forever exist between you and your College.

A Tlingit Brother of Alpha Chi

by RICARDO WORL

⋙ This excerpt is from a chapter in the book *First Person, First Peoples* (1997), containing contributions by more than a dozen Dartmouth alumni and subtitled "Native American College Graduates Tell Their Life Stories." Ricardo T. Worl 1984 (whose career upon returning to Alaska was to be, initially, in publishing and, subsequently, banking) relates something of his undergraduate experience at his alma mater, this within the context of the College's late-twentieth-century reemphasis of (as expressed in its 1769 royal charter) "the education and instruction of Youth of the Indian Tribes in this Land . . ." (to which identification of primary institutional objective the charter's specification adds "and also of English Youth and any others").

W HEN I THINK about my childhood and the place I grew up, I marvel at how I ended up at a liberal arts college in the northeast. When I was small, I thought that everybody lived like Tlingit Indians. Juneau, my hometown, is a small town built on the site of a Tlingit Indian village. Tall mountains, blanketed by a lush rain forest, drop steeply to the green-tinged saltwater channel. Houses and buildings are nestled close together on the slopes. [. . .]

The romantic notion that everybody was brought up like Indians faded when we moved out of Juneau and I quickly learned that non-Indian people think differently. My family relocated to Anchorage in 1970 so Mom could complete her undergraduate degree. Anchorage was the first city I had seen, so I was awed by the lights and the tall buildings. About three years later, Mom received a fellowship to attend Harvard. We moved to Cambridge, where we lived for three years while she worked on her graduate degree in anthropology. [. . .]

Just when I thought my exposure to diverse cultural experiences had reached a climax, Mom asked us what we thought of moving to Barrow, Alaska, so that she could study Eskimo whaling. The next thing I knew, we were hundreds of miles above the Arctic Circle, living in a one-room shack with no running water, television, or flush toilets. For the next three years we lived in this community of less than one thousand primarily Inupiaq Eskimo inhabitants. [. . . .]

Whether or not to go to college was something I never had to con-

319

template. The fact that we would attend college must have been drilled into our heads at birth. My brother had started college a few years earlier, my sister was in college, and Mom had finished graduate school and was working on her dissertation. I was fortunate to have so many role models and people with high expectations around me. [. . .]

I arrived in Hanover for the first time in the fall of 1980. My aunt, her husband, and my two younger cousins gave me a ride from Boston, where they were living at the time. It was warm, humid and overcast. The campus was still green, and turned out to be much smaller than I had envisioned from studying the map sent to me by the admissions office. I was somewhat familiar with the geography, climate, and architecture of the region from having lived in Cambridge ten years earlier.

When my aunt drove away, it struck me that this was the first time in my life that I was alone without another family member. I was in a community where I did not know a soul. It took all my willpower to overcome my nervousness. It got easier when I thought about having the opportunity to test my independence.

I recall many insecure moments in my freshman year when I didn't fit in or understand what was going on. For instance, the guys in my dorm were always talking about a singer referred to as "The Boss." I had never even heard of Bruce Springsteen or his music until I arrived at Dartmouth. The way the guys were talking about him, and the frequency with which I heard his music, made me wonder how many other things I had never heard about while growing up in Alaska. [. . .]

On numerous occasions, my being from Alaska was a novelty to others. I remember being at a friend's dinner party in his summer home in upstate New York. One of the guests was absolutely fascinated with me because I was from Alaska. The whole table had been listening to our conversation when she looked at me with a straight face and asked, "Well, if you're from Alaska, where did you learn to speak English so well?" I looked at my friend for help because I didn't know if she was serious or if I should laugh. After a long silence, her husband elbowed her and politely changed the subject. My friend and I get a kick out of that story now, but at the time I was at a total loss for words.

Regardless of these differences and difficulties, I was able to succeed in college. I had learned to convert being eccentric into being exotic and to capitalize on my differences. Besides, there were so many fun experiences during college that I didn't have time to be consumed by the insignificant or negative events.

My dormitory, Smith Hall, was a small, all-male dorm with about fifty guys. We were adjacent to an all-female dorm, Woodward, which faced another small all-male dorm named Ripley, our rivals in any sort of dorm competition. My freshman-year room was a one-room double. There was just enough space for the bunk bed, two desks, two dressers, and a small refrigerator. My roommate, Marty, was from Boston. He had sent me a letter at the end of my senior year in high school to introduce himself so we wouldn't be total strangers when we met in college. Marty had attended prep school and was a pretty good hockey goalie. His father was a Dartmouth grad. Marty was the perfect roommate for me. He was very patient with my naive questions about East Coast culture, sports, music, books, and protocol. Marty was always on top of the important stuff like freshman meetings, academic requirements, and registration paperwork. He knew which fraternities were having parties and he was an excellent role model when it came to study habits. My Dartmouth experience would not have been the same if I had ended up with a roommate who wasn't responsible or kind enough to show me the ropes. Marty played an important role in my effort to balance the Indian world with the Dartmouth/non-Indian world. The short time we spent as roommates made a lifelong impression on me. During that time I learned to communicate and interact effectively with non-Indian people. My family and my experiences at Dartmouth taught me that social and economic contrasts between Indians and non-Indians may get in the way sometimes, but should never prevent you from learning from and enjoying life.

I would venture to say that an equal amount of my learning in college came from my social experiences outside of the classroom. The variety of individuals I became friends with provided me with knowledge and lessons more valuable than any textbook. Certainly some of the more memorable moments took place at parties and during play time. However, the more meaningful experiences occurred during uncensored dorm room discussions or during student organization meetings. I had four years of watching America's finest in action; we became masters in diplomacy, goal setting, and problem solving.

I didn't truly understand the significance of Dartmouth's being an

Ivy League school until I began to understand the quality of individuals I worked with and became friends with. I was able to determine what was important to know and what wasn't. In high school I had learned to watch for cues of proper etiquette and other social nuances. I learned to differentiate between those who were sincere, and those who were not, and what was appropriate behavior and whom I could trust. However, the Dartmouth community and social sphere were far more complex than the public high school I had attended. Throughout my four years at Dartmouth, I somehow managed to become comfortable and fit in without sacrificing my Indian identity or values. I suspect that my values and childhood in Juneau, Alaska, were not typical of most other Dartmouth students. I was expected to return home and put my skills to work for the benefit of the Indian community. I remember fellow classmates asking me what I would be doing after graduation. I explained to them that I would be returning to Alaska. They couldn't understand why I wanted to return to Alaska, where there seemed to be few career opportunities and not much social life. Many of my friends had interviewed for jobs in New York City, Boston, and Chicago. They were willing to live wherever the best job offer placed them. The concept of living anywhere but Alaska had never crossed my mind.

Many Dartmouth students viewed college as a stepping stone or a prerequisite to building a successful career for themselves. For me, it was different. My mission would be accomplished by graduating. My upbringing didn't prepare me to maximize the academic and career opportunities available at this college.

I had no idea what my major would be when I arrived in Hanover. Many first-year students already knew their major, and some had even selected their courses for the next four years. My high school counselor advised me to try a wide range of classes when I got to college. He felt I should find out what I was good at and what I enjoyed the most. By the middle of my sophomore year, I discovered I didn't have a strong desire to pursue any particular area of study. However, anthropology was a natural choice for me. Mom was an anthropologist. I grew up around anthropologists. I had even participated in my mother's fieldwork on Eskimo whaling. My grades were average when it came to all my other courses. I got clobbered in introductory economics, was skeptical of my religion course, and just barely reasoned my way through philosophy. Although I could manage science courses, I didn't have any real interest in them. By process of elimination, I determined that anthropology would be my major.

Dartmouth did a wonderful job of creating a sense of community. Our sense of devotion and sense of pride in the college was established during our first term on campus. Freshmen participated together in camping trips, sat together at football games, and constructed the homecoming bonfire. We felt this same unity within our dorms and with the college as a whole. Students had plenty of opportunity and choices for joining clubs and participating in campus activities. [. . .]

My transition from Alaska to college would not have been as comfortable, nor as successful, without other Indians. My friends through the Native American programs became my surrogate tribal members. Without connection to other Indians, my self-confidence and identity would have been severely challenged. Some members were uncertain about my participation with the Native American group because of stereotypes associated with my fraternity. Since graduation I've learned that this type of skepticism is not exclusive to Dartmouth, nor is it uncommon among Native American tribes.

I was fortunate and thankful to have had Indian mentors like Arvo Mikkanen, Steve Healey, Professor Michael Dorris, Grace Newell, director of the Native American Program, and my classmate Mark Chavree. My four years at Dartmouth were the only time in my life I was not around other Indians on an everyday basis. There were so many instances where I would be at a social function, restaurant, convention, or meeting where I was the only Indian, and sometimes the only minority, attending. For nine months at a time, I would live, eat, study, and party with guys whose values and priorities contrasted with my own. Being with Indian friends helped me keep my values, my humor, and my life complete.

I made my life more complicated when I joined a fraternity that had earned the reputation of being "pro-Indian symbol." Dartmouth's unofficial mascot at one time was the Indian. The administration had officially discouraged use of the Indian symbol. However, Dartmouth has a history and a taste for "old traditions." Students who wore Indian-symbol hats, jackets or T-shirts, and who used the "wah-hoo-wah" and "scalp-'em" cheers at football games were perceived to be rebels defying "the administration" and trying to keep a Dartmouth tradition alive, regardless of the fact that the symbol and cheers were offensive to Native Americans. It was an example of institutional racism at its worst. Pro-Indian symbol students believed themselves to be somehow detached from their irresponsibility and insensitivity because it was a college tradition. Alumni seemed to encourage its use, and "everyone else" seemed to be wearing Indian jackets.

I spent hours, usually on a one-on-one basis, with my fraternity brothers trying to understand them and then trying to explain to them why using the Indian as a mascot was wrong. I know that my efforts and the words that came from my heart made an impact. I let my friends and classmates know I objected to the use of the Indian symbol. But I refused to let the issue consume all of my time and energy because Dartmouth and Alpha Chi Alpha had so much more to offer.

I joined Alpha Chi because of its many positive attributes and because of its members. Alpha Chi had an extensive membership of campus leaders, scholars, and athletes, as well as a history of community service. My best friends today were my brothers in Alpha Chi. Some of the best experiences in my life were with them, and some of my most meaningful lessons came from them. A good portion of my time outside of studies was spent at the fraternity or in fraternity-related activities. Vacations, ski trips, football games, dorm parties, movies, meals, workouts, and campus functions or ceremonies were usually done in the company of one or more of my fraternity brothers.

My senior year, I lived in the fraternity house with twenty other guys in my class. Unlike in dormitories, where the college took care of everything, we were responsible for everything—cleaning, maintenance, financial management, fire inspections, college standards, and security were all in the charge of residents of the house. Our parties were always fun, but we had to deal with the mess and the exotic smells the next morning. We knew how to have fun and we would play hard, but we also knew when it was time to work and study hard. The discipline and intensity my fraternity brothers had when it came to studies was a positive influence on my own work habits. Their attitudes toward work helped me establish a high standard, which carries over into my career today.

Graduation was a mental and emotional blur for me. Commencement was loaded with pomp, ceremony, tradition, and personal reflection. After four years of fun, independence and personal growth, I found it difficult to accept that I was about to give up the security and comforts of Dartmouth and my friends. I was too busy thinking about all the good things I would be leaving in Hanover to really think about the significance of my accomplishments, the details of the graduation ceremony, or my immediate future. I was envious of my classmates and fraternity brothers who had landed jobs in Boston or New York City, where a substantial number of Dartmouth alumni worked and lived. They would be able to room together, get together after work, and attend Dartmouth football games in the fall.

When I moved back to Anchorage, I was no longer surrounded by twenty of my best friends. I no longer had the daily exposure to intellectually stimulating experiences. I was no longer part of a community whose members had similar interests or were socially compatible with me. I remember feeling lonesome for the longest time. I had made my choice. I wanted to come back to Alaska, which my friends could not understand. They questioned the availability of any meaningful work experiences. I could have looked for work in one of the cities, but my commitment and desire to serve Alaska Native people was stronger than my desire to live in a city, away from home, where my work would only benefit me and not others in my community.

I was passing up the opportunity to live in a big city with a competitive, fast-paced, cosmopolitan lifestyle. Instead, I would be living in Alaska, where access to the great outdoors, the long, dark winters, and seasonal industries influenced the pace of work and life. I have no regrets about my decision. In the ten years since graduation, I have kept in touch with my fraternity brothers. Although at times I am envious of their professional success and personal growth, they tell me that they are envious of me—that they wish they could live in a place as peaceful, safe, clean, and breathtaking as Juneau. [. . .]

The Best Part of
My Academic Life Here

by HAROLD L. BOND

≫> A highly regarded member of the English Department for nearly four decades, Prof. Harold Bond 1942 was accorded the tribute of being invited by Seniors in the academic year 1983-84 to be their Class Day Orator. This is what he said to them on June 9, 1984, as published in that month's number of the *Alumni Magazine*.

W E MEET TODAY in the Bema for two reasons: one is to celebrate the Class of 1984. The other is to prepare in our own way to say farewell for a while to Dartmouth, you after four years, I after 46 years. I say "for a while" because I know you'll be back.

We have already had celebrations of 1984, and I want to add to them by saying that it has been a privilege to share with many of you a reading of some wonderful literature, most particularly Keats, Shelley, Wordsworth, and the other romantics, and also the writers and translators of the King James Bible. Moreover, the best part of my academic life here has been the association with students. I am always astonished by their energy, vitality, talent, and sometimes their brains, and also by their remarkable diversity. I see before me artists and poets, champion skiers and outstanding athletes, playwrights and novelists, birdwatchers and hikers, physicists and geologists, candidates for leadership in law and business, men and women who will grace the professions, men and women who have become and will continue to be part of the Dartmouth family.

It is fitting, too, that we meet in the Bema. This amphitheatre was constructed 102 years ago. The seniors in the class of 1882 wanted a private place for their class day celebrations. Ever since that year, Class Day has been held here (weather permitting), and for a great many years the commencement ceremony, too. Commencement was moved to the lawn of Baker Library in 1953 when President Eisenhower received an honorary degree. The crowd of 10,000 people could not be accommodated here; but Class Day has remained in the Bema with its lovely trees, the New Hampshire granite, the glorious sunshine, reminding us of the wilderness from which the College grew.

The word *Bema* comes to us—like many good things in our civilization—from ancient Athens. Literally meaning a step, it was the speaker's platform from which statesmen addressed the Athenian Assembly. Since then the word has been used to designate the platform from which services are conducted in a synagogue, and, in the Greek Orthodox Church, the enclosed area about the altar. The connotations of something sacred in the term have remained; and, if you won't mock at my thought in an age when it is pretty hard to say that anything is sacred, our Bema is Dartmouth's sanctuary. D. H. Lawrence, when visiting the great Benedictine Abbey at Monte Cassino in Italy, said that it was one of the quick spots of the earth—living, energizing, vital throughout the millennia. The Bema, too, is one of the quick spots of the earth, even though Dartmouth has only a little over 200 years of history.

Yet, in reality, our roots go back much further than 200 years. Like the mandrake, a symbol of fertility and creativity, we have *two* great taproots for our College, roots which started growing over 2,500 years ago, one in Athens and one in Jerusalem. And in our time, when all we hear is talk about change, accelerating obsolescence, the value of innovation (always assumed to be good), it does not hurt to recall that important things do not change, things like love and hate, freedom and tyranny, peace and war, life and death, and things like our roots.

When Eleazar Wheelock selected *Vox Clamantis in Deserto* as the motto for his college, he almost certainly was thinking of the real wilderness that was this country in 1769. But the motto has much more to do with truth than with wilderness; and the term which was once relevant to uncultivated and unsettled parts of the earth, almost from the beginning had the metaphorical meaning of what Dante, Spenser, Milton, and Bunyan would call the wilderness of the unenlightened world. The whole verse in Isaiah 40, from which the motto is taken, reads (in the King James English):

> The voice of him that crieth in the wilderness,
> Prepare ye the way of the Lord, make straight
> in the desert a highway for our God.

The voice speaks through the prophet to a people in slavery by the rivers of Babylon where they had been in captivity for 50 years. It comes at the beginning of what was to become another exodus. Just as Moses led the chosen people out of slavery in Egypt, so the Lord will lead his people back to the Promised Land. "The Lord will come with a strong hand, and his arm shall rule for him. . . ."

> And he shall feed his flock like a shepherd: he shall
> gather the lambs with his arm, and carry them in his
> bosom, and shall gently lead those that are with young.

From slavery to freedom with "the word of our God [which] shall stand forever," this faith almost certainly was the foundation of our College.

To turn briefly to our other root, and the second Bible of Western civilization (I mean the literature of classical Greece), we might mention only the great oration by Pericles at the Bema in Athens at the end of the first year of the Peloponnesian War. He spoke proudly of the ideals of the Athenian state; and although Athens was to lose this terrible war, she won the honor of becoming one of the major civilizing forces of the Western world. Here are some of the ideals. They lie behind not only the foundation and purpose of our College, but also behind the birth of the United States:

> Our administration favors the many instead of the few;
> that is why it is called a democracy. Our laws afford
> equal justice to all. . . . Advancement in public life falls
> to reputation for capacity, class considerations not being
> allowed to interfere with merit. We cultivate refinement
> without extravagance, knowledge without ostentation;
> wealth we employ more for use than for show. . . . Our
> ordinary citizens, though occupied with pursuits of
> industry, are still fair judges of public matters. . . . Instead
> of looking on discussion as a stumbling block in the way of
> action, we think it an indispensible preliminary to any
> wise action at all. . . .

Well, these ideals and this faith are in our roots, and they provide rich nourishment even to this very moment.

I have said that the important things do not change, but the surface of our lives is always changing. And so it is with Dartmouth. If my ancestor, William Bond of the Class of 1812, could return to Hanover today, he would recognize virtually nothing on the campus.

But our activity, described by some as the pursuit of truth among friends, he would recognize; and he would not have any trouble meeting his old friends on the shelves of our library.

Yet one serious worry I have about the future here and elsewhere in this mechanized, computerized, nuclear world is that surface change may become so great as to render us unfit or unable to read the great books, and to partake of the great tradition of a truly human life and spiritual health. You will remember that citizens of Huxley's *Brave New World* were unable to read the classics. When they tried to read of the love of Romeo and Juliet, they burst out in uncontrollable laughter. Well, to make no greater claim, graduates of Dartmouth can still read Shakespeare, and we even ask our freshmen to try *Paradise Lost*.

Let me conclude by remembering my own commencement here in the Bema, 42 years ago. Pearl Harbor struck us in our senior year, and a campus that was largely pacifist knew overnight that it had to go to war. Spring break was cancelled and Commencement was moved forward one month to May 10th, to enable us to join the services all the sooner. From here we did indeed go 'round the girdled earth: England, North Africa, Italy, France, Burma, the Philippines, Guadalcanal, Okinawa, and many other places. Forty years ago last Monday, I was riding in a jeep behind the leading tank in the American and British taking of Rome; and 40 years ago last Wednesday, American forces with Dartmouth men among them stumbled ashore in the bloody landings at Normandy. Thirty-three members of my class did not return from that war. The president of our class was last seen diving his attack-plane on a Japanese battleship. Another member of the class whom I once watched schuss the headwall at Tuckerman's Ravine, lost his life in the mountains of northern Italy. But all of us were better able to do what we had to do in those years, and even more importantly in the years of peace that followed, by what we gained from Dartmouth. We took with us the memory of Dartmouth's

sharp and misty mornings,	the crowding into Commons,
The clanging bells,	The long white afternoons,
the crunch of feet on snow,	the twilight glow. . . .
Her sparkling noons,	

We took all this, but even more, the voice that we heard then and still hear now, crying in the wilderness. It is still a guide.

A Relocation of the
Dartmouth Medical Center

by PAUL D. PAGANUCCI

❯❯❯ While a Vice President of the College, during the years 1977–85, lawyer-educator-financier Paul Paganucci 1953 was central to the projections and negotiations that he chronicles here—involving what he has described as "one of the two most important decisions voted by the College's Board during the twentieth century."

THE FALL OF 1985 was a momentous time for Dartmouth and its Medical School, as well as for the Mary Hitchcock Memorial Hospital, the Hitchcock Clinic, and the Town of Hanover. After almost a decade of planning, negotiations, threats, setbacks, revisions, and leadership changes, the goal of the Hospital to achieve a major expansion on Maynard Street in Hanover proved unattainable. Such was the case because the Clinic, the local group of nearly two hundred physicians, was unable to secure from the Town, for reasons of potential traffic and parking congestion, a permit to build a new facility on the Dewey Fields, just north of the Hospital and Medical School. There did exist for the Clinic an alternative of creating its own out-patient facility on land it had acquired southeast of the village, adjacent to the road to Lebanon. However, a continued close proximity of the Hospital and Clinic was deemed to be essential for efficient patient care, as was the maintenance of a nearness of the Hospital and Clinic to the Medical School, for purposes of clinical education.

Accordingly, the development of a plan to move all three entities—the Hospital, the Clinic, and the Medical School—to a single site, together, became a top-priority objective. In fact, this was undoubtedly the largest question of a non-programmatic sort that Dartmouth's Trustees were, within memory, called upon to resolve. Programmatically, coeducation (achieved in 1972) was of course the most important change at Dartmouth. But the Medical Center move was surely the other of the two most important decisions voted by the College's Board during the twentieth century. And the 1985 Medical

Center decision was made within the context of a period of tremendously acute pressures—pressures associated with an end-of-year deadline (imposed by a pending change in federal tax law) the meeting of which was essential to financing the overall, highly complex undertaking involved in recreating the Medical Center in an entirely new location.

From the time it opened in 1893, Mary Hitchcock Memorial Hospital had more or less steadily expanded. But its biggest growth had occurred after the Dartmouth Trustees' 1956 decision to build a new physical plant for the Medical School, to double the School's enrollment, and to enlarge its faculty. Then a decade later the School extended its two-year curriculum to a three-year program, and in 1979 it went to a full four years—transitions that especially required expansion on the part of the Hospital, the existing number of teaching beds being critical to the clinical instruction of third- and fourth-year medical students. In addition, during 1973 the Veterans Administration Hospital at White River Junction, Vermont, had been invited to make its beds available, by joining the Hospital, the Clinic, and the Medical School, in the formation of the Dartmouth-Hitchcock Medical Center.

By the early 1980s the Hospital felt that in order to stay competitive it needed a substantial upgrading and expansion. The result was a proposal to spend $63 million on the existing Maynard Street facility. When this was brought forward, however, many of us knew that if such an investment were made, it would be virtually impossible ever to change the location of anything in that part of Hanover where the College is located. We didn't know at this point what a wholly new Hospital would cost, but we were sure that $63 million had to be a big percentage of the total cost of an all-new facility.

The idea of moving the Hospital to land in Lebanon that the College had purchased during 1981 originated within my own office. At the time, I was Financial Vice President of the College. Cary P. Clark 1962, the College Counsel, and I would typically spend time at the end of a workday brainstorming ideas. Between the two of us, we had this notion long before anyone else did, and whenever the subject of expanding the Hospital and Clinic on the old Maynard Street site came before the Dartmouth Trustees (usually within the context of reporting more delays and frustration), Cary and I would lobby selected members of the Board, urging a relocation of these facilities to Dartmouth's Lebanon acreage instead. (Indeed, I find that I first suggested to the Trustees' Investment Committee in June of 1981, four months before Dartmouth even agreed to buy the land in question, that "one ideal use of a portion of the land might be to persuade both Mary Hitchcock Memorial Hospital and the Hitchcock Clinic to relocate to the outskirts of Hanover.")

To understand our thinking, one has to step back to the late 1970s, when John Kemeny was still President. Traffic pressures on campus had become more and more oppressive, and in order to document what was happening, as well as to make some predictions for the future, Dartmouth retained the services of the consulting firm Barton, Ashman, whose findings proved to be in agreement with the judgment of the Medical Center's planners, Payette Associates: The bulk of the traffic that was overwhelming the Dartmouth campus was coming from the Hospital and the Clinic. Both the Barton, Ashman and the Payette reports were of a type the College routinely shared with the Town of Hanover, because of major projected or potential impacts. In fact, the oversight committee set up in 1981 to monitor the Barton, Ashman study was comprised of Town of Hanover, as well as Dartmouth, officials.

A second problem Cary Clark and I often focused upon was that the Hospital and Clinic were, essentially, confined to very limited space north of Maynard Street (about 12.5 acres in all), a circumstance that led to persistent attraction for the Hospital to develop into the area south of Maynard Street—the block involved being the most logical area within which the College itself might someday grow.

These factors of pressure relating to the land south of Maynard Street were intensified when the Occom Inn, on North Main Street, north of Kiewit Center, came up for sale. Dartmouth bid for its purchase the property's appraised value, which was very high. The Hitchcock Clinic, however, offered an eye-popping sum over and above the appraised value; and the Clinic thus gained some power that came from owning a key piece of real estate in the area—a power of ownership which later became part of a very complicated scenario.

With regard to Dartmouth's major land purchase in Lebanon in 1981, first President Kemeny and then his successor, President McLaughlin, encouraged me in something that many others at the time thought was absolutely crazy. It was a plan to buy 2,006 acres that belonged to a Hanover resident, Jack H. Nelson. Nelson had initially intended to develop a community on this holding—a holding which was in its extent almost half of the total wooded and open area between Lebanon, West Lebanon, and Hanover. (It could have been another town about the size of White River Junction, and it would have had profound effects—in my opinion, negative effects—on our whole Upper Valley area.) It was first offered to the College, in the late 1970s, for about $6.5 million. Then, when the prime interest rate jumped to over twenty percent in 1980-81, the price of land declined rapidly. Nonetheless, Nelson felt he still wanted to sell, and in September 1981 he called me to let it be known that his land could be bought at a much more reasonable price. We wound up, in November, paying $1.5 million in cash for it—less than twenty-five percent of the original asking price.

In that Dartmouth has only 265 acres or so that make up its core campus—with the whole College on it—these 2,006 acres in Lebanon, at $750 an acre, seemed somewhat akin to the acquisition of Alaska by the United States! At any rate, it was this move that permitted the whole chain of events that led to relocating the Medical Center, and basically to a regaining of Hanover Plain for the College.

Soon after David T. McLaughlin was elected and before he had taken office as President, I wrote him, on March 23, 1981, about problems related to the growth of the Hospital and Clinic. I sent him parts of the 1977 Payette report, which was the official long-term plan that had been adopted for the Medical Center, and I said: "The planning report indicates that by the year 2000 or so the present site will be saturated. Lord only knows what traffic congestion will be in the area of the undergraduate college! If only some way could be found for its ⌜the Hospital's⌝ new facilities to be built in stages in the large, open area south of Hanover, the character of Dartmouth would be preserved. If at some point when you and I are long gone the entire Medical Center, except for the basic science years of the Medical School, were located south of town, your presidency would be long lauded for this alone! . . . I hesitate to burden you with all this, but you will readily see that it is a project for a strong CEO if there ever was one!"

And I remember an evening with the President-to-be, on April 1, 1981, during one of his first trips to Hanover following his election. After we had attended a dinner, he and I were talking at my home and got into these questions of the location of the Hospital, the traffic problems, and what were going to be his major challenges in office.

At the end of that night, I took him up into the Hospital parking lot, and we walked around. It was then between nine and ten o'clock, and of course the cars were wall-to-wall there. I recall saying, "Dave, this is going to be one of your biggest problems—to try and get this relocated."

By the fall of 1985, the dual problems of traffic and the finding of land for Medical Center expansion stimulated Dartmouth to pursue actively the desirability both of helping the Hospital and the Clinic to relocate and of purchasing the Mary Hitchcock real estate.

Dean Robert W. McCollum of the Medical School and his faculty wanted the entire School to move if the Hospital and Clinic were to relocate. But because some undergraduate departments shared with the Medical School reliance on the Dana Biomedical Library and on certain equipment, powerful opposition emerged from the College's science departments. The biology faculty in particular was opposed to any move of the basic-science component of the Medical School.

David McLaughlin provided steadfast and courageous leadership to all components of the Dartmouth-Hitchcock Medical Center following the collapse of the plan to expand the Hospital's Maynard Street site and to build a new Clinic facility nearby. His staunch optimism was needed time and again during the late summer and fall of 1985, to marshal support for the move to Lebanon, as well as to rebuff a heavy stream of skeptical critics. Having been a Trustee of Dartmouth for a decade before being elected President, he was thoroughly aware of the complications, frustrations, and setbacks that had attended the planning of major new facilities for the Hospital and Clinic around Maynard Street. He had also viewed with alarm the ever-rising encroachment on the undergraduate College by heavier and heavier traffic generated north of the College Green.

In the crisis that developed during the autumn of 1985, Dartmouth's major contribution at the outset was to promise to give land to the Medical Center for its new site. Initially 100 acres were offered, subsequently increased to 225—amounting to somewhat over ten percent of the property purchased in 1981 from Jack Nelson. And how did it come about that Dartmouth was able to buy for $25 million the Hospital's Hanover real estate—seventeen buildings and the land on which they stood? Such was made possible by a dramatic change in financial philosophy, a philosophy that had been embraced by the College within only the previous two or three years.

During the Dickey and Kemeny presidencies many of our sister institutions relied on the sale of tax-exempt bonds in order to leverage the assets they had in their endowments and to use the proceeds to provide needed facilities. When, for example, they wanted to expand their student bodies, they borrowed money through state financing authorities and sold tax-exempt bonds, so that they could build additional dormitories; then, they paid back the bonds, over a period of time, out of rental revenues, rendering the new properties self-financing. This was thoroughly acceptable financial practice within the realm of higher education. Dartmouth's Trustees, however, had long resisted putting any debt on their balance sheet. (The fact that the College declined to leverage its assets, as I understood the history from my predecessor as Vice President and Treasurer, John F. Meck 1933, is what led to the "Dartmouth Plan," in which the College went to a year-round operation at the time women were admitted in 1972.) Thus, when David McLaughlin became President, in 1981, he inherited a virtually debt-free balance sheet, which meant that Dartmouth had a lot of borrowing power.

The College did not deliberately set out with any objective of borrowing major amounts of money, in order to leverage up the Dartmouth balance sheet. But the College evolved into that arrangement gradually, and this constituted a major structural change in its financial *modus operandi*. During 1980, upon exploring the possibility of using tax-exempt bonds to finance student loans, and having discovered that New Hampshire had a law which permitted colleges and universities within the state to sell tax-exempt bonds only for bricks-and-mortar projects, we had started a legislative effort to get the New Hampshire law amended. Thomas D. Rath (an alumnus of the College, Class of 1967, and a prominent lawyer in Concord), Cary Clark, and I were central to that effort. The Governor at that time, Hugh J. Gallen, proved to be interested in the answer to one question only: Would what was proposed cost the state any money? When we were able to assure him that what nominal costs were involved, Dartmouth would pay, he backed the change; and a revised statute whistled through the General Court in June of 1981.

The College's first bond issue was sold, and $13 million of some $30 million in proceeds went to the Dartmouth Educational Loan Corporation—something that cut the loan-interest rate charged to students roughly in half—with the balance of the money being used for facilities (such as renovations of the Thayer dining-hall facility and the River Cluster dormitories). It was the skills and knowledge acquired through a series of such financings and refinancings, from 1982 to 1984, that instilled in us confidence to undertake in 1985 the purchase of the Mary Hitchcock properties, and thereby help to finance the move of the Medical Center.

The purchase of the Hospital properties was developed in negotiations conducted principally by President McLaughlin and me, for Dartmouth, and James W. Varnum, President of the Hospital—who felt all along that the Hospital needed to get $25 million for its Maynard Street properties (which was at least one-eighth of the cost of the all-new facility) and that it also needed to get free land at the new site.

Dartmouth vigorously challenged the initial findings of the Hospital's consultants who held that moving the Hospital was not economically feasible. During the critical effort to get these consultants to change their assumptions and to view the prospect in a positive manner, both Dean McCollum and John C. Collins, CEO of the Clinic, played key roles. When at last that piece fell into place, Dartmouth could see its way clear to commit itself to the $25-million purchase, to be covered entirely by the sale of tax-exempt bonds. However, the situation then confronting us was that the requisite tax-exempts could be offered for only another three months or so. Moreover, and perhaps more critically, it would become impossible after December 31, 1985, for the Hospital to make its bond offering, which was intended to finance virtually all of its new facility.

This presented an extremely unusual timetable for such far-reaching decisions. Usually a faculty would take many years to evaluate anything this important (and, in fact, various committees of the Dartmouth faculty had indeed already been studying questions involving the future of the Medical Center for years and years—without making any really measurable progress).

In anticipation of the two faculty meetings—of the faculty of Arts and Sciences and of the general faculty (the latter being Arts and Sciences, plus the professional schools)—which were to be held on December 2, 1985, to advise the President and Trustees on the proposal to move the Medical Center, Provost Agnar Pytte issued a memorandum summarizing what he regarded as the advantages and the disadvantages of such a move. On the plus side, he considered it would permit retention of an integrated academic medical center on a single site, entailing maximum educational and clinical, as well as operating, efficiency; and the College would also have room to expand, when necessary, into the institutionally zoned area north of the existing campus, opening up possibilities not previously available to Dartmouth. Also, Provost Pytte felt that relocation of the Medical Center to the Lebanon site would enhance the future value of the remainder of the College's land holdings there.

The disadvantages he outlined were: that the medical faculty would be two to three miles removed from the other faculties of the College; that the cost of renovating the present Hospital facilities would be high; that Medical School fund-raising could not take place until after the Hospital's drive was completed; and that the College's annual operating budget for carrying the old Hospital, if it could be saved for conversion to other purposes, would be about $500,000. However, in summing up, Pytte said: "I have become convinced that the plan before us, or something close to it, is in the best long-term interest of both the College and the Medical Center."

To assess the potential economic impact of the projected $25-million purchase on the undergraduate faculty, a task force was appointed, with Prof. Alan L. Gustman as chair. President McLaughlin, the College administration, and Professor Gustman's group all relied heavily, during the fall of 1985, on work done by campus master-planner Lo-Yi Chan (Dartmouth Class of 1954), from the New York architectural firm Prentice, Chan & Ohlhausen, whose study dramatically revealed that the cost of converting the massive 400-plus-bed Hospital facility, either for faculty housing or as a dormitory, would be prohibitive. This added to the anxiety and disappointment of all involved. In frustration, Professor Gustman proposed that the main building, the bulk of which was less than twenty-five years old, be destroyed as soon as the Hospital moved, this in order to reduce the cost to Dartmouth of carrying such a white elephant, as well as to eliminate any future temptation to undertake a conversion at what would necessarily be exorbitant expense.

On December second the two heavily attended faculty meetings convened. In my own remarks, as Vice President, I stressed that the timing of the proposed purchase of the Hospital properties was fortuitous, within the context of Dartmouth's strong financial position, which at the time was the healthiest in twenty years. And I pointed out that:

• The Dartmouth endowment then exceeded $434 million, and the Dartmouth Medical School component of that had risen to over $37 million.

• The stock market was at an all-time high (the Dow Jones Industrial Average was close to 1500), with the bond market at a six-year high.

• Consideration of any renovation of the Hospital building had been abandoned, in favor of the more economical choice of razing it.

• Professor Gustman and his subcommittee projected the financial impact to be from $5.7 million to $26 million, which Dartmouth had the financial strength to handle quite comfortably.

• There should be no negative impact on present or future operating budgets of Arts and Sciences or the professional schools, except for the contingent expense of less than ten percent of the Dartmouth Medical School's endowment.

• The arbitrage profit of $4 million on Dartmouth's $25 million tax-exempt bond sale would grow to at least $9 million from rents to be paid to the College by the Hospital before it moved.

• It was critical to act before December thirty-first, in order to sell tax-exempts under the expiring tax law, so as to gain the arbitrage profit, even though no one liked so tight a timetable.

Continuing, I went on to plead that opportunities like this could come but once in a lifetime and to express my earnest hope that the Trustees of the College would in fact make a decision to purchase the Hospital properties under the tax-exempt financing option about to expire.

Other speakers, including President McLaughlin, Dean McCollum, and Dean of the Faculty C. Dwight Lahr, focused upon both the advantages and disadvantages that had been summarized by Provost Pytte in his memo; and Walter Burke, as chair of the Trustees, made an appearance before both faculties.

The general faculty at its meeting acted to support the relocation plan by a vote of more than three to one. The undergraduate faculty was considerably less enthusiastic, and its affirmative vote entailed a seeking of assurances that would protect certain priorities for the undergraduate College.

The College's Trustees proved not yet inclined to approve moving of the Medical School. The Board did, however, vote at a special meeting on December nineteenth to purchase the Maynard Street properties for $25 million and to sell a total of $34 million of tax-exempt bonds to provide financing. This vote cleared the way for the Hospital to authorize and sell its own $163 million tax-exempt issue prior to the end of the year.

Although many other matters still had to be studied, planned, and resolved in the months and years that lay ahead, by the close of 1985, the Hospital and Clinic had raised the sums needed to build superb new facilities on the land in Lebanon donated by the College; and Dartmouth, for its part, had borrowed the funds to complete its purchase of the Hospital properties. Thus ended one of the most frenetic and eventful periods in the history of the College, the Medical Center, and the Town of Hanover.

Sports Talk

by SEAVER PETERS and RICHARD JAEGER
with JACK DeGANGE

⋙⋗ Seaver Peters 1954 was captain of the Dartmouth hockey team that played the first game on the "artificial ice" surface of Davis Rink, predecessor facility to Thompson Arena, and he served as Dartmouth's Director of Athletics from 1967 to 1983. Richard G. Jaeger 1959, a three-sport athlete while an undergraduate, was an admissions officer at the College for twenty-five years before he became its Director of Athletics in 1989. In this edited transcript of a taped discussion, the two men reflect on a half-century of athletics at Dartmouth, with Jack DeGange, who was Sports Information Director for nine years during the Peters incumbency.

eGange: Describe athletics when you were undergraduates at Dartmouth.
Peters: Winter sports were fun. Winter Carnival was great. There was always a hockey tradition on Carnival weekend: that you played on Thursday night and Saturday morning. Dartmouth was at home. Period. Carnival was really very big then. My freshman year I worked forty hours on Carnival sculptures to get tickets to the four big events.

DeGange: Who were the coaches?

Jaeger: When Bob Blackman came here in 1955 to coach football we had notable coaches: Doggie Julian in basketball; Eddie Jeremiah in hockey; Karl Michael in swimming.

Peters: Tommy Dent in soccer and lacrosse; Red Hoehn in tennis and squash.

Jaeger: Tommy Keane out at the golf course; Ellie Noyes doing track. Venerable guys. You revered them as more than just coaches. They were here for the long spell.

DeGange: And Tony Lupien in baseball, who was fairly new at the time.

Jaeger: Even Tony. He cut me after three swings, my sophomore

340

year, but I still loved him. He saw Ralph Manuel and said: "They both play first. Jaeger's a lefty and Manuel's a lefty, and I'm going with Manuel." I had a great freshman baseball year, with Eddie Jeremiah as my coach. I had a great freshman basketball year, with Al McGuire as my coach—until Rudy LaRusso, who later starred in the NBA, stuffed me about six times, and that ended my career.

Peters: Dick raised a good point about the coaches. Most of them coached at least two seasons and two sports: Hoehn . . . Doggie . . . Jerry . . . Lupe . . . Dent. . . .

Jaeger: And Elmer Lampe, who coached football and basketball.

Peters: I have to tell a story about fall baseball practice. The football team practiced where Leverone Field House now stands. And Penn ended a twenty-three-game losing streak against Dartmouth, 14-7, in the fall of 1956. Somebody hit a line drive into football practice, and Blackman yells in to Lupe, "Hey, Lupien, the baseball season's over." And Lupe yells back, "So's the Penn losing streak." They were not close!

DeGange: Who had significant influence on you as an athlete and, then, as an administrator?

Peters: As an athlete, Eddie Jeremiah. As the Athletic Director, John Meck, the Vice President of the College.

Jaeger: For me it would be Bob Blackman. Tough guy. Demanding. No humor. The bullhorn. Lots of studying.

DeGange: What about crowds and local support?

Jaeger: In many respects Dartmouth athletics was the only show in town. One of the great experiences was a Saturday night, with hockey at seven and basketball at nine. You'd go from Davis Rink over to the gym. It was standing room only—in both sports.

DeGange: Dick, before you were Athletic Director, you spent twenty-five years in the Admissions office. What was your view of athletics over that period—from an all-male institution to a coed one; from seventeen sports then, to thirty-four now?

Jaeger: Athletics was a tremendous source of pride for the institution. It was something positive we could talk about, because the kids we were getting in were good students, productive on the fields, getting national records and awards. You could always point to a strong, vibrant athletic program, from skiing and football right on down.

DeGange: Seaver, when you were Athletic Director, coeducation arrived, and you had to develop the program. What were the challenges?

Peters: First of all, the institutional commitment was there. Budget aside, our charge was to determine in what sports women had interest. And we hired a wonderful woman in Aggie Bixler Kurtz, who did a terrific job. Basically, we understood that athletics for women are just as important as they are for men. We provided the opportunity, and we did it right. We literally had the benefit that Princeton and Yale had started a year before us. That was a real plus. We learned a great deal from them. Our whole institution did, not just in athletics. And the caliber of women we got was just fantastic. We tended to attract not only bright, but outdoor-oriented, athletically oriented young ladies. That's just the nature of Dartmouth.

DeGange: Dick, twenty years later you've got a women's program that's reasonably mature. What are the issues and challenges today that are any different than Seaver saw at the advent, twenty-five years ago?

Jaeger: A good bit of it is predicated on what I call Title IX realization—our realizing the full implications of the federal legislation requiring colleges to offer equal opportunities to men and women in intercollegiate athletics. The awareness—what it meant—took a while to dawn on people, with everything from strength of schedule to the same number of recruits, to coaches having similar offices, to coming into parity on coaches' salaries. That puts huge pressure on the overall program and the overall budget. You have to pay attention to all those considerations.

To me, the biggest single impact on Ivy League athletics, in terms of the national fabric, is when the nation went to equal opportunity and the doors opened for a whole lot of amazingly talented minority kids. That whole reality changed everything. That was the beginning of the huge separation between the super powers—or whatever they call themselves—and where the rest of us are.

DeGange: What about the legacy women athletes?

Jaeger: My best example is the Hannigan family. Jud, Class of 1946, played football; a World War II veteran, he was captain of the '47 team. And Timmy and Mike, both 1971s, played baseball and football, respectively. And then came Mike's twin daughters, 1997s. Kelly was a fine lacrosse player, and Elizabeth was a manager. There are several cases like that, where there are daughters who came here and played sports and are now hard-core Big Greeners.

DeGange: Among coaches, you don't get the longevity you had with Jerry and Dent and Doggie and others anymore.

Jaeger: Not as many, but you've got guys like Carl Wallin in track and Chuck Kinyon in men's tennis. And Chris Wielgus, who coached basketball here, left and came back.

Peters: It used to be that a coach in the Ivy League had reached the top of his profession. Now that isn't the case.

DeGange: Over thirty years, do some name-dropping, recall some events as memorable.

Peters: I remember the 1971 Cornell-Dartmouth football game, when we beat the Ed Marinaro team. I remember beating Yale, for the first time ever, in swimming in 1972. And going to the NCAA baseball College World Series in 1970 was clearly an event of great magnitude.

Jaeger: The undefeated football teams of 1970 and 1996 were special. There were a number of NCAA appearances by our cross-country teams and by our women's lacrosse and women's soccer teams. They are proud moments. I think of that wild basketball game up here when we beat Penn, when John Bean threw in the half-court shot.

Peters: We went to the Final Four in hockey a couple of years in a row.

Jaeger: I think about the runner Bob Kempainen. And Adam Nelson, who played football and set the NCAA shot-put record. The late Sarah Devens was an amazing athlete, playing in three sports. And Jay Fiedler at quarterback.

Peters: I go back to Murry Bowden.

Jaeger: And Reggie Williams, who went on to play in a Super Bowl.

There was Gail Koziara Boudreaux in two sports, basketball and track (where she was the Ivy champion shot-putter). There was Judy Parrish in hockey.

Peters: And Ross Brownridge and Dennis Murphy in hockey.

DeGange: Where is the Ivy League's influence today?

Jaeger: My perception, from attending NCAA meetings and being part of Ivy League initiatives in that realm, is that we're still the voice of reason. But all too often we're the little snots who argue against athletic dorms or adding four more hockey games. So, we become the little goody-two-shoes types. Many times for good reason. I don't see any of the others being converted back to the philosophy we have.

Peters: I think the Ivies contributed tremendously, primarily with people and their thinking. Asa Bushnell of Princeton was ECAC [Eastern College Athletic Conference] commissioner. There was deLaney Kiphuth, the Yale athletic director, and Ken Fairman, the Princeton athletic director. They were the foundation of the NCAA.

Jaeger: But then the big bucks came along, and most football and basketball coaches now are making eight times what the deans or the athletic directors are making around the country. I remember Vince Dooley, the former Georgia coach (now athletic director), getting up on some big issue—voting on some football-related subject—and saying, "Fellas, it's time for the big dogs to howl!"

Two Valedictory Addresses

≫ A feature of each year's Commencement exercises is the "Valedictory to the College," delivered by the academically top-ranking member of the graduating class.
Here presented are extracts from one such presentation made in the decade of the
1980s and another from the '90s.

I. by W. BRIAN BARNES 1985

A s YOU CAN SEE, I brought along a personal cheering section in
the guise of the Dartmouth College Glee Club. Though I have
been a member of the Glee Club through all my years here, it has
only been during this last year that I fully appreciated how important
it has been to me, and how much I'll miss it. Thank you all very much.

Partly in recognition of the fun that we have had singing here, and
partly as a means of exhorting me to originality in this oration, one
of my friends in the Glee Club went so far as to suggest that I sing the
valediction. Now, quite apart from the unorthodoxy of such a plan
(which would defy the very meaning of the Latin words *vale dicere*,
"to say farewell"), in light of the competition I would be exposing
myself to on this platform . . . well, I decided that really wouldn't be
such a great idea. ⎡Opera-singer/administrator Beverly Sills was the
Commencement's guest speaker.⎤ Nevertheless, I would like to do the
next best thing, to read you the second verse of the "Twilight Song,"
which has been the introduction to nearly every one of our concerts
and which is therefore familiar to many of you, I'm sure. The words
are simple, but they are, I think, singularly suited to this occasion.

> Brothers, while the shadows deepen,
> While we stand here heart to heart,
> Let us promise one another
> In the silence ere we part:
> We will make our lives successful;
> We will keep our hands from shame,
> For the sake of dear old Dartmouth
> And the honor of her name.

Brothers and sisters we are and have been for the last four years,
but the shadows we have cast here are waxing as the sun of our college days sinks now beneath the horizon which is our graduation.

345

Despite the best efforts of the Alumni Council to bring us together, this is undoubtedly the final time that our entire class will "stand here heart to heart." The time is now, if ever, then, to take a look at that sun and—like sailors—to determine our course for tomorrow by the aspect and colors of its setting.

For the privilege of four years' attendance at one of the finest liberal arts institutions in the nation, we are profoundly in debt—some of us quite literally, in fact. We are, first of all, deeply grateful to each of the various agencies here assembled on our behalf; to our parents, who in most cases paid the bills and who were also ready with the other less tangible but more important kinds of support that saw us through final, after final, after midterm, after final [. . .]; to our faculty and administration without whom there would be no College, and for whom we at Dartmouth can be particularly grateful for their dedication and availability to us the undergraduates; and to our classmates, who helped us in ways and at times that our families could not, and who are perhaps the single greatest asset of the College, though they would not be here but for its other attributes.

Our obligation is far greater, though, than can be expressed on a price tag, and it is owed in large measure to ourselves, for with this education comes the responsibility to fulfill its purpose. From us to whom much has been given, much is already and far more will be expected in the future. This is, I think, the meaning of the pledge in the verse I have read. Yet when we promise to "make our lives successful," we do not vow to return to our tenth reunion each in a Mercedes-Benz, brandishing the full panoply of other symbols that mark the achievement of a position and salary commensurate with the investment made here. The shame from which our hands must be kept clean is not embarrassment for having won an inferior income or notoriety relative to our peers; it is the realization that our decisions have been ill-made, our choices ill-founded. We may surely err, but let us err boldly. When Franklin Delano Roosevelt said, "To train a man in mind and not in morals is to train a menace to society," he underscored one of the essential features of an education in the liberal arts: it is free in precise relation to the number of choices it demands of us, and the benefit of such an education is to be found as much in the process as in the ostensible goal.

Although the burden of the responsibility is primarily a personal one, it is further characterized by the degree to which we share it and by the ways that a choice made by one of us will rebound to affect the rest. This is particularly true for us at Dartmouth, where the unifying spirit is so pervasive, and where tradition plays such an important role in maintaining it—hence the added incentive to live up to our pledge, "for the sake of dear old Dartmouth." The "honor of her name" is in many ways intimately tied to that of our own. In referring to our responsibility to foster the traditions we have shared here, I do not mean that we must pass them on without alteration. Change is, after all, a prerequisite to progress, and if something as time-honored as Coke can change, then I suppose there is always hope for Dartmouth, too. We are, however, the continuing tradition of the College, and what Dartmouth will be is largely of our making.

In singing then the twilight song of our departure, taking our final bow, as it were, in this pageant which began at Convocation four years ago and ends here now with Commencement, we might only hope to achieve the same perspective—on both our accomplishments and our expectations for the future—that the immortal wit Chuckles the Clown had when he said: "a little song, a little dance, a little seltzer down your pants." We must continue to sing our songs and to dance our dances, and if we do get seltzered along the way, well, we'll always dry out again.

II. by KAMALA DEVI DANSINGHANI 1994

I SPENT A fair amount of time this past week thinking about what I should say today, what "message" I wanted to get across in my address to you. Then I realized there was no *one* single, all-encompassing idea that would both sum up our four years here at Dartmouth and give us direction to guide us in the days and years ahead. If what you're looking for is some earth-shattering insight about the "meaning of life," sorry to disappoint, but I don't have the answers, at least no more than any one of you. . .

Instead, I would like to share with you some thoughts about our soon-to-be alma mater that have been swirling around in my head during our last week here. Before I do that, though, I'd like to tell you a story about a little girl, about the mistakes she made and the lesson she learned about what is truly important, and what is not so important. . .

This little girl was ten years old, and in the fifth grade, when she won her school spelling bee. You can imagine how excited she was, and it wasn't because of the $25 check she received for winning; rather, it was the chance to represent her school in the town spelling bee that made her eyes sparkle and her stomach knot in anxious anticipation of the event. She practiced and practiced for weeks beforehand, until she knew the list of words backwards and forwards, in order and out of order. Finally the big day came. She was so nervous she could barely sit still for a minute. Maybe it was nerves that got to her, or maybe she didn't know that list as well as she thought she did, but whatever the reason, she didn't win the spelling bee. In fact, she didn't even make it to the finals, and she was absolutely devastated. I know you're probably thinking, "So she lost—there are worse things in life that could happen. . ." But to this little girl that spelling bee was *the* most important thing to her in her life at that time. She got over the loss, of course, but the stinging memory of her crushing defeat remained with her.

The years passed quickly, and the little girl grew up. Soon, she entered high school, and during her four years there, she worked her very hardest, this time with a new goal in mind—to graduate first in her class. Now, there is nothing inherently wrong in having such a goal; however, in her case she sacrificed all else in the attempt to fulfill this ambition, and in the end, only came in second. She had been shooting for number one, and once again, victory had eluded her, just as it had seven years earlier. This time, however, defeat dealt a much harder blow—so hard, in fact, that it nearly destroyed her. Here again, you may be saying to yourselves, "Why did this girl make such a big deal out of being second instead of first? This is not exactly a tragedy here." You're right, of course, but this girl's entire identity was tied up in being first—to her it was a symbol of winning and achieving—and when she failed, she lost more than just the title of "valedictorian". . . she also lost part of herself.

By now you are probably wondering where this story is heading, and why on earth I told it to you. As you may or may not have guessed, that ten year old girl who lost the spelling bee was me. Yes, and it was I who graduated as salutatorian of my high school class. But what is the point of all this? Well, let me explain. . .

When I first got to Dartmouth, I threw myself completely into my work. . . I spent most of my first two years secluded in the Tower Room, which is why many of you out there are probably wondering who this person is standing here. But even though I may have done well academically, I missed out on a lot of what college life is all about, and I wasn't really happy. It was not until last year that I began to realize that there was much more to Dartmouth than just academics. With the help of someone very special to me, I was able to overcome not only the eating disorder that I had suffered from for four years, but also the protective wall I had used for so long to insulate myself. It was only then that I truly began to enjoy Dartmouth.

It has taken me nearly twenty years, but I think I have finally learned a lesson from all of this. You were right, Mom, when you told me in high school that "Five years from now, this isn't going to seem like such a big deal to you." Success—be it academic or financial or whatever—is not what it's all about. We are all here today to celebrate an important achievement in our lives—our graduation from Dartmouth College. However, it is not just the attainment of this goal that we are celebrating, for in and of itself, it has little meaning. . . rather, it is the individual paths that have brought each of us here today.

I once read that "There is not one big cosmic meaning for all, there is only the meaning we each give to our life. . ." I would argue that this is true of what people call the "Dartmouth Experience" as well, for in these four years, each of us has given our own meaning to, and created our own unique, "Dartmouth Experience." Yes, we will all go forth from here with memories that we share as the Class of 1994, but Dartmouth has left its impression on each of us in different ways. And that impression is more than just midterms, finals, and papers. . . more than just the snow and cold of the North. . . more than just the Ivy League name (and the price tag that goes along with it!). . . and yes, more than just frat parties and beer. What is it, then? That is something each of us has to answer for ourselves, in our own way. . . and I will leave it to you to do just that. [. . .]

I began by telling you about how I learned what the meaning of success is *not*; I would like to end by sharing with you what I have found so far to be the best definition of what success *is*, from Christopher Morley's *Where the Blue Begins*: "There is only *one* success—to be able to live your life in your own way." As we have each lived our Dartmouth lives in our own individual ways, so now we prepare to go out into the world and do the same. . . But, in order to do that, we need our diplomas, so without further ado, good-bye and good luck to the Class of 1994. Thank you.

A Commitment to Excellence

by JAMES O. FREEDMAN

⇜⇝⇝ On October 6, 1986, David T. McLaughlin announced his intention to leave the presidency. The following spring James O. Freedman, then president of the University of Iowa, was chosen to be his successor. These are the remarks made to the Dartmouth faculty by the President-Elect on April thirteenth, immediately after the Trustees' formal announcement of his selection, indicating that he would take office on July first of that year. "A Commitment to Excellence" is reprinted from the collection of President Freedman's 1987 addresses, entitled *Speaking at the Outset.*

I FEEL PRIVILEGED to have been offered one of the most important opportunities in American higher education: to work with the faculty of Dartmouth College and the entire Dartmouth community to strengthen this institution's intellectual distinction and to enlarge the contributions it makes to the lives of its students and the life of the country. I thank all of you for offering me that opportunity.

Having grown up virtually in the shadow of this College, I have a special appreciation of the fact that it has been served by a series of remarkably able and devoted Presidents. I speak especially of those who have served within my own lifetime: President Hopkins, President Dickey, President Kemeny, and President McLaughlin. I hope to be worthy of their outstanding example. And I want to add a particular word of esteem, on my first public occasion in Hanover, for the extraordinary contribution that David T. McLaughlin has made during his tenure as President of Dartmouth.

As all of you know, this is my second college presidency; and, with regard to that fact, I have thought in recent days of Samuel Johnson's comment on second marriages: that they represent the triumph of hope over experience.

I want to assure you that I begin this second presidency with the highest of hopes—and the deepest of beliefs—that Dartmouth College is on the threshold of an era of great opportunity and achievement. Several years ago John Kenneth Galbraith said that universities are becoming, at the end of the century, what banks were at the beginning: the suppliers of the nation's most needed source of capital. The

350

greatest challenge of Dartmouth's present era is to continue to meet the highest standards of intellectual distinction in discharging its responsibility as a supplier of that human capital and as a citadel of liberal education.

There are, of course, many specific challenges facing Dartmouth in the here and now. It is much too early for me to comment in any detailed fashion upon those challenges. But it is not too early to join with all of you in a conversation based upon a common commitment to intellectual excellence at Dartmouth.

I deeply admire the central role that Dartmouth College has always accorded to liberal education and the high importance that it has placed upon the teaching of undergraduates. The "Dartmouth experience" has forged a special identity among its faculty, its students, and its alumni. This College has demonstrated a capacity, virtually unequaled in American higher education, to inspire its graduates with a love of the institution. It will be essential in the years ahead that we preserve the fundamental nature of the Dartmouth experience, at the same time that we continually seek to refine and strengthen it.

One of the special traditions of Dartmouth College has been its ability to maintain strong undergraduate and graduate and professional programs, side by side. As we seek to maintain Dartmouth's stature as a major research institution, we will want to continue to explore how, and in which new areas, the College may be able to make an enlarged and distinctive contribution to graduate education—a contribution that will be consistent with the Dartmouth tradition and will enrich the Dartmouth experience.

The considerations currently being addressed regarding the quality of "residential life" are essential to the future of Dartmouth. Residential life must be an integral part of the Dartmouth experience, in the contribution it makes to the intellectual, moral, and social development of our students. I expect this discussion to be both vigorous and fruitful, and I look forward to listening to it, as well as to participating in it.

Clearly, however, we must insist that all of our conversations about the future of Dartmouth, involving subjects that by their nature are controversial, be conducted in a climate of civility, because civility toward one another and the tolerance of maddeningly different points of view are essential to the maintenance of a community of scholars and to the passionate exchange of ideas. As Justice Oliver

Wendell Holmes, Jr., once said, freedom of speech must mean "not free thought for those who agree with us but freedom for the thought that we hate."

I undertake my new responsibilities with two fundamental premises in mind. The first premise is that *ideas* matter—and matter in the most important and fundamental of ways. The French writer and surgeon Georges Duhamel wrote, in a volume of essays entitled *The Heart's Domain*: "Great ideas have . . . radiant strength. They cross space and time like avalanches; they carry along with them whatever they touch. They are the only riches that one shares without ever dividing them." It is the function of colleges like Dartmouth to examine ideas, to develop ideas, and to teach ideas. Ideas and intellectual inquiry matter, and colleges are society's most critical institutions for the creation of new ideas, the examination of established ideas, and the teaching of both.

The second premise is that *people* matter. In a college like Dartmouth, people matter most obviously in generating, testing, and disseminating ideas. They matter in their collegial influence and interchange—and in their stubborn resistance and endless argumentation—as they create an environment in which ideas can flourish. They matter in the wit and flavor and energy that they invest in their scholarship and teaching. They matter in their passion for learning, discovering, sharing, and taking risks on intellectual ventures of uncertain outcome.

In a world where knowledge and talent count so heavily, it is people—faculty and students—who matter most to the quality of a vital educational institution. That is why we must look so carefully toward the quality of the faculty we are forming now for the next century. That is why we must insist that the standards we apply in appointing new faculty members and in granting tenure to junior faculty members are as rigorous as we can make them. And that is why we must work so tirelessly in assembling a student body of young men and women with the intelligence, ambition, and idealism to make significant contributions to American life.

I do not share the conventional wisdom that today's generation of college students is lacking in idealism and seeks only pre-vocational education, in the heady pursuit of commercial success. Perhaps such pessimism has always been present. (Henry Adams, in reflecting upon his own college Commencement in 1858, observed "If any one of us has had an ambition higher than that of making money; a motive better than that of expediency; a faith warmer than that of reasoning; a love purer than that of self; he has been slow to express it; still slower to urge it.") Yet I believe that today's undergraduates possess an untapped capacity for idealism and altruism, for which our society does not provide adequate outlets. I have been delighted to learn that Dartmouth has addressed this problem so effectively, and I hope that we will continue to do so in the years ahead.

As we assemble an outstanding student body, we must also emphasize the role that great universities should play in preparing students for the responsibilities of citizenship and leadership. Dartmouth College has an historic obligation to educate the leaders of this nation, persons whose courage and wisdom and energy will build the sense of community upon which the maintenance of our democratic institutions and the fabric of our social life depend.

Alfred North Whitehead warned in *The Aims of Education*: "The tragedy of the world is that those who are imaginative have but slight experience, and those who are experienced have feeble imaginations. Fools act on imagination without knowledge; pedants act on knowledge without imagination. The task of a university is to weld together imagination and experience." And let me add to Whitehead's formulation that it is the task of all of us, as scholars and teachers, to nurture those of the younger generation whose ideas, in time, will displace our own.

We must also respond vigorously to Whitehead's further challenge: "Do you want your teachers to be imaginative? Then encourage them to research. Do you want your researchers to be imaginative? Then bring them into intellectual sympathy with the young. . . ." We must follow Whitehead, as Dartmouth so notably has done heretofore, in urging our most distinguished senior faculty members to teach and inspire entering freshmen. And we must encourage every professor who teaches an undergraduate course, to clarify the relationship between that course and the larger concerns of the discipline, and between the discipline and the larger body of knowledge embraced by the entire College, whether within the liberal arts or one of the professions. In so doing, we will make certain that the men and women of Dartmouth discover, above all, the exhilaration of the intellectual life—a taste of what Justice Holmes called "the secret isolated joy of the thinker, who knows that, a hundred years after he is dead and forgotten, men who have never heard of him will be moving to the measure of his thought."

We want our students to move to the measure of the scholar's thought—in the rich and intellectually diverse disciplines of the liberal arts, which by their power encourage students to understand their common humanity and to seek out their authentic selves, and which by their haunting resonance compel students to confront what William Faulkner, in his Nobel Prize address, called "the problems of the human heart in conflict with itself."

We want our students to move to the measure of the scholar's thought—in interdisciplinary studies, as they come to appreciate that many of our most baffling problems are beyond the competence of even the most advanced thinkers in any single discipline.

We want our students to move to the measure of the scholar's thought—in international studies, as they participate in a cross-cultural trade in ideas and, thus, widen their angle of vision on the human community.

Now, as we join hands for the years ahead, I ask your help and colleagueship and friendship—in working together to meet the challenges of Dartmouth College's future, in serving as curators of the Dartmouth experience and of its intellectual distinction.

The Alma Mater

by BARBARA L. KRIEGER

❧❧꞉ Dartmouth Archival Specialist Barbara Krieger here traces the history of how the College's current alma mater came into being.

O N MARCH 31, 1887, Henry M. Baker, Class of 1863, wrote to Prof. John King Lord submitting "a general plan for prizes which," he said, "I hope may secure a very acceptable 'Dartmouth Song.'" Then, toward the end of April, Baker dispatched to the College his check in the amount of two hundred dollars, intended to cover, as he declared, "two prizes of $100 each."

The projected competition, according to a still-surviving outline of its terms, was "to be announced on or before Commencement 1887" and would involve one prize rewarding "the best original music" and another "the best original words" for the desired song. Eligible to participate in the contest would be "all undergraduates and alumni of the College." Beyond this, there was stipulated the appointment of "a committee of three gentlemen skilled in musical and literary matters who shall consider the music and words submitted for competition and shall award the prizes, or either of them, if in their judgment the contributions justify an award." And it was further specified, "If the Committee shall decide that no contribution is worthy an award, or to award only one of the prizes, then the prizes or the unawarded prize, shall remain open for competition at each succeeding Commencement until both prizes are awarded. . . ."

It was not until more than eight years later that the prize for suitable lyrics was finally bestowed. In September of 1896, Baker wrote to President William Jewett Tucker:

"Having been advised that the Committee of award on the prizes offered by me for a distinctively Dartmouth song have awarded the prize for the words of the song to Mr. Richard Hovey of the Class of 1885 and have rejected all the music submitted; after careful consideration, I suggest that the terms of the competition be enlarged so as to permit composers everywhere to compete for the remaining prize to

DARTMOUTH SONG.

I.

Men of Dartmouth, give a rouse
  For the college on the hill!
For the Lone Pine above her,
And the loyal men that love her, —
  Give a rouse, give a rouse, with a will!
    For the sons of old Dartmouth,
    The sturdy sons of Dartmouth—
Though round the girdled earth they roam,
    Her spell on them remains;
They have the still North in their hearts,
  The hill-winds in their veins,
And the granite of New Hampshire
  In their muscle and their brains.

II.

Then were mighty men of old
  That she nurtured side by side;
Till like vikings they went forth
From the lone and silent North, —
And they strove, and they wrought, and they died;
    But — the sons of old Dartmouth,
    The laurelled sons of Dartmouth —
    The Mother keeps them in her heart;

And guards their morning altar-flame;
The still North remembers them,
  The hill-winds know their name,
And the granite of New Hampshire
  Keeps the record of their fame.

III.

Men of Dartmouth, keep a watch
  Lest the old traditions fail!
Stand as brother stands by brother!
Dare a deed for the old Mother!
  Greet the world, from the hills, with a hail!
    For the sons of old Dartmouth,
    The loyal sons of Dartmouth —
Around the world they keep for her
    Their old chivalric faith;
They have the still North in their soul,
  The hill-winds in their breath;
And the granite of New Hampshire
  Is made part of them till death.

Richard Hovey.

Boston, Easter Day
1894.

Manuscript of
"Men of Dartmouth"
by Richard Hovey
Class of 1885

the end that the best possible music be secured and the heart of every Dartmouth man be made glad."

In addition to garnering the prize established by Henry M. Baker, Richard Hovey, who by 1896 was already well established as a poet and man of letters, had received another award for this same composition (initially called simply "Dartmouth Song"). Edwin O. Grover, Class of 1894, states in a letter published in the October 1931 number of the *Dartmouth Alumni Magazine*: ". . . The poem was written at the suggestion of a member of the Dartmouth Lunch Club of Boston, which offered a prize for the best poem about Dartmouth. Some months later the poem won a $100 prize offered by Henry M. Baker . . . for the best poem suitable for a Dartmouth song." And Grover went on to declare, "I had the pleasure of first publishing 'Men of Dartmouth' in the June 1894 issue of the *Dartmouth Literary Monthly*, of which I was editor."

Dated "Boston, Easter Day 1894," a manuscript of the Hovey poem (two of its three stanzas carrying crossings-out and verbal emendations) is now preserved within the College Archives.

Grover's June 1894 publication of the text in the *Literary Monthly* contains—either because of his not having the original manuscript in hand or through exercise by him of editorial license or by some undocumented discussion with the poet—a few minor divergences from the Easter Day 1894 manuscript. For example, the final two lines of the first verse read, as printed, "And the granite of New Hampshire / In their muscles and their brains." Whereas this passage in Hovey's manuscript has "muscle," singular—which indeed does change the meaning somewhat. And in the third verse, where the printed version reads "Men of Dartmouth, set a watch," Hovey's manuscript has "keep a watch."

Certainly neither of these were substantive alterations, but they constituted, at any rate, ones that were to persist over the years that followed.

Whatever the wording, the Richard Hovey poem appeared to have no trouble in winning wide approval. On the other hand, the securing of a suitable and enduring musical setting would prove to take many years, and involve many different composers. Among those who tried their hands at setting music to "Men of Dartmouth" were Addison F. Andrews 1878 (whose version appears in the first edition of *Dartmouth Songs*, published in 1898); Frederic Field Bullard; Marie

Wurm (who set a number of Hovey's poems to music); Charles H. Morse (Dartmouth music professor, whose version was sung at the laying of the cornerstone of Webster Hall in 1901); and Louis P. Benezet 1899 (whose setting was performed in 1904 when the cornerstone was laid for the rebuilding of Dartmouth Hall).

In 1908, Ernest Martin Hopkins, then Secretary of the College, approached Harry R. Wellman 1907, who was at that period serving as Secretary of the College Club in Hanover, and asked him to attempt a new musical setting for Hovey's poem. Prof. Paul R. Zeller (Director of the Dartmouth Glee Club 1947–79) in his 1950 edition of the *Dartmouth Song Book* records Wellman's reminiscence, provided more than forty years later, of what ensued:

"I went to my room, sat down at the piano, fastened the poem to the music rack and went at it. The first few lines went fairly easy, since they lent themselves to broad, homeric chord treatment. In fact, up to the phrase 'with a will'—it wrote itself. Then Mr. Hovey had changed his meter beginning with 'For the Sons' and I was left swinging on the stool! Not being a trained musician or even a musician, I didn't know what to do. So I kept fooling around doing one phrase at a time, until I had completed the changed meter. It sounded terrible to me; it didn't make sense. So, to cover it up, I wound up the last few measures as I had started, with broad, full chord structure. It wasn't until 30 years later when I was introduced by the head of the Music Department to a real composer, that I learned that 'the treatment of the recitative was nothing short of genius!'. . ."

The Wellman setting was sung at Commencement in 1910, a tradition that was to continue with few exceptions—including 1942, when "Dartmouth Undying" was sung, and during the years of World War II, when there were no Commencement exercises—from that time onward.

From the time of the Wellman composition, the only serious competitor of "Men of Dartmouth" for the role of Alma Mater was one the words of which begin:

> Come, fellows, let us raise a song,
> And sing it loud and clear;
> Our Alma Mater is our theme,
> Old Dartmouth, loved and dear.
> Dartmouth! Dartmouth! challenge thus we fling!
> Dartmouth! Dartmouth! Hear the echoes ring.

Of this Professor Zeller has written: "In the fall of 1891, W. B. Segur '92 set out to satisfy the Glee Club's need for a distinctive Dartmouth song to use as a finale for its programs. He wrote the lyrics for 'Come, Fellows, Let Us Raise a Song,' and together with Guy W. Cox '93, Glee Club pianist, worked out a tune for it. Known as 'The Dartmouth Song' it was the College's first Alma Mater and held this position until 'Men of Dartmouth' superseded it. . . ."

A vote of the senior class in 1918 indicated a preference for "Men of Dartmouth," and in 1926, with the urging of President Hopkins, it officially became the College's Alma Mater. In a whimsical letter published in the November 15, 1926, number of *The Dartmouth* Mr. Hopkins said, in part:

". . . It has been said that the secret of good administration is to decide quickly, and sometimes right. On this particular matter, however, I have been so solicitous not to aid and abet any lurking sentiment that might be existent somewhere in behalf of the old song that I have tried to school myself to a complete neutrality of feeling. The contention at the present time, however, has so definitely appealed to my desire to see a change that with all the risks of doing so, I am impelled to state my position.

"Personally, I can see no argument for the use of the old Alma Mater song as compared with 'Men of Dartmouth' for any occasion which demands an expression of worthy College feeling. My antipathy to the older song began nearly 30 years ago with my first enrollment in the College, and has consistently held ever since, with only this difference, that for the last two decades we have had an alternative in 'Men of Dartmouth,' set to appropriate music, which we did not have before.

"I have sometimes reflected in more recent years that perhaps the older song had a use in that it made defeat in athletic competitions more terrible than it would otherwise have had to be in anticipation of the necessity of singing the older song. . . .

"I am not as enthusiastic as many of the undergraduates of the present day for the overthrowing of all tradition and the eliminating of all color and dramatic fire and pungent atmosphere from College life. When, however, the undergraduates of the present College turn on the administration a half decade or so hence, and urge the restoration of many of those things for whose elimination they have been largely responsible, it would be a source of immense satisfaction to me if amidst the much harmful violence which had been done to tradition, it should be found that so worthy a purpose had been achieved as the obliteration of a song wholly inadequate to and unworthy of the College in whose behalf it had been presumably sung from time to time."

Nearly half a century later, in 1972, responding to the coeducation decision of the Board of Trustees, Dartmouth admitted its first class to include women. President Kemeny opened the College that year by addressing the "men and women of Dartmouth," and the Convocation ceremony was closed with the singing of "Dartmouth Undying."

Kemeny's decision to substitute "Dartmouth Undying" for "Men of Dartmouth" was of course made out of sensitivity to the presence of women in the new entering class, and was arrived at by the President with the approval of the Chairman of the Board of Trustees. It did not, however, meet with the full approval of the student body. After Convocation, *The Dartmouth* decided to poll the women for their feelings about the College's decidedly male-oriented Alma Mater. Although few of the women responded to the questionnaire, the majority of those who did favored retaining the Hovey lyrics. (As one respondent noted, "If men want to sing about rocks in their heads, it's fine with me.") The Trustees took the survey results into consideration at their October meeting and voted to retain "Men of Dartmouth" as the Alma Mater.

The issue of a gender-inclusive College song arose again in 1980 when Cobra, a women's senior society, composed an additional verse for "Men of Dartmouth." The verse, placed between verses one and three of the original version (Hovey's second verse had been rarely sung, except in time of war or at memorial services), was introduced at the Commencement exercises that year—the one and only time the Cobra verse appeared in a Commencement program.

Several years passed before serious consideration of revising the Alma Mater would be revisited. Then, in its May 1986 report, the Council on Diversity offered this recommendation:

"Because 'Men of Dartmouth' is an inappropriate school song for a coeducational institution, the College community should explore three possible ways to address the situation: a) through modification of the present language and/or the creation of wholly new verses to replace the old ones; b) through the substitution of another traditional Dartmouth song that is not sex-specific; or c) through the creation of a wholly new song. . . ."

The report also suggested that until such changes could be made, only other traditional Dartmouth songs be sung at formal College functions.

The Council's report was issued too late in the spring to have much impact on the 1986 graduation exercises, and accounts of Commencement that year do not indicate that there was any significant protest over the inclusion of the traditional version of "Men of Dartmouth" in the printed program. This would be, however, the original song's last solo appearance in that publication.

Convocation in September of 1986 was another story. Protest fliers, as well as active protest at the ceremony itself, evidenced an increasing desire for change in the College's official song. In response, President David T. McLaughlin requested the creation of a committee, formed from the Student Assembly and the Alumni Council, to investigate the Alma Mater issue. Despite results of their own poll, which showed that sixty-one percent of the students supported retention of the original song and lyrics, the Committee on the Alma Mater recommended revision of the original verses.

Still under the title "Men of Dartmouth," both the traditional version and a revised set of lyrics (offered by the senior class executive council) appeared in the 1987 Commencement program. The Dartmouth community was invited to join in singing either of the two versions presented.

Another year would pass before the lyrics as they are sung today would make their official appearance. Worked on by Prof. Charles Hamm, Lynne Gaudet, '81, Douglas Wheeler, '59, Caroline Luft, '89, and Dean Edward Shanahan, the new version provided eight changes to Hovey's original poem. On May 28, 1988, President James Freedman announced these changes to the College, and in the Commencement program that year the new version, and only the new version, was printed. The title? Simply "Alma Mater."

> Dear old Dartmouth, give a rouse
>   For the college on the hill!
> For the Lone Pine above her,
> And the loyal ones who love her,
> Give a rouse, give a rouse, with a will!
>   For the sons of old Dartmouth,
>   For the daughters of Dartmouth.

Though 'round the girdled earth they roam,
    Her spell on them remains;
They have the still North in their hearts,
    The hill-winds in their veins,
And the granite of New Hampshire
    In their muscles and their brains.

Dear old Dartmouth, set a watch
    Lest the old traditions fail!
Stand as sister stands by brother!
Dare a deed for the old Mother!
Greet the world, from the hills, with a hail!
    For the sons of old Dartmouth,
    For the daughters of Dartmouth,
Around the world they keep for her
    Their old undying faith;
They have the still North in their soul,
    The hill-winds in their breath;
And the granite of New Hampshire
    Is made part of them till death.

Tribute to John Sloan Dickey

by DAVID T. McLAUGHLIN

≫⸲ Following a stroke, suffered in 1982, the final years of President-Emeritus Dickey's retirement interval were spent as a patient at Dartmouth's infirmary, Dick's House, where he died in February of 1991. The following April a "Service of Commemoration" was held in Rollins Chapel, with two of his successors in the presidency, David T. McLaughlin and James O. Freedman, as the principal speakers. Their addresses were subsequently published, together, in booklet form. Here presented, drawn from that source, is the major portion of President-Emeritus McLaughlin's memorial expression.

FOLLOWING HIS 1945 installation in the presidency of this College, and over the ensuing twenty-five years, more than seventeen thousand students were told by John Sloan Dickey, in what became much celebrated as the counsel with which he closed his annual Convocation address: ". . . as members of the College you have three different, but closely intertwined, roles to play:

"First, you are citizens of a community and are expected to act as such. Second, you are the stuff of an institution and what you are it will be. Thirdly, your business here is learning, and that is up to you.

"We'll be with you all the way—and good luck."

In the fall of 1950 I was one of the pea-green Freshmen who heard that message.

As I look upon this congregation in Rollins Chapel today, I recognize many of John Dickey's former colleagues. Among the remarkable abilities of the President was his capacity to judge well his fellow man, and I am confident he would be the first to insist that his accomplishments as President were due in full measure to the people who worked with him: trustees, faculty, administration, staff, alumni, and students. So, all of you former colleagues, and many others who are not with us, become, with him, the cause—or, to use his word, the "stuff"—of our celebration today.

Each of you who knew him can, of course, frame your remembrances of President Dickey in your own terms. But permit me to speak, just briefly and quite informally this afternoon, of a few of my personal recollections and reflections, which I hope may be worthy of this occasion.

My undergraduate interval coincided with what some have called the Dickey Administration's "vintage years" on the Hanover Plain (at least, they may have been such in all respects except with regard to football). It was the time when the innovative Great Issues Course was flourishing. International Relations was one of the most popular majors, and high on a graduate's list of career preferences was entering public service. Academic programs and departments were then rebuilding with an emphasis on the concept of teacher-scholars, and Dartmouth's achievement in the percentage of alumni-giving led the nation.

I remember well the sincerity of manner, the incisiveness and eloquence of expression with which the President spoke to the student body. The titles of his Convocation addresses during my years in College suggest something of the forceful nature of John Sloan Dickey when engaged in the exercise of educational leadership. There was in 1950 "The Hard Business of Facing Front." The following year he addressed the proposition that "A Free Man is Answerable." In 1952 it was "The Business of Being a Gentleman," and the year after that, "The Measure of Maturity."

Then, the last Convocation address I heard him deliver (when I was at Tuck School) was entitled "The Liberating Arts"—a favorite theme of a President in full stride. Let me this afternoon quote just two short passages from the Convocation ceremony, opening the College's 1954–55 academic year.

Early in the talk, Mr. Dickey referred back to previous Convocation messages of his, when he specified some of the qualities requisite for responsible adulthood and citizenship: humility, loyalty, integrity, a cooperative and moral outlook, manners, and "that ultimate discipline of self," called maturity. Next, he went on to relate these to the undergraduates themselves and to the purposes of the College:

"The words have been said at other Convocations, but the relevance of these qualities is timeless—except that for you and me the time is now, the place is Dartmouth, and the doing of these things must be yours at every point where you touch Dartmouth and she touches you." And he continued: "I say these things flatly, gentlemen, because it is only such men Dartmouth dare endow with the power of higher learning, and only unto such hands ought her purposes be entrusted. I must tell you, and remind myself, these are not mere sentiments of convenience; they are the conditions and commitments which sustain the existence of this College. Without them it would soon be empty of purpose. . . ."

And later in his text, in one of his most insightful passages, the President declared:

"In a free land the never-ending frontier of freedom's forward thrust is each man's mind. I suggest to you, and I avow for myself, that in our American society it behooves institutions of the liberal learning to take a dynamic view of their mission. Ours is the task to free, as well as to nourish, men's minds. This is why, as I have sought to understand the nature of Dartmouth's obligation to human society, I have come increasingly to think of our commitment of purpose as being to the *liberating* arts, rather than just the liberal arts. It is the active, liberating quality of these arts, I believe, that makes them the best bet for Dartmouth's purposes."

As I reflect on my own undergraduate exposure to President Dickey, I never fail to be impressed by his singular pursuit of the "liberating arts" and by his abiding concern for the total learning experience—for that which should take place outside the classroom, as well as within.

During Freshman trips at Moosilauke, for example, he would speak about *why* we were there. And I vividly remember one comment of his, during such a trip, to the effect that ". . . the essence of your college experience is an everwidening opportunity of choice."

As a student, I worked with the President in my role on the College's Undergraduate Council. In that context John Dickey gave us opportunities of choice, indeed—entrusting to students decisions on College policy, in matters about which he, obviously, felt strongly himself. Whether it was a question of the disciplining of an individual student for infraction of some College rule or the issue of disavowing discriminatory clauses imposed by national fraternity charters, he would listen to our position, state his own views, and then, after mangling an unlit cigarette (which was at that period his custom, as part of a rather ritualistic demonstration—to himself and others—that he had conquered "the smoking habit"), he would look up and say, "Well, have at it."

That faith in others to reach a proper, a correct decision—to "have at" the hard business of learning—is a mark of the man and of the great educator that he was.

Some years later, following my graduation from Dartmouth and Tuck, I returned to the campus, and quite by happenstance I met President Dickey striding across the College Green. (It was in the spring of 1961.) He gave me a hearty greeting and warmly urged me to tour with him the Hopkins Center, which was then under construction.

To my delight, we were joined at the entrance of the Center by none other than Ernest Martin Hopkins, and for the next unforgettable two hours, the three of us poked about in every room and corridor and alcove of that magnificent facility, while Mr. Dickey described enthusiastically, as well as in great detail, the concept and significance of each component of the structure, and their relationship to liberal learning within Dartmouth's program. (Not a bricks-and-mortar man, Mr. Dickey saw buildings as helping to constitute the means of achieving a comprehensive learning experience; and never was there a better example of such provision than the Hopkins Center, a project to which he devoted infinite personal attention and care. He was an educator who was perhaps at his best when "hands on" and relating warmly and personally to others.)

Needless to say, that was for me an unforgettable afternoon—and, as a matter of fact, one that ended around the Dickeys' kitchen table at One Tuck Drive.

Nearly two decades later, in 1979, my class's twenty-fifth reunion coincided with John Dickey's fiftieth. The President was the principal speaker at both events. He had then been out of office for approximately a decade, but he was no less disposed, then, to speak freely and emphatically about issues close to the heart.

In the Bema on that June morning, before the Class of '54, he elected to educate those of us who were gathered there, about the context and meaning of the great Dartmouth College Case. Speaking without notes, he described exquisitely the emotional appeal Daniel Webster made, before the Supreme Court of the United States, on behalf of his "small College." He explained how Chief Justice Marshall's decision had molded into the spirit of Dartmouth an abiding sense of individual and institutional independence (in John Marshall's words, institutional "immortality and individuality").

His fifty-year address to his Class of 1929, given later that same day, was no less memorable, for on that occasion he invoked movingly Dr. Tucker's message that the spirit of fellowship is grounded in loyalty to place—to which he referred as "place loyalty," a great fashioning and shaping force of this College.

This quality—loyalty—is one of the primary tenets by which this extraordinary man, John Sloan Dickey, lived. And he himself once defined loyalty as "that quality in a man which carries the bond of human solidarity beyond the reaches of knowledge and belief—indeed, even beyond the normal bonds of faith itself."

I personally experienced a demonstration of the depth of his conviction in this regard, when I was considering the possibility, which had arisen during 1980, of my election to the presidency of the College. I visited President Dickey and sought out his counsel and advice. We sat together on his deck at 11 Lyme Road, at an early-morning hour, and I shared with him candidly some of my reservations about the proposition then being contemplated.

Part of President Dickey's response centered upon loyalty. He spoke of *his* loyalty—to the cause of education, to the cause of Dartmouth. He said that serving as Dartmouth's President was the greatest calling he could ever imagine and that ". . . anyone who was fortunate enough to have some experience with dedication to the ideal of education is the beneficiary of a great, great human impulse."

He revealed that during his quarter-century as President of the College he had received many offers that involved opportunities to leave, but that he possessed a firm conviction that there was no more rewarding post to be had, no more worthy or important work to be done than right here on the Hanover Plain, in the presidency of Dartmouth—or, as he modestly used to phrase it, by "the fellow on this job."

President Dickey, the educator, taught us a great deal about Dartmouth College, about liberal learning, and about ourselves. He demonstrated to each of us in this chapel—and to Dartmouth—a sense of loyalty that binds us one to each other and to our College, no matter where we may be, the "girdled earth" around.

Perhaps this was best stated in one of John Dickey's last talks to Freshmen at Moosilauke. On that occasion he said, in part: "This is what an institution is all about—when you learn to love an institution, you'll be loving something much larger than yourself. That's a special kind of liberation from provincialism of self that I hope may be part of your college experience at this place we call Dartmouth."

Today we have gathered at this place called Dartmouth—this place he so deeply loved and so well served. We are gathered to accord special remembrance and to express enduring thanks—to celebrate the life and accomplishments of John Sloan Dickey: one who, both on "the job" and within a myriad other contexts, over the years touched countless lives and made each of them the better, the richer, the fuller—this extraordinary and worthy traveler and friend.

In the words of the College's Alma Mater, President Dickey was, indeed, one who "set a watch, lest the old traditions fail"; momentous and unrelenting were the deeds he dared "for the old mother"; joyously, he greeted "the world, from the hills, and with a hail"; always and everywhere, he kept for this institution the "old chivalric faith"—the "old undying faith." He had "the still North" in his soul, "the hill winds" in his breath; and "the granite of New Hampshire" was, without question, part of him "till death."

Now, as he so often averred, and as he demonstrated by the example of his dedication and doing, "the word is 'so long,' because in the Dartmouth fellowship there is no parting."

A Civil Voice in the Wilderness

by JAMES DODSON

֍ Such was the titling for *Yankee* magazine's June 1991 article treating of President James O. Freedman and the first four years of his administration.

A FEW HOURS AFTER American smartbombs began raining on Baghdad last January, James Freedman, Dartmouth College's 15th president, answered an unexpected knock on his door. Standing there were three students, young men who were infants during America's last war, who needed someone to help them make sense of what was suddenly happening in the Persian Gulf.

Dartmouth presidents, it's been said, have always behaved more like headmasters than administrators, but Freedman did not know these particular students personally. They came to see him because, since his first day as president four years ago, Freedman has championed a "climate of civility" that encourages open debate on great issues, but insists on a "tolerance of maddeningly different points of view."

As Freedman, 55 years old, a stocky intellectual who looks and sounds like a warmer version of John Sununu, roamed the Hanover, New Hampshire, campus that week, such a debate was under way. There were mock gravestones and yellow ribbons, vigils for peace and demonstrations in favor of the Allied assault on Iraq.

"The thing that struck me was how powerfully opinions and viewpoints differed," Freedman reflected later. "And yet, as I listened to the unfolding debate, I was immensely pleased about one thing—the way in which people who completely disagreed on this most important issue discussed their feelings in a civil manner. After what this school has been through, I think it said something very good about Dartmouth College."

If so, it was a welcome change from the "moral and intellectual civil war," as *The New York Times Magazine* has described it, that has fractured the Ivy League's smallest college for the last decade—a war in which Freedman's own commitment to civility, and to freedom of speech, has been hotly questioned.

369

The struggle for Dartmouth's soul goes back at least 20 years, to the administration of John Kemeny, who presided over the sea changes of the seventies: coeducation, increased recruiting of minority groups, and the first assaults on the entrenched power of the fraternities. But according to conservative critics like *National Review* publisher William F. Buckley Jr. and former cabinet member William Simon, Freedman has accelerated Dartmouth's liberal tilt. Dartmouth under Freedman, they say, has abandoned its defiantly independent motto — *Vox clamantis in deserto* ("the voice of one crying in the wilderness")—to become a left-wing rookery where conservative ideas, free speech, and Western culture itself are systematically suppressed. This might come as a huge surprise to those who have long thought of the school as the Ivy League's most visibly conservative, clubbish institution, an elite bastion of athletic WASP scions who preferred their drinks strong and their women weak.

Freedman has made no secret of his desire to attract more minority, foreign, and female students and faculty to Dartmouth. Women, who were not admitted until 1972, now make up 44 percent of first-year students, and the percentages of foreign and minority students have also risen. The most common surnames at Dartmouth these days, says one administrator, are Kim and Lee.

Aiming to squash the school's "smart jock" stereotype, one of Freedman's first acts as president was to launch an aggressive "Presidential Scholars" program that woos academic achievers the way other colleges seek out power forwards and wide receivers. Despite protests from students who feared the campus would eventually be overrun by "geeks with pocket protectors," the school now harvests a larger crop of gifted student scholars every year from an ever-dwindling talent pool. As one professor put it, "Dartmouth wants the creative oddball as well as the smart kid who majors in Budweiser and basketball."

To the delight of the faculty and the dismay of his critics, Freedman has also presided over a major broadening of the school's curriculum, added Arabic and Japanese studies, overhauled the administration, increased the numbers of full and tenured professors, and deepened the institution's commitment to graduate study and scientific research.

But there are powerful factions, mostly alumni and political conservatives outside Hanover, who are infuriated by Freedman's civil liberation of Dartmouth. Some of them have struck back by funneling vocal and financial support to the *Dartmouth Review,* an independent off-campus newspaper that began publishing in 1980. Depending on your political point of view, the *Review* has added a refreshingly irreverent—or malignantly provocative—new voice to the debate over Dartmouth's destiny.

In 1982 the *Review* attacked affirmative action in an article headlined "Dis Sho Ain't No Jive"—an article so offensive that conservative congressman Jack Kemp resigned from the paper's board of advisers. In 1984 the *Review* published the names of Dartmouth students it claimed were homosexuals. When antiapartheid students built shanties on the college green in December of 1985 to protest U. S. investments in South Africa, *Review* staffers tore them down the next month—on Martin Luther King Day. [. . .]

These well-publicized stunts have focused waves of unflattering media attention on Dartmouth and complicated Freedman's efforts to diversify the college community. Faculty recruiters say that one of the first questions prospective candidates ask is whether racism and sexism are as blatant on the campus as they've heard.

The answer, based on an unscientific sampling of Dartmouth students, seems to be no. But the school's "Animal House" image, engraved by the film that was written by a Dartmouth grad, dies hard. "In preparing Dartmouth for a more intellectually stimulating future," says professor Jere Daniell, an expert on New England history, "the greatest challenge to Jim Freedman may be coming to terms with the school's romantic and stimulating past."

[. . .] Dartmouth has always inspired passionate devotion among its graduates. [. . .] That much seems to hold true even today. Routinely ranked among the top ten colleges in the country academically, Dartmouth ranks number one in overall student satisfaction according to an annual poll taken by *U.S. News and World Report.* A good measure of that satisfaction stems from rustic social traditions that would seem prehistoric on other campuses. Every year 85 percent of the incoming class of 1,050 students agrees to participate in a mass hunter-gatherer ritual known simply as "The Freshman Trip": two days of hiking to Mt. Moosilauke and the famed Ravine Lodge, a giant log edifice overlooking the Baker River. There, gathered around blazing bonfires, they learn the school's rough-and-tumble history, hear ghost stories and Indian legends. They are taught sacred school anthems such as "Dartmouth Undying" and "Men of Dartmouth."

Usually the president shows up to greet the newcomers, and in the morning everybody eats green eggs and ham à la Dr. Seuss (class of 1925).

"The trip is pure indoctrination," says one of the group leaders, "but it amounts to the making of a solemn covenant. You feel you've been selected, you are part of a historical continuum. Those who aren't hopelessly alienated by the experience—and few seem to be—fall helplessly in love with the place for life. They aren't just bonded to Dartmouth. They *are* Dartmouth."

It's difficult to imagine this kind of orientation taking place at, say, Harvard or Yale, and it is precisely that distinction, some believe, that first attracted the conservative celebrities who bankrolled the *Dartmouth Review*. Attempts to organize similar dissenting conservative organs at Yale and Harvard had flopped. "Basically, they couldn't get a toehold anyplace else," says sociology professor Ray Hall. "Dartmouth's image and history and isolation made it a perfect target for the *Review.*"

The *Review* has skillfully exploited the passions of Dartmouth grads whose allegiance to the college's traditions outweigh their deference to racial, ethnic, or sexual sensitivities. For example, when Dartmouth began to admit more Native Americans during the 1970s, some of those students protested that the Dartmouth mascot—an Indian—was demeaning. They also called for the removal of the Hovey Murals, a set of hokey paintings in a college dining hall that depict scantily attired Indian maidens and warriors cavorting drunkenly in a romanticized woodland setting. In due time, the college authorities agreed to disavow the Indian mascot—it had never been the *official* mascot, they said—and, eschewing outright censorship, covered the murals with removable panels. Traditionalists never forgave the administration for caving in and have campaigned to have their symbols returned ever since. The *Dartmouth Review* obligingly distributes free Indian T-shirts to first-year students.

Ironically, when Jim Freedman was growing up in Manchester, New Hampshire, it was just such hallowed traditions that persuaded him to attend Harvard instead of Dartmouth. "Dartmouth was one of the schools I applied to, and I came and had a look," he recalls. "Its image was all male, woodsy, WASP-y, with a heavy emphasis on athletics. The world I grew up in dictated that I needed a little more breathing room than that."

His father, an English teacher at Manchester's Central High, liked to call their neighborhood "a little United Nations" because of the mingling of Lebanese, Irish, French-Canadian, and Jewish families. "From the playground on up we learned to talk to each other," Freedman says, "because survival often meant you had an ability to get along."

His taste for diversity came from the old neighborhood, and he inherited his love of books and "the life of the mind," as he calls it, from his father. But some of his deepest-held ideas about honesty, responsibility, and fair play evolved while working part-time in the newsroom of William Loeb's *Manchester Union Leader*.

"I worked there after school and in the evenings on the weekend. At night, you know, is usually when you'd get calls about accidents or suicides and such. There was always a police call or a fire. You grow up fast listening in an environment like that. There were only a few of us, and I learned that if I didn't do my job, I let down everyone else. And honesty. I remember fierce debates over how, ethically, to play a reported suicide. These were life-and-death issues. I recall doing a Little League roundup one night, and someone—it may have even been me—wrote that one team had 'shellacked' another. I remember the sports editor said we had to change that. These were only kids, he argued, and saying they got shellacked was just too strong. That had a tremendous impact on me. I realized what words could do to people. Anybody. And I never forgot that lesson."

Later, when he was at Harvard, he recalls with amusement that William Loeb—the master of American newspaper invective—sent him "nice little Horatio Alger" notes urging him to grow up and do something positive. Today, the newspaper where he learned his first lessons about ethical journalism routinely blasts its former copyboy—though with a more-in-sorrow-than-anger tone—for what it perceives as his liberal leanings and especially his treatment of the *Dartmouth Review*.

Oddly enough, Freedman began his presidency in the good graces of the *Review*. Upon his arrival in July 1987, the newspaper hailed his vitae: Harvard, Yale Law, former dean of Pennsylvania Law School, and president of the University of Iowa, where he presided over a large growth in the school's endowment and academic standing as well as five football bowl appearances. For probably the first time in its existence, the *Review*'s editors agreed with Dartmouth's Board of Trustees that Freedman was just what Dartmouth needed—an intellectual who liked sports. [. . .]

But in 1988, six months after Freedman took office, that abruptly changed. A black music professor named William Cole was a frequent target of the *Review*, which questioned his qualifications. The newspaper's hounding of the jazz biographer took an ugly turn when four *Review* staffers approached Cole in his lecture hall. The details of who did and said what to whom are still in dispute. But in the small melee that ensued, obscenities were exchanged and a *Review* photographer's camera flash was broken. After a two-day hearing before a campus judicial body composed of students, faculty, and deans, the *Review* staffers involved were suspended for disorderly conduct. They filed suit against the college, claiming their rights had been violated. A state judge eventually ordered the students reinstated; Professor Cole left the College.

The Cole incident brought Dartmouth's new president into the fray for the first time. "Nothing has disturbed me more than reports from students of the climate created by the *Review*," Freedman told the faculty at a special meeting a month after the suspensions. "In this climate, some of their classmates have been emboldened to assert that minority students and faculty members do not belong at Dartmouth—that somehow they occupy an illegitimate place within our community. Such assertions are patently false and entirely malicious."

Moreover, Freedman accused the *Review* and its famous patrons of "poisoning" the Dartmouth environment by creating a culture of racial hatred. "What the *Review* has done on this campus has not been decent. What it has done has been irresponsible, mean-spirited, cruel, and ugly."

The faculty gave him a standing ovation. "He finally put brilliantly into words what many of us had been thinking for years," says one faculty member.

In October 1988 the *Review* retaliated with an inflammatory piece entitled "Ein Reich, Ein Volk, Ein Freedman" (alluding to the Nazi slogan "One Reich, One People, One Fuehrer") that accused Freedman of engineering a "final solution to the campus conservative problem." The phrase "final solution" was an echo of the Holocaust, underlined by the timing of the story, which appeared only a month before the 50th anniversary of Kristallnacht, the night the Nazis began rounding up Jews.

The crude attempt at satire was condemned by the Anti-Defamation League of B'nai B'rith. Eleven faculty members wrote to the *Review*'s advisory board charging that the paper was guilty of anti-Semitism, noting that Freedman is Jewish. One professor referred to *Review* editors as "prefascist thugs."

Like some volcanoes, the *Dartmouth Review* tends to erupt every two years. Last fall, on the eve of the Jewish holy day Yom Kippur, a quote from Hitler's *Mein Kampf* appeared on the *Review*'s masthead: "Therefore, I believe today that I am acting in the sense of the Almighty Creator: By warding off the Jews, I am fighting for the Lord's work."

Once again, Dartmouth College found itself trying to contain a media meltdown. President Freedman issued a statement denouncing the use of the quote as "appalling bigotry." He said that for ten years the *Review* had been attacking "blacks because they are black, women because they are women, homosexuals because they are homosexuals, and Jews because they are Jews."

The *Review* strenuously denied the charges, arguing that blacks, Jews, women, and other ethnic minorities had served in top editorial positions at the paper. Its editor at the time, Kevin Pritchett, was black. It pointed to its pro-Israel foreign policy stance. But the damage to the *Review*'s credibility was devastating. Over 2,000 students and faculty signed a petition condemning the newspaper, and two of its own editors resigned in protest. [. . .]

Insisting it had been the victim of sabotage, the *Review* asked the Anti-Defamation League to investigate the bizarre incident. After completing the probe, the ADL concluded that an unnamed *Review* staff member had indeed inserted the Hitler quote. The report rebuked the *Review* for creating "an environment that not only condoned but encouraged the inclusion of such a quote." [. . .]

National columnists of conservative stripe sprang to the defense of the beleaguered publication and lambasted Freedman. One of them, Dartmouth professor Jeffrey Hart, who serves as faculty adviser for the *Review*, branded Freedman a liar and predicted that he would be gone in less than a year.

Gone where? "Clearly," says Pritchett, "Freedman wanted to pad his resumé with the death of the *Dartmouth Review*; he was really using Dartmouth as a stepping-stone to somewhere else." That somewhere else, *Review* supporters insisted, was Harvard, Freedman's alma mater, which was looking for a new president.

The assertion fits neatly into what might be called the Crimson Conspiracy theory. Some Dartmouth alumni have suspected ever since Freedman arrived with his talk about diversity and intellectual rigor that his hidden agenda was to make broad-shouldered Dartmouth into an effete North Woods version of Harvard. Freedman, however, insisted his future lay in Hanover, which presented his critics with an even more vexing possibility—that he really is planning to stick around.

The week war broke out in the Persian Gulf, Kevin Pritchett sat in his off-campus office, surrounded by pictures of icons like Bill Buckley, Richard Nixon, and Pope John Paul II [. . .]. Freedman's "enlightened agenda is really a form of trendy political correctness," Pritchett explained, and he insisted that the college president had "been weakened by this controversy, I think, because he has been shown to be a liar." He denied rumors that the *Review* was faltering financially: "If anything, our subscriptions are up."

That may be, but several Hanover stores pulled their advertising from the *Review* in the wake of last autumn's events, and many professors now refuse to speak to *Review* reporters when they call. Worst of all, few students seem to read the paper anymore. Ask them about it, and they will tell you they are tired of all the commotion. [. . .]

In late January Freedman and his wife, Bathsheba, flew to Washington, where he was to give the keynote speech at a dinner honoring Thurgood Marshall, the Supreme Court's aging war-horse of affirmative action, for whom Freedman clerked after law school. They watched as thousands protested the war by marching down Constitution Avenue. Freedman's thoughts returned to Dartmouth and the reaction of its students to the war. "I was moved by the emotional power and complexity of the voices I heard," he reflected. "And I was deeply pleased at the civil manner in which we disagreed."

That night Freedman saluted his old boss in the words of another great justice, Oliver Wendell Holmes Jr.: "A hundred years after he is dead and forgotten, men who never heard of him will be moving to the measure of his thought."

Though he didn't say so, Freedman might have had his college in mind when he talked about how America will someday embrace the ideals of equality and justice that Marshall has championed. For all the ideological warfare it has suffered in recent years, Dartmouth may yet emerge a better—or at least a more civil—place for those who love it.

Big Jump

by DAVID BRADLEY

≫⟫⟫ The demolition, in the spring of 1993, of Dartmouth's venerable ski jump caused physician-author-teacher-skier David J. Bradley 1938 to produce an expression that is partly nostalgic reminiscence and partly memorial homage. "Big Jump" was initially published in the Winter 1993 *Alumni Magazine*, from which this excerpt has been taken.

SKI JUMPING IS pure physics. As heavenly bodies must follow Newton's laws, so must the earthly. Good jumping hills conform to these laws. There is a steep in-run to give the skier speed, then a curve to a somewhat hanging takeoff. In air the jumper will go out and down in a parabola of fall. (He may enlarge the parabola by catching the air, surfing on it; or he may narrow it, obstructing the air.) Whether smooth or struggling or upside-down, he will fall 16 feet in the first second, 64 in two seconds. The landing hill must shadow this parabola down to the longest jump and then flatten out through the dip to a level outrun.

When Dartmouth's big jump was constructed in 1921, last of a long line of lesser hills, it was designed for jumps of up to 135 feet. An 85-foot tower was erected beside the bowl to provide the necessary speed. Some nutty ideas also went into the design, improvisations by the Minneapolis engineer: a bell-curve at the top, a mid-section 45 degrees steep (too steep to hold snow), and a long flat run to the takeoff.

The steep section could be crudely fixed by building two wooden troughs for the skis, packing in snow, and putting the watering cans to them, but the racket would daunt the deaf: bang—bang—bang into the troughs—Hell's own uproar down the ice—wait—wait—wait for the lip. Even a blind jumper could tell the only safe place on that contraption was out in the air.

So in 1929, two years after Baker Tower went up, the big jump was rebuilt to the graceful lines we remember. All troubles vanished. For 64 years the two towers stood as landmarks—glad reaffirmations of the two Dartmouths (the indoor and the outdoor) born together in Eleazar's log-cabin college.

Ski jumping looks dangerous, but it is not, if the hill follows its physics and the humans pack the snow hard and smooth. Skiers fear sticky snow on the takeoff, gusty winds aloft, and soft snow or ice on the landing and dip where, struggling for balance, they may catch an edge and crash. For all the spectacular falls over 72 years, the big hill at Dartmouth produced nothing more serious than two broken arms.

There are times, however, when even Sir Isaac wouldn't know what to advise: as when Donnie Cutter '45 sailed out and found one ski dropping off in midair. Great gasp from the Carnival crowd! In less than a second, Donnie invented his maneuver, placing the loose foot behind the other, makeshifting a landing, doing a contortion ballet in the dip, and riding it out all standing.

Or once when Omer Lacasse was opening the Carnival competition. Down he came from the top, squatting low and happy in the sport he loved. Just then a red setter full of Carnival spirits started straight down the landing hill. Omer couldn't see the dog, nor could he hear the warning yells from everyone around the hill. Out he came—Omer was a beautiful jumper—and over the knoll; then he saw the wagtail dog running interference for him.

"Oh nooooo!" he sang out at this trick of fate, but his voice was lifting into a laugh. He landed alongside the setter, the dog transmigrated and Omer rode to a stop shaking his head. "You never know," he said, still laughing. "You never know."

Around home in Wisconsin I found a 1920 copy of the National Geographic which rhapsodized over "Winter Sports at Dartmouth," all sorts of winter sports including ski jumpers doing somersaults on purpose. Sounded like an excellent institution. Father agreed. He wanted only to be sure the college laid on some education during the off seasons.

So, in September 1934, I disembarked at the Lewiston Station across the river, clumped through the old covered bridge, and entered Dartmouth. That was frightening, all those muscles running around, all that yelling.

President Hopkins—a calm friendly force of a man—enrolled me. After that it was books, classes, evade the predatory sophomores, and sign up for fall training with the ski squad. Through a long fall of dimming sun and changing colors we ran the hills, cleared trails, fixed jumps, and engaged in some disorganized brutality called soccer.

Naturally we freshmen were splattered with the blood of the God-like upperclassmen, survivors of monstrous cross-country marathons and insane downhill races. And we were told the solemn old legend: "Did you hear about the two guys who went off the big jump in a baby carriage?" "No—what happened?" "They're still in the hospital." (I went up to the hospital to learn the details, but the doctors only looked cross-eyed at me, and the nurses laughed.)

Everyone here skied four events, but I knew nothing of cross-country racing, nothing of the black magic of wax, and had never heard of slalom and downhill. Although I didn't know it, I was joining a cavalcade of skiers already recognized throughout snow country. (Over seven decades, starting with John Carleton in 1924, Dartmouth would graduate 65 skiers to the Olympics.)

Work on the big hill was fun, a way of getting acquainted. But the weekends among the boulders and downed timber at Moosilauke were nightmarish. We were clearing up Dartmouth's new downhill racing trail, "Hell's Highway," a two-mile gash down the mountain, in the middle of which was a long precipice obstructed by islands of trees. It was vertical. At the bottom a "cowcatcher" of logs had been piled up to strain out the falling bodies.

This was crazy. Tip the whole state of Wisconsin up on edge, schuss it from the copper ranges in the north to Illinois and you'll find nothing like Hell's Highway unless you miss your turn at the bottom and skid on through Chicago.

But—there was Sel Hannah '35, our captain, a four-event throwback to the Norse God Ullr (with contributions from the Irish and Abenaki), a scholar, a poet. And Bem Woods '36, a shy slender fellow, flawless in the air over big hills. As a freshman he had won the first National Downhill Championship on the old carriage road on Moosilauke. These two didn't seem like suicidal types.

And there was Otto, our renowned ski coach, Otto Schniebs, from Germany and the mountain troops of World War I. Four times wounded, Otto had come to this country an inspired prophet. He had his God: Saint Peter, and his religion: skiing. He said that had the Kaiser been a skier, with only a "lousy Schtemm Krrristy" to soothe his soul, there would have been no war. Otto radiated divine assurance. He didn't convert me; he rebuilt me from the junk parts left over from Hell's Highway.

"Hokay, Dahveed, so you're a chumper. Gut. Also dann a runner . . ."

"Oh no, Otto. Nix on that cross-country stuff."

". . . and a little slalom and downhill machen too, nichts?"

"Please, Otto. Not downhill. Not cross-country."

"Vat!—You vant to be nur Spezialist? Inschteed of real Skier? In der voods going, in der mountains going . . . all your life!"

"Well—all right, Otto—if you say so."

"Dot's der sschtuff, boy. Now you're talking."

Impossible not to love the old hill. It had plenty of height and air for the long jumper, yet stayed close and easy for the youngster of ten or 12, determined to go off because "that's what all the big guys did." (He might barely reach the knoll and carom off for a second jump, but he'd be right back up all toothy eagerness.) It oversaw the midnight revelers riding the landing on toboggans and dining-hall trays. And it waited with special solicitude for the beginning skiers who, on a fraternity dare or determined to force a personal rite of passage, slid out of a Sunday when nobody was around: Well?—It looks awfully high—Other guys have—Yup—It's crazy, but I will if you will—Well, you go first.

I remember when my brother Steve and I, during a break in exams —those severe upper-level disturbances—went out in crystal weather to jump, just to get ourselves back down to the uncomplicated earth. New snow had come overnight; we jumped soundlessly on silk.

And once, when a full moon blazed over the golf course, black pines all around, black shadows lacing the in-run. Well—Why not? To pour down the flickering slide, to lift out over that bald knoll and then drop into penumbra, falling, falling till the hill banged up under our skis and made us lurch for balance. That was good, as Frost says, both going and coming back.

In early February, when the sun began to warm, came the year's great celebration: the Winter Carnival—the College bursting out of steam-heated exams, ice sculptures everywhere, dancing, hockey games, ski and skating races, Outdoor Evening on the golf course under an exploding sky.

At Carnival time, the big jump was naturally the central attraction: flags streaming from the top of the tower, cold hot dogs and cold coffee at the bottom, people from all over the North Country, dog fights, snowball fights, officials, police, and a shivery trumpet call to herald each jumper starting down.

Pure fun. Here was one event everyone could walk or ski to, the one event which they could see top to bottom. Spectators were much too enthralled to be partisan. Whether they were skiers or not, they shared everything that was happening. They shouted for the classy jumper while he was still in air; they ducked for the poor fellow caught in an inter-fraternity snowball barrage; they groaned with the unfortunate who pretzelized himself in mid-air; and mightily they cheered for the impressed Harvardian facing his moment of Veritas in downhill boots.

Skiers from all over New England came to Carnival. Also, skiers from Wisconsin and Michigan, Seattle, Denver, Norway, Finland, even from Florida. After 1915 the great Red Birds of McGill were perennial favorites; in 1937 the Swiss universities sent over seven expert amateurs to race at Carnival and tour the western circuit. The Swiss may have won the Carnival, I don't remember. Among such exuberant sportsmen, winning numbers added nothing.

Often the Carnival side shows were as exciting as the main event. In the twenties it was Bill Robes turning somersaults; the thirties, double and triple jumps were put on to please the crowd. (No one got skewered.)

But of all the extraordinary spectacles the big jump put on for us, none ever matched the day when two of the world's best jumpers appeared: Birger and Sigmund Ruud of Norway. Birger had won three Olympic titles, Sigmund had set the world's distance record at 283 feet. Compact bundles of energy they were, with broad smiles and that lilting-drawling Norwegian way of speaking. The hill was only half-size for them; no matter, jumping was for fun.

Five thousand people and not a sound when the trumpet called them from the top. Sigmund came first, rolling out into an effortless streamlined flight, his skis perfectly together, body curved over them, down, down, to land well beyond the hill record. The impact was so sharp, part of a ski tip snapped off. He rode on out, then turned to warn his brother, in shouts and laughter, not to go on them too hard.

Birger came tightly coiled: an explosion on the take-off, a high arching eternity in air, down and down to land 18 feet beyond the hill in the curve of the dip. His catlike landing made it look easy and his jaunty tail-wag christy showed us it was.

Those were perfect jumps—curves of high art drawn across a wintery Hanover sky which not even Leonardo could have imagined.

Farewell then to Carnival jumping, the heart of winter exuberances at Dartmouth. Something local and precious. Yale has its incomparable Whiffenpoofs, Harvard its Head-of-the-Charles. At Dartmouth it was Carnival and convocation of the big hill.

It's down now, the gorgeous length of that great jump junked—the first big college hill in the country, for decades the best, and, as it turned out, the last. Students of the future will not notice the dreadful emptiness among the pines on the golf course; little will they hear beyond some weird fable about jumping in baby carriages.

In 1980 the NCAA decreed that ski jumping was no longer a sport. Insurance costs were claimed to be the main reason, but that was a smokescreen. College insurance premiums have not dropped a penny following the elimination of jumping.

The one insurmountable reason was team travel. Many teams, unable to build their own jumping hills nearby, had to drive long distances in all sorts of weather to practice: UVM to Middlebury, UNH to Laconia, Colby to God-knows-where. Out west in the Rocky Mountain States the travel problem was much worse.

A final reason, well-known but never mentioned, was that, if a college or university were out to buy an NCAA championship, it had to import Norwegian jumper-scholars. By eliminating jumping, the school could, at one stroke, save time and money and free up athletic scholarships for other sports. The decision was inevitable.

One dissenting vote was cast during that crucial NCAA meeting: Dartmouth's Seaver Peters '54, a hockey star, and our athletic director at the time, argued that ski jumping after all remained a popular Olympic sport. He knew that jumping was a spirited part of skiing, which over nearly a hundred years had brought international fame to this small college. At Dartmouth at least, it called the community together and lit up the festivities like the autumn bonfires.

So ends the era, or almost. Four days before the crane and acetylene torches moved in, we held a last celebration on the old hill. This was no solemn Requiem Mass, but a snowy sendoff, an enskyment.

Three winters of slop and frozen grass had frustrated all attempts to use the jump; then in late March the hill winds blew us down an old-fashioned blizzard, piled up the drifts and brought out the skiers as though summoned by Richard Hovey himself.

The Ford Sayre gnomes came, the local high-school and junior-high jumpers rattled up in their vans, a busload drove over from Lake

Placid; some older riders showed up, 54 years and younger, still with the gleam in the eye if wanting reflexes in the legs.

They came for one last jubilant salute, to tramp the hill hard, to lug snow in bags up the windblown tower, to fuss and fidget over their bindings, finally to climb to the lofty platform and test themselves, as it has always been, alone with their fears and hopes.

Warren Chivers '38, up from Vermont Academy, and Ev Wood '38 and I, all of the 1938 team, may have been the oldest skiers around. We were still good for marking distance and patching shell holes.

Many a youngster soloed that day. (They weren't listening when someone told them that jumping was supposed to be dangerous.) One six-year-old, no bigger than a candlepin, kept shooting the landing and cussing because he wasn't allowed to go from the top.

Chris Hastings and Joe Holland, recent Olympic skiers, were there for the celebration. They showed us that even on a 40-meter hill the new V-shape style (flat down on the skis like a hang-glider without fabric) works beautifully. Three times the old record of 165 feet was equaled. Then: haul down the flags, pick up the rakes and shovels, wind in the measuring tape, pass out prizes, drink a toast of Akvavit, and home to a lesser world.

Why do they come, the young, the old, with shining faces, lugging those heavy five-grooved skis? Because—Vox Clamantis—this is the most beautiful thing they have ever done, or are ever likely to do.

Yours in Peace and Struggle

by ZOLA MASHARIKI

≫≫ᵒ The full title of this essay by corporate attorney Zola Mashariki 1994 is "Dear Old Dartmouth: I am yours in Peace and Struggle. Love, Zola." It treats of her own undergraduate years and reflects broadly, also, upon the African-American experience at Dartmouth.

WHEN I GRADUATED from Dartmouth in 1994, I swore I would never return. The stress of being an African-American woman activist at Dartmouth had demoralized me. The sixteen year old extrovert that I was when I entered Dartmouth bears little resemblance to the cautious woman I've become. Only now, years later did I begin to confront my Dartmouth demons.

My time at Dartmouth was the most exciting, exhilarating, remarkable, and difficult period of my life. My Language Study Abroad program in Spain was a thrill-seeking adventure where I explored cultures and lifestyles far different than my own New York City upbringing. During my senior year, membership in Casque and Gauntlet provided endless enjoyment and fellowship. And the numerous friendships I have made and maintained increase my awe of the amazing and talented men and women that Dartmouth attracts. Simply put: Dartmouth made me happy.

In spite of all this happiness, I know many Dartmouth alumni of African descent have not chosen the easiest path. But I never asked for Dartmouth to be easy. I only asked for my own survival and dignity. And have survived.

If endurance marks our existence as New World Africans of Dartmouth, then the question for the future is: how much more will we have to endure to prove that we belong, and where does the struggle end? How many more obstacles before we achieve the ultimate goal— acceptance, fusion, and some semblance of control over our Dartmouth destinies?

My heart breaks for all the freshmen who each year are told by their classmates that their admission and inclusion at Dartmouth is solely because of affirmative action. Do those people know that they are saying, *"The only reason why you are included is because of race. Save race, you have no value to us. We would never let you in."*? Black students are constantly asked in classes taught by their highly intelligent, well-meaning and white professors if they can add the "black perspective" to the discussion. Clearly, the struggle lives in the halls of Dartmouth.

Several times during my Dartmouth career, I have been approached by an ordinary white Dartmouth student who, longing for a color-free society, wanted to know why I was always hanging out with other blacks. Though he admits that he knows nothing about black hair, can't stand the sound of hip-hop music, and has no idea who The Lost Boyz are, he can't understand why we "segregate" ourselves. I hope someday he will finally understand that, among other blacks, my humanity is presumed and accepted. I seek out blackness because the struggle beckons.

It was nothing short of a miracle when the first black student, Ernest Everett Just, entered the Dartmouth community in 1908. I am proud of the African-American men and women who have survived their Dartmouth experiences and come to inspire others to do well.

Dartmouth's greatest victory does not lie in the rapidly changing statistics, percentages and demographics of the student body. I believe the victory lies in the fact that African-Americans of Dartmouth continue to devote themselves to changing Dartmouth's ugly history of exclusion and ignorance, while cherishing the great Dartmouth traditions.

African-Americans at Dartmouth, like all African-Americans at large, are (to borrow phraseology from LL Cool J and LeShaun), *doing it, doing it, and doing it well.*

I'm not arguing that blacks have always been martyrs, and whites have always been demons; that's far too simple and misleading. The point is simple: My Dartmouth experience was marked by activism, education, and a commitment to change. This is also the greatest legacy of the African-American sons and daughters of Dartmouth. May the struggle continue.

Advice to the Graduating Class

≫≫ The College's annual Commencement exercises typically include an address by a guest speaker, an individual selected from among those to whom honorary degrees are being awarded on the occasion involved. Here follow parts of three such presentations, from the latter half of the decade of the 1990s, the orators being: the President of the United States, in 1995; journalist-author David Halberstam, in 1996; and historian-biographer Doris Kearns Goodwin, in 1998.

I. by WILLIAM JEFFERSON CLINTON

ASOCIETY IS NOT a collection of people pursuing their individual economic, material self-interests. It is a collection of people who believe that by working together they can raise better children, have stronger families, have more meaningful lives and have something to pass on to the generation that comes behind. That also is the purpose of education, and we need it more than ever today.

And so, my fellow Americans, and those of you who will live and work here, you must decide, what is this new world going to be like? You can probably do fine, regardless. You have a world-class education at a wonderful institution. You have the luxury of deciding: Will you devote your lives and your compassion and your conviction to saying that everybody ought to have the opportunity that you had? Will you believe that there is a common good and it's worth investing a little of what you earn as a result of your education? Will you believe that education is more than economics, that it's also about civilization and character? You must decide. Will you work for more equality and more opportunities? [. . .]

I've had the privilege of representing you all over the world, and I think all the time, every day, about what it's going to be like in 20 or 30 or 40 or 50 years, when you come back here for that remarkable reunion that they're celebrating today. And I am telling you, if you will simply use what you have been given in your lives, from God and the people who have helped you along the way, to rebuild this country and to bring it back together, and not to let us be divided by all these forces, to lift up these forces of opportunity and to stamp out the seeds of destruction, you still are at the moment of greatest possibility in all human history.

Your late president, John Kemeny, who came to this country after fleeing Hungary, told the last Commencement he presided over in 1981, the following: "The most dangerous voice you'll ever hear is the evil voice of prejudice that divides black from white, man from woman, Jew from Gentile. Listen to the voice that says, man can live in harmony. Use your very considerable talents to make the world better." Then he ended the speech with, as I understand, the words with which he ended every Commencement: "Women and men of Dartmouth, all mankind is your brother. And you are your brother's keeper. Do not let people divide you one from another."

Do not let people make you cynical. And do not think for a minute that you can have a good, full life if you don't care about what happens to the other people who share this nation and this planet with you. Good luck and God bless you.

II. by DAVID HALBERSTAM

THE TRUTH TODAY, which I suspect you already know, is that you are among the fortunate. You have been given a priceless education in an age where work is increasingly defined not by muscularity but by intelligence, and so you are already advantaged. More, you have not only been given an exceptional education but perhaps more importantly, you have been part of a rare intellectual community where the intellectual process is profoundly valued not just for what it can do for you economically but as an end in itself. Learning is not just a tool to bring you a better income; learning is an ongoing never ending process designed to bring you a fuller and richer life.

In addition you are fortunate enough to live in an affluent, blessed society, not merely the strongest but the freest society in the world. Our courts continue to uphold the inherent rights of ordinary citizens to seek the highest levels of personal freedom imaginable. In this country as in no other that I know of, ordinary people have the right to reinvent themselves to become the person of their dreams, and not to live as prisoners of a more stratified, more hierarchical past. We have the right to choose: to choose if we so want, any profession, any venue, any name. As much as anything else this is what separates us from the old world, the old world across the Atlantic and the old world across the Pacific, where people often seemed to be doomed to a fate and a status determined even before their birth. [. . .]

So what do we do with all that freedom? Freedom after all, does not come without burden and without responsibility—for if we make the wrong choices, we have no one to blame save ourselves. We cannot rant against an authoritarian government which deprived us of our rightful possibilities. So how do we handle the burden of being responsible for our destinies? That is what I would like to talk about today, for you are at the threshold of one of the most important choices that most of you will make in your lives, the choice of your careers. We have after all in this country an inalienable right to life, liberty and the pursuit of happiness. Notice that wording, we are not guaranteed happiness—merely the pursuit of it. Notice, as well that the wise people who authored that phrase did not say 'pursuit of wealth,' for the pursuit of happiness and pursuit of wealth are by no means the same thing, nor do they by any stretch of the imagination generate the same inner sense of contentment, and personal validity.

This is a critical decision for you. For other than the choice of a lifetime partner, nothing determines happiness so much as choosing the right kind of work. It is a choice about what is good for you, not what is good for others whom you greatly respect, your parents, an admired professor, your friends, a significant other, whom you suspect may be dazzled by a greater or loftier choice of profession. The choice is not about what makes *them* happy, but about what makes *you* happy. Not what seems to show that you are successful by the exterior standards of the society. Not what brings you the biggest salary—particularly in the beginning when those things seem so important—and the biggest house, or the greatest respect from Wall Street, but what makes you feel complete and happy and makes you feel, for this is no small thing, like a part of something larger than yourself, a part of a community. [. . .]

The choices for you out there are not simple. It is, for example, possible to be immensely successful in your chosen field, and yet in some curious way to fail at life, to get to the top and yet fail to enrich yourself. [. . .]

So try and use your lives wisely, and try and make choices—even in your professional lives—that are of the heart. Do not be too readily caught in the material snare of this society. If you want to be a botanist, poet, actor, teacher or nurse, if that is what your heart tells you to do, do not go to law school or some other graduate school on the theory that it is a great ticket, and that it will get you to a higher level in the society, that you'll make some money for a while, and then you can go on and do the things that you really wanted to do in the first place.

It doesn't work that way. You will, I suspect find it surprisingly hard to escape the life you have chosen and go back to the career you originally intended. For you will almost surely become a prisoner of a lifestyle that you did not particularly seek out in the first place: an ever larger house, a fancier car, a more luxurious vacation. [. . .]

Do not be afraid to take chances when you are young, to choose the unconventional over the conventional. Often it is experience in the unconventional which prepares you best for the conventional. Be aware that it's all right to make mistakes, and it is all right to try at something and fail. The price of failure when you are young is much lower than when you are older. I suspect that you in the audience may look at us upon the stage and see people who seem like we have always succeeded, men and women who have led professionally flawless lives. Would that it were true. What you do not see is our own anxieties, not just when we were your age, but throughout our careers, when again and again—in our own minds—we seemed to be on the edge of some new failure.

You do not see me, at the moment a few days short of my 22nd birthday when the editor of that small daily in Mississippi came to me and told me it was time for me to leave, that in fact he would pay me for that last day and that he wanted me to be gone from the office and from the town by the next morning. He had already hired my successor who was scheduled to show up the next afternoon and he did not think it a good idea if we overlapped. Fired as it were from the smallest daily in Mississippi after less than a year. What an auspicious start to a career!

So I am telling you to trust your instincts—no one else will know them so well. If you are unsure of yourself and somewhat scared about your future, look at us, and know that we were often—and still are—unsure of ourselves, and scared of the future; if we look confident and self assured today, it is only one of our many faces. And I am suggesting as well, that you not defer your lives—that from the start you should try and live them with enthusiasm and truth. Years ago I interviewed Senator Wayne Morse for one of my books, and I asked him why he was one of only two men in the Senate who had voted against the Tonkin Gulf Resolution in 1964—a blatantly flimsy piece of paper that allowed Lyndon Johnson to go ahead with the Vietnam war. At the time perhaps as many as 80 of his colleagues had their own serious private doubts about what the President would do with so ambiguous a piece of paper. But the others went along, much to their regret later on while Morse did not. So I asked Morse, a curmudgeonly man, what had made him different and I think his answer is applicable to you here today.

"I vowed when I first went to the Senate," he said, "that every term was going to be my last one and that I wasn't going to worry about re-election, and that above all else, I was never going to shave my conscience on any issue just to get one more term. And that made life in the Senate much easier. Because of that I always voted my conscience, I never cut corners. So when the Tonkin Gulf Resolution came up I could tell it was a phoney and it was very easy to vote against it. Because I had decided that I was going to lead my life without regrets. I was always going to trust my instincts."

So let me leave you with Wayne Morse's words of wisdom. In all things in life, choose your conscience, and trust your instincts and lead your lives without regrets. It's simply easier that way. I mention that because life, under the best circumstances, even if you're lucky, as I have been to choose the right profession is very hard. First you have to choose the right profession—and then you have to work hard for the rest of your lives to sustain yourself in this choice which you happen to love. As the noted philosopher, basketball player and sports commentator, Julius Erving—Dr J—once said, "Being a professional is doing the things you love to do on the days when you don't feel like doing them."[. . .]

III. by DORIS KEARNS GOODWIN

I WOULD LIKE this morning to turn time on its head, in order to focus on old age looking backwards, instead of youth looking forward, the more typical theme of graduation speeches. I would like to share with you at the outset the experience I had with President Lyndon Johnson in the last years of his life, during his retirement at his ranch, as he looked back on the choices he had made, wishing he had chosen differently, feeling despair and terror at the thought of death.

I started working with him when he was still in the White House, when I was (I admit with some trepidation these days) a 24-year-old White House intern. But our relationship had a less promising start. Indeed, the very next day after a ball at the White House to celebrate the selection of the White House Fellows, the President discovered that I had been actively involved in the anti-Vietnam War movement and had written an article entitled "How to Dump Lyndon Johnson." I thought for sure he would kick me out of the program, but instead he said, "Oh, bring her down here for a year, and if I can't win her over, no one can." So I worked for him in the White House his last year of the presidency and then accompanied him to his ranch to help him on his memoirs.

Now on the surface he should have had everything in the world to be grateful for: His career in politics had reached a peak with his election to the presidency; he had all the money he needed to pursue any leisure activity he wanted; he owned a spacious ranch in the country, a penthouse apartment in the city, a half-dozen cars equipped with traveling bars, a sailboat, a speedboat, a movie theater in his own home, and an incredible swimming pool equipped with floating rafts, on top of which were floating desks and floating notepads and floating sandwiches and floating drinks; he had servants to answer every whim and the opportunity to travel anywhere in the world.

And yet the man I saw in his retirement had spent so many years in pursuit of work, power and individual success that he had absolutely no psychic or emotional resources left to commit himself to anything once the presidency was gone. So dominant had politics been, constricting his horizon in every sphere, that once the realm of high power was taken from him, he was drained of all vitality. Years of concentration solely on work meant that in his retirement he could find no solace in recreation, sports or hobbies. As his spirits sagged, his body deteriorated, until I believe he slowly brought about his own death.

A month before he died, he spoke to me with immense sadness in his voice. He said he was watching the American people absorbed in a new President, forgetting him, forgetting even the great civil rights laws that he had passed. He was beginning to think his quest for immortality had been in vain, that perhaps he would have been better off focusing his time and attention on his wife and his children, so then he could have had a different sort of immortality through his children and their children in turn; he could have depended on them in a way he couldn't depend on the American people. But it was too late. Four weeks later he was dead. Despite all his money and power, he was completely alone when he died, his ultimate terror realized.

As I understand the implications of this story, it reinforces a central wisdom I learned years ago at a seminar taught by the great Harvard psychologist Erik Erikson. And he taught us that the richest and fullest lives attain an inner balance of work, love and play, in equal order—that to pursue one to the disregard of others is to open oneself to ultimate sadness in older age, whereas to pursue all three with equal dedication is to make possible an old age filled with serenity, peace and fulfillment.

As for the first sphere, of work, I've come to realize, the older I get, that the key is enjoyment of the process itself, notwithstanding the end result. Perhaps Johnson's retirement might have been less difficult if all his life he had enjoyed the process of politics for its own sake, for that process could have continued even in his retirement in his hometown. But for him, sadly, it was the end result that mattered —the victories won, the power achieved—and once that was taken away, everything was lost.

Eleanor Roosevelt's last days provide a sharp contrast. All her life she took pleasure in her daily work, in using her power and celebrity to help others less fortunate than she. As First Lady she provided a voice for people who did not have access to power, poor people, migrant workers, tenant farmers, coal miners, blacks and women. Indeed, at her weekly press conferences she invited only female reporters, knowing that newspapers all over the country would be forced to hire their first female reporter, in order to have access to the First Lady. (An entire generation of female journalists got their start as a result.) And after her husband's death she remained a powerful inspiration to activists in the civil rights movement and the international struggle for human rights. As a consequence, at the close of her life, she was neither haunted nor saddened by what might have been. On the contrary, she sustained an active engagement with the world until the very end.

So as you figure out the kind of work you want to do, the challenge is to find work imbued with meaning, work that provides enjoyment on a daily basis. If you choose a career for money or prestige or security but dislike going to work more days than not, it will never be worth it in the long run.

As for the sphere of play, I've learned over the years that even with sports and recreation and hobbies, there's a need for a level of commitment of time and energy deep enough to really enjoy something and be able to derive relaxation from it. In my research on Franklin Roosevelt, I concluded that a central aspect of his leadership during World War II was his ability to relax at the end of the day, to cast off his worries and enjoy himself for a few precious hours, thus replenishing his energies to meet the struggles of the following day. Because of his paraplegia, he was unable to relax in traditional ways, by playing golf or tennis or taking long walks, so he found his relaxation through conversation with friends and associates.

At the end of each day he loved nothing more than sitting in his study, over the cocktail hour with his friends, telling old stories and jokes. Indeed he had a rule in his cocktail hour that nothing serious could be brought up; discussion of the war or the problems of the day was strictly forbidden. [. . .]

On a personal level, I will always be grateful to my father for instilling in me an irrational passion for baseball, so deep that it remains a large part of my life today and gives me a field of play that occupies me for more than half the year. I can still remember as if it were yesterday sitting on our porch when I was six or seven years old, waiting for my father to return from work, so I could share with him the results of that afternoon's Brooklyn Dodgers game, which I had preserved, play by play, inning by inning, in the red score book he had given me. No doubt my love of history was planted in those nightly sessions when he sat by my side in seemingly rapt attention as I recounted, in excruciating detail, the entire history of that afternoon's game. [. . .]

And even in these past years, as I settled in Boston and became an irrational Boston Red Sox fan, I have found myself following many of the same rituals with my sons, at Fenway Park, that I followed with my father, who died before any of my children were born. It may all sound a little crazy, but such is the spell cast by these rituals that if I close my eyes against the sun at Fenway, I picture myself back at Ebbetts Field with my father [. . .].

And as for the final sphere, of love and friendship, I can only say it gets harder once the natural communities of college and hometown are gone. It takes work and commitment, demands toleration for human frailties, forgiveness for the inevitable disappointment and betrayals that come even with the best of relationships. For me the most moving moment in the story of Franklin and Eleanor's life was Eleanor's ability to forgive Franklin, in the months after his death, for the deep hurt she had endured upon discovering that he had been with a woman he once loved, Lucy Mercer, when he died. Though it seemed at first as if the hurt would be too much to bear, she was eventually able to come to terms with the combination of flaws and enormous strengths that her husband possessed. With a strength of will that never faltered, she deliberately chose to remember only the good times that they had shared, never the estrangement and pain, which allowed her to go forward in life without bitterness, to build on the foundation of love, respect and affection that they had shared for nearly half a century.

What is more, beyond the difficulty of engaging oneself deeply in each individual sphere of love, work and play, it is extremely hard to find the right balance over time. I know that my own life was far too tilted toward work and ambition in my twenties, and then the painful experience of watching Lyndon Johnson die tilted me back toward family and friends. I got married, had children, was a professor at Harvard trying to teach and write and be with my kids—doing nothing right. I finally decided to give up teaching so I could have time to write and be at home with my family. [. . .]

To be sure some opportunities were lost. [. . .] But the point is, even if some opportunities were lost by the choices made when the children were little, there's still plenty of time now to move in new directions. It was just a matter of trusting in the choices that were made.

So in closing I would leave each of you with the hope that as you make your own choices over time, you will choose in such a way that allows your drive for achievement to be balanced by an equal commitment to love and to play, to family, to friends and community. I hope that none of you, no matter how successful you become, ever have to experience the sadness and the loneliness that Lyndon Johnson experienced. For nothing, no amount of power or success, is worth that. I hope instead that when you are "old and gray and full of sleep," as the poet William Butler Yeats once wrote, that you can say that your goal in life was not the perfection of work alone, but the perfection of a life. It is that wish I leave you with today, along with my heartiest congratulations on this day that means so much to you and to your families.

Teaching and Research:
A View from the Humanities

by NANCY K. FRANKENBERRY

꙳꙳꙳ Nancy Frankenberry, John Phillips Professor of Religion, writes of the highly creative tension between teaching and research that animates the modern Dartmouth.

I T WAS VOLTAIRE who was ready to vouch for the sincerity of his professed belief in God, but who added "as for monsieur the Son and madame His Mother, that's a different story." Many professors at other universities give lip service to the belief that teaching and research are both important, but when time devoted to teaching starts to erode upon time for research and publishing—well, that's a different story. At Dartmouth, for as long as I've been on the faculty, the imperative to do both with equal excellence has been drummed into me by senior colleagues, by deans, by several presidents, and, above all, by my undergraduate students, whether they realize it or not. Peer pressure is nothing compared to the pressure of having the fruits of your intellectual labors subjected to the daily hour-long scrutiny of very bright and easily bored eighteen to twenty-two year olds. Their high expectations, respect for competence, audacious questions, and immediate *need to know* continue to cause me as much lost sleep, hours searching in the library, and agonized headscratching as the tenure process ever did. From the point of view of students, the scholarship a professor does—or does not do—shows up live every lecture.

Everyone, of course, agrees it is a grave mistake to regard research and the education of students as separable activities. The most familiar rationale for their belonging together is, however, too one-sided. It offers what I call the "bee and pollen" picture of research and teaching. Busy faculty bees stick their noses into all sorts of nectar and then flit from flower to flower, student to student, classroom to classroom, pollinating as they go. But that's a "top-down" model. Real synergy between teaching and research means that "bottom-up" influences affect and permeate the whole system, giving rise to novel and unpredictable emergents. In the humanities, this means that undergraduate scholars at Dartmouth can frequently contribute as much to setting a research agenda, defining the questions, and tackling new territory *for faculty* as we do ourselves.

This is not a simple matter.

I came to understand it better in my second year at Dartmouth. A senior colleague, going on sabbatical, passed along to me a Religion major who had approached him about doing an honors thesis. When the student first appeared in my office, halting and hulking, he resembled a football player more than a Religion major. (It turned out he was both.) The topic he wanted to research—Max Weber's concept of charisma—was far outside what I then, barely out of graduate school, considered my field. Not only did I know very little about Weber's sociology of religion, I knew much less about *everything* than I was supposed to know. Would either of us be equal to this joint venture? Fortunately, he was more equal than I. Over the course of those terms of intense reading and talking together, writing and rewriting, he produced an intellectual *tour de force* that encompassed not only Weber, but also Durkheim, Marx, and Freud. And I was obliged to cover new ground, research that took me into areas surprisingly congruent with an introductory course I was developing on "Modern Religious and Anti-Religious Thinkers." Soon after, the first scholarly paper I published, although it had nothing to do with Weber and was quite lacking in charisma, owned its premise to an idea that dawned in working with the student. Eric Ziolkowski '80 went on to earn his Ph.D. at the University of Chicago and now teaches, publishes, and directs honors theses in the Religion Department at Lafayette College.

Not every Dartmouth student does honors work in the major, but every department and program now requires its majors to fulfill a specified "culminating experience" in their senior year. Here is another site at which the synergy between my own teaching and writing has been fueled as much by students as by collaboration with a colleague. The "culminating experience" course Professor Hans Penner and I created was on "Language, Truth, and Religious Belief," dealing with controversial theories and methods in the study of religion which were, in our judgment, crucial for any Religion major to master. Coming to that judgment together, however, involved a long journey. What did we have in common intellectually and what could we agree we wanted Religion majors to know about the study of religion? Could we even agree on the major issues and most important readings? These questions took us to very basic and often contentious levels of discussion in the six months preceding the course. The other half of the journey was taking our students there. In the course of the seminar, which was gifted with some exceptionally able students, we discovered that one particular classic essay, Clifford Geertz's "Religion as a Cultural System," acted as a lightning rod for all the criticisms of other readings we were discussing. Spurred by our students' interest in and response to that essay, we two professors collaborated on writing an article for publication that exposes some of the methodological and theoretical problems with Geertz's influential definition of religion. Our essay will become required reading in the next version of the course, to be critiqued along with all the other readings. Finally, *Language, Truth and Religious Belief* is also scheduled for publication as a volume edited by us, with superb assistance from Jennifer Walker-Johnson and Ross Wilken '99, for scholars at other institutions to use in the study of religion. Quoting Casey Stengel, we will tell a new group of majors that we "couldn't have done it without the players."

Ginger Rogers, it has been said, did everything Fred Astaire did, only backwards and in high heels. When it comes to research and publishing, the Dartmouth humanities faculty does everything our colleagues in the natural sciences do, except without graduate students or huge grants. Performing our difficult gavottes, we endure the popular impression that, unlike expensive, controlled, and vanguard research in science, which leads to real discovery and the growth of knowledge, professors of literature and languages, classics, philosophy, religion, etc., simply do armchair research, animated only by our (soft, unrigorous) imaginations and requiring only a few well-thumbed tomes (which we oddly call texts).

There is some truth to this. Missing, however, is the most important part. Our imaginations are not stirred by texts alone, but by teaching, by the company of students in whose presence we flourish, and with whom we carry on internal dialogues even in our solitude. At least some of what we are imagining during sabbatical labors of reading and writing is: "How will I teach this?" "Would this work in next term's course?" "Oh! here's a source Claire should know about for her independent reading course." The revelation—conferred on me by several generations of Dartmouth's undergraduate scholars— is that our students are our best critics, most reliable litmus test of half-baked or overly-determined ideas, and freshest, most unjaded source of inspiration. If some professors at large research universities are so hermetic that they never flourish in the presence of students, they should be re-directed to employment in non-educational research institutions.

The twin perceptions—that research means the subordination of teaching and that teaching interferes with research—ignore the way we actually live. Some of the most highly active research faculty I know are also the ones most deeply interested in engaging and being engaged by a wide variety of student and faculty colleagues on campus. The truth is that the love of teaching and the love of one's intellectual discipline mix and mingle in indefinable doses, and both bring their own brew of surprises and disappointments, moments of breakthrough, frustration, and joy. The other plain fact, beyond all the platitudes, is that achieving excellence in both teaching and scholarly publication is tremendously difficult, but we do it at Dartmouth.

Only the most empathic, sustained, and careful coordination between faculty, deans, and students will maintain the balance we have achieved where humane teaching and research reinforce each other. As long as a Dartmouth education amounts to much more than *instruction*, in the mode of imparting information, as long as it is also a reciprocal and quite personal process of transaction between learners, some older, some younger, there will be no substitute for human relationships and presence, for listening, for sharing insight and wonderment, and for caring.

Knowing Our Place

by DANIEL M. NELSON

❦❧ Here Daniel Nelson 1975, Senior Associate Dean of the College, reflects upon the College's setting and its impact on and meaning to the sons and daughters of Dartmouth.

LEAZAR WHEELOCK HAD good reasons for wishing to move his school for Indians north from Connecticut. The achievement of his purpose depended on proximity to a population of native people, and he needed to be located in a place where he might find more students for his mission than remained in Connecticut. He needed access to the kind of convenient transportation made possible by the Connecticut River, and foresaw the advantages, historian Ralph Nading Hill observes, of being at some safe remove "from the restraints of parliaments and clerics." He also understood that the school's isolation would enhance the education of his pupils. In Wheelock's words, the school's location in the wilderness was "most favorable and friendly to the studies of the youth, free from a thousand snares, temptations and divertissements which were and would have been unavoidable if this seminary had continued where it was, or been fixed in any populous town in the land." The place he chose was one where he anticipated that the "voice crying in the wilderness" would be heard and heeded.

It was indeed a wilderness, although perhaps less idyllic than Wilder Quint's description in *The Story of Dartmouth*: "To the westward flowed the Connecticut . . . To the east were rugged, densely wooded hills, presently to rise into bare and towering mountains. On the level plateau selected as the location for the college, giant pines nearing three hundred feet in height shut out the very sun, save at noon, and calmed the fiercest blasts of the upper air into a cathedral quietude . . . The good doctor had desired a place for his college 'removed from the allurements of more populous towns.' He had surely found it." In response to the many outraged objections from land speculators who had hoped to profit from the siting of the College at other locations, and who accused him of less than noble motives, Wheelock pronounced that "The site for Dartmouth College was not determined by any private interest or party on earth, but the Redeemer's."

Whether it was divine providence, presidential prudence, or simple luck, more than two centuries have proven the prescience of Wheelock's sense of place. The place was so integral to his original purposes that it became inseparable from the College's continuing and evolving sense of mission. Hewing a site for the College out of the woods, huddling in poorly heated huts that first winter, and gathering together for prayer outdoors before the construction of a suitable place to worship, gave enduring meaning to the place for the first and succeeding generations of students and teachers. Something of that connection between place and purpose, at first because of practical necessity, was what an early professor, Edwin Sanborn, discerned when he wrote that "there is something in being part of an adventure that has hewn its way into a wilderness at first physical and later symbolical to accomplish an exalted purpose."

What that "something" is defies description, but what emerged, beyond the physical College, was a defining sense of continuing and close community. "Dartmouth men were compelled to be clannish when old Eleazar's ax-wielders slashed the room for their huts and cabins out of the virgin forests of a wilderness," Wilder Quint explained. "They were compelled to be clannish for years afterward in the hard struggle for existence. The feeling of loyalty and oneness got into the blood, and it has never gotten out. Today the geographic aloofness of the college still works its ancient spell."

Over time, the place became not only the setting but also a player in the Dartmouth myth celebrated in story and song. William H. McCarter '19, a regular columnist for the *Alumni Magazine* in the 1950s, observed that "the core of alumni devotion is at least fifty percent a blind love for the hills and valleys and unkempt streets of the Hanover locale . . . Some intangible of local geography creeps into our bones and being to weave the town, as well as the college, into the spell assigned by Richard Hovey to the roamers of the girdled earth." What makes Hovey's songs distinctive, McCarter observed in another essay, "is the specificness of his references" to the physical features of the place. "[E]ven in such a stately and formal piece as *Men of Dartmouth*, he works in 'hill winds,' 'Lone Pine,' 'still and silent North,' and 'the granite of New Hampshire.'"

The place inspired what is now the oldest outing club in the country, still Dartmouth's largest and most active student organization, when Fred Harris '11 engaged the imagination of his fellow students by asking and answering the rhetorical question: "what is there to do at Dartmouth in the winter?" with the proposal "that we might take better advantage of the splendid opportunities which the admirable situation of our College offers." The enthusiasm of its students for the outdoors, and its continued isolation, was responsible for its attractiveness to applicants and their parents, *The Story of Dartmouth* instructed readers: "[T]he glories of 'Dartmouth out-o'-doors' are beginning to impress themselves far and wide, and fathers and mothers appreciate the situation of a college that has no easy access to the flash fascinations of metropolitan evil . . . This 'magnificent isolation' is the chief glory and hope of those who rule the college—and that means the alumni of Dartmouth, as well as its trustees and faculty."

What of the College now, no longer so situated in such splendid isolation? Do students, and those of us who live and work here, still know our place? Is it the same? Although far from urban, the setting is much less rural than it was. Traffic jams on Main and Wheelock are a daily afternoon phenomenon, not just a football-weekend rarity. There are more opportunities in Hanover to shop for real estate, a home-equity loan, or Chinese food than for a pair of skis or an ax. The White Mountains are crowded with hikers from out of state, and New Hampshire is far from wilderness, although even suburban Hanover, with its confident skunks and marauding raccoons, can sometimes seem wild and inhospitable to students for whom home is the city.

And yet we still do know our place. Students still cherish the Bema, where they gather on their first arrival in Hanover to meet one another and assemble in groups for their freshman trips, where they go for solitude or quiet conversation, and where they gather again Commencement weekend to celebrate friendship and the accomplishments of classmates. The D.O.C. trips still take freshmen up the Appalachian Trail to Moose Mountain and Smarts, and over Cube to Moosilauke. When trips are ended, students still gather at the Ravine Lodge to learn the Salty Dog Rag, to doze through edifying remarks from deans after a raucous dinner, to shake the rafters with their square dancing, to hear about Doc Benton haunting the mountain, and to eat green eggs and ham after a hike to the summit to catch the sunrise. They run in Pine Park and roller-blade around Occom Pond. They paddle canoes on the Connecticut and kayaks on the Mascoma. Some still drive through Lyme and Orford, to Bath and Littleton, and up past Whitefield and Lancaster on their way to the College Grant for hiking and skiing, fishing and hunting, mountain biking and canoeing, stopping each way at the Errol Restaurant for pie and a "moose burger." They still build cabins and maintain trails, and they still ski at the Skiway. They still admire Dartmouth Hall in the moonlight, and when alumni are in town, they look up to see if a green light is shining in Baker Tower.

In a contemporary essay, "Landscape and Narrative," Barry Lopez recalls an evening spent in an Inuit village in the Brooks Range of Alaska, listening to hunters and trappers tell stories about the behavior of animals, the weather, and the details of memorable hunts. As he walked outside at the end of the evening, and as he looked at the village and the surrounding mountains, the place assumed a vibrancy in his understanding. "The landscape seemed alive because of the stories," he said. Late in the essay he reflects on the relationship between geographical landscape and the "speculations, intuitions, and formal ideas" that constitute our minds, our "interior landscape." "The shape and character of these relationships in a person's thinking," Lopez notes, "are deeply influenced by where on this earth one goes, what one touches, the patterns one observed in nature—the intricate history of one's life in the land . . . These thoughts are arranged, further, according to the thread of one's moral, intellectual, and spiritual development. The interior landscape responds to the character of subtlety of an exterior landscape; the shape of the individual mind is affected by land as it is by genes."

Education at Dartmouth is precisely concerned with the development of students' "moral, intellectual, and spiritual" lives, so no wonder generations of students continue to be profoundly shaped by the College landscape. We retell to newcomers the stories of how the College came to be in this place, and we converse incessantly about how best to understand the here and now. We stake claims to the College of the future. By adopting this place, and then being adopted by it, each generation of students makes this place its own, keeping the place the same and ever new.

"It is not necessary to be either a geographer or a sociologist to know that place rubs off on people," John Dickey said in his 1957 Convocation address. "And conversely it is not necessary to be a historian to know that over the years the past of an institution becomes as much a part of the place as its physical setting." Dartmouth's "sense of place" has defined the institution as much as "the Dartmouth spirit" or "the Dartmouth family." Perhaps the sense of place accounts for most of what makes our sense of spirit and community possible. Our particular place in the world, how and why we are geographically situated in the Connecticut River valley and in the foothills of New Hampshire's White Mountains, is intertwined with our educational situation, our mission as a college.

Although an enduring sense of place involves loyalty and faithfulness to something concrete, what we ultimately sense in this place is not the architecture and geography, the external landscape. Rather, we sense the impression that has been made on our inner landscapes, the spaces of our hearts and minds, by the purposes that brought our predecessors here and that we still pursue. Knowing our place is important not primarily because of benefits to the College—the affection, loyalty and faithfulness the place inspires—but because of our purposes for students. Our place at Dartmouth, our mission here, is to help students know and make their place in the world, and to make the world a better place for others. Here, at Dartmouth, the sense of place remains the same, and strong.

Remarks to the Community

by JAMES WRIGHT

>>> On April 5, 1998, Dartmouth's Trustees elected as sixteenth President of the College, in succession to James O. Freedman, James Wright, who had at that point already served the College for nearly three full decades—as a teacher of American history from 1969 onward, and also in the capacity of a top-level administrative officer (having been, successively, Dean of the Faculty and Provost, in addition to a six-month period in 1995 as Acting President). On April sixth a hurriedly arranged gathering was held in Alumni Hall of the Hopkins Center, in order to make to the College community a formal announcement of the action taken by the full Board the previous day at Boston. The President-Elect and his wife, Susan DeBevoise Wright, were accorded hearty congratulations by the assembled audience, and here follows the main body of what he said that afternoon in acknowledgment and response.

THIRTY YEARS AGO this coming fall, I made my first visit to Dartmouth—indeed, my first visit to New England—for a job interview in the History Department. I was very pleased to accept their offer, and thought I would be here for a few years.

I was encouraged from the very beginning by a group of colleagues who were supportive of each other, colleagues who took both teaching and scholarship seriously. And I was captured by an environment in which faculty, students, and staff cared about each other and cared about the broader world of which this campus was only a small part. It is important to know that I still today consider myself—and always will consider myself—first and foremost a faculty member, a teacher, and a historian.

Dartmouth is a far more complicated place than it was when I came here, but I believe the basic themes and values remain. This is a place where all members of the community take seriously their responsibilities to each other and are committed to the values of this institution.

I have asked three special friends to join Susan and me today, three people who have worked closely with me and who personify that commitment: Gail Vernazza [Administrative Assistant, Department of History], June Sweeney [Administrative Assistant, Office of the

404

Dean of the Faculty], and Jeannine McPherson [Administrative Assistant to the Provost]. They have supported me over many years, and are colleagues deeply committed to the purposes of Dartmouth. Even the most complicated organizations finally come down to people, and I would salute all of the people, from faculty to those who take care of our superb facilities, who make this place true to its principles and give me great confidence in the assignment I will assume.

There will be ample time over the next several months for me to share with you in detail my vision for Dartmouth and the objectives of my presidency. I expect to engage in a wide discussion of who we are and what we aspire to be, sharing with you my perspectives and learning from yours. For now, let me outline some of the important principles that will inform my presidency.

President William Jewett Tucker said that the "risks of inertia are far greater than the risks of innovation." I have no interest in inertia. We end the twentieth century in a position of real strength, thanks to the commitment and efforts and vision of my predecessors. John Dickey raised our aspirations and reminded us of our common obligations to our world and to others. John Kemeny moved us through a period of significant change and enlarged in every way our sense of who defined this community. David McLaughlin enabled us to rededicate the residential experience and secured our financial strength. Jim Freedman reminded us that our primary commitment and obligation is to the life of the mind. And it has been the very special support of Dartmouth's alumni for this place and its values that has enabled our College to thrive and excel.

Our legacy is wonderful, but our task is unfinished—it will always be unfinished. Now we must focus upon the next century and prepare ourselves for the challenges that it will surely bring. We need to affirm the importance of the liberal arts in this world of change.

My vision of Dartmouth is of a research community that is committed to attracting and retaining the very best faculty and recruiting and engaging the very best students. A place marked by learning rather than teaching, learning in which students are full participants rather than passive observers. A place where the out-of-classroom experience fully complements the formal classroom learning. A place where students enjoy the freedom and independence to shape their own lives. Freedom and independence entail responsibility. Being a member of a community involves necessary negotiations between our personal interests and the values that bind us together. I expect to participate fully with the Board of Trustees, with faculty and administrators—and especially with students—in a full discussion of what membership in this community means.

Our shared responsibility is to assure a place that attaches the highest priority upon learning, to assure a community that is open to everyone, a community that does not demean women—indeed that does not demean anyone. A community that does not tolerate the harming of others and that tries to prevent the harming of oneself. Let us celebrate all of our members and understand our obligation to the world in which we live. As we discuss the way to secure these things, understand that I think we can do no less. My sense of this community is that we need to come together to discuss our common purposes, and I intend to be an active participant in this discussion.

I also told the Board of Trustees that I fully intend to participate in debates that have a national resonance. One has to do with the value of research. Research in the academy is not a pastime that competes with teaching, but a critical activity that informs the best teaching. It is too easy to dismiss research by focusing on things that have failed or projects that critics deem foolish. The American research university is the most successful in the world, and we should never forget the importance of this to our national well-being—not simply in those critical research fields which we hope make our lives safer and our world more familiar, but in the arts and the humanities that make our lives fuller and richer.

Dartmouth is a research university in all but name, and we are not going to be deflected from our purposes. This is a place that is marked by flexibility, by a sense of community, and by full opportunities for interdisciplinary work bridging not only arts and sciences departments, but also including the strong programs we have developed in the professional schools. I hope to work with the deans and with the faculties to strengthen these ties. For, finally, it is the strength of the faculty and their work that makes this such an attractive place for the very best students. And the very best students attract an even stronger faculty.

I have particularly enjoyed over the last fifteen months my involvement with the three professional schools. I am impressed by their strength and by their sense of excellence. I am excited about the prospect of looking for new ways to build upon their accomplishments and to expand even more their ambitions. We have the potential here to develop new models of academic medicine and of health-care delivery, to strengthen engineering as a professional field while enriching its ties to the liberal arts, and to build upon Tuck's position as a residential business school committed to new models of business research and education. Dartmouth's venerable professional schools and her impressive graduate programs are fundamental to the special character of this College.

I strongly reaffirm our commitment to Affirmative Action and to diversity. This is not simply due to some sense of long-standing obligation, although this is important. This is not simply due to our need to provide opportunities to minority students, although it is hard to imagine our society if we neglect this responsibility. Most importantly, our commitment to diversity is rooted in the fact that we are an educational institution. It is hard for me to imagine education going on without a richly diverse student body and faculty. The world is diverse, and so must we be. I will see that we do not let up in our recruitment efforts. But recruitment is only the first step. This community needs to do still more to welcome and salute difference.

A personal note may underline my commitment to this principle. My path to Dartmouth was not a direct one—I didn't commence my college education until I was twenty-one years old, because post-secondary education was not something that was part of my community or its values. One of my grandfathers was a miner and the other was a farm worker. Neither finished eighth grade. My father was a bartender. He dropped out of college during his first semester, because the Depression blunted his aspirations. I worked for a time myself as a miner—a powderman in 300-feet-deep hardrock mines.

I know well the distance from there to this spot for this occasion. Once I began to study, I found a world of excitement and of opportunity. I have been fortunate, and I have benefited from the support and encouragement of teachers, mentors, friends, and family over the years. I recognize personally the power of education and the capacity of institutions like Dartmouth, at their best, to enable full opportunities and rich lives. The post-war democratization of American higher education has been a wonderful story, and I have been pleased in my time at Dartmouth to see this extended to be fully inclusive. I can assure you that on my watch there will be no letting up in this College's commitment to a diverse and rich student body, faculty, and administration and to a financial-aid program that will sustain this.

Some of you will know that Emily Dickinson has a special and personal importance to Susan and to me. We were married in her house. Emily Dickinson wrote:

> "Hope" is the thing with feathers—
> That perches in the soul—
> And sings the tune without the words—
> And never stops—at all—

I am privileged to be at a place whose soul is indeed filled with hope, and I will be honored to be the president of an institution so richly endowed with people who share in that sense of optimism and promise.

This book was designed by Roderick D. Stinehour (Dartmouth Class of 1950) and printed at The Stinehour Press, Lunenburg, Vermont.